Yours affectionately,

Elisha Yale

The Model Pastor.

THE

LIFE AND CHARACTER

OF THE

REV. ELISHA YALE, D. D.,

LATE OF KINGSBORO',

DRAWN MOSTLY FROM HIS OWN DIARY AND CORRESPONDENCE.

TOGETHER WITH

THE DISCOURSE PREACHED AT HIS FUNERAL,

JANUARY 13, 1853.

BY JEREMIAH WOOD,

PASTOR OF THE CENTRAL PRESBYTERIAN CHURCH, MAYFIELD, NEW-YORK.

WITH A PORTRAIT.

ALBANY:
JOEL MUNSELL, 78 STATE-STREET.
1854.

CONTENTS.

CHAPTER IV.

HIS COMMUNON WITH GOD.

CHAPTER V.

HIS SPIRITUAL CONFLICTS.

CHAPTER VI.

HIS ANXIETY FOR THE SPIRITUAL WELFARE OF HIS PEOPLE.

CHAPTER VII.

SEASONS OF DISCOURAGEMENT AND DEPRESSION.

CHAPTER VIII.

HIS STRONG RELIGIOUS AFFECTIONS AND SPIRITUAL COMFORTS.

CHAPTER IX.

HIS PASTORAL FIDELITY.

CHAPTER X.

MEANS EMPLOYED TO PROMOTE A REVIVAL.

CHAPTER XI.

HIS TREATMENT OF INQUIRING SINNERS.

CHAPTER XII.

HIS SHINING EXAMPLE.

CHAPTER XIII.

HIS ENTIRE DEVOTEDNESS TO THE SERVICE OF GOD.

CHAPTER XIV.

THE DUTIES AND RESPONSIBILITIES OF THE GOSPEL MINISTRY.

CHAPTER XV.

PASTORAL COMMUNICATIONS.

CHAPTER XVI.

INTERESTING INCIDENTS.

CHAPTER XVII.

HIS REGARD FOR THE SABBATH.

CHAPTER XVIII.

HIS GREAT INDUSTRY.

CHAPTER XIX.

HIS DOMESTIC HABITS.

CHAPTER XX.

HIS PULPIT PREPARATIONS, AND THE CHARACTER OF HIS PREACHING.

CHAPTER XXI.

INTERESTING VIEWS OF SCRIPTURE TRUTH.

CHAPTER XXII.

PLANS OF USEFULNESS.

CHAPTER XXIII.

HIS INTEREST IN THE CAUSE OF BENEVOLENCE.

CHAPTER XXIV.

MEANS USED TO PROMOTE MISSIONARY OPERATIONS.

CHAPTER XXV.

HIS HAPPY OLD AGE.

THE RIPE CHRISTIAN, DYING.

PREFACE.

Says a friend not long since, "There are so many religious biographies now a days, that it sometimes makes me almost sick to think of them." And it is no less true now than it was in the days of Solomon, that "of making many books there is no end." To make a book simply for the purpose of adding to their number, in this age of the world, is indeed very undesirable; and there are doubtless biographies written which in no way subserve the cause of Christ, or tend to promote the spiritual interests of men. Yet there are men whose life has been so spotless, and whose Christian character has been so much an exemplification of the genuine spirit of Christianity, that it seems desirable that some memorial of their piety should be preserved for the benefit of survivors. As their sun shone with such brightness while living, it is proper that its rays should be elongated after death. Such was the case with Dr. Yale. It may be truly said, that he was no ordinary man. Whoever came within his influence, felt that there was something about him to inspire awe. He might not have realized what it was. There was a cheerful piety in his whole demeanor which made one feel that he was in the presence of one who was in correspondence with heaven. His every day walk was only the outward expression of the inward feelings of his soul. His face shone because he held such intimate communion with God. He drew daily supplies of grace from the fountain head; he daily burnished his gospel armor, so that he was always ready for action as a leader of the hosts of the Lord. His spirituality of mind seems to have been habitual (however much he did at times deplore his languor of feeling), so that whenever one came where he was, he appeared like one who had just come down from the mount.

In preparing this memoir, it has been the author's purpose to draw as largely as possible from the productions of Dr. Yale's own pen. He kept a memorandum through the greater part of his ministerial life; and during portions of this time it is very voluminous. There is much in this memorandum of surpassing interest, as it serves to introduce the reader into the inner chambers of his heart, and to give him a most striking, an unerring likeness of himself. There we are enabled to see the man as we could see him nowhere else. He shows us his heart as we had never before seen it; and furnishes us with a measuring line by which we may fathom the depth of his piety, as we had never been able to do. A man of ordinary religious attainments, when reading these records of his religious exercises, his conflicts with the corruptions of his heart, his strugglings after holiness, his earnest wrestlings with God, and the intensity of his religious emotions, will be likely to have a very diminutive view of himself, and feel, as we may suppose a pigmy would feel, when standing by the side of a giant. Yet he never looked upon himself as any thing else than "less than the least of all saints."

Dr. Yale occupied his pen for the last few months of his life, in preparing a work which he called a Review of a Pastorate of Forty-eight Years; and which he had just finished at the time of his decease. He had finished it, though it had not then gone to the press; and it is not known that he intended to give it to the public during his life. The readers of that work, should it ever be published, need not be informed that it is a book of great interest. It contains very many incidents connected with his pastoral labors, and very many hints suggested by his experience, which will be found of great practical utility. Yet, in such a work as that, while the writer was narrating circumstances of thrilling interest, and uttering sentiments of the deepest wisdom, it was not to have been expected that he would open the sanctuary of his own bosom for the inspection of the world. This was no part of his design, and this his delicacy of feeling and Christian modesty, would have forbid. Upon examination of that work, in manuscript, it was believed in no sense to occupy the place of a memoir; though there are some things in it, which, if they had not been there, would properly have come into such a work. In preparing the following pages, it has been the compiler's design to exclude from them everything which Dr. Yale had previously inserted in the Pastorate. This he believes to have been done, so that it is not known, that, in a single instance, the same matter is contained in the two books. Having said thus much, my purpose shall be, as far as possible, to give an outline of his character, and labors, and religious sentiments, in the language in which he has himself expressed them.

THE MODEL PASTOR.

INTRODUCTION.

There is a way in which the living may hold communion with the dead. It is not by receiving communications from the invisible world, nor by invoking responses from the spirits of the departed. We would not, if we could, disturb the slumbers, or break in upon the repose of our sainted friend. Nor would we desire him for a moment, to suspend those holy aspirations which he is breathing forth before the throne of God, for the purpose of communicating with us. We rejoiced in his company while living; and we take pleasure in calling to mind his excellencies, now he is dead.

But after a long and toilsome life, spent in the service of God and in labors to benefit his fellow-men, it is his privilege to rest without molestation or disturbance; and so may he rest until the time appointed for him to awake.

We know, too, that this was in accordance with his long-cherished desire. He was willing to labor through the day; nor did he, through the spirit of indolence, desire to have the day come to an end, so that he might be released from toil. Yet did he anticipate the termination of his conflicts and his toil with satisfaction, and felt willing to lay aside his armor, and to rest from his labors whenever God should see fit to order it. He communed with death as with a friend, and he looked into the grave as the place of his repose.

Several years before his death, and while enjoying his accustomed vigor, considering the uncertainty of human life, and impressed with the idea of his own frailty, he solemnly penned and properly executed his last will and testament, in which he gave to this thought a prominent place. An extract from this document is here introduced, for the purpose of illustrating the piety of his character, even in those things which were not strictly religious; and also of showing the light in which he looked upon death, and his expectations of a future state. It commences as follows:

"In the name of God, amen. I, Elisha Yale, of the town of Johnstown, in the county of Fulton, and state of New York, being of sound and disposing mind, memory and understanding, and in good health, but considering the uncertainty of human life, do hereby make, publish and declare my last will and testament, in manner and form following:

1. I commit my soul into the hands of my ever-blessed Lord Jesus Christ, the only Redeemer of men, my Lord and my God, to be pardoned of sins innumerable through his blood, and clothed with his righteousness, to be accepted before God, and to be sanctified by his spirit, and made perfectly holy to be fit to dwell in his eternal kingdom—all my salvation and all my desire.

2. I commit my body to the dust from whence it came, to be kept by my glorious Lord in union with himself, in a good, sound, unbroken sleep, till the morning of the resurrection, and then to hear the voice of the archangel and the trump of God, and come forth in the glorious resurrection to be united again to my spirit, and to be forever with the Lord."

Having thus committed his soul into the hands of him on whom alone he rested his hope of salvation, and his body to the dust, he proceeds to make a distribution of his effects among some of his friends; but giving the most to his surviving widow, to whom above all other survivors it properly belongs. To the execution of this will, in all its parts, we most heartily assent. We love to think that since it has pleased God to remove him hence, his body lies by the side of his father, and in the midst of his people, in undisturbed tranquility, and that his soul is with the blest in Heaven. So be it, amen.

Yet, is there a way in which we may hold communion with the dead.

Two enquiries here present themselves:

1. How is such communion to be held?

We hold communion with the pious dead by thinking of their virtues; by recounting their deeds of charity; by calling to mind their acts of beneficence; by remembering their instructions; by recollecting their pious examples; by repeating their admonitions; by practicing their counsels; and by cherishing that spirit of devotion to God, which gave type to their character while living.

2. What is the benefit to be derived from such communion?

It is not to supersede those communications which God is pleased to address to us in his word. It is not to reveal to us those secret things which God has not seen fit to reveal. It is not to impart to us a superstitious reverence for the lifeless dust of departed friends. But it is to exhibit and illustrate the nature of true piety; to furnish us with examples for imitation; to excite survivors to holy action, to diligence and fidelity in the service of God; and to magnify God's grace in the Christian walk, and holy deportment, and consistent example, and humble piety, and peaceful end of God's devoted people.

This is the end of biography. Not to praise the dead. They are deaf to our praise, and receive from it no advantage. But to benefit the living, and to commend a life of religion, a life devoted to the service of God, by a reference to the life and deeds of his departed people. If the following pages do but answer this end it is all that is desired in their behalf.

CHAPTER I.

HIS EARLY LIFE, HIS RELIGIOUS EXPERIENCE AND HIS PREPARATION FOR THE MINISTRY.

Elisha was the son of Justus and Margaret Yale, and was born in the town of Lee, in the county of Berkshire, and State of Massachusetts, on the 15th day of June, 1780. His mother's maiden name was Margaret Tracy; and his ancestry on the side both of his father and mother, were professors of religion, and believed to have been pious and praying people. His own parents, however, during his childhood, were not either of them members of any Christian church. His father made a profession of religion many years after; and his mother died when Elisha was but fifteen years of age. But though she was not a professor of religion, some of her most intimate friends believed her to be possessed of genuine piety. Elisha, in early life, was the subject of many serious impressions; was subject to parental discipline, and was held in restraint by parents who always vigilantly guarded his morals; and he afterwards believed that he was often remembered before God, in the prayers of pious friends.

At the time of his mother's death, his mind appears to have been a perfect chaos, and so destitute of all proper religious feeling, as that he afterwards thought of it with the deepest amazement. In view of it, he enters upon his journal the following record: "Alas! I have often reflected with horror on my thoughts, exercises and views at that time. What a heart was then within me! and at that time, how insensible was I to its horrid vileness!"

His childhood was marked by some incidents of which he was accustomed to speak, in after life, with the deepest interest. In two or three instances he narrowly escaped death, in which he afterwards recognised the merciful interposition of his Heavenly Father. Once, when a little boy, was he tempted to the commission of theft, by taking a sled which belonged to a neighbor. In speaking of it, he says: "I took it and drew it home. My father met me at the door, and questioned me about the sled. Finding that I had stolen it, he made me understand that it was wrong, and immediately sent me back with it. I do not remember that from that day I ever had a thought of stealing any thing whatsoever. That parental admonition was very effectual."

Though he passed through the entire period of childhood and youth, before he became the subject of God's renewing grace, during this time was he frequently exercised with serious thoughts, and deeply awakened to a sense of his spiritual necessities. "One day when I was very young," he writes, "being at play in a field with two or three little boys, one of them said that there would be a day of judgment, and that this world would be burnt up. This deeply impressed my mind, and I often remembered it afterwards. Whenever the thought of it returned I felt serious; and even to this day the thought of it is solemn. This was the first religious impression which I remember to have been made upon my mind. In my succeeding days of childhood and youth, I used frequently to dream that the day of judgment had actually come. Perhaps this might have been the effect of that deep impression." Again he writes: "A short time before my mother's death, I heard of Christ, and of conversion, by means of the conversation of two men who were laboring with me in the field. I had doubtless heard of them many times before, but they never before made such an impression upon my mind as to abide, and even then they did not abide so as to make me serious. I can hardly have an idea of the greatness of my stupidity. It is a wonder that I was not always left in that situation."

From his childhood, he had a great fondness for reading; and among the books which he read, there were some which in their character were decidedly religious; such as the sermons of President Davies, and Baxter's Call to the Unconverted. The reading of these books made a strong religious impression, so as sometimes to make him tremble greatly. "For about a fortnight," says he, "I was full of fear at times, and it seemed as though there was but a little space between me and the bottomless pit." Yet was his seriousness then but of short duration.

Among the things which contributed much towards driving away his serious impressions, and producing a state of thoughtlessness in respect to the things of religion, was the influence of worldly companions and his love of worldly pleasure. Of this he speaks as follows: "From my twelfth to my sixteenth or seventeenth year, the company nearest to me, and with which I frequently met, was such as tended not to form my mind to virtue, but the contrary; yet, through the good providence of God and the care of kind parents, I was restrained from those excesses of wickedness, to which many are suffered to run." In view of this, he many a time marvelled at that kindness of God, by which he was preserved from those fleshly indulgences, which have proved the snare and the ruin of so many.

Mention has already been made of the serious impressions which were made on his mind by reading the sermons of President Davies. His sermon on the resurrection and final judgment, in particular, affected him very much. In reference to this period of his life, he writes as follows: "During the time of this seriousness, I was invited to attend a ball, the first to which I was ever invited. My mind was so much impressed that I wished for some excuse that would be satisfactory; but I found none. I wished that my companions would become serious. It appeared to me that I had much rather attend a religious meeting than a ball. However, the love of evil companions prevailed; and being advised by a young man older than myself, I resolved to go. I went, and with this went all my seriousness."

During the autumn of 1798, and the winter of 1799, he taught a school in Richmond, with a good degree of success; and as to his religious state at that time, he has given us the following account; "During all this time, my mind was grossly stupid as to religion, and yet

I seldom slept without praying. This was purely through a fear which had remained on my mind for a number of years, and especially after my terrors in reading Davies' sermons. In the spring I returned to Lenox [the place of his father's residence], where I found my companions uncommonly engaged in the pursuit of pleasure. A small number with whom I was specially connected, had been in the habit of meeting frequently during the winter, for dancing. I joined them. But after having been dancing till midnight, I did not very well know how to go home and pray. The thoughts would come into my mind, but I would suppress them. Thus I had many struggles in my mind."

Finding such to be the influence of dancing upon the religious state of his mind, it is not to be wondered at that he felt decidedly opposed to the practice during all his subsequent life. It was his settled conviction that an attendance upon dancing parties, and the amusements of the ball-room, were inconsistent with the seriousness of a religious profession, destructive to the enjoyment of vital religion, and directly calculated to dissipate all serious religious impressions. Dancing and praying appeared to him to be decidedly hostile to each other, so as that the two can never be made to harmonize.

Dr. Yale was accustomed in after life, to take a retrospective view of the past. He often looked back upon the days of his folly and impenitence, with mingled emotions of amazement and thankfulness. He was amazed at his own stupidity and heedlessness about his soul and the interests of religion; amazed at the matchless mercy and grace of God by which he was preserved in being and finally led to repentance. And he was thankful for God's long suffering and forbearance, and benevolence in his regeneration. His thoughtlessness, and neglect of religion, and abuse of the means of grace, and failure as to the proper observance of thè sabbath, filled him in after years with the bitterest regret, and prompted to the exercise of the the deepest self-loathing.

The eleventh day of November, 1830, was set apart by the General Assembly of the Presbyterian church as a day of fasting and prayer, in view of the extensive desecration of the sabbath, which is chargeable upon the people of our land. This day was observed by Dr. Yale with feelings of peculiar interest, and at this date he made an extended entry in his journal, in which he takes a view of his early life, and speaks with the deepest humiliation of heart, in respect to his sins in the profanation of God's holy sabbath. Sabbath sins he always regarded as among the most heinous; and the remembrance of his sabbath profanation, even in the days of his youthful folly, and only in such ways as are common to the young, filled him with the deepest shame. To these sins he applied the expressive word, "abominations," and it was in this light that he regarded them.

Yet it is not to be supposed that he exceeded other young men in thoughtlessness, or his love of worldly pleasure, or his inattention to the claims of the sabbath. Indeed he speaks of himself as being derided and abused by others; and seems rather to have been enticed into that course of folly by the influence of vain and worldly companions. Yet was it also in accordance with the inclinations of his own corrupt heart and hence it produced in his mind such feelings of remorse.

Dr. Yale has stated above, that upon his return from Richmond to Lenox, in the spring of 1799, he found the young people very much engaged in the prosecution of worldly pleasure. It was proposed to establish dancing parties, to be continued once a month through the season. The account which he has given of this arrangement is as follows: "This appeared to me to be a fine thing. Accordingly, being invited, I gave in my name as a subscriber to this school of Satan. In May the first was attended. I thought this was doing well. This joined me still closer with several young friends whom I greatly esteemed.

I promised myself much satisfaction in this new

mode of amusement, and gloried in it greatly. But in the beginning of June scenes opened which brought in a new train of thoughts, and eventually produced a very great change in my character and conduct."

It does not appear that these dancing assemblies were held through the season, as was anticipated; or if they were, our friend had experienced such a change in his feelings as to have lost his relish for the amusements which were there afforded.

At that time there was in progress in some parts of the state of Connecticut a remarkable revival of religion. The Rev. Mr. Shepard (afterwards Dr. Shepard), the pastor of the church of Lenox, paid a visit to some of those places which were then enjoying the reviving influences of the Holy Spirit; and upon his return ,with his heart uncommonly warmed up with a spiritual influence, and possessing an uncommon measure of the Spirit's presence, he entered upon a system of labors which resulted in a revival of religion among his own people. He preached with peculiar fervor; and established meetings for prayer and religious conference, which were blest by the Spirit as the means of great good.

The mind of young Yale, then thoughtless and specially occupied with the pleasures of sense, was arrested. Being invited by a particular friend whose father was a professor of religion, he attended the first conference meeting which was appointed, and as he believed, the first which was ever attended in the place. Of this meeting and the state of his mind subsequently, he gives the following account:

"The subject of discourse was the Being and Perfections of God. It seemed new. My attention was awake. I began to think. I was convinced that there was a God in reality, and saw some evidence of it more than I had ever seen before; although I do not remember that I ever doubted the Divine existence. The next week I attended another conference, when people flocked together from all parts of the town. The divinity of the Scriptures was the subject of discourse. I assented to this. My attention became more fixed. I rode home in company with a wise and influential Christian, who conversed considerably and helped to lead on my mind. Conferences were continued—young people were desired to write on the subjects. I wrote —entered deeply into the spirit of them, so that they engrossed all my thoughts, and occupied the chief of my conversation. As my views often enlarged, I became more acquainted with myself; and though I was often puffed up with pride, yet my views of myself tended to abase me in my own eyes.

"Sometime in the summer of 1799, I am not able to mention the day, I obtained hope of an interest in Christ. I had been mourning because I had not been more deeply convicted of sin. For though I had felt myself a great sinner, yet I had not felt that terror which many feel, and therefore it seemed as though I had not been suitably prepared for regeneration. Some obtained hopes before I did, which increased my anxiety, and gave opportunity for the exercise of envy. I remember well, one sabbath when in company with a few such, I envied them so that I could scarcely bear their sight. Then indeed was my soul in the gall of bitterness and under the bonds of iniquity. About the same time, a question was proposed about prayer which gave my soul great anxiety. It seemed as though I could not pray right, and yet I could not live easy without prayer. Several times I met with great terror when I attempted to pray. Being one day in my chamber alone, thinking on my condition, the 51st psalm, 1st part, L. M., of Watts' version, seemed to be exactly right to me, and the very language of my heart. Then I could pray like a perishing sinner who had nothing to depend upon but the sovereign grace of God. It seemed to be easy with me; and yet I had not the most distant imagination at that time that I was a Christian. Indeed, till two or three days after, thought nothing about having experienced grace, and then the thought was first suggested by a friend to whom I had been speaking of my exercises. Then I began to hope. But I was very much afraid to depend on what I had experienced, and the more because I did not think of its being gracious, till my friend had mentioned it. I was afraid of depending on his word for it. However I have many times thought since that it was rather favorable than otherwise, because my exercises spoken of above, did not in the least proceed from an idea that I was a subject of mercy. I always have looked upon my beginning as very small, and have sometimes doubted from this very circumstance. But I judge more by the fruit, than by the bud."

I am happy to have been able to present this account of Dr. Yale's early life and religious experience from his own pen. It was written by himself at different times, much of it more than forty years ago, and interspersed in his diary without any particular regard to the order in which the events took place; and yet, beyond all question it is a truthful exhibition of the state of his own mind and his religious exercises at that period to which it refers. Though he speaks of the beginning of his religious experience as very small, yet small as it was, the change at the time was very decisive. The change was apparent in his whole moral character; in his feelings, his train of thought, his theme of conversation, and his habits of life. He was effectually cured of his love of sensual pleasure; to him the ball-room had lost all its charms; his prayers were no longer a heartless form; and he felt no disposition to spend the sabbath as a day of recreation and idleness. He had become a partaker of that grace which moulded and modified his whole moral character.

From the time of his conversion, he was the same conscientious, exemplary Christian, that he continued to be through life. One who was on terms of great intimacy with him at a very early period of his religious history, and who ever after retained that intimacy, in a recent letter to the compiler of these memoirs, used the following language: "Mr. Yale was the same decided, uniform Christian at twenty, as at seventy.

Ready for conversation, good in the prayer-meeting, Bible with him in every religious service, careful in his daily walk, never uttered a foolish word, studious, systematic, laborious, advancing constantly, humble, unblamable."

It has been already remarked, that from early youth, Dr. Yale was particularly fond of books. The books to which he had access at that period of his life were by no means numerous. Yet did he read all that came into his possession, and improved all the facilities for improvement in literature which were within his reach. For years before he experienced a change of heart he had earnestly desired to devote himself to literary pursuits. He says of himself: "I had early very strong desires of becoming learned, and of being a minister. No object excited my admiration so much as literature; and I little envied any but learned men. And of all the professions, the ministerial only had any charms for me. But I used to endeavor to suppress my desires, because I supposed it impossible that I should ever obtain a liberal education. It was not that I might do good, however, that I wished to be a minister; but I thought ministers so good and happy, and so honorable that I wished to be one."

After his conversion he retained his love for literary pursuits, and his desire to become a minister; though his motives for desiring that office were not only greatly modified, but thoroughly changed. It is true that he always regarded the office as more honorable than any within the reach of mortals; yet did he also cherish an impressive sense of the fearful responsibility which it involves; and he desired to enter upon it and to discharge its duties that he might thereby be enabled to do the most for the glory of God, the good of the church, and the salvation of men.

At the time of his conversion he was possessed of such an education as that he was thought qualified to teach a common school; and at the time that he determined to undertake the attainment of an education for the gospel ministry, his circumstances would not admit of his pursuing a regular collegiate course of studies. From that starting point his whole course, both literary and theological, was embraced in a period of less than three years in a private school taught by the Rev. Nathan Perkins of West Hartford, Connecticut. During this short period of preparatory study, he was so diligent and laborious, that he made greater proficiency than most young men would in the same time; yet did he regard himself as but poorly qualified for the work when he was licensed and entered into the field.

In his journal he has given an account of his license in the following words:

"Feb. 15th, 1803. This day, in company with Messrs. Osborn and Wetmore, presented myself for a license to the North Association of Hartford County. After examination it was voted that we should be approbated, and licensed by that body to preach the gospel. The day following, Feb. 16th, we received our licenses. When this was done, Rev. Mr. Hawley, moderator, addressed us in a short but very friendly and pious speech, inculcating an entire devotion to our work, great diligence in the cause of the Redeemer, and that we might be successful he recommended frequent and fervent addresses to the throne of grace.

Dr. Strong then made somewhat of a lengthy speech, in which he urged in the strongest manner the necessity of attending diligently and thoroughly to classical studies. He reminded us of the responsibility which that body had taken upon themselves, and the critical situation in which they were placed by licensing those who had not been liberally educated. He moreover recommended great care and caution that we might not speak diminutively of collegiate education; but do all in our power to promote institutions so profitable and honorable to our country. Surely his observations were very weighty, and I am sure they pressed down my very soul. How poorly qualified to preach the gospel to poor ignorant immortal souls! May I remember the Doctor's advice as long as I continue to preach the gospel, should it be to the day of my death. Rev. Mr.

Washburn made some remarks to the same purpose, and concluded by assuring us of the friendly assistance of the association as far as their aid would be beneficial."

Dr. Yale never did undervalue the advantages of a collegiate education; nor did he ever cease to regret that his own early advantages had been so limited.

Yet such were the powers of his mind, and he entered upon his work with so much of the spirit of devotion, and he was so systematic in his labors, and he pursued them with so much diligence and industry, that he took a most respectable place among his brethren in the ministry, and was honored as a very successful laborer in the vineyard of his masters. He after received the honorary degree of Doctor of Divinity from one of the leading literary institutions of the country, and though the honor set as lightly upon him, perhaps, as upon any man who ever wore it, yet very many are far less deserving of it than he. He was a great biblical scholar, and became an acute theologian; while his literary attainments were such as to command respect even from the learned.

CHAPTER II.

THE TYPE OF HIS PIETY.

That Dr. Yale was an eminently pious man, none doubts who has had the benefit of his acquaintance. The character which the pen of inspiration gave to the early companion of Paul, was in a high degree applicable to him; "He was a good man and full of the Holy Ghost and of faith:" The design of this chapter is to present some things, by which his piety was particularly distinguished.

1. It was eminently characterized by the low opinion which he had of himself, and the humiliating view which he took of his own innate corruptions. If the estimate which others form of him, is to be graduated

by that which he formed of himself, it would by no means be of an elevated character. He was perpetually struggling with sin, and perpetually mourning over the remains of corruption within him. This fact it is proposed to illustrate by some extracts from his journal.

1829, March 22. "Pained in view of my sins and imperfections. Sorrow, sorrow, sorrow continually on this account; yet not so deep as it should be, or so entirely godly; 'Godly sorrow worketh repentance unto salvation, not to be repented of.' "

1831, Sept. 4. "In the morning felt ineffable distress on account of my internal pollutions. Could find no language to express the horrid, horrid, horrid sins of my heart—my neglect of duty—my wicked performance of duty—my contaminations of others by my pollutions. Cried to God, and delighted to know that Jesus saves from sin—takes away the stony heart—gives a heart of flesh—cleanses from all sin. But the thousandth part cannot be said, nor felt, nor conceived by me, nor by man."

Sept. 16. "Set apart this day as a day of private fasting and prayer—particularly to recollect myself, and prepare to preach, and to do all the duty incumbent upon me in this solemn time, and also to intercede in behalf of many perishing souls. In the course of the day meditated much on the 1st chapter of the 1st epistle of John, on fellowship. Some delightful views. Then on my sins. At first I seemed to have but little sense of them. But they came upon me as a flood, overwhelming all my thoughts, without number, or measure, or bound. It seemed for a time as though I could distinguish nothing in the immensity. But I took the ten commandments and looked them all over, and found particular sins against every one. Then I looked over my past life, and saw sins in every period, childhood, youth and riper years. Then I looked on the ministry, and saw amazing sins against God, and against souls. My distress and confusion in view of them were inexpressible, yet I knew that the number and aggravations of my sins were inconceivable by me. God only knows them. How true his holy word! My heart is deceitful above all things and desperately wicked; who can know it? I tried to fix upon the passage in close connection with fellowship; but for a time could not, to much advantage. 'If we confess our sins, he is faithful and just to forgive us our sins, and to cleanse us from all unrighteousness.' I wished for a sense of pardon, and assurance that my sins should be all cleansed away. I was not troubled with a fear of wrath, but with the immensity of my sins, which seemed not to be removed away.

"Cleanse me, oh Lord, and cheer my soul."

I read the fifty-first psalm, and also Watt's version. It was precious. Surely there have been other souls oppressed with sin. After struggling for awhile I went to the mercy seat with my soul, and committed it to my Savior, to be cleansed by him. O Lord, my only Savior, I bring my soul to thee. Besides thee there is no Savior. I despair entirely of doing anything without thee. All my doings to come to thee are polluted, my prayers, my reading, hearing, endeavors to repent, believe and trust. All are like the leprosy of the leper, when he came to be healed—all unclean; like the services of the worshipers offering sacrifices and oblations, all needing to be washed. To thee I give up my soul, to be saved, to be washed in thy blood, to be purified by thy spirit, to be saved from the world and the devil by thy power. It is said that thy name is Jesus, for 'he shall save their people from their sins.' Thou hast said, 'Him that cometh unto me, I will in no wise cast out.' I come to thee just as thou hast said, a sinner to be saved from sin by thee, in thine own way. O Lord, thou wilt not cast me out. Thou wilt save me as I need, as thou art able, and as thou hast promised. Amen."

Similar extracts might be copied from his diary, to any amount; but I will give but two or three more, and these shall be very brief. Though they breathe the same spirit of deep humility, on account of sin, and though they present him as engaged in severe and earnest struggles with his own depravity; they do at the same time, give us some additional features of his Christian character.

1822, April 6. "O! how barren my soul! I seem to have no desires, and my prayers do not ascend over my head. I have not a spirit of prayer. 'God, be merciful to me a sinner.'"

1824, July 4. "My heart—how vile—pride—ambition—self—envy—these enemies—O Lord, bring them out and slay them.

"O, for a closer walk with God."

To walk with God—this is, to believe as he teaches —to obey his commandments—to go as he directs—to aim as he aims—to shun what he hates—to delight in what he loves."

July 13. "Selected for preaching in the evening, a sermon on the case of the wicked woman forgiven. Blessed be God, it was an encouragement to my own soul, particularly as to prayer. I had been so sinful, so remiss, so guilty, that my confidence in prayer was gone; but this renewed my confidence. My sins did not seem to be so great a bar—no bar at all. I mourned over all my imperfections, and sins, in this respect. My success in the ministry seemed little—my work difficult —as though great efforts were necessary to do anything. Others seem to do their work easier than I. Indeed, it has seemed so a long time—my prayers not heard—my preaching not blessed. I mourned over this, wept, besought God to correct all my disorders, and make me right. I did beseech him to bless my labors, my people. O, that God would subdue my heart, and bring me to himself."

2. His religion was characterized by his earnest desires after holiness. His conscious imperfections were productive of the bitterest grief, and he sighed, earnestly sighed for deliverance. His convictions were strong that the work of sanctification was progressive; and the idea that a Christian believer becomes perfectly sanc-

tified, as the result of a single struggle with his corruptions, was not in accordance either with his theology or his experience. He fully believed it to be a work which, for its completion, requires the whole period of a man's natural life. He had no doubt that his warfare as a Christian, would continue as long as he dwelt in the flesh , and that it would only be as he passed into a state of immortality, that all his sins would be washed away. Yet, if there was one desire which burned in his bosom, with greater intensity than another, it was that he himself might be altogether free from sin.

1829, Nov. 10. "When I awoke in the night, the beauty of holiness delighted my soul. I felt some of my unholiness, and longed to be holy as God is holy. Oh, how hateful did all that religion appear which is not holy!"

1831, June 19. I have tried to preach three sermons this day. But it seemed as though I could not preach. Yet people were pretty attentive. Yet oh! the terrors of my own soul! What it is, I know not, but usually preaching is my greatest terror. Lord wilt thou not afford me relief? Is this because I am so prone to be proud and vain, and self-sufficient? Dost thou employ these inward trials to keep me low? Anything, O Lord but sin. Let me be filled with horror rather than pride. Thou knowest what I am, what I need, what is good for me. O, do teach and help me to preach as I ought. and let me look at what I preach, and the spirit by which I am actuated, rather than my own joys, or sorrows, comforts or terrors. Let my soul be subdued unto thee, and be sanctified and pardoned through Jesus Christ, and all shall be well. Amen.

1829, Aug. 22. "Search me, oh God and know my heart; try me and know my thoughts, and see if there be any wicked way in me, and lead me in the way everlasting." I do not desire to cover my sins. O God, do I not desire to discover them? Wilt thou not lay them all open to me, and enable me so to see Christ, as to be able to bear this dreadful sight? O, my God, take away all my sin. Sweep, wash, tear away all my pollution. O make me holy, even as thou requirest me to be holy. Why should I love the praise of a man that shall die? Of man, a sinner? Of man, who is only convalescent in a hospital, to say the best of him? Of man, more than half blind, unholy, unfit for anything, except to be purified by the grace of God? Shall such beings praise one another? Shall such beings be tickled with each other's praise? O, what folly! O may I evermore be pained, instead of pleased at such praise. O, may I be deeply abased, and loathe, and abhor myself."

3. His piety was characterized by a remarkable degree of self-vigilance, and a close inspection of his own heart. He was a most rigid disciplinarian—and more especially in regard to himself. He seemed constantly to have before his mind the injunction of wisdom, and it seemed ever to be his purpose to fulfill that injunction, to its very letter: "Keep thy heart with all diligence, for out of it are the issues of life." This point shall be illustrated by further extracts from his diary.

1829, Oct. 29. "Felt some anxiety in the morning, about myself, the church, the hoping, the awakened and others; and endeavored to lay all before God. Troubled some with myself because I meet with no enemies in my heart just now. Fear they are lurking in the walls to deceive me. I know they are not all dead, and that I must never put off my armor so long as I live. Entreated the Lord to keep me awake, and active, and watchful day by day, that the enemy may get no advantage."

Sept. 7. "I must talk some with my own heart. I have seen in thee, O Heart, some of the most deadly enemies of my soul; pride, self-complacency, vanity, ambition. These like serpents lift up their crested heads, and flatter that they may deceive; and try to deceive that they may destroy me. I could find no relief but in Christ. O Lord, deliver me for thy mercy's sake."

1835, Feb. 28. "I have preached to-day on this text, Ps. 71, 16," "I will go in the strength of the Lord, I will make mention of thy righteousness, even of thine only." This is my purpose, and is well adapted to my case. This is just the strength I need; just the righteousness in which I can safely appear.

"Who exposed to others' eyes,
Into his own heart never pries,
Death's to him a strange surprise."

I will now endeavor to pry into my own heart. This is so much the age of action, that the temptation is very great to neglect one's own heart. I fear I have fallen by this temptation. The inevitable consequence is leanness of soul, self-ignorance, and a loss of communion with God. But where shall I begin?

1. My views of truth—My doctrinal views—My spiritual views.

On examination, I find that my doctrinal views do not differ very materially, from what they were thirty years ago. I am satisfied that they are agreeable to the word of God. Yet am I not hereby justified. God is my judge. Perhaps many are satisfied that they are right, who are yet totally wrong. But I do think that my views accord with the plain teaching of God's word, without addition, without diminution, and without variation.

Were I as well satisfied with my spiritual views, I should not have much room to doubt. Is it then anything more than intellect? Than reason exercised correctly about revelation? Are my affections engaged so that I do truly esteem, admire, love, delight in, submit to and cordially receive God's truth as revealed in the word? There is a receiving of the truth in the *love of it.* Is it so with me? I think it is.

2. My profession and duties.

I have long professed religion, and performed its duties. Without them I could not consistently think myself a Christian. But with these, I am not, unless I have something more. There is a duty of the spirit. Does my *heart* perform duty? I am in the closet, the family, the sanctuary, every place. But this may be professional belonging to my ministry, or it may be by habit.

Or it may be to keep up my profession or appearance of consistency. Or it may be to be seen of men. Or it may be to gain the favor of God. Is it none of these?

Suppose all these considerations to be blotted out of my thoughts. Is there anything else to keep up my profession, and to stimulate me to duty? Suppose it were all to be done again, would I make a profession of religion and engage in duty? I think I would. But why? What moves thee, O my soul, to think this? Do I love this religion? Do I love the author of it? Do I feel myself bought by Jesus Christ? Am I desirous to honor him? Am I governed by his will in duty? And do I with my heart, in the spirit feel and act in my duty? In this ordinance of the Lord's supper, what is it which induces me to partake of it? My Lord's command is the outward inducement. But is it because I love him? Do I feel my need of him as a whole and complete Savior? And do I partake of this ordinance so as to partake of Christ? Do I view it also as the seal of the covenant? And do I partake of it so as to seal my covenant with God, and renew my entire devotion to him? Do I view it also as a feast in the wilderness, not for the body, but for the soul? And partake of it for my spiritual nourishment and growth in grace? and that I may serve the Lord more spiritually truly, fervently, and effectually? And do I also view it as an amazing token of the Savior's love? And do I receive it with lively gratitude and thanksgiving?

Furthermore, do I see in this the most lively expresion of the evil of sin! And do I abase myself the more deeply before God my Savior on account of the extreme evil of sin against one so good and gracious? And do I take occasion from this view of sin to oppose it more effectually, entirely, sincerely and prayerfully?"

The above is but a sample of the fidelity with which Dr. Yale dealt with his own heart. He looked upon the heart as full of deceit; and there was nothing from which he shrunk with such an involuntary shudder, as the thought of being deceived in respect to his religious state and his acceptance with God. Therefore it was that he was in the habit of subjecting his religious character to the most rigid scrutiny. He looked at himself with an eagle eye; and there was nothing in the state of his affections, the feelings of his mind, or his motives of conduct, which escaped his notice. Whatever else he knew, or did not know he seemed to regard it as unpardonable for a man not to be familiarly acquainted with himself.

4. Dr. Yale's life was, in an uncommon degree, a life of faith.

He habituated himself to the exercise of faith in the whole of God's character, and the whole of God's word. Unbelief he regarded as a heinous sin; and it was a sin against which he guarded his heart with the greatest diligence. His doctrinal views of truth accorded with the standard of the Presbyterian church of which he was a member. His firm reliance for salvation and acceptance with God, was upon the vicarious sacrifice of the Lord Jesus Christ, and there were few errors from which he shrunk with greater horror, than the denial of the essential Godhead of the Savior. On this subject he uses the following language, in a letter to a friend, under date of Dec. 16, 1850.

"I had rather that a teacher should be any thing else than a denier of the proper Godhead of our Lord Jesus Christ. No man that walks the earth is so offensive in my view. He pretends to be a Christian, and yet strips Christ of his divinity, and exposes him in the nakedness of his humanity. Oh! I can not endure it. Let him be Pagan, Mohammedan, Jew, Papist, Atheist, Deist, anything—but let him not pretend to honor Christ, and strip him of his glory. This I can not endure."

Nor was the faith of Dr. Yale a mere assent of the understanding to religious truth. Faith in him was a vital principle, which controlled the affections, and prompted to a life of obedience. He leaned on the grace of Christ, as a child leans on the arm of his father, or an invalid on the strength of his friend; and his eye rested on the word of God, as the eye of the mariner upon the needle of his compass.

Take a few more extracts from his diary.

1830, Dec. 4.

> "The Lord can clear the darkest skies,
> Can give us day for night."

"Trust him, O my soul, with all thy wants, with all thy cares. "Believe when nothing is to be seen." "Offer thy prayer unto him without ceasing, and with just the same confidence, when he hides himself behind the dark cloud, as when he gives the visions of his glory. For he is the Lord, he changeth not."

1829, April 4. "In the morning, several things which I can not do, led me to think of walking by faith. O how delightful! Spiritual supplies, healing mercy for my diseased soul, bodily supplies, sermons, preaching, reading, visiting, promoting Christ's cause by societies, contributions, &c., all I have to do, all I would have others do, seemed to be the proper business of faith. Oh, let me live by faith, and work by faith. The second Psalm seemed peculiarly beautiful. 'Christ is all, in all,' Amen.'"

1840, Aug. 17. "Awoke between twelve and one, and was up nearly two hours, pondering over the condition of my neighbor, the church generally, and myself. Amazing unbelief! Heb. xi, was the guide of my thoughts and prayers. I saw clearly that the great thing I need is faith. I entreated the Lord to work in my heart this precious grace. The words of Garrick the comedian, were in my mind, which he said to the prelate: 'I make fiction appear like truth, and you make fact appear like fiction.' I saw that the only remedy is faith; such faith as that of Abel, of Enoch, of Noah, of Abraham, of Sarah, Isaac, Jacob and Moses. I prayed over these examples. I felt that the full and experimental belief of the realities revealed in the word of God, would lead me to do my duty. I tried to get a plan of operations, so that I might daily live by faith, and carry into practice what I feel."

If faith in principle, faith in feeling, and faith in action constitutes a Christian, then was he a Christian in a preeminent degree. His faith was the governing principle of his life; faith led him to rejoice in the government which God administers over the world, and implicitly to follow the Divine monitions.

5. His piety evinced itself in his most scrupulous exactness in the performance of whatever he believed to be duty; his conscientious regard to the requisitions of the law; and the prompt discharge of all his legal pecuniary liabilities.

Things which might seem to be of small importance, and which by many, perhaps, might be thought but little of, always commanded his attention.

Of this he speaks in the following passage from his memorandum.

1822, Oct. 20. "Rose at four o'clock. In prayer was affected with my imperfections, especially in not attending suitably *to little things*. 'He that despiseth small things shall fall by *little and little*.' I can see how I have fallen in my family, and among my people, and before my fellow-men, by not attending to little things. 'O this is a small matter—it will not do much good or harm. I am in haste and have more important business—let it go.' This is an error. I have prayed that I may be entirely altered in this respect. This is, however, the work of the closet. It only shows me what I should be. This is the morning of the sacrament day. O, may it be the beginning of a new life!"

His religious principles prompted him to render obedience to the requirements of the civil law. There were laws which his judgment did not approve, and which he desired to be modified or repealed; yet while they continued to be laws of the land, he believed that they ought to be obeyed. Civil rulers he regarded as "the ministers of God," and he believed it to be an unwarrantable assumption of rights for individuals to set themselves up in opposition to the requisition of the statute. He ever adhered to the principle that government should be maintained, even though it might be at the sacrifice of one's private interests.

Time was when the postal arrangements of the United States were such as to impose an additional amount of postage for every additional piece of paper, though it might be enclosed in the same envelope, without regard either to its weight or its value. It was thought by many, that an evasion of this law, where it could be done without detection, involved in it no moral wrong; and many good men had no misgivings in enclosing bank bills, or other valuable pieces of paper in letters, without paying the amount of postage required by law, provided they were so concealed as not to be discovered by those who were employed in the post office department. This subject, at one time, occupied the attention of Dr. Yale; and in respect to it he expresses himself in the following terms:

1822, Jan. 23. "An occurrence has recently happened, that has brought out a kind of depravity that I did not suspect to be lurking in my heart. It is considered as a kind of allowable fraud to conceal money in letters, and not pay the full amount of postage. But God has showed me that an honest man is honest before God. I must make inquiries on this subject, and understand the law exactly, and then conduct accordingly. It is a sacred duty to go exactly according to law. If I can not keep the law of the land, when it is good, how can I keep the law of the Lord which is far more strict and spiritual?"

Dr. Yale was strictly honest in all his pecuniary transactions with others. On the subject of the contracting and the payment of debts, he has given his views at length in a letter to a friend, from which I am permitted to make the following extracts.

"KINGSBOROUGH, *April* 17, 1849.

Dear Friends: As you think proper to consult me in regard to some temporal matters, I will give you the best counsel I am able to give, and I wish you to use it as Mr. Scott desired his friends to use his counsel—to help them to make up their own judgment. No man can shape his course specifically by the mind of another, unless he be a soldier, or a slave, or unreasonably willing to obey or believe what others command and teach. If I give you good reasons for what I say, you can appreciate them—if I do not, you ought not to regard them.

CONTRACTING DEBTS.—I like the apostle's rule very well. 'Owe no man anything, but to love one another.' Rom. xiii, 8. What Mr. Henry says on this subject you know, or you may read in his Commentary. I will give the substance of Mr. Scott's comments, which are about the same thing. He says: 'It can not be supposed that the apostle meant to prohibit the contracting of debts on *any account*, which is next to impossible to the greatest part of mankind; but only to direct Christians to pay all legal demands without needless reluctance and delay, and with great punctuality; and that they should avoid all superfluous expense, that they might be preserved from debt, and from the danger and discredit of not rendering to all their dues. Yet when all such demands were answered, they would still owe love to all men, with all the duties that would result from its enlarged exercise.' Mr. Scott continues by referring to the learned Erasmus, who thought the passage might be rendered in the indicative mode—'Ye do owe'—instead of the imperative—and he queries whether after all that subsequent commentators have written, the passage ought not to be indicative.

'The apostle was exhorting Christians to render to all their *dues;* and having branched out the general precept into a few particulars, he closes by adding, ye owe no man anything, &c; as if he had said: All that I would inculcate is reduceable to this. Obey the law of love to others in all its branches, and then you will render to all their dues.' He says the other construction, viz., the imperative, as it is in our version, 'may embarrass the minds of the most upright.' 'No doubt it is the duty of all Christians to avoid contracting debts, which they have not a reasonable prospect of discharging punctually.' This is as much of Mr. Scott as my spare time will allow. I would just observe in regard to this mode of translating the words of the original, that they are the same in the indicative as in the imperative. As that in the 14th of John: 'Ye believe in God, believe also in me.' It might just as well be rendered in the imperative in both clauses, as in the indicative, and vice versa. Thus; 'Believe in God, believe also in me.' Or, 'Ye believe in God, ye believe also in me.' In such cases the translator does not depart from the original, or force it, let him render it as he will. The words themselves can not determine which way they should be translated. Therefore the translator must have recourse to the scope of the passage, and other parts of scripture, which throw light upon the subject.

So far as I am concerned, I have always aimed to live within my income, and have done so. I have sometimes found it impossible to be out of debt; and yet have always made it a point to have property enough over my debts, to satisfy every demand, and to meet every demand when due, or by an arrangement with my creditors. I have sometimes been in debt nearly a thousand dollars, but was never afraid of defrauding any one. My debts are all paid now. And I wish to pay for everything when I purchase. It is not always easy to do so; nor is it needful to do so. A doctor's bill for instance, can not well be settled daily, or weekly, and so of some others. Sometimes I have hired money for current expenses, rather than pay the credit price. In doing so, six or eight per cent is saved above the interest of the money. Still I wish, and think it best when I can, to owe no man any money. Yet if I meet my payments, or if my creditor is willing to wait, I do no wrong.

I think these views are about right.

Yours, E. YALE."

Many years ago, Dr. Yale was appointed by the Presbytery to perform an important service, which seemed somewhat to flatter his pride; and which for that reason gave him some trouble, and led him to inquire whether, on the principle of self mortification, he ought not to decline its performance. After serious and prayerful consideration, however, he enters upon his journal the following decision: "In this I fear the working of my evil and depraved feelings. Though I have nothing to glory in, and have much more reason to be ashamed than to be proud, yet such is the state of my heart, that the love of the praise of men gives me much trouble. I have even doubted some whether I should not stay at home, for this sole reason that my heart is not prepared for this service. But I can not admit this principle. My duty is unalterable. My mind must be made right, if it is not right. I am to bring my mind to my duty, not my duty to my mind. O God, I beseech thee to purify my mind, and bring me into the very frame which is agreeable to thee."

6. Another thing by which his piety was characterized, was his non-resistance of injuries received, and his gratitude for favors conferred.

"But I say unto you that ye resist not evil; but whosoever shall smite thee on thy right cheek turn to him the other also." An injunction of the sin-forgiving Son of God, which, in the experience of his disciples, it is found to be most difficult to fulfill. To resent an injury is far more in accordance with the promptings of man's unsanctified heart, than to forgive it. A disposition to return good for evil, a blessing for a curse, is indicative of a high state of religious attainment. Yet even this was a grace which adorned the character of Dr. Yale. To be satisfied of this, one needs but to read those parts of his diary in which mention is made of certain individuals who had taken offence, and exerted an influence in opposition to his ministerial and pastoral labors. Though he speaks with great decision, and sometimes with strong disapprobation of their conduct; yet there are no imprecations, but an expression of an earnest desire that they may be made sensible of their sin, and repent.

As an illustration of this spirit of non-resistance of injuries, I will transcribe a single passage from his diary:

1829, April 11. "Wrote two letters—one to a man from whom I received one on Wednesday, in terms of most unmeasured abuse. I thought at first that I would throw his letter into the fire. Then I sealed it up, scratched out the superscription, and wrote his own name upon it, to send it back again just as it was. But finally I concluded to endeavor to overcome evil with good. So I wrote to him as kind a letter as I possibly could."

And while he thus refrained from resentment of injuries, he always cherished the feeling of gratitude in view of acts of kindness. The incident which follows, was in itself a mere trifle, amounting to but a few shillings; yet it was enough to call forth the religious sentiments of his own mind. It occurred when he was engaged in a course of family visitations.

1829, Sept. 24. "In one incident I saw an expression of kindness which was truly gratifying. At Mr. H's they gave my horse some hay. When I came away Mr. H. took up my bridle, and said: 'It appears to me you want a new bridle.' 'O my bridle and saddle will do to go together. But Deacon R. said the other day, he thought it was time my bridle should be lost.' Mr. H. took it and went into his saddle and harness room, and brought out a good bridle, almost new, and put it on my horse. I said, I am much obliged to you. 'You are very welcome.' When coming home I fear my pride was flattered; but I tried to be thankful to God, and to implore a blessing upon my benefactor. 'It is more blessed to give than to receive.' May he enjoy the blessing in this, and may I enjoy it in imparting such things as I have."

7. The character of Dr. Yale's piety may further be seen in his submission, under the afflictions of God's providence. The spirit of God within him prompted him to say: "*Not my will, but thine, O God, be done.*" His life, to a great extent, was a life of prosperity. It was his privilege to walk in the sunshine of God's favor. Yet he was sometimes called upon to drink of the cup of sorrow, and to sigh under bereavements.

He never had any children of his own; yet at different times did he receive youth into his family, who were blest with his training and his counsel. Among these was a lovely, promising lad, the son of a relative, whom he had adopted as his own. To him he became strongly attached, and if he had been his own child he could scarcely have loved him with stronger affection. The child bore the name of his foster-father, and Dr. Yale's happiness seemed to have been very much bound up in the lad. But it pleased God suddenly to remove this amiable and promising youth by death. A severe blow was it to him, and he bowed himself down under it, as if carrying a load which was well-nigh insupportable. Yet did grace triumph, and he was even then enabled to say: "Thy will, O God, be done."

His interest in the child commenced at a very early period of his existence, as will appear from a brief extract from a letter to his parents soon after receiving intelligence of his birth. It is under date of April 5, 1836.

"I am very much gratified indeed, that you called your son after my name. This was unexpected; but I thank you most sincerely, and hope he may live, and grow up, and be a minister of the gospel, to bear the name of Jesus to the nations. If the Lord would accept him for this service, and bless him in it, I should esteem it a greater honor and favor, than if all nations should become one empire, and he become emperor over the whole. O pray that the good Lord would condescend to accept him for this service. Since you have dedicated him to the Lord, you will desire to have him employed in the way best suited to promote his glory. But how short-sighted are we! How little do we know what is best and what the Lord will do with us and ours? It becomes us to be very humble, and say: 'Not as I wilt, but as thou wilt.' This lesson I have long been trying to learn; and yet, every new trial shows me that I need to learn it over again."

This child, afterwards, became an inmate of his own dwelling, and a member of his own family; beloved by them, and beloved by all. But God, in his inscrutable providence, was pleased to remove him hence, while yet the bloom of youth was in its freshness. "Even so, father, for so it seemeth good in thy sight."

The following from Dr. Yale's memorandum has reference to this afflictive event.

1849, Lord's day, March 25. "The dealings of God with me during the last few days have been memorable. On Monday morning last, about two o'clock (if I remember right), I was awake about two hours. I meditated, and arose and prayed. It seemed that I had been very deficient in duty, and I was distressed on that account. I pondered over my deficiencies and sins, and tried to get forgiveness for the sake of the Lord Jesus Christ. In the same connection the query came to me: Will you avoid what will displease God? And will you do what is agreeable to his will? I pondered it all over, and prayed over it, and came to the result that I would do so, by God's assisting grace. Something very pleasant came to my mind in connection with these words:

'I follow where my father leads,
And he supports my steps.'

I was settled, and undertook to act accordingly.

In the morning I went abroad—&c—

On my return home from preaching on Friday evening, found E. Y. West very sick. With some difficulty he seemed to get sweating, and on Saturday morning appeared better. Afternoon worse. At 2 P. M., when I went away to church meeting he appeared distressed, and asked me: 'Do you think this will pass off?' 'O yes, I think so.' When I returned, in about two hours, he was in inconceivable distress, and totally unconscious. So he continued nearly two hours. Then easier. Two men sat up with him. He took medicine. It operated well. In the morning he was easier, but knew nothing. I went and preached at the usual time. At noon I nearly gave up all hope. Went to church again and preached. About a quarter before three returned and found him breathing his last.

Just as he expired, I said: 'Let us pray,' fell upon my knees and said; 'Father into thy hand, we commend his spirit.' A few more sentences acknowledging the reign of Jehovah, saying among other things; 'We have said thy will be done; We do not take it back. We now say; 'Thy kingdom come, thy will be done on earth as it is in heaven, Amen.' I had before, in the morning and at noon, been earnestly pleading with God for body and soul in secret, and had given him up. Thus my experience has led me to realize at every step:

'I follow where my father leads,
And he supports my steps.'

O what trials since Monday morning last at 2 o'clock! But God has brought me through encouragements and discouragements. But the last trial—Oh! But thanks to God not a murmuring word or thought.

'I follow where my father leads,
And he supports my steps.'

I am come just so far led by my father. He is my guide. I hold his hand. I know not where he leads till I am at the spot. Thus I go as a little child—my hand in his. My father leads—supports.

But it is not a dream. It is a reality. My dear boy is gone."

Monday, March 26. "A day of great trials. The remains of my dear boy in the house, laid out upon a board, cold, motionless, and I am writing to his bereaved parents. O what a difficult task! O how could I tell them the melancholy truth? Yet I did it as well as I could.

Tuesday, March 27. "At 2 o'clock P. M. the funeral. Brother Wood preached, and a great concourse, young and old, was present. Many of his companions and associates wept. We took the last view. We saw the coffin closed, and followed it to its resting place. We left it there. But my solemn thoughts pry open the coffin, turn back the lid, and the linen covering over his face. I behold his pale visage, his light hair, his closed eyes, his sealed lips. How solitary he is there alone! How dark his chamber! How cold his bed! No more will he awake and arise till the Archangel's trump shall sound. Then will he awake and hear, and burst all bonds, and come forth and live again. Sleep on, then, dead, and cold, and silent clay. My father by thy side will wake with thee, and I and aunt near by, shall also awake and spring forth to immortality.

'O what amazing scenes!'"

On the day after the death of this youth, he wrote an account of it, and sent to his parents who resided some two hundred miles away. The whole letter is an admirable specimen of epistolary correspondence, and, in itself, shows remarkable skill in the manner of communicating such intelligence to afflicted relatives. But as the facts in the case are contained in the above extracts from his diary, I will transcribe of this letter only a few of its closing paragraphs.

He concludes as follows:

"And now dear weeping friends, join us and say as Job said at the loss of ten children at one stroke: 'The Lord gave and the Lord hath taken away: blessed be the name of the Lord.'

My dear friends, this is no dream, it is a reality. But, 'our Father and our Saviour lives.' And I entreat you to do as I have done, leave the soul of our dear boy in our Father's hand. I am silent; I can not say one word. Our father is the Father of spirits. In his hand we leave it, even as we committed it to him. Your aunt says she has nothing earthly to live for. May she and I live, as we ought always to have lived—to the glory of God. May you also be quickened and comforted in the Lord. We have remembered the words, Heb. xii, taken from Solomon: 'My son, despise not the chastening of the Lord, nor faint when thou art rebuked of him.' 'Is any among you afflicted, let him pray.' 'Pray for us.' We greatly need the Lord's help. ELISHA YALE."

A few extracts from another letter to these afflicted parents, written a few days later, and containing further particulars concerning their deceased and much-loved son, will farther reveal to us the depths of his sorrow, and also His spirit of submission to the doings of his heavenly Father.

KINGSBORO, Fulton Co., N. Y., *April* 4, 1849.

Dear Friends,—Your favor dated Saturday morning March 31, and post marked April 2, has just been received. We are not only glad but thankful, that you bear the great affliction so well. Writing that letter to you on Monday, the 25 of March was the hardest task of the kind that I ever undertook. But I thank the Father of all mercies, that he has enabled you to bear the shock so well. I purposely forbore to say much about the character of our dear boy, till I should write again. On Tuesday at 2 o'clock P. M., his funeral was attended. Rev. Mr. Wood of Mayfield, preached on Mat. xxii, 30., last clause; "But are as the angels of God in heaven." Three other ministers were present and offered prayer. We enjoy greatly the sympathies and prayers of our people, and so do you. It was vacation in the Academy and most of the students were away.

But their companions here took pains and sent as far as fifteen miles, though the traveling was very bad. His class-mates were all here, and the sabbath school and Bible class scholars, and the youth in the neighborhood generally. Many sat and cried as soon as they heard he was gone. One little boy cried all night at times. Elisha was a great favorite among his mates, and the youth and children generally. He had an influence very remarkable for one of his years. He was active, strong, laborious, kind, obliging, ready to do any service in his power, for the relief, benefit, or comfort of any one. You say, 'I hope he was always a good boy, and a comfort to you while he lived.' He was more than we ever expected. He never forgot the good you did him when he was very small. He was easily managed, and always ready to do anything he could do. He would leave his table at any time cheerfully to do what was needful. He was remarkably cheerful and happy. It was his usual practice as he passed my door on his way to bed, to say: 'Good night uncle.' And I used to say: 'Good night, sonny.' I feel what no one else feels at the loss of that 'Good night, uncle.' It was so cheerful, and pronounced with a feeling so kind, that it was charming.

On Monday, the 26th, the day I wrote you that letter, you can not think how we felt. It happened that only your Aunt and I, and Rebekah were at the table. The other place was empty. We wept. And when we read, his place was empty, so was every place empty, which he used to fill. ' His cap, his coat, his books—I can not specify—all brought him before us. I was prepared, in a measure, for the last look on Tuesday, and for the scene for the narrow, cold, dark, silent house. But my thoughts visit that house often. When I lie down on my bed, I think of our dear boy in his bed. I can easily pry into his little chamber, and look upon his pale, cold, placid face. I love to do so. I am not melancholy, but solemn and cheerful. God keeps us from murmuring, though we weep often.

We do thank and praise Him that not one murmuring thought has passed our mind. Oh! may there never be one. We left his spirit with God, just as I wrote you; nor have we desired to pry between the folded leaves of God's records. You gave him up to God in infancy. You have repeated the dedication often since. There we leave him in our Father's hand. I preached last sabbath on Job, x, 2, 'I will say unto God, do not condemn me; show me wherefore thou art contending with me.'

I observed the following things, after reference to certain facts, besides those in the case of Job:

1. That it is no new thing for men to be afflicted.
2. That it is proper to inquire why God afflicts us.
3. That God may have designs secret to us, and yet very important in his kingdom. So in regard to Job—to baffle Satan—to show his grace in us—to teach the world. So it may be in regard to us.
4. That we may bless God, and confide in him still. Job blessed God, and then he said: 'Though he slay me, yet will I trust in him.' I hope God is doing good by this heavy affliction upon us.

But a cloud is over our beloved boy. We do not think we idolized him. Perhaps we did not know ourselves. But be sure we do not murmur, though we often weep. Do not you murmur either; but bless the Lord. Our earthly hope is broken; but our God is the same. On Wednesday morning, the 28th, my heart began to sink at our empty house. But the blessed

Spirit, the holy comforter, showed me very gently, and made it plain that our Father would lead me to be more faithful in duty, and more spiritual in doing it. So I have gone about my work, and God finds me enough to do. I have felt no sinking since. How kind and gracious our Father, in restoring Mrs. West so far before the heavy tidings reached her. Oh! friends, be comforted in God, the author of all comfort.

I have made haste to finish the letter to-day, so that it may go on its way to-morrow morning; for I want to comfort your sorrowful hearts with the comfort which we have in God. Do not be swallowed up in overmuch sorrow. Heb. xii., 'My son, despise not thou the chastening of the Lord, nor faint when thou art rebuked of him.' Avoid two things, viz: trifling and fainting. His chastening will do us good, if the Lord adds his blessing. Write again before long, and let us know your comfort in tribulation.

Our love to the boys. May the Lord bless them.

Yours, very affectionately,

ELISHA YALE."

The death of this beloved foster-child was never forgotten. In all his after communications to his parents, which were very frequent, he speaks of him and of his death, much in the same strain as in the letter which has been copied above. But, though he never forgot him, and deeply mourned his loss, he uniformly spoke of him with the spirit of the most unfeigned submission. "*Thy will, O God, not mine be done.*"

Thus have I endeavored to present from his memoranda and his correspondence some of the leading characteristics of his piety. I have thought it best to specify several particulars. His piety was marked by his spirit of meekness; or the humble and lowly views which he had of himself—by his spiritual warfare with his spiritual foes; or his struggles with the corruptions of his own heart—by the close and active inspection which he maintained over his own religious state; or his watchfulness against the first risings of sin within him—by the vigor of that faith which he exercised both in God and the revelations of his word—by his conscientious regard to the demands of duty, in all his relations in life—by his spirit of forbearance and forgiveness in relation to those who might have sought his injury, and by his recognition of God's hand in all the dispensations of his providence, and submission to his will in seasons of the deepest affliction.

Yet, perhaps, there may be some who desire to know more definitely what those evidences of piety were on which he placed reliance, and by which he was led to regard himself as in a state of acceptance with God. Dr. Yale was not a visionary fanatic. He never looked for "visions and revelations of the Lord," in respect to his own religious state. He judged of himself by the exercises of his own mind; and judged of those exercises by their correspondence with the revelations of God in his word.

But as to what those particular evidences were on which he relied, we are not left to conjecture. Some further extracts from his diary will present this matter in a clear and satisfactory light.

1829, Dec. 11. "My meditations on the character which God approves, were peculiarly interesting, founded on II Cor. x, 18, and Heb. xi. I was satisfied of possessing this character in some small degree. Surely, if I know anything of myself, I do trust in the sacrifice of Christ; I do walk with God; I do fear and take refuge in the ark of safety; I do obey God's commands; I do feel and live as a stranger and a pilgrim on the earth; I do choose affliction with the people of God rather than to enjoy the pleasure of sin for a season. Thus I am satisfied of being a child of God. But I am not satisfied with my attainments, and feel very imperfect and sinful. I have not felt to-day that deep and lively, and humbling sense of sin, which I have sometimes felt, and which I need to feel now. I have rather an abasing sense of my great deficiency, than of my active sinful exercises. In all things I seem to be lacking in the vigor and fervor of the graces of the spirit. I feel not that lively, and holy, and powerful activity in the service of God, which becomes me."

1831, Nov. 6. " 'Tis a point I long to know, &c.

'Am I to the Lord inclined?'

On a careful examination, I do think I am, for,

1. I do think I truly love and trust the Lord Jesus Christ.

2. I do think I hate and turn from all sin.

3. I do think I continue in the Apostles' doctrine.

4. I do think I continue in the fellowship of the saints.

5. I do think I delight to continue in prayers.

6. I do think I delight in God's ordinances.

7. I do think I love to do good with such things as I have.

8. I do think that I am patient under insults and injuries.

9. I do think I love my enemies.

10. I do think I care, and labor, and suffer, and deny myself for the sake of the souls of men.

11. I do think I seek God's glory supremely.

12. I do think my treasure and home are in heaven. In some of these I am clearer than in others. But in regard to every one, I am, to a good degree, satisfied. I am imperfect, very imperfect in all; and I have many times, severe trials with the pride and self-seeking of my heart, those deadly enemies of God. Yet, if I know anything about myself, I do love holiness and lament my sin, and rely on Christ, and his Spirit, and the Father's grace for salvation; and hope in God's mercy in the gospel. The covenant of God's love is all my salvation and all my desire. I need no more. I wish no more. This is all sufficient, and altogether desirable and lovely. Amen."

1834, July 5. "In meditating on my condition this morning, I was convinced of being very far away from God, especially on this question—Do I know the Lord Jesus Christ? I answer, I know him to be the true God; I know him to be a true man; I know him to be one person, the Mediator, possessing these two natures; I know him to be the only true and all-sufficient Savior, as his name is Jesus, to save his people from their sins; I know him to be the anointed one, to be the prophet, priest and king of his people. But there is another sort of knowledge of which I feel some doubt—an intimate acquaintance, consisting in a constant, pleasant, delightful intercourse, more attractive than any other, than all others—intercourse drawing me to him, leading me to seek frequent interviews and enjoyment, so that he may say as to Moses: 'I know thee by name, and thou hast found grace in my sight'—so that he may own me as an acquaintance at last, and not cast me off, saying: 'I know thee not.' In this I am very defective, if not entirely destitute. And yet it seems to me that I have known something of this sweet intercourse. But oh! it is so long since, it is so long gone by, that I feel very doubtful. It seems as though the guards of the Lord's army hail me, and bid me to stand and answer some questions before I approach the King.

1. Do you know Jesus Christ, the Lord?

2. Do you believe in him, with a genuine, cordial faith?

3. Do you truly repent of all your sins?

4. Do you truly love the Lord Jesus Christ above all?

5. Do you truly, from the heart, obey all his commands?

I paused long at the first question, as stated above, and retired without gaining much satisfaction."

CHAPTER III.

MEANS OF *GROWTH IN* GRACE.

Dr. Yale was never satisfied with those religious attainments which he had been enabled already to make. His motto was: "Not as though I had already attained, either were already perfect, but I follow after." There are few men who are believed to have progressed farther in the life of piety than he; yet are there few who seem to have been more deeply anxious for still further advances. The nearer a man gets to heaven the more enraptured he may be expected to be with its glories; and the more like Christ he becomes, the more anxious is he to be perfectly transformed into his image. Dr. Yale, however, while he relied altogether on the efficacy of sovereign grace, ever recognized the necessity of appropriate means. He never believed that grace in the heart, like thistles by the way-side, would spring up of itself, uncultivated and uncared for.

The means which he employed for his own progress in holiness, did not differ in kind from those which are employed by others, and which, in some other cases, have also proved efficacious to the attainment of eminent piety. They differed not in kind; yet in the use of those means was he uncommonly diligent and conscientious.

Yet those who desire to imitate him in the Christian walk, will wish to know definitely the methods which he employed for his own religious improvement.

1. He often found his own spiritual state benefited by his efforts to benefit others. In this respect did he realize the fulfillment of the promise of inspiration, "He that watereth shall be watered also himself." He did not always see that fruit of his labor which he desired in the conversion of sinners; and the vineyard which he cultivated sometimes seemed to him to put on the appearance of barrenness: yet in the midst of all his labor, and toil, and fatigue, to promote the interests

of the church, he felt encouraged by this consideration, that if none others were blessed, the more he did for others, the greater was the blessing which he received in his own soul.

At one time he alludes to the experience of the eminently pious Brainard on the subject, as being the counterpart of his own:

1834, Oct. 14. "Brainard speaks frequently of being most spiritual when most strenuous and active in every duty. So I find myself. Is there not a good reason for it? Is not the mind more active? Do not we cooperate most with the Holy Spirit? He speaks often of the effects of the tender mercies of the gospel on his Indians, even more to produce conviction than terror has. So have I found it in my preaching."

He sometimes labored long and labored hard to promote the spiritual interests of his people, without realizing the results desired. One such period was near the close of the year 1849. He then engaged in a series of long continued and laborious efforts for the salvation of souls in one particular section of his congregation. Besides visiting families and holding personal conversation with individuals, he preached nearly every evening for several successive weeks. He was unwearied in his efforts, and spared no pains or toil to secure the end in view. During a portion of this time the meetings were numerously attended and peculiarly solemn. There seemed to be every promise of a powerful revival of religion. His own soul, at times, was in an agony; yet it was not known that there was a single conversion. The cloud dispersed which had been hanging over them; the hopeful appearances subsided; the meeting closed, and all put on the aspect which they had previously worn. Yet did he regard that very effort, though it was a time of deep humiliation, as productive of great good to himself. As to the results upon the people, they can never be fully known until the revelations of the judgment. Possibly some may have received impressions which will result in their conversion and salvation; while the condemnation of others may be heightened and their future misery increased. About the close of this period, he entered upon his memorandum a record, which, in a most interesting manner reveals the state of his own mind:

1850, Jan. 4. "Rose at five, after a very pleasant and refreshing sleep. Made arrangements by attending to things necessary, so that I was ready at six for the prayer-meeting in the closet. But oh! what a time! The devil with his whole army of doubters was upon me, darkening, perplexing, confusing my mind; and for nearly an hour and a half I was in a terrible conflict. At length I obtained some relief and was in a measure composed. But oh, how I was obliged to cry for succor to him who knows how to succor them that are tempted! I thought of our High Priest, I thought of Isa. lxiii. 9: 'In all their affliction, he was afflicted,' &c. I thought of the pity of the Lord, and of the text and sermon last evening. But oh! it seemed at times that my mind was all confusion. I was reduced to the necessity of being with Christ in the agony of the garden. I felt a great trial at the prospect of giving up at the North-West without a convert. What will the enemy—what will the people say? Among the multitude of my thoughts, it seemed as it did once before, that God might well cast me into a ditch, and cover me over with clods, and say: 'I have no more use for thee.' Could I complain? I never deserved any good; I have been very unprofitable. Now if he cast me away as a broken vessel, what can I say? 'Thy will be done.' I was calmed down in a measure. But I thank God I did not repine, or despair. When I ceased praying I was much exhausted.

During the day, one brother suggested the propriety of discontinuing every-day preaching at the North-West. I had come to the same conclusion yesterday. In reflecting on the subject, it seemed right to me to leave all my labor with God. He knows what to do with it. About forty sermons have been preached there since the 28th of October 1849. I did what seemed my duty to do, and God will use it as seems good unto him. I have derived great good from it myself, and I hope that Christians have had some considerable benefit. As to the impenitent, I know not who has received any saving good, or whether there ever will be any. God only knows. I leave all in his hands. So be it. Amen."

The results of that effort—who will venture to predict what they may yet prove to be? "My word shall not return unto me void." Yet, even though a sinner may not have been converted, nor a Christian edified, the man who took the most prominent part in it, and who performed the most of the labor, was himself most abundantly blessed. He might have said with David, "I humbled myself with fasting, and my prayer returned into mine own bosom." Nor was this a solitary instance in which a blessing to himself resulted from his labors for the benefit of others. It was the ordinary effect of such labors.

2. He derived great advantage, and took great comfort in serious meditation; and found it to be an important means of grace. His estimate of this may be seen from the following:

1820, Nov. 8. "Last evening I failed in spending a suitable time in devotion and contemplation, after my return from lecture. I see how I grieved the Holy Spirit. What a poor creature I am! I do feel as though heavenly contemplation was life to the soul. The little that I practice it convinces me that it is a most profitable and comfortable exercise."

In his private devotions he was accustomed to fix his mind upon some passage of Scripture, and meditate upon it with peculiar profit. He found it to be an important means of exciting hope, in seasons of despondency; of inspiring him with sacred confidence, in times of difficulty; and of furnishing him with spiritual weapons in his spiritual conflicts. He delighted to dwell in his thoughts on the sovereignty of divine grace, and the amazing mercy of God as exhibited in the sacrifice of his Son. He thought with the deepest interest upon the promises of the gospel, and the rich blessings which those promises encourage us to hope for. Indeed, the promises of God's word were to him like springs in the desert, cold water to a thirsty soul. He fed upon them. He feasted upon them; he lived upon them.

He speaks above of "heavenly contemplation;" and the phrase as used by him was full of meaning. His "conversation was in heaven"—for there was his treasure, his inheritance, his affections. He spoke of heaven. He thought of heaven. He found also that such thoughts were well calculated to promote his own spirituality.

3. In his efforts to promote his own spiritual improvement, he made great use of the word of God. He was a great Biblical student. God's word was like manna to his soul. He spent much time in reading it. Nor was it merely as a theologian and a critic; but as a Christian. It is true that be aimed at a critical knowledge of the volume of inspiration; such a knowledge as would enable him to explain, and expound, and enforce it in his public ministrations. His desire was to feed the people "with knowledge and with understanding." Yet did he also read the Bible as a treasury of knowledge in relation to Christian experience, and for the purpose of deriving profit to his own soul.

He had great confidence in the influence of the word of God in moulding the human character, and in controlling human passions; as well as a means of perfecting the graces of his people.

Several years ago he had in his family, and under his care, two lads, in whose welfare he felt a very great interest. These lads were by no means vicious; but, like other persons of their age, they did sometimes indulge in things which were exceedingly trying to his feelings. He talked with them, and prayed with them; and on account of the moral influence which he hoped thereby to produce upon their minds, did he give each of them a passage of scripture, daily, to be transcribed into their journal. Among the passages which seemed to have been designed to correct some fault, or to excite to some duty, were the following: "Not slothful in business, fervent in spirit, serving the Lord." "Wherewith shall a young man cleanse his way? By taking heed thereto according to thy word." "Let us hear the conclusion of the whole matter: Fear God and keep his commandments; for this is the whole duty of man." "In all thy ways acknowledge him, and he shall direct thy paths." "What shall it profit a man, if he shall gain the whole world and lose his own soul?"

While, therefore, he had such confidence in the efficacy of Bible truth, it is not to be wondered at that he devoted so much of his own time to its study.

See his estimate of the Bible in the following:

1832, July 15. "Felt distressed in view of my neglect, and set myself immediately about a reform. In reading the Bible and secret prayer, I am resolved by the grace of God to begin a new life. That I may be definite, I will read, generally, one chapter in the Old Testament, and one in the New Testament daily, and three Psalms of David by myself, with meditation and prayer, besides what I may read in studying the Bible; and on the Sabbath read no other book but the Bible, or some one that tends directly to explain and enforce it."

It is true, also, that both in the reading of the word of God by himself, and in the public exposition of it to others, he was accustomed in a remarkable degree, to make a personal application of it to his own particular state.

1830, June 20, Sab. "Examined my own heart on the subject of my sermon, particularly in regard to the principle of life. Am I truly alive? I have a name to live. I am thought to be orthodox, moral, liberal, zealous. But do I truly live? Have I living faith? Do I desire the glory of God? Is my supreme affection in heaven? Having a name to live, I have a name to keep alive. This may be the only motive which governs me. If it be, I am certainly dead. Let me, then, be very careful, very impartial, very faithful in searching into my mind, in the light of God; for it is in his light only that I can stand in the invisible world, in the last great and trying day. Christ says: 'I know thy works.' 'Search me, O God, and know my heart; try me, and know my thoughts, and see if there be any wicked way in me, and lead me in the way everlasting."

1829, Nov 9. "Attended inquiry meeting. A peculiar solemnity prevailed while I read and remarked on the 6th of Isaiah. Scarcely ever in my life did I feel such an impression of the holiness of God, and of solemn delight in contemplating it. Surely God was in the midst of us. The coal from the altar seemed to be applied to the lips of some. Oh, may the Holy Spirit purify all our hearts!"

Furthermore, was it true, that the word of God was most skillfully used by Dr. Yale, in repelling the assaults of his spiritual foes. His warfare with sin and with Satan, was most faithfully maintained; and in it he found an advantage in resorting to the truths of the Bible. Unsheathing the "sword of the spirit," and making an appeal to the authority of God, was usually found efficacious in driving back and disarming all those spiritual enemies by which he was assaulted.

Take a single example:

1840, Aug. 9, Sab. 'Temptation commencing in a vile dream by night, this morning carried my soul away to think of things proper on week days, but not on the sabbath. Found the whole armor necessary, with all prayer, to resist the devil, lest he should remain at my right hand to resist me. Then came other wicked thoughts, like fiery darts, ready to set on fire the wicked combustibles within me. Then I cried unto the Lord, 'Iniquities prevail against me!' 'For thy name's sake, O Lord, pardon mine iniquities.' 'As for my transgressions, thou wilt purge them away.' 'A fountain opened to wash in from sin and uncleanness." Precious words! Those operated as thrusts to the adversary. But I perceive that a conflict is before me. God permits the devil to come near me. Now I try to do as he says: 'Draw nigh to God and he will draw nign to you.' 'Resist the devil and he will flee from you.' 'Cleanse your hands, ye sinners, and purify your hearts, ye double minded." Surely I have enough to do. Lord grant me the grace I need. Help me to hide in the secret of thy pavilion. Be thou my great shield, my target. Help me to use thy sword well, to watch, and to pray. Then all shall be well. Found the 141st and 142d psalms peculiarly adapted to my case, and part of the 143d. Yet I am not so low now as David represents himself in a part of that psalm. But how soon should I be if the Lord should leave me! Yea, I should be as one shut up in prison and enclosed in hewn stone. But I am not so now. I do not now despair; though I should in a moment, if God should leave me in the hands of the giant."

Thus "Mr. Great-heart" struggled with the conqueror, and himself conquered, by the use of those spiritual weapons which are furnished in the word of God

4. Another means on which he greatly relied for growth in grace, was earnest, importunate prayer.

Prayer he found to be one of the instrumentalities of God's appointment, both to promote the interests of Christ's kingdom in the world, and to keep alive the fire of holy love, in the hearts of individual Christians. His closet he has called his "earthly paradise;" and there he seems to have talked with God, as a man talks with his friend. He was often there, and there, too, at hours when most others were locked in the deepest slumber. "And in the morning, rising up at a great while before day, he went out, and departed into a solitary place, and there prayed."

Nor was there anything which grieved him more than a conscious want of the spirit of prayer; and whenever such was the case, he diligently set himself at work, to inquire after the cause.

1824, Feb. 2. "I have to lament my want of a spirit of prayer, and nearness to God. I sometimes fear that all is vain for want of that holy intercourse with God which is the life of all religion and action."

1849, May 3. "As I was going to my study early, about half-past four A. M., I said to myself: 'If I had a spirit of prayer, I could offer such prayer as God would accept and answer. A stern question came to me: 'Whose fault is it?' I was withered in a moment. For here is a throne of grace. I said long ago, if I do nothing else, I will endeavor to pray. Luke xi, 1,-13, shows me how, and affords all the encouragement I need. In Romans viii, it is said: 'The Spirit also helpeth our infirmities.' 'Whose fault is it?' I am deeply in fault—awfully deficient—do not pray as I ought—nor as much as I ought—especially when afflicted. I tried to humble myself and pray. Then I said to my wife, as I met her afterwards: 'Whose fault is it?' Said I to another person whom I met alone: 'Whose fault is it?' May the Lord search and make us of a contrite, and humble spirit, trembling at his word."

"I said long ago, if I do nothing else, I will endeavor to pray." This is a resolution which is found recorded in his diary, in the most solemn manner. Prayer was his life.

1836, Nov. 22. "Among the thoughts of this morning, the importance of prayer, which I have felt partially for some time, was urged with much force, and I now feel that if I do nothing else, this must be done—that I must do as Daniel when he set himself to seek the Lord by prayer and supplication. *This is now my fixed purpose, that by the grace of God I will live a life of prayer if I do nothing else.*

So help me God, Amen."

In addition to his ordinary closet devotions, he frequently observed seasons of private fasting and prayer. This he found to be an important means of grace. At times they were observed with great frequency—sometimes as often as once a week, and not unfrequently not less than six times in the course of a year. These seasons were observed with great solemnity and spiritual profit; though it was not uncommon for him to have, on these occasions, severe struggles with himself, and to find his soul shrouded with the deepest darkness.

As a sample of the manner in which these seasons were observed, take the following:

1824, March 6. "Set apart this day for special fasting and prayer.

1. Because religion is low in my soul, and I have greatly declined in the spirit of prayer.

2. To implore a revival among my people, and especially in the church, that God would stir up all to duty, and bring about a great revival and convert all the people.

3. Especially that he would direct and bless the means about to be used.

Spent considerable time in examining scriptural uses of fasting and prayer—Moses—Joshua and Israel—the eleven tribes before Gibeah—David—Elijah—Jehoshaphat and Judah—Ezra—Nehemiah—Esther and Mordicai—Daniel—Christ—the Apostles—Paul often.

About 12 o'clock I tried to pray, but all appeared dark, and cold, and senseless. At two I went to church meeting, endeavored to say something, but my mind was not clear. Just at evening I seemed almost prepared to pray. At a little prayer-meeting in the evening, I felt more freedom than for a long time. Tried to pray again in the family, and in the closet, but it seemed as nothing. Yet I could not feel distressed at my condition. It seemed to me, however, that this must be no more than the beginning of the work, and that I must go on and abound more and more. By the grace of God I will not rest, but will abound more and more."

Sabbath morning, March 7. "God has given me more light and exercise in prayer than for a long time. I feel as though I must not view fasting and prayer as a penance, but as a privilege; not the fasting as delighful in itself, but as a source of improvement and a means of nearness to God.

Oh, may God quicken me, in great mercy."

March 13. "I have set apart this day for private fasting and prayer for the same reasons that I did Saturday last. In my first address had particular nearness to the throne of grace, plead the promises, besought the purifying influences of the spirit, especially as I am seeking a universal revival among my people, that he would deliver me from all selfish feelings and aims, such as pride, vanity, ambition, ostentation, envy, and every desire to be known and distinguished; that he would grant me his Holy Spirit for this purpose, and work the right exercises in me; that he would dwell in me as his temple, and make me fit; that I might be holy as the angels and the spirits of the just; that I might love my neighbor as I am required to love him, and seek his salvation as the salvation of my own soul.

I rejoiced that God had required this, for it not only *authorized* the work I am attempting, but *required* it. I can not love my neighbor as myself, unless, as I have ability and opportunity, I seek and labor for his salvation as my own. I rejoiced to plead for the Holy Spirit as a child for bread, and with God who is incomparably more willing to give it to them that ask him, than parents are to feed their children. My soul went to God in confidence of his ability and his love. I saw that nothing was too hard or too much—the spirituality of all my brethren, the conversion of all my people, ministers, churches, colleges, legislators, officers, factories, merchants, and men in places of public resort.

Indeed the great work seemed to be under the hand of God, and able to be done. I desired and prayed to be wholly free from all other business, to engage in this. I felt as though I had just begun to pray, and knew not how to keep on; but God is a fountain inexhaustible.

Between eleven and twelve, I besought God to enlighten, by his Spirit shining into my mind, so as to discover my sins, wherein I had declined in a spirit of prayer, and how I might rise again and recover.

1. My sins—ambition—pride—envy—sensual appetites. Sensual desires are beastly; the sins of the soul are develish. The brute keeps close to the devil. These detestable sins must be mortified and removed, for they oppose all good, and God hates them.

2. Wherein I have declined in a spirit of prayer. Neglect of reading the Bible, neglect of secret prayer, very often in the evening and when away from home. Praying very often without a spirit, and remaining so. Praying without watching, and without careful meditation. Hence it is more frequently my task than my pleasure. Lamentable truth! What need of deep humiliation? No mechanical system will answer. I must pray always with all prayer and supplication in the Spirit, and watch thereunto with all perseverance.

3. How I may rise again and return.

This is not so easy to tell. 'Facilis decensus averni, sed revocare gradum—hoc opus.' How shall I so recover as to come into the presence of God and obtain what I ask?

1. *Cast out iniquity.* For the Psalmist says: 'If I regard iniquity in my heart, the Lord will not hear me.'

2. *Do always what pleases God.* The Savior says: 'I do always those things that please him.' 'I know that thou hearest me always.'

3. *Desire what is lawful, and desire it from pure motives.* 'If we ask anything according to his will, he heareth us.'

4. *Ask in the name of Christ.* 'Whatsoever ye ask the Father in my name, he will give it to you.'

5. *Rely on the Spirit.* 'The Spirit itself helpeth our infirmities.'

In the afternoon was encouraged to implore a universal revival among my people by the following considerations, viz:

1. *God loves every soul.* I do not know that every one is elected, nor that it is not. I do not know but that God has turned away from some finally, nor that he has.

2. The provisions of the gospel are equally adapted to the wants of all.

3. The spirit pervades all, and is able to move all hearts.

4. God has not restricted me, but has commanded me to love my neighbor as myself. Therefore, I not only *may* ask, but if I love as I ought I *must* ask.

5. God may be glorified, these souls made happy, they may be used to do good to others, angels and heaven will be happier, and I shall be happier myself."

April 3. "Set apart this day for fasting and prayer, to seek the blessing of God, especially upon my people. I do not feel that spirit of intercession which I need and which I have felt in former times. I would seek help in this. But Oh, let it not be a penance, or work of self-righteousness. On reviewing, March 13th, and comparing it with two facts which have since come to my knowledge, I am some surprised. That was my second day of fasting and prayer. During the night after, a neighbor, an excellent Christian who was sick, was greatly distressed by the sensible hiding of God's face. She told me three days after, it was the most dreadful darkness she had ever perceived—she could not get one ray of light. The next day, another neighbor, a very pious woman, at meeting had a more clear and awful sense of her sinful heart than she ever had before, so that it seemed to her she must die on the spot. She told me this last evening with great solemnity, and expressed an earnest desire that her family might all know the evil of their hearts, and not be deceived.

It is remarkable that these should be so near my day of fasting and prayer. I am afraid my evil heart will receive injury from the discovery of these facts. O Lord, humble me. Yet may I not hope that my prayer has begun to be answered? I scarcely dare to think of this. I am afraid the thought will so injure my mind as to provoke God, and to prevent his blessing. O what a heart I have! What need of being humbled and purified!"

CHAPTER IV.

HIS COMMUNION WITH GOD.

"And the Lord spake to Moses face to face as a man speaketh to his friend." After having been in the mount with God for a succession of days, when he came again into the camp, the skin of his face shone so that the people "were afraid to come nigh him." Such as held intercourse with Dr. Yale often felt that there was such a luster about his person, as that they were exercised with feelings of peculiar reverence in his presence. The reason may not always have been apprehended, yet it might have been found in the fact that he held such intimate communion with God. "*The skin of his face did shine.*" He seemed to live in the atmosphere of prayer. He realized the truth and acted in view of it, that the life of the soul can no more be supported without prayer than the life of the body without nutritious food. Prayer in him was a daily and habitual exercise; and he frequently regretted the necessity of being away from home, chiefly because his stated seasons of communion with God were thereby interrupted. "There is the place," says one when pointing to Payson's pulpit, "there is the place where Payson prayed." But it was not the pulpit chiefly which marked the fervor of Dr. Yale's devotions. Away from all human eyes, and not unfrequently when the eyes of most were closed in dreamless slumber, did he pour out his soul to God in the most earnest and importunate supplications.

Though mention has already been made of his habits of prayer as a means of his own religious progress, yet he was so preeminently a man of prayer that the subject requires a separate chapter. The views which he entertained of the nature of prayer and the spirit with which it should be offered, he thus expressed in his diary, under date of Oct. 18th, 1826:

"This morning I am sensible that most of my feelings in prayer are totally wrong. To feel that prayer is a task is to feel wrong. To feel that prayer is a task which must be performed, is to feel wrong. To feel that prayer is a task which, when performed, will secure God's favor is to feel wrong. To feel that prayer is a task which, when performed, will have the least tendency to secure God's favor, is to feel wrong. To feel that prayer is a task which, when performed, lays God under any obligation to show us favor, is to feel very wrong—it is an abomination. To feel that prayer is a task which, when performed, may encourage us to look for divine favor, is to feel wrong.

I ought to feel that God is infinitely righteous, and might righteously rive my soul with lightning, and send me to instant death. I ought to feel that his infinite mercy has wrought great things to render it consistent for a sinner to pray—devised the way of salvation—sent Christ to die—revealed the way—given the encouragement—bestowed the Spirit. Sinners may pray to God by virtue of this amazing system of mercy. But we must feel that it is amazing mercy which allows us to pray. And we must feel that when we are thus allowed to pray, we should improve the allowed liberty, as a favor of the greatest magnitude—to plead for the life of souls—to plead as intercessors for others. Illustrate this by a criminal approaching a king—how vile—yet how needy—will he make a merit of it? Endeavor to have and to promote such feelings. How Abraham felt when he approached to plead for Lot and Sodom! What an immense difference between right feelings and the common feelings of men in regard to prayer!"

The sincere and earnest desire of his heart was to maintain intimate communion with God; and when he failed in so doing he felt depressed and cast down, as success in it was ever regarded a cause for gratitude and joy. His earnest desires for such holy intercourse with God, and his enjoyment of such intercourse, are expressed in the following:

1824, June 16. "In secret prayer God seemed to be actually present, and to impress my mind with this, that if we would live, and pray, and speak, and write, and converse, and act, just as though he were by, and we realized it as we do the presence of man that we converse with, it would be our rule of prudence in all things and at all times. Then truth as it is in his word and in fact would prevail. Then duty would rule. Then sin would be put down, because the presence of God would so overawe us, that we should have no fear of man. This view seemed to be an answer to our prayer last evening, for we can not be at a loss before God. We dare not speak anything but exactly agreeable to his truth, in all its extent before him. O that I might always feel this! As this is the commencement of my forty-fifth year. O that I might this day and every day of my life, live deeply and fully under this impression. This is walking with God, as Enoch and Noah. This is having God with me as he was with Joseph and others. This is having the fear of God before me all the day long. In this way I shall be wise and holy, and successful, just so far as it may be desirable to be successful. 'Whatsoever he doeth shall prosper.' O my God, grant me and all thy servants this grace, Amen."

1829, May 1. "Feeling confused, distracted, unprepared for anything, and yet knowing that much is to be done, I devoted this day to special abstinence and prayer. I want to gird up the loins of my mind so as to be the better prepared for my duty. I feel lost when I get away from God, and I need time for recollection, forethought, and contemplation. The Lord's supper is near. This month is also one for my journey. I expect to be much in company. O how much do I need the guidance and influence of the Holy One. O Lord guide and influence me. Having spent the day I am hardly roused from lethargy. Have, however, been thinking about keeping the heart, am but little impressed with divine things. Know but little of myself. Must preach to myself."

Estimating prayer as he did, it is not to be wondered at that he spent much time in this exercise. He called to mind the practice of the German reformer, of praying three hours in each day, and resolved to practice it himself.

1830, April 1. "Resolved to commence this day endeavoring to spend three of my best hours in prayer, as my ordinary practice.

1. From five to six in the morning, for myself and my friends.

2. From eleven to twelve A. M., for my church and people.

3. From nine to ten in the evening, for all the world.

I expect it will be impossible to observe these times always: but I shall observe them as well as I can. I do not include prayer only, but a little reading of the word of God, and meditation on it, and the condition of the subjects of prayer, directly to the point. This reading and meditation may be half the exercise or more. I am not to be always on my knees, but standing, walking, sitting or any suitable posture. At times a Christian friend may be with me when suitable. Indeed I think as much variety as possible consistent with the design, should be studied, that it may be a most profitable and delightful, and intelligent intercourse with God."

How far he was enabled to carry out this design does not appear; but that he was enabled to execute it, at least for a while, with some degree of success, may be seen from what follows.

April 2. "Rose at five and retired soon to my closet. Found so much in myself that was bad, that I hardly found time in my hour to pray for my friends. It seemed that my time was rather too short than too long. God gave me an abasing view of myself. O how deeply am I polluted! I prayed to be washed and cleansed in the blood of the Lamb."

April 3. "Attended to my seasons of devotion, and found generally much more of a spirit of prayer than usual."

The fact is that Dr. Yale's closet seasons were among the most precious of his life. It was when thus engaged that he drew near to God, and his soul was not unfrequently fired up with feelings of pious ardor. He was not among those who regard prayer as a task, but a precious, a delightful privilege.

1828, March 16. "Tried to preach this day on depravity, and on the unwillingness of sinners to accept of mercy and salvation. Some solemnity. After returning home I tried to pray. The thought occurred how shall I know when I have prayed enough? The question reproved me. Prayer is too apt to appear as a duty to be performed, out of regard to which God bestows his favors. False! Altogether false! It is a favor which he allows us, and we have asked enough only when we have obtained the blessing."

Yet, though he prized prayer so much, and performed it so conscientiously, there were times when he mourned over his coldness, and felt deeply humbled because of his conscious imperfections.

1827, Aug. 5. "Am fully convinced that I do not pray as I ought, and that the blessings of God delay, because our prayers delay. O God, move my heart in this sacred and holy exercise."

On the 10th of April 1836, in his own peculiar manner, he entered upon his memorandum what he called the testimony of his closet. It is as follows: "I felt much more than common, the great and precious blessing of the Father's promise of the Holy Spirit. Surely I must seek the Spirit as the great agent. Surely prayer is the great means of revival. May my closet no more bear witness against me, for the very little real prayer which I offer in it, before God. It does testify against me now. *Now let me record its testimony.*

For thirty-five years and more, says my closet, you have generally been on your knees twice a day, and sometimes oftener. At some seasons you have found prayer very interesting and profitable, and have prayed much. But many, many, many times you have prayed more as a ceremony, than as a serious business, a duty to honor God, and a privilege to procure benefits to your own soul. For a long time past you have made secret prayer a very formal and superficial business. As you have not allowed it much time, so it has not much engaged your deep affections. But in particular the following things are true concerning you.

1. *Your prayers are very short.* A few minutes, probably not more than five on an average, will measure the length of your prayers each time.

2. *Your prayers are crowded by other business or avocations.* Business or avocations take up the time before you commence. And before you are really engaged, you are arrested by some call, or by the hour of repose.

3. *Your prayers are interrupted by unseasonable thought.* Very often such thoughts intrude upon your mind, and lead it away after other subjects, while your words are praying and your knees are bended.

4. *Your prayers are generally dry and heartless.* However fervent the expressions, your feelings are not much interested, and your frame of mind is often such as God can not approve and accept.

5. *Your prayers generally leave your mind in darkness.* It is difficult to tell when any clear light has shone into your mind, or when you have derived any sensible benefit from prayer.

6. *Your prayers receive no answer.* It is a long time since you have so clearly obtained any blessing in answer to prayer, that it is doubtful whether the Lord hears you at all.

These are some of the items in the testimony of my closet in regard to secret prayer. How truly, then, am I in a deplorable condition!"

In his seasons of devotion, he frequently had the most abasing views of himself, and was at times almost "overwhelmed with a sense of his imperfections and sins." His langauge at one time was: "I appeared to myself so much like nothing that I should be, that I was almost led to despair of hope."

Yet, while thus abased in view of his own unworthiness he always had the strongest confidence in God, and in the efficacy of prayer.

1826, June 18. "At the rising of the sun I began to contemplate our situation: saw that I did not really pray with earnestness and hope for my people at this consecrated hour. I kneeled on my knees before God, acknowledged my unworthiness, guilt, pollution, poverty, and helplessness; but being encouraged by the 55th of Isaiah, which was in my mind last evening, and by other parts of scripture, I asked God to bestow, not for anything in me or my people, but for what there is in him.

Wouldst thou invite us to a fountain and then refuse to give us water, because we are thirsty and have none, and are unworthy and ill-deserving? Wouldst thou invite us to thy table, richly spread and abundantly furnished, and then refuse to give because we are hungry, and have no food, and are unworthy of any? Wouldst thou invite us to thy wardrobe which thou hast provided and opened, and then refuse to clothe us because we are naked and unworthy? Wouldst thou invite us to come and take of thine eye-salve, and then refuse to give it because we are blind and unworthy? Wouldst thou put words into our mouths and teach us to say, 'Take away all iniquity,' and yet refuse to take away our iniquity because we are guilty? Wouldst thou invite us to seek, ask, and knock for the Holy Spirit, to apply redemption to our souls, and to restore us to thine image, and then refuse to give the Spirit, because we are polluted and have never cleansed, nor never can cleanse nor attempt to cleanse ourselves? Surely none, nor all of these evils shall cause me to doubt or fear that thou wilt bestow what we need; because thou dost not bestow for the sake of our goodness or worthiness, but for thine own mercies, for thine own name's sake. Thus I was enabled to plead with God, and to entertain some hope that I should be regarded. The more entirely I laid aside all self-worthiness, and all hope from anything in me, the greater was my confidence in God. I prayed for the church—for Christless families—for the youth—for the children—and for a blessing on all the means of grace. I was enabled to plead more earnestly and with more hope than common. But surely God can not give anything for my sake. I am worse than nothing. I do not ask or expect it. May he keep me ever and forever at his feet. Amen."

His confidence in the efficacy of prayer may be seen from the following brief extracts of letters written to his much-loved friend the Rev. Joab Brace, of Newington, Conn. The first from which we extract was written on the first Monday of April, 1818, a day in which the monthly concert of prayer was observed by the churches, for the conversion of the world.

"*The first Monday.*—Should I have a share in those prayers which are ascending into the hand of the angel before the throne, you might have a better epistle than if written at the time appointed. As Campbell observes in his travels in Africa, that he received a favorable answer from the king of Latakoo on the first Monday in the month, would it not be a good day to begin a sermon? to drive some good work?to seek relief from some embarrassment? to strive for the victory over some spiritual enemy? to supplicate an outpouring of the Holy Spirit on our own people? Is it not a good time to present our petition while our King is engaged in hearing petitions from morning till evening? Need we fear being overlooked among such a crowd? O what a being is he that can as easily attend to the minute affairs of all his creatures as the greatest interest of one! Who does not forget the number of our hairs in the day of his greatest business, or to feed the ravens while he spreads a table for angels!"

Another letter under date of June 9th, 1820, contains the following: "Great are the blessings of divine grace which have been recently sent down in this region, and I trust they are descending still. The glorious work still advances in some places, and I do hope we shall be favored with a refreshing shower. We are dependent and unworthy; but God is rich in mercy, and I hope he will treat us, not as we deserve, but as we need, and make the riches of his grace and the wonders of his love appear in our salvation. Dear brother, permit me to request you to remember us *once* especially, in your secret place, after reading this letter, and I will endeavor this evening to bear you and the dear people of your charge before the throne. O, let us pray and labor, and labor and pray, but be sure to depend neither upon our labor nor our prayers, but on the agency of the Holy Ghost."

The Savior taught his disciples to expect that in the world they should have tribulation; and though the life of Dr. Yale, on the whole, was a life of prosperity, he did sometimes experience sore trials. In seasons of adversity he was peculiarly comforted by carrying his case to God; and indeed he was accustomed to regard afflictions as directed by the hand of a kind and affectionate Father.

There was no subject in which he felt an interest,

which he did not make a subject of prayer. He passed through some seasons of great pecuniary embarrassment, and at such times it was his constant practice to carry his case to God. It was not with the expectation that God would work miracles for his relief, but from the belief that all hearts are in God's hand, and that all supplies are under his control. Nor was it unfrequent that he found occasion to notice the remarkable manner in which his prayers, even for pecuniary supplies were answered. Take the following as illustrations:

1820, June 6. "About 10 o'clock, P. Mills, whom I owed about $40 called and told me he wanted thirty of it to morrow morning. This was rather unexpected. I had in my possession about $15 received about two days before, but was much hurried in business and knew not where to go for $20 which I needed for this and another engagement. I went to God and thought I praised and trusted him. This passage was precious to me as it ever had been before: "Be careful for nothing, but in everything by prayer and supplication with thanksgiving let your requests be made known unto God;" Phil. iv, 6. I asked him for what I needed. Before noon a man of whom I had not thought as owing me anything, sent me $3; at 6 o'clock, I received $1·50 at a wedding, and two dollars from another man. I applied to one of the trustees and he procured for me $13. Thus more than enough for immediate use came to me, through the kind hand of God, before I wanted it, and without turning me out of the way of duty, which I had marked out in the morning. O how kind is my Heavenly Father!"

1840, June 6. "I felt the need of some supplies soon, as I borrowed $17 yesterday. I therefore asked the Lord last evening and this morning, to stir up the minds of two or three men, in an adjoining county, to send me two or three small sums, due some time. About 11 this morning, the son of one of them came and brought me $11. O, that I might be suitably thankful. I did return thanks and take courage."

There was nothing which he more earnestly desired,

and nothing for which he more fervently prayed, than the spiritual welfare of his people. It was for their good that he lived and labored, and for this also he prayed.

1830, Nov. 12. "At eleven, the hour of prayer for my people, I had more than ordinary assistance. I tried to shut out the world, and to shut up myself with God, and to get up the ladder to heaven. Seemed to be more successful than common. I did plead with God for the spirit of preaching, and that he would bless my preaching. It seemed as though he had long been angry, and justly angry with my preaching, and would not bless it. I entreated and besought him to forgive me, and to wash my preaching, and to enable me to preach so as to meet his approbation and enjoy his blessing. I besought him also in behalf of all my people, that he would save them and use them for his service and glory. It seemed almost presumption in me to pray so, because it was asking what God had never granted to any man; why then should he to me? This almost confounded me. But I tried to set myself right, by resting on his word. He had directed me to intercede for all men—surely then for all my people. I entreated him to fit me for the work and for the blessing. When I had finished, I inquired whether I had prayed so as to be accepted. I could hardly tell. I was afraid of self-complacency. Prayed for humility."

It would be difficult to find one who was more diligent and faithful in all his ministerial duties than he—yet after all his diligence in preparing his discourses, and all his fidelity in delivering them, he uniformly felt that it was only the blessing of God, attending the truth, which would secure the results desired. Man may sow the seed, but God makes it grow. Paul may plant, and Apollos water, but it is God that gives the increase. Keeping this truth before his mind, he was accustomed always after having delivered his message, earnestly to implore the divine blessing to make it successful. See the following:

1829, Sept. 27. "We had a greater number than

usual at the house of God. In the morning I preached from Prov. i, 28, 29, to show that sinners do not choose to be converted—*not cho se the fear of the Lord.* In the afternoon, on John vi, 39, to show that Christ is not to be disappointed, but will have a people according to his Father's will. I made an effort to present these subjects in a convincing light. May the Lord grant his blessing. Felt anxious and did cry to God that he would bless this day's labor. In the evening I preached in a school house, on Mat. vii, 7, 'Ask and it shall be given you.' The house was full and the attention uncommonly good. When I came home, I came praying almost the whole way, for purity in myself, in the church, in the sabbath-school, in families connected with the church, and in dead families. I felt greatly encouraged in the Lord, while I felt no courage in myself, or in the members of the church. It seemed that all fullness is in God. I could hardly cease crying unto him."

1831, Sept. 4. "In the evening preached in a school house, to an overflowing assembly. When I saw them flowing in and filling the house I was deeply oppressed. Seeing that God only can help, I wanted to cry unto God, and call upon every believer to cry unto him also, for his Spirit. In returning home I wanted to pray all the way."

It is known that Dr. Yale was a warm friend of all those benevolent operations in which God's people are engaged, with the view of extending the kingdom of Christ through the world. But he never expected that the appeals of the agents to the churches would fill the treasuries of the missionary boards, or the labors of missionaries among the heathen would result in their conversion, unless attended with the blessing of God. Hence it was that in respect to these matters also, he cultivated the spirit of prayer in his own bosom, and urged it upon his brethren. His feelings on this subject were clearly expressed in the following passages, from a letter written to his friend Rev. Mr. Brace, under date of Dec. 30th, 1842:

"To the Lord, then, we may lift up our soul. 'Not by might nor by power.' I admire much the spirit of Mr. F's address near the close of the special meeting of the Tract Society in October. We are to look up. We have not looked around too much; but we have not looked up enough. Now we see not how the Lord will help out of the barn-floor or out of the wine-press. We see not whence the money is coming for foreign missions, or for home missions, or for the Bible Society, or for the Tract Society, or for the Education Society or for any other mode of operation. Often do we ask, how shall we do? Peal after peal comes upon the Christian ear for help in the work of the Lord. All the agencies echo the cries of the perishing, while we become more and more enfeebled and crippled in our means. Many times since I saw you have I been pained at the aspect of our affairs. Yet upward we may look with just as much confidence as ever. As Jehosaphat said, so may we say: 'Our eyes are upon thee.' 'Some trust in chariots,' said the Psalmist, 'and some in horses, but we will mention the name of the Lord who made heaven and earth.' Said Moses to Israel at the Red Sea, 'Stand still and see the salvation of the Lord.' Yet we are not to be inactive. We have more to do, to deny ourselves more, and to bear a heavier cross. That will bring us to the very point to which we need to be brought—'to follow Christ as a hard laboring, self-denying, and suffering Savior.' Then may we expect that the blessing will come, the universal blessing, which shall reach all the earth, and turn all the people to the Lord. We shall be *compelled* to pray more. As our help comes from the Lord who made heaven and earth, so must we seek it with all our heart and all our soul. It will come. The Lord will bless his people, and hear their prayer."

His prayers both for himself and his people, and the world, were characterised by great importunity.

1829, Aug. 3. "L. J. came to me with tears and desired me to pray for him. I said, 'Cursed is the man that trusteth in man, and maketh flesh his arm.' Yet I promised to pray for him, while I warned him not to rely upon anything but Christ."

Aug. 4. "Sometime in the night I awoke and could not sleep. I went into the study, feeling as though I had not slept enough, and fearful that I could not pray. When I began there seemed to be a clearness in my views quite uncommon. I commenced intercession for the young man who had sought my prayers. From him I went to others, some members of the church, and some of the worst, oldest, and most hardened sinners among us. I came to one at whose dreadful situation I was shut up for a time. I thought perhaps God was going to silence me. But at length the question which the Lord put to Abraham, 'Is any thing too hard for the Lord?' prevailed, and I could plead with him. I wrestled till I was very weary, going from one to another, and took a chair, turned it down, laid a pillow on the back of it lengthwise, reclined upon it in the easiest manner I could, and continued my supplications. At length I lay down with a view to sleep if I could. After some cries to God in that position I fell asleep, and continued till about the usual time of rising in the morning. I felt exhausted, and also felt the want of sleep; yet I went about my work as usual. I fear I shall glory. But I saw in the beginning of my supplication a little of this sin, and begged God to cleanse my heart from it."

Placing as he did such an estimate on the value of prayer, it might have been expected that he would seek to promote a spirit of prayer among the people and to stir up his brethren to the faithful discharge of this duty. This was, indeed, one of the principal objects which he aimed at in his pastoral labors.

1827, April 27. "At 2 o'clock yesterday afternoon attended the church conference. Not so many present as I expected. Yet I felt intensely, and to me the meeting was interesting. Felt and said among other things, that we *should make haste and bow before the throne of grace with our eye fixed on heaven and hell, lay our right hand on the head of a Christian, and our left on the head of a sinner, and pour out our souls for them to the God of mercy.*"

He desired each of the members of the church to spend a quarter of an hour each day in saying, 'Thy kingdom come.' And to promote a spirit of prayer in the church, he proposed a plan which is mentioned in the following extract from his memorandum:

1821, Nov. 1. "I have been organizing prayer-meetings. Six are in a train. I attend three in a week. I am about to institute in them, an inquiry into all the prayers of the Bible, with a view to promote a spirit of prayer and of sacred research. My plan to edify praying people is, to begin and go through the Bible with a view to take notice of all the prayers in it. A suitable portion of the prayers to be attended to at each meeting. Such as attend are invited to note in a blank book, made for the purpose, all the passages, book, chapter, and verse. This will be an index by which they can readily turn to any prayer as they please. I have been edified myself in what I have done. I hope others may be."

In closing this chapter I will introduce two short extracts of letters, bearing upon this subject, written to his friend Mr. Charles H. West. The first is under date of December 15th, 1849.

"I am working hard since the 28th of October, trying to revive religion in a section of our church and of our place. I have made some discoveries which almost overwhelm me and those who are my helpers. Our church and ourselves as a part of the whole, are sunk so low that we are beyond (I had almost said) a conception of what the effectual, fervent prayer of a righteous man means. What does it mean? Is it like that prayer which is offered daily in the closet, in the family, and on the sabbath in the sanctuary? Is it like that prayer which is poured forth from the lips, but vanishes then into thin air, without any to inquire whether it is regarded by any one in heaven, or earth, or hell? Oh! those careless, heartless formalisms, which are often called prayers! Alas! may not God well say, 'Bring no more vain oblations?' Oh what need to repent of the sins of our prayers! We need not wonder that there is no revival."

The other letter from which I extract is dated July 2d 1851. "I am learning some good lessons—one, that the chickens I feed have more faith in me than many men have in God—another, that whenever we go to God in prayer we should expect to receive—another, that God is as able to make us happy in affliction as in any other way—another to trust God in all things implicitly, and that faith in Christ is the first and the last—first in justification—last in giving up the soul to God."

CHAPTER V.

HIS SPIRITUAL CONFLICTS.

With his garments always clean, and his countenance always wearing such an aspect as betokened the intimacy of his communion with God, a looker-on may have supposed that Dr. Yale was free from those fierce combats with his spiritual foes, which have characterised the religious experience of many. Yet when we are permitted to look into the inner chamber of his heart we find that this was far from being the case. Indeed, Satan often makes his strongest and most vigorous assaults upon such as are most determined in the service of God, and most vigilant in guarding against the corrupt affections of their own hearts.

There is no occasion to alarm a sleepy sentinel; and when one manifests a disposition to harbor and cherish his foes rather than to seek their destruction, why should they assault him?

Dr. Yale's principles led him to give no quarters to the devil—and the fixed determination of his mind was, that Satan should not only be dethroned, but expelled. "Giving no place to the devil," he uniformly maintained a vigorous warfare with this prince of infernal spirits.

The assaults of the wicked one were sometimes most terrible; and were made by the injection into the mind of evil thoughts, by the production of great spiritual darkness, and by the presentation of strong temptations. The adversary, however, was promptly met and vigorously repelled. Take a few examples.

1824, March 20. "This morning I have been in a terrible conflict. I set out, as my practice has been lately, to attend to my own concerns with God, as though I were the only creature in existence. Distraction of thought commenced. I was running on everything. But I determined to attend to the subject. At the same time there seemed to be one striving to counteract this determination. All my meditations were unavailing. I was dark, agitated, pent up as one taken hold of by another, could get no enlargement; betook myself to my knees, determined to resist, but only one thing appeared encouraging—that was staying on God. It seemed as though I would hold fast to him; and I had a little ray of light, in repeating passages of his word. After struggling for some time, there seemed to be a little more enlargement. I was not afraid, but distressed with straitness and distraction. Has not God permitted this as a chastisement for my neglect in times past? It is an awful truth that I have blended my personal concerns with my official duties. I have within two weeks undertaken to separate them. It is right that I should be tried. Oh how dreadful to be given over to Satan! Yet this temptation, terrible as it is, is not so dangerous as those which are congenial to my feelings. These are distressing—those are polluting. In the course of the day I thought, moreover, that this temptation might be permitted to counteract spiritual pride."

April 1. In the morning my soul was cast down within me. I chode it. I asked, "Why art thou cast down, Oh my soul! why art thou disquieted within me! Hope thou in God." It comforted me some to think that God was answering my prayer on Tuesday evening, and yesterday morning—to show me the evil of my heart and destroy spiritual pride. Blessed be his name I was not utterly cast down."

Sabbath, April 4. "All this day could not obtain a spirit of prayer or preaching. Emptiness, distance, dryness. In the afternoon my subject was very solemn, 'No man cared for my soul'—but I did not feel more than a chip."

April 5. "In trouble on account of being unable to pray for my people, on the day of fasting and prayer, set myself to find out the cause. Read part of Psalm lxxvii: In trouble cried unto the Lord, sought the Lord. It struck me that I could not pray for my people because I had not the spirit of prayer for them, and that I could not expect an answer till I prayed. Here then is the case.

1. Ultimus—My church and my people may not be expected to be moved till I pray for them.

2. I do not pray for them without a spirit of prayer.

3. A spirit of prayer is what I now need, and am now to seek.

But here is my difficulty now—why can't I pray now? I have not the spirit. What hinders the spirit? This question remains to be answered. Saith the Psalmist; '*My spirit made diligent search.*' So must I *make diligent search*. During the day I labored some on this subject, and obtained some light, but not clear."

April 6. "During the whole day I have been in trouble—in darkness, darkness, darkness—no light—no spirit of prayer—no discovery of my difficulty, though I besought the Lord to show it me."

April 7. "Awaked in trouble—darkness—searched, but discovered nothing. Read the 77th Psalm with Scott—meditated on God's wonders, and on Israel's conduct. God led his people, supported, and defended them through the wilderness; he settled them in Canaan They were not first in it. Men are never first in their salvation, or in any good work. It originates with God. Is it the sending of the Gospel into the world, the spread of it among the heathen, the revival of religion at home, the conversion of one soul? All begins and is carried on by God.

1. *The design originated in him.* 'God so loved the world that he gave his only begotten son, that who-

soever believeth in him should not perish, but have everlasting life.'

2. *The determination to extend it through the world is made by him.* Thus he said to Moses; 'As I live all the earth shall be filled with the glory of the Lord.'

3. *The call to repentance, faith, and salvation is from him.* 'He now commandeth all men everywhere to repent.'' 'Look unto me, and be ye saved, all the ends of the earth.'

4. *The commission to spread the gospel is from him.* 'Go ye into all the world, and preach the gospel to every creature.'

Men are not before our gracious God in any part of this blessed work. We do not outgo him in good desire and action, and then pray to him to come up to us, and help us; but he infinitely outgoes us, calls upon us to come forward to the work—to the help of the Lord against the mighty. He is not backward; but we are. He is not unwilling to bless; but we are unwilling to put ourselves in the attitude and place to receive a blessing. Here then I discover several wrong views:

1. That the cause of spreading the gospel is the work of any man, or society. It is the cause of God, in which a man, or a society may engage, and in which they do engage when they do their duty.

2. That the Lord does not work so fast as we wish to have him. We do not work so fast as he wishes to have us.

3. Despondency: As though the work were dependent on man.

4. Pride: As though the work were performed by man. As though we had done much, when in fact we have not come near our duty.

5. Indolence: God calls us to action, and we refuse. We are about our business, or about nothing. In view of these things, I think I see one thing which has brought me into darkness—viewing myself forward, unable to obtain God's blessing, while I am far behind what he requires me to do for him and distustful of his goodness

and mercy. From this search I think I found some relief."

Sabbath, April 25. "This has been one of the most terrible days I ever saw. I was distracted and could not preach. My soul is tossed with storm. Oh, what shall I do? It seems as though my preaching were altogether vain. I am at my wits' end. When I look towards God I see no light."

"6 P. M. Being tossed to and fro, not knowing what to do, the inquiry arose: 'Now were you delivered from pride, ambition, envy, self-righteousness, and self-sufficiency, would you be so agitated.' No. 'Then take your place broken-hearted, humble, patient, diligent, obedient, doing all you can in the work to which you are called, trusting in the wisdom, power, and grace of God and you will follow Christ and his servants.' This seemed right. I confessed my sins and prayed for the very grace which I need. Then my mind became in some measure calm. I read Jeremiah xii, 'If thou run with the footmen,' &c. A scene opened to my view as possible, which might truly be terrible. But I am harnessed. Oh God, gird me for the conflict, and strengthen me to do thy will."

1826, May 21. "I feel this morning exceedingly low. I feel so guilty that I can not come with confidence to the throne of grace. Yet I attempted to unite in the concert at sun-rise.

'My soul lies cleaving to the dust,
Lord give me life divine.'"

1827, Dec. 8. "In the afternoon and evening spent some hours in trying to pray. But oh! what darkness, distraction, deadness, in all the powers of my soul! No light, no order, no encouragement in prayer. All I could say or think of seemed like nothing. What power of great darkness overspreads my soul! I can not pray for anything, for myself, or for the church, or for any creature. I seem to be shut up in hewn stone, so that I can not get out, nor see anything to encourage me where I am. I see in my heart and my life, pride, ambition. too much thought and care about the world, unbelief, stupidness, prayerlessness. Surely I deserve to be left. Yet I am not without hope that God will yet send me light from above, and help me with his salvation. But it is altogether from another source than anything in me. It must be for his name's sake and for his rich mercy. Oh that I might indeed look away from myself, and derive help from God."

1849, Dec. 14. "Yesterday I had many trials but went along through them. At the close, and after nine in the evening, I spent a season in secret prayer. The wicked one came with his terrors to make me afraid, as he did many years ago. He seemed to be near, though he did not seem to touch me. My flesh crawled with shivering, and my hair seemed as though it would stand up. But I thrust him with the word of God, as I had done years ago in a similar case. 'Resist the devil, and he will flee from you; draw nigh to God and he will draw nigh to you.' I told him of the conflict with Jesus, in which Jesus said, it is written. Yet three times did he come near me with the same impressions, though rather feebler each time. I was, indeed, in an agony. Yet I thanked God for it, as he then taught me that there was one in hell that cared for my prayers. Thus was explained that power which I felt on Wednesday, and the seeming shutting out of my prayer. The devil had been permitted to do it, thus rebuking me as God permitted him, for my coldness, stupidness, neglect of prayer. I said, moreover, 'Rejoice not against me, oh my enemy, for when I fall I shall arise.' So I did, after some time, through God's grace; and though in a measure exhausted, yet I could not but rejoice and give thanks; because God thus taught me that he did regard my prayers. For if he had not, then the devil would not have cared for them. I was then encouraged to hope that God would bless our endeavors to promote his cause. Will he not give us the real spirit of prayer? This temptation seemed a foretaste of it. In prayer this morning my thoughts ran on at a great rate, anticipating God's glorious work, and the result of it in much good to his people, through my trials. Now these more than ten years I have suffered greatly, and sinned grievously. I have sinned in the neglect or careless performance of duty. But I have all the time remained steadfast in the conviction that God revives religion in the use of his word and prayer, and the holy living of his people."

"Put on the whole armor of God that ye may be able to stand against the wiles of the devil."

CHAPTER VI.

HIS ANXIETY FOR THE SPIRITUAL WELFARE OF HIS PEOPLE.

"Oh that my head were waters, and mine eyes a fountain of tears that I might weep day and night for the slain of the daughters of my people."

Few people realize the deep anxiety which is felt by the devoted minister of Christ in behalf of the people of his charge. They may listen to his stirring eloquence, and witness, at least, an occasional tear as it steals down his cheek; yet perhaps they may regard it only as *professional* eloquence, and as a tear which is the result of misplaced sympathy. Yet there is, in reality, the kindling up of the fires of the soul, and an intensity of anxiety which is produced by nothing less than a realization of the worth of man's undying spirit. Such were the feelings of Dr. Yale. Nor was religious feeling in him like the occasional flashes of light artificially produced in the laboratory of the chemist; but like the light and the heat which emanate from the sun, constant, permanent, and abiding. He longed, he wrestled, he agonized for the salvation of his people: and he might have appropriated to himself the pathetic language of the Apostle Paul: "My little children of whom I travail in birth again, until Christ be formed in you." The last tears which he shed, were for sinners; but these were not the only tears which a sense of their wretchedness and prospective ruin called from his eyes. He wept because of the view which he entertained of their deep-rooted depravity, and obstinate perverseness.

Sin, whether in himself or others, appeared to him most odious, and the very sight of it affected his heart with sadness. His feelings with regard to it, he once expressed in the following emphatic language:

1829, August 10. "Sin appeared most odious. The carnal mind resembles a solution of arsenic. Put a piece of bread in it, and how deadly! So the mind, body, and all that belongs to a sinner, are steeped in sin. O how offensive to a holy God!"

Like other pastors it was his lot sometimes to fall in with persons upon the verge of the grave, not only without hope, but without any realizing sense of their true condition. The sight of such men filled his soul with agony. We may see an expression of his feelings in the following.

1830, January 7. "In visiting called on a poor old man who is just gone with cancers. He seems to be one of the most wretched men I ever saw. He says nothing about a future world, is in much pain, and evidently has no comfort. He has searcely been to meeting in twenty-five years, and has had nothing in view but to make money. He is not rich, but every year made money. I would not be in his condition for ten thousand worlds."

Oh, how intensely did he desire the welfare of the church, and the salvation of men! There were times when the church was in a low, languid state—destitute of that spiritual energy which contributes so much to the vitality of gospel ordinances; and then his feelings found vent in tears. He labored hard, he prayed fervently, he warned sinners of their danger, and excited the people of God to activity; and yet his efforts seemed to be paralyzed, by a want of zeal, and fidelity, and cordial and hearty cooperation among the members of the church.

Such a state of things was to him deeply affecting, as may be seen from the following paragraph:

1850, January 5. "To-day it has occurred to me that our church is more like a poor sickly mother, than one dead—can not nurse. Our church is like a sick mother. She takes no care of her children. She gives them no nourishment. They are very feeble. They cry indeed for milk, but they get none from their mother. They must go to another nurse, or be fed by a bottle. Alas! for this sick mother! She brings forth no more children, and nourishes not those that are lean and sickly. Call a physician. Entreat him to send health and cure. O, that he would heal us, for we have no remedies."

Indeed he was frequently so deeply anxious in view of the state of his flock, that he found himself unable to enjoy his accustomed sleep. Take the following for examples.

1829, March 12. Much distressed during the night on account of the state of the church, For a long time in the night I could not sleep. The condition of some of the members of the church pained me at my very heart. I tried to cry unto God, yet it seemed as though I could not cry. In the morning I read in Henry's Exposition some of the trials of our Savior while his disciples were asleep. I seemed to know something of his trials. I sought for his spirit of meekness, gentleness, kindness. Oh! Lord Jesus, all I want is to be like thee."

March 13. "Troubled in the night as before. Oh! Lord, show me what to do. In the devotions of the morning, searched my own heart, and gained evidence of grace, but saw my indwelling enemies in dreadful array—pride, ambition, vanity, envy. I can not say as Jesus said; "The prince of this world shall find nothing in me." He does find those friends of his, and my traitors. Get ye hence."

In fact his anxiety for his people was so intense, that he sometimes regarded it as excessive, and was led to call in question the propriety of indulging it.

1830, Deccember 8. "I have been thinking of late that probably I give myself too much anxiety, in regard to God's dealings with my people. I can not tell what are his plans, if I try. Let me rather do my duty, and leave all with him. 'How unsearchable are his judgments, and his ways past finding out! His judgments are a great deep." He giveth account of none of his matters. It becometh me to resign all up into his hand, and leave all at his disposal. Yet I am not to be stupid, negligent, or indifferent about the salvation of souls. Oh Lord, help me to cast all my care on thee."

Still, however, he had such a sense of the worth of of souls, and his faith in the realities of a future state was so undoubting, that he could not suppress his anxiety. The following extracts from his diary are presented for the purpose of showing the intensity of this feeling. They are selected from records made at different periods, embracing a considerable portion of his ministerial life:

1821, March 26. "Language can not express the anxiety which is in my heart for this people. I fear, I tremble for them. When I consider that many are yet stupid, that those who are awakened may become so, and that thousands may perish from among them, I can not but tremble. 'My heart's desire and prayer to God for ' Kingsborough ' is that they might be saved.'"

1821, March 26. "People attentive. Encouragement enough to use the means of grace. A young man desired public prayers. Poor young man! How vain has been his past life, though moral. Was affected with the duty of being more earnest with people in health. At the close of the evening meeting, was affected with a sense of the folly and madness of sinners. It seemed as though I wished to seize hold of some, and cry out: 'Oh what madmen you are!'"

1822, Feb. 3, Sab. "A very pleasant day. Many at meeting. But oh, how awfully stupid! Though some appeared to shed tears, yet the most appeared to be blind, and deaf, and dead, and lost. My soul is in deep distress, and I fear I am impatient with God and with man."

March 3. "This morning it seemed as though I could come up to the Most High and confide all the affairs in which I am concerned to him. Comfortable time. In the afternoon I went to Deacon Hall's. We spent some time in prayer. My soul was lifted up to God and solemnized. Had some ideas of the nature of faith in prayer. Oh may the God of mercy shake and quicken the dry bones. They are very dry, but nothing is too hard for the Lord."

April 15. "Could scarcely sleep last night on account of a pressing desire of the Holy Spirit upon myself, and my church, and my people. I do not know as my desires are right, but they are strong. I was also distressed very much with the conviction of one member of the church. He seems to be totally destitute of grace."

Nov. 13. "Read of the compassion of Jesus in feeding the hungry, and poor and fainting multitude. I wept at his kindness, and pleaded for his spirit to satisfy perishing souls. My heart was distressed for stupid sinners. I felt that God only could save them. Yet I was induced to look around and see, among many careless ones, some who, I hope, will be 'my joy and crown.' This comforted my heart, though it did not satisfy it."

1824, April 14. "Saw and groaned over the low state of religion in the church. Sunk down in secret prayer. In family worship the last verse of the thirty-first Psalm gave me courage: 'Be of good courage, and he shall strengthen your heart, all ye that hope in the Lord.' This led me to cry to God for help."

May 16. "This morning, and some days past, have been ready to ask, where are my days of fasting and prayer? Four days have I spent in this exercise, in little more than two months, but what is the benefit? I do not pray, my people are uncommonly stupid, and it seems as though every thing was going to ruin."

Aug. 26. "Very evident that Christians are in a deep sleep, and sinners in the sleep of death. Burdened very deeply. Great heaviness and sorrow in my heart."

Aug. 30. "Called to visit a young man, just on the brink of eternity. It wounded me to the heart to see this lovely flower fading. But oh! the soul! Without hope—poor parents wretched! No religion—yet thought once they were Christians—false religion."

1827, July 5. "Very much affected with the conviction of an old man who has attended the worship of God for many years. He rests on the fact that few or none can know how it will go with them, till they go into the eternal world. He does not know but he may be a Christian, and few are sure that they are. So it may be as well with him as with them."

Aug. 13. "Awoke a little past twelve last night. Felt pressed very much with the conviction of my people. Having occasion to rise I went into the study and spent some time in prayer. I tried to plead with God. But some how or other my prayers soon came to an end. I cried to God for myself, my family, my church, the prayerless families, the multitudes of youth and others that have no grace. Need very much the teaching and aid of the Holy Spirit in prayer. Oh that the Lord would work in me to will and to do of his good pleasure."

1828, March 18. "Troubled towards morning with the state of my people. This condition is dreadful, and most of all because the church is so low and so much after the world."

March 19. "Read a few chapters in the beginning of Judges, where we learn that the Canaanites were not driven out by Israel. Their state resembled ours. Only now and then they did any thing for God, and the Lord delivered them. God did for them; not they for God. So with us."

There are many other passages in his diary which are equally expressive of this deep anxiety of feeling in behalf of his people; yet as they are somewhat lengthy and contain but little that is new, but one more will here be introduced.

1830, June 21. "Awoke before one o'clock, and was deeply distressed in view of infidelity—the practical infidelity of the church, and of my own heart and life. Did we practically believe the word of God, that there is a heaven for some and a hell for others; that a few are of God, and that the whole world lieth in wickedness; that the few are bound by the law of Christ to let their light shine, and that the whole world must be converted or perish forever—how differently should we live and act? I was distressed as one on a dying bed at the thought of my own neglect. I cried in my spirit unto God. I was led in the morning to inquire why the mind is more deeply impressed at such a time than at ordinary times. The impressive truth or fact is unattended with ordinary circumstances. It comes when the mind is just awake, divested of associations; in the stillness and solitariness of night; under the eye of God, in view of the eternal world. The singleness of the impression, in such a condition, is deep. I try to believe. I entreat God to continue this impression. Oh how shall I live, if I truly believe! 'Lord I believe, help thou my unbelief.'"

This great anxiety for the spiritual welfare of his people, was expressed repeatedly in letters which he addressed to some of his friends, in the course of a regular correspondence, in which he gave full scope to the feelings of his own heart. A few extracts from some of these letters will be here introduced.

The first from which I extract was dated April 1, 1824, and was written to Rev. Mr. Brace:

"MY DEARLY BELOVED—Your closing remark has done me good this morning, and perhaps it may do you good in the reperusal. 'We must *love* our work, and when we meet our hearers cold, and vacant, and estranged, we must not be contented, till they and *we* are made to feel.' A word in season, how good it is! This has lain by now three months; but I needed it this very morning. Lately, for about four weeks, I have been endeavoring to seek the Lord on some occasions, by prayer and fasting (I would not say this to any but an intimate friend, and I hope I do not say it from ostentation), to obtain a spirit of grace, and supplication, and his blessing on my people and labors. Blessed be his name for help. But I see more of my own dreadful state, and that of my people. I can not move my people. Yet I feel your good word—'*must not be contented, till!*'—may the gracious spirit grant us this grace. How few of our people, comparatively, are converted! How far short of the words of our prayer—'add daily'—I have seen only the thirtieth part of this—it has been only *one in a month*, on an average, that has been added to this church since my ministry commenced. Great work indeed compared with nothing; but small compared with the population around me. I feel the need of more—more wisdom, grace, fidelity, zeal, faith, humility, boldness, and an unconquerable firmness and perseverance. How many are defiled with leprosy! Yet may we not come to Jesus and say: 'Lord, if thou wilt thou canst?' Are not our churches laboring under a *paralysis;* the limbs benumbed, the eyes set, the ears heavy, the tongue dumb, and the very current of life sluggish, almost to congelation? Yet if they are living, may we not bring them before Jesus? We need not put them upon a bed. No crowd will prevent our approach, no roof need be broken up. Here in our study, there in the sanctuary, or the prayer-meeting, may we lay them down before his face and at his feet. Blessed privilege, fully enjoyed, miserably improved by me. One has a withered hand, some are laboring under fever, many are possessed with devils, among unbelievers. Yet who ever came to Jesus, or was brought, without receiving mercy? This is all plain, and it reproves my unbelief. But, brother Brace, when I look upon the particular cases of difficulty around me, my faith staggers, like Peter's in view of the waves. It seems impossible that many should be saved. I am 'at my wits' end.' I know not how to gain access to some men; and if I do, every effort seems like plowing upon a rock, no impression; or like the track of a vessel through the waters, it closes and is lost. Yet are not all hearts in the Lord's hand? Is he not able to move them? May not the most unlikely be saved? May not a way of access be opened to any? May not the rock be broken and a passage be opened for the waters? What shall be done for the salvation of all our people, to bring them home to God, that they may be holy stones in the building, useful in the church, do good to the world, become monuments of our Savior's praise, and give joy in heaven? Do answer these questions. I am trying to do something—to do more—to preach and pray better—to converse—to catechise—to instruct in Bible classes and sabbath schools. But the spirit is wanting. Yet will not the Lord bless his own means? Is he not able to increase the means, to vary the means, to adapt the means to particular ends? Another thing alarms me. People die around me, every little while; die without religion. They are gone. No more for them. Others follow step by step, and I among them. No return to hear, or embrace the gospel after death—or to preach, or pray, or warn. When these things press me, I seem as one ready to be distracted with solicitude. But when opportunity offers, I am so dead that I do nothing for God and souls.

In my study I can talk, and preach, and pray, and labor, as though I would carry all before me; but when I go out, contact with the world is like the touch of the torpedo—every effort is paralyzed—my purposes are withered, and I come back again to mourn my ignorance, deadness and folly.

I have a thousand trials in my ministry, which I have never heard, or read of in any minister's life. I wish a great many times, that I knew how Paul would have conducted in such or such a case. Indeed I believe there are many parts of ministerial duty, not understood by any man living. When I look at the sinful mass around me I see vast quantities of chaotic matter, on which the Spirit does not seem to have moved. To this ministers and Christians have not approached, by anything like adequate means. No place on earth is fully evangelized. We have no data before us, which can guide us up to that course of application to sinful men of every class, which will answer the purpose. Preaching and praying are the means. But what preaching is there to a large part of Christendom's population? Enough indeed to render them inexcusable—to increase their future misery; but not enough to bring the gospel home to their souls. It needs to be carried to them—to every son and daughter of Adam. Do communicate all you know about carrying the gospel home to every heart. In Connecticut you know most about these things. There you have many laborers, you are near together, and frequently in consultation. Let me know some of your plans in detail. I want the minutiæ; for the least thing is important that is connected with the welfare of immortal souls."

The following are extracts from a letter under date of April 1, 1823:

"How tremendous the responsibility of our station! The thought which you repeated, representing some of our people as already lost beyond recovery, should affect my heart more than it does. At times I look over my people; count our numbers; consider how many do not even profess religion, while some who do profess, bear little fruit or none at all; and I say oh how unprofitable am I! how little have I done! how little has my ministry been blessed! I have been laboring here now twenty years, and only about two hundred and thirty have been added to the church. Of these, four have been excommunicated, and a few more give no signs of life. How my time flies—forty-three years old—soon seventy—soon laid away, and my work done. How many shall I leave unconverted when I die? Such thoughts make my flesh crawl, and for a moment I feel as though I would fly in every direction, if I could, and cry unto all about me to make haste to be saved. Yet I make but a snail-like progress in my work. What you state of the calamities of ministers, and the changes in your association, might rouse any one but a dead man, or one sunk into a deep sleep, or one who is diseased so that he can scarcely move."

In another letter we find the following language:

"Your remarks about our perishing people affected my mind a little. They should affect it much. How dreadful to think, as I do often think—some of my hearers, my people, my neighbors, are now, and will be to all eternity in hell!"

At a much later date he writes as follows:

"One evening last week I was so burdened that I could not sleep. I rose about 11 o'clock, and for more than an hour tried to cast my burden upon the Lord, as directed, Psalms lv, 22. I did so, and he took it, to my great relief. Now I leave my burden with him and try to cooperate in his work. Doubtless you know a minister's burden. Mine is a burden of burdens—one compound burden, made up of many particular burdens. One, of members who seem to have no religion; one, of Anakims, old sinners, tall and mighty; one of prayerless families; one of neglecters of public worship; one of hardened young men and women, baptized in infancy and brought up in religious families; one of the great class of careless ones; and finally, of a few thoughtful ones, very, very critically situated."

I will here give a brief extract of a letter, bearing upon this point, written the week after he resigned his pastoral charge. June 30, 1852.

"I feel but one pang in resigning my charge, except the consciousness of sins and imperfections innumerable, and that is caused by the fact, that many have perished under my ministry, whom I shall see at the last day, trembling at the left hand of the judge. Had I done more, and in a better spirit, I know not how many more might have been saved; but I trust that I have preached more to them all, than Jonah preached to Nineveh. Had they repented, they would have been saved. Alas! it is too late for them to be saved, or for me to do more. I trust their blood will not be found upon me. 'God be merciful to me a sinner.' In this way only I hope to be saved."

His great anxiety for the progress of religion, both among his own people and elsewhere, caused him greatly to deplore those political commotions which have sometimes existed in our country, and also certain delusions which some professedly good men have felt disposed to propagate, and by which the public mind has been, at times, so much occupied as to be unfit to engage in anything of much utility. The following extracts are taken from a letter written October 19, 1844; a year in which our country was uncommonly agitated with questions connected with the presidential election, and a year also which immediately succeeded the explosion of what may be called the Miller delusion. And it is introduced here principally on account of its allusion to these things.

"It becomes us in these times of political excitement, and while many are running to and fro, some Millerites, some Mormons, some one thing, some another, to be watchful and prayerful, that we may withstand in the evil day. This is, indeed, a terrible year for ministers. For what can we preach that will be profitable? The most spiritual subjects are suited, neither to our present state of mind, nor to that of our hearers. If we preach any thing that is interesting, it must be something about politics, and then some will say that we are preaching politics. But surely, we as a nation are in a most peculiar condition—all still on the subject of religion. If there be anything solemn on the sabbath, the day is no sooner over, if over at all, before the political whirlwind comes, and carries all away. Often have I been led to inquire what shall I preach next? Ministers long to have the election over, so that we may labor again with hope. In the meantime, all things are running down—the sabbath day, temperance—the cause of benevolence, sabbath schools, other schools, and all our interests which have in them any spirituality. How shall we ever arise, and recover that tone of religious feeling, which is the peculiar characteristic of a religious revival? At the late meeting of the Synod of Albany, we took into consideration the state we are in, as destitute of any revivals. We tried to mourn and pray over our condition, and recommended the 20th of November, as a day of fasting and prayer in our churches, to desire mercies of God on account of our low and helpless condition. We felt unwilling to put off the day so long, but thought it would be no use to commence any public, special action till the public mind should have a little time to become composed.' So that one more long month from this time, we must plod along, and make our way as we can 'through waves, and clouds and storms.' The poor Millerites in this region are now expecting the great catastophe before that time, even on the 23d inst. Mr. S. J. is going from place to place, to give the churches, and his friends warning. so that they may be ready for the day. He appears to be a real monomaniac. But why should the believer fear, even if that day should come at once? They that are alive and remain shall be caught up to meet the Lord in the clouds, and so shall they be ever with the Lord. Comfort one another with these words. The truth is, that if we are truly ready, the Lord's coming will be to our everlasting joy. Hallelujah! Even so, come, Lord Jesus. So may confirmed believers sing in view of death and judgment, come when they may. But an unbeliver is under the wrath of God, and is just as liable to die every moment and sink into hell, as if the world were to come to an end. The Miller system and the second advent system, though differing from Millerism, are only devices of the devil to divert Christians and others from the quiet business of life—real preparation for all events, and the spreading of the gospel. Well are we cautioned by John in the Revelations, to watch and keep our garments, while the unclean spirits like frogs are going out of the mouth of the dragon, aud out of the mouth of the beast, and out of the mouth of the false prophet. These are the spirits of devils, going forth to gather the kings of the earth to the great day of God Almighty. In these times we have no security but in keeping close by the word of God, and by the God of the word. In this way we are safe. What a happy thing it is to be rooted and grounded in the word! Those who are not are carried away by every wind of doctrine, by the sleight of men and cunning craftiness whereby they lie in wait to deceive. "To the law and to the testimony, if they speak not according to this word, it is because there is no light in them." How accurately are these events foretold in the scriptures! So their occurrence may turn to us for a testimony. Many will be infidels as the result of Miller's dreamy interpretation of the prophecies; but real believers will be confirmed the more, because the Lord Jesus and his apostles have told us of these things. While the wicked stumble at the stone, and while some are ground to powder by the falling rock, they that build their house upon the rock become more firm and stable."

CHAPTER VII.

SEASONS OF DISCOURAGEMENT AND DEPRESSION.

Looking, as we sometimes do, at the cultivated field and the waving harvest, we may not realize the amount of labor which has been expended, and the numerous discouragements which have been experienced, in the cultivation of that field, and in the production of that harvest. Many a looker-on has been tempted to envy the successful pastor in the prosperity of his church, and the amount of fruit which he has been permitted to gather in his Master's vineyard. In this respect, perhaps, few pastors have been regarded as occupying a more enviable position than Dr. Yale.

For many years past, the church of which he was pastor has been in an outwardly prosperous state; its members had become numerous, and were possessed of a good degree of wealth; the people were enterprising and intelligent; in proportion to their means they were supposed to surpass most others in the amount of their contributions for the various objects of benevolence; they were ordinarily punctual in their attendance upon the means of grace; and he was himself highly esteemed, and loved, and revered, not only among his own people, but by the surrounding community.

What, then, could there be lacking to fill his cup of joy? When we have looked at the fruit of his labors, perhaps we may have lost sight of the toil, and fatigue, and discouragements by which that fruit has been produced.

Dr. Yale was subject to such like discouragements and trials, as fall to the lot of other men of the same profession, and who are employed in the same kind of labor.

It is true that he was cheered and supported by his confidence in God. He loved to call God's grace to mind, and to confide in his promises. And though the sun did not always shine into his soul, nor upon his path, when he turned his eye heavenward, he ordinarily saw something to encourage him. Few men look up more intently than he did, and few have received more comforting communications from on high. His soul was so bound up in God that he could most sincerely apply to himself the language of one of Dr. Watts' hymns:

> " In darkest shades, if thou appear,
> My dawning is begun."

Yet, a man that has to do with earth, must sometimes feel upon his soul the influence of earthly things; and Dr. Yale also was affected with these things as are other gospel ministers in like circumstances. "As in water face answereth to face, so the heart of man to man." And the principal object had in view in introducing the matter contained in this chapter, was to show his brethren in the ministry that their trials and discouragements are only the counterpart of those which have been experienced by others.

One of his principal sources of discouragement was the limited success which attended his ministry. It is true that he was permitted to rejoice in several interesting and powerful revivals of religion. Souls were born into the kingdom, and God's people were made glad by the sun-shine of his favor. In such seasons his soul was filled with gladness—and at the close of his pastorate he was comforted at the thought that six hundred during his ministry, had been added to the church under his care. But he was by no means cheered with a continued revival during his connection witb that people. Far from it. There were long seasons of religious declension—the ways of Zion mourned—the night was dark and dreary—God seemed to frown—Christians were stupid—sinners were careless. He preached, but without the success desired; and when he returned from the pulpit to the closet, he involuntarily cried out: "Hath God forgotten to be gracious? Is his mercy clean gone forever?" "Lord, who hath believed our report? and unto whom is the arm of the Lord revealed?"

While he was gathering in the fruit of those precious revivals with which his people were blessed, he rejoiced as the busbandman when he returns laden with his sheaves. But oh! the blight which sometimes overrun his field of labor! The frost—the drought—the mildew! His hopes were blasted; and his heart made sick—so stupid, so unfeeling, so hardened, so insensible, so heedless to the truth, and so indifferent to their souls' best interests, were the most of those to whom he ministered.

But on this subject, as on others, shall he speak for himself.

1822, March 17. "Distressed in the conference of youth this evening, because all seemed to be so stupid. They heard, but did not seem to feel anything. They seemed to say: 'You may try what you can do to move us.' When coming home I thought of the prophet crying to the dry bones. So am I."

April 16. "Find myself amazingly depressed in spirit. Every thing around me appears unpromising as to spiritual things. No life among Christians, no life in my own soul, no motion among the dry bones. When I pray and cry unto God he does not seem to regard my prayer or my cry. It is a dreadful state. I have no reason to complain, because I have never deserved any thing only evil. All goodness is from the Lord. From him it must come, and all my hope is in his fullness. Yet it seems in vain to call upon him. I do not pray so as to please him, and therefore he justly leaves me to myself—to nothing."

1828, April 26. "So much stupidness apparent, that I feel really sunk down very low—seemed ready to faint away."

1822, November 14. "I would comfort my heart against discouragement. These trials of little success in my ministry (only about ten persons on an average having been added to the church, each year of my ministry) I belive will do me good. They make me feel my dependence, and push me down in the dust before God. But oh! how I should lament that the state of my heart makes it necessary for God to withhold! I have often lamented that my public preaching has been so little blessed."

1829, March 22. "I felt pained very much that so few are converted by my ministry, and that I am so little successful. I wished to put my mind down continually to the work, to preach, converse, and do all my duty, relying on God, and leaving all with him. Tried to do so in prayer."

Those feelings of discouragement which he sometimes felt, in view of the limited success of his ministry, and the impenitence of many of his people, he once expressed in a letter to his cousin, the Rev. Cyrus Yale, of New Hartford, Conn., from which I purpose to make some extracts.

It is under date of Sept 7, 1840.

"In your last, some things appear very much as my thoughts and feelings are when I am discouraged—when I ask, 'Are his mercies clean gone forever; and will the Lord be favorable no more?' 'I cry unto him in the day time, but he heareth not, and in the night season, and am not silent.' Yet it is good to 'remember the years of the right hand of the Most High.' How many times did I ask before the autumn of 1838, 'Are his mercies clean gone forever?" Conscious of so many defects and sins, it seemed to me that the Lord would look no more towards me. But you and I have learned that the Lord does not deal with us, according to our deserts, nor reward us according to our iniquities. Therefore 'it is good that a man should both hope, and quietly wait for the salvation of the Lord.' Your letter is not so sombre as my thoughts have many times been. I sympathize with you, and I agree with you that such sombre musings are wrong. But as you say, 'yet, here we are.' We are not fatalists, nor atheists; and yet, if we were both, could we be much different from what we are? I see now, among the members of my church, those who need special attention on various accounts—but do I give them special attention? I see among the members of the congregation, many, both old and young, who need warning and admonition from me, as a watchman, as a friend of souls, as one who will soon meet them at the bar of God—but do I perform pastoral duty as I ought? I have seen times when I did speak to men, when I did warn them. Why not now? Moreover I pray for individuals, amd see that it becomes me to deal faithfully with their souls. I do sometimes take men alone and talk with them on the welfare of their souls. They weep, and I weep. They do not hate, nor forsake me, on this account. But I do not follow up this as I should. I do not feel about, talking with such, on the danger of their souls, which I see, as I do about their temporal interest, if I see that in danger. I do not go to them as often as I should in any case, nor at all to a great portion of my people, and tell them plainly all I know, and all I fear about them. How, then, can I be a faithful minister? *I am not*, and I many times fear that God will put me to shame before the universe. I am ashamed to tell *you* how unfaithful I am—I often confess it to God. 'But here I am.' I have no excuse. Surely I must say, God be merciful to me a sinner.' Is it thus with you? From your writing I should suppose you know a little of the unlimited evils that are in me, and often distress me. Oh it will be great grace, that shall blot out my sins—such neglects of duty. This is the thing that cuts me to the heart more deeply than any other sin.

I think of Baxter, who blamed himself for neglecting to warn sinners. Indeed I do fear the awful displeasure of God againt this sin. Yet I am the less cxcusable, because I know my duty, and because I know too that God has encouraged me greatly whenever I have attempted to do anything in this way. I am too on my last decade, since the 15th of June. Sixty-seventieths of the life of man are gone; only ten seventieths remain. Sometimes I sink down in discouragement when I think how old I am, and how many infirmities are likely to encompass me, and to render much of the remains of life of little service to myself or others. No way remains for me, but to double my diligence, do the work of the day in the day, pray much, and trust God for all."

A few more extracts will here be given from his diary:

1849, Feb. 22. "Felt very low and very helpless; hardly courage and resolution enough to call upon God.

What will become of my people? They are very thoughtless. Oh what a world! Yet God is saving men of just this sort, transforming them into his image. Very low are we indeed. I can not arouse them. I am ready to halt myself. My feet have well nigh slipped. Oh Lord, hold me up, lest I backslide, and fall, and be ruined! Oh Lord, have mercy on us, for thy great name's sake."

March 11. "Last evening and this day I have been exceedingly exercised under a sense of unprofitableness. Last evening I had an afflicting sense of having labored in vain, and spent my strength for naught, so far as saving sinners is concerned. It seemed that my conversation, my preaching, my writing, my living, and all about me, and all I do, were of no use. I labored hard in prayer, and confession, and struggling to resign myself to God, and to await his will."

There were few periods of his life when he felt more deeply, when he labored more unweariedly, when he prayed more fervently, and when he deplored his want of success more earnestly, than near the close of the year 1849. It was at this time that he engaged in a series of protracted efforts for the promotion of the interests of religion in a certain section of the congregation; and though there was much promise of good, during a portion of the time, his expectations were not realized. Then it was that he made in his diary the following entry:

"This meeting was very attentive and solemn. Yet one thing is wanting—such powerful operations of the Spirit as shall cause the impenitent to cry for mercy, and fall at the footstool. Returned home thinking and praying. The Spirit taught, by the help of Bunyan's Holy War, to understand and apply some facts and truths of the Bible. I was thinking on the condition of the people, and was led to ask, 'What shall I do?' On reflecting, I find that eye-gate, and ear-gate, and feel-gate are open, while mouth-gate is shut, and the citadel is in the hand of Diabolus. I considered the facts of the New Testament. John the Baptist's hearers saw, heard, felt, and asked: 'What shall we do?' The woman with the issue of blood, touched the hem of his garment secretly, and was healed. He inquired after and at length she came, and fell down, and told him all the truth. 'Daughter, be of good comfort.' On the day of Pentecost, the eyes, the ears, the feelings were engaged, and at length they spake out: 'What shall we do?' Saul of Tarsus asked: 'What shall I do?' The jailor: 'What shall I do?' Such truth and power strike the heart, and so strike it that mouth-gate flies open. Last evening my discourse came to this point, that the enmity of the carnal mind keeps the impenitent from coming to Christ. The Spirit seemed to teach me very plainly, that the terrors of the Lord must be thrown in upon the mind, till conviction causes the heart to tremble, and mouth-gate to fly open. 'Lord who hath believed our report, and unto whom is the arm of the Lord revealed?'"

Yet, disheartened as he sometimes was, for want of that success in his labors which he desired, still did he persevere in his efforts, nor did he ever regard his want of success as a reason for the suspension of his labors. It is true also that discouragements, and encouragements were sometimes found to follow each other in rapid succession. He was ever encouraged and comforted at the thought of God's universal dominion, and that his purposes of grace to his people will be fulfilled, in opposition to the united malice of earth and hell.

"Found in the American Tract Magazine the following sentence: 'If you are about a good work, Satan will do all he can to discourage and hinder you; but he can not break his chain, nor go beyond it.' This is good. Thanks to God for the man who wrote it, and for putting it in my way. I know by my own experience, that discouragement hangs about every good work I undertake."

Like other gospel ministers, Dr. Yale was sometimes greatly tried on account of the absence from some important meetings, of many of the members of the church. On the ordinary services of the sabbath, there was usually a good attendance; and on other occasions it is believed that the members of that congregation are quite as punctual as people in other places. Yet there were times when, at sacramental lectures, and meetings for prayer, he felt very much depressed on account of the absence of members whom he believed might and ought to have been present. Of this he speaks as follows:

1823, Oct. 18 " After a busy week I went to the house of God to preach a sacramental lecture. But a small number of the church present. My soul sunk down within me. It seemed as though I could not preach. I could think, indeed, of several of the aged and infirm, and of a few that might be sick, and be detained themselves and detain others, and of some that were absent on journeys; such I could not expect. But that much more than half the members should be absent through necessity, seems incredible. The painful conclusion rushed upon my mind, that they did not care enough about the service, to leave their business and take the pains to come to the house of God. The thought distressed me exceedingly, and I inquired, is our religion of so little consequence? Do we care so little about the interests of the church? Is it so easy a matter to prepare for the Lord's supper? Alas! what a fearful prospect is before us! Thus I attempted to preach, with a heavy heart, and went home exceedingly depressed."

He regarded an attendance upon the instructions of the Bible class as an important means of grace; and at a certain period of his ministry, they were frequently held in different neighborhoods, so as to accommodate the people in the various parts of the congregation. These meetings were often full of interest and profit. There was also ordinarily a good attendance; yet the pastor's heart was sometimes made sad in view of the non-attendance of members.

1829, March 11. "In the evening, attended Bible class. Many attended, and many members of the church who have not been used to attend. Yet I was very much grieved at the absence of members near the house. It was sinking to my spirits to consider where they might be, and what they might be doing, while they ought to have been with us, in reading the word of God and prayer. I have been fully satisfied of the slumbering state of our church. Oh, it is dreadful—dreadful. Lord, have mercy on us."

And at the prayer-meeting, too, whenever there were such vacancies as to indicate the want of a desirable state of religious feeling in the church, his own feelings were saddened by the aspect.

1728, April 30. "At half-past four o'clock attended prayer-meeting. Four men and four women besides myself. Truly this looks very little like asking help of the Lord. But it was rainy, and this may have been one cause of this non-attendance."

1826, Nov. 23. "At evening went to the place of prayer, but no body to pray. Deeply depressive sense! Oh God, I beseech thee, strengthen my heart."

There was another cause of grief, which Dr. Yale

had in common with many other of his brethren in the ministry. Men will sometimes sleep in the house of God! Alas! that good men should convert God's house into a dormitory, and worship the goddess of sleep when they ought to be worshiping the God of heaven! Yet so it is. Such a mind as Dr. Yale could not look upon such a profanation of the sanctuary with any other feelings than those of sorrow.

1829, March 22. "Some slept. Painful fact, that even Christians, eminent Christians sleep in the house of God, under his word. How distressing to me that I can not preach so as to keep Christians awake!"

April 26, Sabbath. "A pleasant day. Many at church. Lamented that I could not engage the attention of Christians. Some will sleep; some, too, whom I view as very pious. How can it be? Oh, Lord, show me what I shall do."

July 12. "Seemed to be able to pray but little, yet needed to pray much. In the afternoon I was distressed. It seemed as though no advances were made—no conversion—not many of the church praying. I feared we should be disappointed. Several members of the church slept. Oh, how was my soul tortured at such a sinful sight! Very few members active. Oh, how dreadful!"

August 9, Sabbath. "In a peculiar state of mind all this day. In the morning preached on the temptation of the Savior to worship the devil. Good attention. Yet it seemed, by my own feelings, as though the Spirit might have taken its departure forever from me and others. In the afternoon some shed tears, and some slept. Oh what a place is the house of God! Lord awaken my soul to attend to its peculiarities. It is truly amazing that such strange admixtures, and such opposite extremes, should meet in the same place."

1830, Nov. 7. "A large congregation, and pretty good attention. But some members slept. Oh how it cuts me to the heart to see members asleep! It is like a shock of palsy to my soul. It hardens the hearts of sinners."

1822, April 28. "Have suffered amazingly this day in public worship. Not one ray of light in my soul. Not one particle of comfort in any one exercise. Amazingly straitened in my thoughts and feelings. My people were drowsy in both parts of the day. I preached as well as I could; but I could not get the attention of my people. They slept. Oh, my soul! what agonies hast thou endured! Since meeting I have endeavored to call upon God under a pressing sense of the need of the Holy Spirit."

It is no part of my present purpose to mention all of those trials which fell to the lot of this devoted pastor, during his long, and laborious and useful life. Sometimes was he tried by the unchristian deportment and and ungodly conduct of members of the church. Sometimes by the personal ill-treatment, either of open enemies or alienated friends. Sometimes by pecuniary embarrassments and the want of means to procure even the necessary provisions for his family. Sometimes by the idea that even his own people cared but little either for himself or his labors. And sometimes he almost became impatient in view of the obstinacy of sinners, and their persistence in sin.

1824, May 25. "On returning home, when thinking of my people, it seemed that they cared nothing about me —they pay me very little—they do not attend on my ministry as they should—and some even of the church go sometimes to other meetings when they should be at their own. My soul sunk down within me."

1830, Dec. 16. "When returning home on the hard and icy ground, with the snow about my head, and without my supper, as I frequently do, I began to have hard thoughts of my hard lot, and the little success of my work. Thought of Jonah, who said: 'I do well to be angry.' In trying to read some interesting missionary intelligence I fell asleep, being overcome with cold and fatigue, and then setting in my study by my warm stove. So I went to bed without much prayer."

April 1. 'Sometimes I am very much tried with the church. They seem to care very little about their own souls or the souls of others. I am ready to be provoked at them, and to say: 'If you care not for yourselves, then go to hell and take the consequences.' But oh! what a wicked thought! Jesus wept over sinners, and prayed for his disciples while they were asleep. My business is to serve God, and do all I can for men, whatever be their conduct. Neither the good or the bad conduct of men is to make any alteration in the discharge of my duty; neither their gratitude, or their ingratitude is to be any rule for my conduct. This is a world of sinners. I must expect evil from sinners. Oh, let me follow my Lord in love, every day this month, and every hour of the day. He may release me this month; and if I am of a right mind, he may even cause it to do good, when I am gone. Oh, may my heart, and words, and conduct be right. Lord, help me to serve my generation by thy will, and to thy name be the glory. Much work is to be done this month. Cause me to be more spiritual, holy, heavenly; ready to go any day, or any hour, and yet laboring and planning to do good even for many years."

It is pleasant to turn the eye away a little from these discouragements; and before we close the chapter, to look at the breaking in upon the picture of a little light. In this world it is nothing uncommon that there should be an intermingling of light and shade. Though he was sometimes depressed, he was not utterly cast down. He toiled on, hoping in God, with his eye upon the rain-bow and the throne, and receiving his reward from his work. It is proposed to illustrate this thought by two or three brief extracts from his correspondence. The letters from which these extracts are taken, were written to Rev. Cyrus Yale of New Hartford.

January 11, 1843. " Who can understand the wonderful works of God? Our very trials prove to be among our choicest mercies. Hence it is said: Rejoice in the Lord at *all* times.

Surely there is never a time when we have not abundant occasion to rejoice in him. We hope ere this you are in the midst of harvest in the middle of winter. But if you have trials, be sure that all things work together for good to them that love God. 'Count it all joy when we fall into divers temptations.' We are sometimes called to toil all night without taking anything. No matter. We are on our master's business, and he knows how to sustain us while we toil, bless unto us his wise delays, and give us many and heavy sheaves as a reward for our sowing in tears. Indeed, the work itself has its pleasures. When we toil early and late; when we go forth in storms of rain and snow and wind, and meet even a few in the prayer-meeting or lecture room, we are amply repaid in the precious hour we spend in prayer and praise and the ministry of the word. I have had much enjoyment since I saw you. On my return home, the next sabbath, I preached on the same subjects as in your church. Very soon after, the thought occurred to me that it is my duty to seek the conversion of every soul among us, and use means for this purpose. On the next sabbath (I believe), I announced this, and began to make arrangements. But, oh! what a valley of bones lay spread out around me! And behold! they were very dry—and so are they yet. But now, more than three months I have been laboring in this cause night and day. One soul was awakened and wholly cut down with conviction the very first week, and has since joined the church. But I know not of another; yet I viewed that one as a drop of mercy to encourage me. I preach three times on the sabbath and twice statedly in the course of the week. Our church do not generally seem to be awake, but some members are striving with me in my prayers. Now all the bones are very dry, and my heart would sink in view of them, did not the word of God afford me all the support I need. I fear I do not labor right, but I trust God will lead me, and guide me, and fit me for this pleasant work. It seems to me, that by the grace of God, I will toil on as well as I can, and expect to see the arm of the Lord revealed."

January 18, 1815. "I am sometimes distressed and perplexed; but never in despair; and I hope I may say, 'Hitherto the Lord hath helped me.' Last year, though attended with great trials, was one of the most fruitful in spiritual blessings. Thirty, in less than twelve months, were added to the church under my care, and about sixty obtained hope of an interest in Christ. There is an apparent abatement in the work of revival, but some of our Jacobs continue wrestling, and I hope they may prevail. We can not expect to be reaping every day; but sowing and watering seem to be favorable omens of approaching harvests. 'They that now in tears, shall reap in joy.' One thing has always been a source of consolation to me; and that is, that God sent me to this place, and continues still to make it plain that it is my duty to stay. Certainly I should rather be thus favored, though fixed in the snows of Greenland, than to doubt God's pleasure in the greatest city on earth. It is a great favor to have a comfortable assurance that God blesses my labors. Nothing earthly can equal this."

Sept. 7, 1831. "As I write you an answer by the first mail, you may think I shall be able to be with you, at your protracted meeting. I thank you for the invitation, and my heart will be with you, but I must not be with my heart at that time. God has filled my hands with labor, and my heart with care and anxiety, in regard to my people. I am almost afraid to speak of it, lest I should have some wrong feeling excited or strengthened, but I cry unto God against it. He has surprised me with the blessings of his goodness. At our communion in July (first Sabbath), I did not know of any special attention. But it soon commenced, and is now extended over a large part of the congregation. About thirty are hoping—some heads of families, and some children, nine or ten years old. Seven united with the church last sabbath, first fruits. Numbers of heads of families are awakened—such as have been long hardened. We see God's hand touching this, and that, and another, in various places. Every day let us pray one for another, and our people."

With great affection, yours,

ELISHA YALE."

CHAPTER VIII.

HIS RELIGIOUS AFFECTIONS AND SPIRITUAL COMFORTS.

A man may sometimes smile, even through his own tears. So, in the midst of all his spiritual conflicts, and while wrestling with his own corruptions, and struggling with remaining depravity, and sighing for deliverance from sin, and groaning on account of the prevalence of wickedness in the community, and praying for God's gracious interposition in the building up of the church, the Christian may be favored with such communications of God's grace, as produce within him that inward peace and comfort, which the man of the world has neither experienced nor conceived. Let it not be supposed that because Dr. Yale had such strugglings with his own heart, and such conflicts with Satan, and such feelings of deep anxiety for sinners, that, therefore, he was unhappy. Nothing is farther from the truth.

He might have said to the men of the world, as our Saviour said to his disciples; "I have meat to eat that ye know not of." "I have joy, which those have never tasted, who know nothing of the sweetness of communion with God."

He had a relish for the society of his friends, as much as is commonly felt by others; he took much comfort in social intercourse with those whom he loved; and he derived great enjoyment, from those providential kindnesses which he viewed as proceeding from the hand of his Heavenly Father. It afforded him peculiar pleasure to recognise God as the author of those blessings which he received. But it is of his *spiritual* comforts, that I now propose to speak.

These sprung from various sources; and yet all proceeded from the same never-failing fountain; e g.

He took great satisfaction in reading and pondering upon the truths of God's holy word—those parts of it which present the character of its author, as the most holy, most wise, most good, and sovereign disposer of all events—those parts which exhibit the grace of God in the plan of salvation through the Lord Jesus Christ—those parts which contain God's gracious purposes concerning his people, and his precious promises to them—those parts which point forward to the period of the Christian's release from sin, and his coronation in heaven. The language of his heart, and the language of his tongue frequently was; "How sweet are thy words unto my taste; yea, sweeter than honey to my mouth," "Oh! how love I thy law! it is my meditation all the day!" "The law of thy mouth is better unto me than thousands of gold and silver."

Another source of very great comfort, was his seasons of communion with God and his people. He loved the courts of God's house—he loved the table of his crucified Lord, and to taste of the memorials of his love—he loved the social circle for prayer—and he loved his seasons of private intercourse with heaven.

Often was he in the mount with God; and often, too, did he cast his eye beyond the river, by which the wilderness in which he dwelt was separated from the Canaan which he loved. This was of itself a source of unspeakable comfort, oh, how his soul was on fire, while he thought of the future glories of God's people!

My readers, however, are expecting that he will still be permitted to speak for himself. So let it be.

1824, April 18. During the night was troubled with such dreams as show the works of the devil in my imaginations. I am convinced of the necessity of watching and praying against his temptations. This morning I do think, amid my imperfections, I find true and genuine love to God, as he is revealed in the Bible, and that I rely on the Lord Jesus Christ as my salvation. This God is the God whom I love; this Savior is the Savior whom I desire. Amen."

April 19. "My mind on revival, at my waking season in the night—first this morning. Very calm and composed. In a sweet frame."

1827, April 16. "Through God's mercy I was enabled to go through the exercises of yesterday with more feeling than common. At the table, especially, I was more free and clear than I have been since my remembrance. I seemed to have command of myself, though not so much of my affections as I could wish. Once under a sense of ingratitude and unfaithfulness, my rising emotions choked my utterance. Oh! how desirable to be humble, and watchful, and prayerful! I do hope that God has helped me in this desire. Now for more zeal, resolution, and boldness in his service."

Oct. 20. "This evening I have been favored, very unexpectedly, with uncommon views. I have seen the nature and excellence of the spirit of revival, especially of intercession, as the subject of it is concerned, as sinners are concerned, and as it gives delighful and glorious views of heaven. I seemed for a little time to enter into the spirit of revival. O God, guide, keep, use me, and cause me to be as I should be. O, cause the church to become such, and glorify thy name. Amen."

1824. March 26. In the morning, meditating on redemption, had most glorious views. The plan appeared greater and more glorious than ever before. O how enrapturing to be swallowed up in it!"

1829, January 31. "I think I have not for years enjoyed myself so well, during a month, as I have during this. I many times wonder what God is going to do with me, or what he is preparing me for. But I am not anxious. Let it be what it may, I can now say, and I hope and trust that he will enable me to say always: "*Thy will be done.*" I felt an uncommonly strong desire to go onward with heaven in my eye, doing the will of God, and bearing it as I go, more and more, whether this year, or another, or another, till I enter into rest. O, what a privilege to serve God, and enjoy him with his people here with the prospect of perfection hereafter!"

Believing as he did in the realities of the future state, and in the future glories of God's people, his mind dwelt much upon it; and in dwelling upon it, he was some times so enraptured, that he seemed to himself to be very near the regions of the blest.

1829, March 31. "Pleasant thoughts on God and heaven, and on the privilege of going to heaven, if it be God's will, not this year only, but this day. This thought animated me more than common. Let me think every morning: 'To day I may go to heaven—if so, I shall sup at night with my brethren and sisters at my Father's table. Oh, how unworthy of such a favor!"

1831, January 9. "Near evening I had some delightful views of heaven. Oh! to be with Christ and all the holy, how desirable! God has promised it to believers. It is therefore more sure than heaven and earth."

Sept. 10. "Felt a sweet frame of mind this morning, especially in the consciousness of having attended faithfully to my duty yesterday, and in view of the advancement of God's work. If my mind be so sweet in a little, Oh! how happy should I be if I were perfectly holy, and where I could constantly, and without sin, or fear of sin or delusion, serve God to all eternity and see his glory. Oh, come that happy day! I trust it will come."

For many years, Dr. Yale was accustomed to familiarize himself with thoughts of death. Nor were they unwelcome and disagreeble thoughts, inasmuch as he regarded death only as the period of his toils and the commencement of his rest. I will here give a few passages from some letters to his friend Mr. Brace.

January 29, 1838. "I trust that I am becoming much more familiar with death. It comes on apace, and draws nearer perceptibly. The time between this moment, and that in which I shall meet him seems nothing, being in my fifty-eighth year. Yet it seemed while reflecting on Dr. Perkins' life, that I would be willing to live as long as he, provided I might be engaged in the service of God, and not stand in the way of some one who might fill my place better. I hope too, I am willing to go this year, if the will of the Lord be so.

Yet I fear my deceitful heart. "Search me, O God, and know my heart; try me, and know my thoughts; and see if there be any wicked way in me, and lead me in the way everlasting."

Jan. 1, 1844 "My thoughts run after the heavenly world, and yet I know I have little of the spirit of heaven. What shall we do there? Whom shall we see there? How far is heaven from earth? How shall we know the way, when the spirit leaves the body? By what means will our spirits proceed to those mansions? Who will be our guides? How long shall we be on the way? Who will welcome our coming? What will be our feelings when we find ourselves there, escaped from all the dangers and through all the enemies of the way? Then comes the more important inquiry: 'Am I ready?' I make the exclamation: 'What if I should fail, after all my hopes and endeavors!' How fearful would be my disappointment! I run to Jesus with greater concern, as I feel him to be my only hope. Am I interested in him? In proof of this, do I renounce every other hope, and cheerfully and joyfully accept of him as he is freely offered in the gospel; my prophet, and my priest, and my king? Nor can I find any peace, till I have renewed evidence of my acceptance in the beloved."

To part with Christian friends was to Dr. Yale, as it is with others, a source of regret; yet when, in the providence of God, they had been removed from earth, he took peculiar pleasure in thinking of them as in heaven. He seemed to see them around the throne, and to listen to their accents of praise, and to be exercised with a sort of holy ecstacy in the anticipation of being with them ere long himself and to unite with them in singing the "song of Moses, the servant of God, and the song of the lamb." Look at a few passages from a letter to his cousin in New Hartford:

July 1, 1846. "We have suffered greatly since the thirtieth of October. Ten of our members have been removed from the world; some suddenly, others by a lingering disease. The last fell asleep on the thirtieth of May. Heaven has grown richer by the gathering of a portion of the glory and honor of the nations into it. That blessed world has more and more attractions to me; and I suppose it is lawful for us to delight in the thought that our pious friends are there. And though the moon grows dim, and stars disappear in the presence of the sun, yet God is pleased to use the moon and the stars for his glory and for the benefit of his creation. It is pleasing indeed to think of our dear Christian friends, as in heaven, in everlasting rest; those with whom we have conversed, and prayed, and rejoiced, and wept, and labored. Abraham and Isaac and Jacob, Moses, Elijah, Samuel, and all the prophets, and apostles, and martyrs, are with the Lord. So are beloved pastors, Hyde, Shepard, and many, many, very dear to us are among the happy company."

I may be allowed also to make two or three extracts from his diary, which have a bearing upon this point.

1829, Sept. 9. "Heard of the death of another member, Eliza F. Poor, humble, patient Eliza! now thou art gone. No more in trouble on account of '*this dreadful heart of sin.* In meditating on the departure of these two believers (Eliza F. and Capt. B.), and their happy reception and meeting, my heart leaped upward. I felt a desire to depart and be with them and all my friends in Christ, and, above all, with Christ himself. Yet I longed to live while I do live so as to please them and above all to please Christ in doing good. *But oh! my dreadful deceitful heart!* Lord help me to keep my heart with all diligence."

1830, Dec. 26. "A pleasant, comfortable day. In the evening, preached on this text, Phil. iii, 20: 'For our conversation is in heaven, from whence also we look for the Savior, the Lord Jesus Christ. It seemed good to be on the borders of heaven. Preaching in reference to the funeral of Deacon Hall, I felt comforted in view of the grace of God bestowed upon him, showing so strikingly the nature of the gospel. I could well and confidently point to him, not as a perfect man, but as a sincere and genuine Christian. I was confident I had the consciences of all on my side. It was a glorious day for the cause of Christ. *Oh, let me die the death of the righteous, and let my last end be like his.* Surely, there has been some true religion among us. But, oh! when shall we see his like again? Lord, let his mantle fall on some of thy servants."

On the 29th of December, 1830, he went to see a ministerial brother who was on the point of death, being cut off in the midst of his days and his usefulness. Upon his return from the bedside of that departing brother, he made a record of some interesting reflections. He says:

"He desired me to speak of the excellency of Jesus, which I did as well as I was able. About noon I returned home, thinking as I came along of these words: '*Be thou faithful, unto death, and I will give thee a crown of life.*' Rev. ii, 10.

An eminent minister, on his death-bed, observed, that 'the point in which he believed ministers failed most, and in which he had certainly failed most, was in doing duty professionally, and not from the heart.'

Inexperienced youth are sometimes amused, when, being delighted with the splendid hues of the rainbow, they are told that they may find a golden treasure, if they will only go to the end of it. For a moment they are on the point of starting to run for the wished for spot. But their rapid powers of reasoning soon induce them to inquire in regard to their informant: 'If what he says is true, why does he not seek the gold himself?'

So the faithful minister. Is God's law holy? he reveres it. Is the law broken? he trembles at it. Is the falling? he is afraid qf it. Is the heart depraved? he mourns over it. Is there none but Christ? he embraces him. Must men be holy? he relies upon the Spirit. Is there a hell? he flees from it. Is the gospel the only hope of man? he endeavors to make it known to every creature.

Jeremiah wept. Our Lord Jesus Christ wept. The Apostle Paul wept. The celebrated Whitfield wept. He often wept in the pulpit till his friends were distressed to see him overcome. But recovering himself, he would say: 'You blame me for weeping so, but how can I help weeping, when I see sinners going to destruction, but unwilling to weep for themselves.'

Many have been alarmed at seeing ministers alarmed for them. But it is no affectation. It is a deep and awful sense of reality. Now this is needful, to be faithful. '*I believe, therefore have I spoken.*'

It is not, however, a minister only who is to be faithful, but a church—the church in Smyrna—every church. Not a church only, but every member. It may be observed, too, that a man is not left at his option, whether he be faithful or not. The blessed Lord and master has commanded, and none can refuse but at his peril. To encourage every one to be faithful, the Lord holds out a *crown*—the highest prize ever held out to man—a crown, not of garlands—not of gold—a crown of *life.*

This animated the Apostle Paul: 'I have fought a good fight, I have finished my course, I have kept the faith. Henceforth there is laid up for me a crown of righteousness which the Lord, the righteous judge, shall give me at that day, and not to me only, but unto all them also that love his appearing.'"

The following extract breathes so much of that Christian serenity which was such an important ingredient of his character, and presents so much in reference to the sources of his religious comforts, that I feel unwilling to withhold it:

1829, Dec. 31. "I think I can truly say in reviewing the year, that it has been the happiest I ever saw. My mind has been at ease, most of the time, in regard to the future world. I have had many delightful thoughts in regard to its excellence and glory. I have had little trouble in regard to the things of this world. I have had enough to supply my wants, but not so much as to burden me with cares. My health and my family's health has been good almost without a day's interruption. I have enjoyed uninterrupted peace in the congregation and the church, except that I have many times been distressed very much with the stupidness of some members of the church. I have enjoyed much pleasure in preaching the word publicly, and elsewhere. I have, in the inquiry meeting, the prayer meeting, and the Bible class, experienced much comfort. Yet, after all, I have had many of the most humbling views of my indwelling sin, that I ever had; and I have felt many painful anxieties in regard to others. I have observed several days of fasting and prayer, and I think I found them all profitable. If I did not experience moral, sensible benefit at the time, I did in a few days. And I have generally thought I have felt sensible benefit in preaching the next sabbath after fasting and prayer. Indeed, if health and other circumstances rendered it suitable, I have thought it would be very desirable to spend every Friday or Saturday in private fasting and prayer.

God has blessed my labors more than I dared to hope, though it was my desire and prayer, that one, at least, might be converted every week during the year, on an average. I trust God has done this and more, though all have not united with the church. Find, on review, some among the converts for whom I felt special desires."

The peace of some good men is greatly marred if not altogether destroyed, not only by adverse providences, but also by fear of approaching ills. Dr. Yale's religion, however, was so much like that of the Apostle Paul, that with him was he enabled to say: "We glory in tribulations also."

It afforded him peculiar satisfaction to look at the hand of God in all his afflictions. He loved to recognize God as the God of providence, and to contemplate the fulfillment of the divine purposes even in those adversities which are experienced by his people.

The following extracts of letters written during the last period of his life will sufficiently explain themselves:

KINGSBOROUGH, Fulton Co., N. Y., *April* 1, 1851.

"MY DEAR COUSIN—Time passes on, and carries into effect the eternal counsels of God. What matter of joy to angels! What matter of joy to men that love God. He says: 'I will do all my pleasure.' I humbly trust that I am humbly pleased to have it so. I think I would not for the world have it otherwise. His infinite all-sufficiency, his infinite love, his unchangeable truth, are the foundation on which all my destinies rest. Would I change them? Not on any account. On the 25th of March, 1849, our beloved one left us for the unseen world. Blessed be God that we have not murmured. Generally, since that time, these lines of Watts have dwelt in my mind:

'I follow where my Father leads,
And he supports my steps.'

On the 16th of this March, I preached twice. On Wednesday morning, a paralysis of my left side made me feel like a shattered earthen pitcher. I have not preached since, nor been to church, nor done any thing worth naming, except trying to bind up the pitcher. The doctor has helped, and friends have helped, and with much success. To-day I rode to Gloversville.

April 2. I give you a kind of diary, as I can write but little. Thanks to God that I can write at all. My mind is clear, but my strength is little. I am obliged to consult conscience often, whether I may write any more. I walk, then lie down on the lounge, then read a chapter, then write a few lines. And sometimes I kneel down here in my study and look up to the eternal hills. To-day for the first time I returned to my beloved study—my little earthly paradise. Oh, how gently, how kindly, my heavenly Father deals with me! I have felt very little pain, and enjoy great peace. I had a very foolish thought several months ago. What shall I do when my pastoral labors among my people shall cease? I had no business with such a thought. It is a secret thing, which belongs to the Lord our God. Deut. xxix, 29. I contemplated this as my last year of pastoral duty. I was strong, vigorous, and able to labor. What shall I do at the end of the year? Foolish thought. God has taught me the folly of it. Before the end of the first quarter he has taught me that he can dash the earthen pitcher at a stroke. Then what is it good for? A shred of it might do to scrape Job's boils with. That may be as much as I shall be good for by the end of 1851. God has taught me this lesson, and I trust I shall learn to let his secrets alone —'Follow where my Father leads.'"

KINGSBOROUGH, Nov. 20, 1852.

"MY DEAR COUSIN—How were we surprised last evening to read in the New York Observer, notice of the departure of Mary, your daughter. What shall we say to you and your bereaved wife and children? Many things we need not say, because you know them better than we can tell you. Indeed we will not attempt to tell you anything new. They are the old things on which we depend in the hour of trial and bereavement. As I have for nearly two years felt myself just on the verge of time, I have found that the one thing is the basis of support and comfort—the one thing—reliance on the redemption in Christ Jesus, especially, as expressed in Rom. iv, 5: 'But to him that worketh not, but believeth on him that justifieth the ungodly, his faith is counted for righteousness.' This is the anchor of my soul. It is the simple fact on which my soul rested first. On this I rest now. On this I expect to rest in my last moment. This is the only thing for me in death. In bereavement, the one thing is the will of God. As we have learned to pray: 'Thy will be done.' When we lost our beloved one at a stroke, the first thing we said, was: 'Thy will be done.' We have often said this—we will not take it back now. 'Thy will be done.' So have we continued to say in the continued trials since I have been laid aside. O how glorious at times does the great truth appear, as declared in these words: 'My counsel shall stand, and I will do all my pleasure.' This is our pleasure too. And another: 'I do always those things that please him.' So said Jesus. So I can not say, but I hope to, ere long. Then shall we be perfect. We can desire nothing more than to be swallowed up in the will of God. This is the perfection of heaven—the perfection we seek after. This is enough. In the eternal, unchangeable counsel of God, our heavenly Father, it was arranged that our Elisha, and your Mary should be removed, just at the time and in the way that it has been done. God brings about what he determines, and all good beings rejoice in his will. We are wounded, weep and mourn, and it was designed that we should, to make our hearts better, and to glorify God.

Do I wound your tender feelings? I hope not. I would sit down by you, and weep with you; but at the same time, I would go with you to the throne of grace, and say all I have said, and more.

Now I commend you to God, and close, so as to send by this mail.

With great affection and regard, your relative in the flesh, and brother in Christ,

E. Yale."

CHAPTER IX.

HIS PASTORAL FIDELITY.

One of Dr. Yale's most fondly cherished sentiments, and a sentiment which seemed to have been interwoven in his entire Christian character, may be expressed in the following sentence. What I am God has made me; and what I do God enables me to do it. His entire reliance upon divine grace was with him a settled principle; and yet, he was not of that class of men, who make their dependence an excuse for the neglect of duty. During his whole pastoral life, he evidently felt that there was a weight of responsibility resting upon him, which it was impossible for him to shake off.

It is true that he did, at times, have an oppressive, and overwhelming sense of his own unfaithfulness, This sense of his short-comings found vent in the following language: "This morning in prayer, my unfaithfulness in the work of the ministry generally, and in regard to Christian duty, overwhelmed me. Years, months, weeks, days, hours, passed in review, and all evidences of unfaithfulness. Had I been faithful, how different had been the state of things! The church have failed with me. So have we neglected duty. We are fit for nothing. Our prayers are good for nothing, because we are under evil influences. We are not hearty, humble, earnest. We wonder why God does not convert sinners. We may rather wonder why he does not destroy us. We must humble ourselves, repent, confess, forsake, and return to the Lord."

But though he thus speaks of his own unfaithfulness it was *comparative,* rather than *absolute;* an unfaithfulness which he discovered in himself, from the high standard of duty which he was accustomed to set before his mind, rather than that which was either discovered or discoverable by others. No man who was acquainted with his course of life, and the manner in which he discharged the duties of the ministry, can fail to see the appropriateness of the text which he selected as the foundation of his farewell discourse to his people, at the close of his pastorate of forty-eight years: Acts xx, 26, 27. "Wherefore I take you to record this day, that I am pure from the blood of all men; for I have not shunned to declare unto you all the counsel of God."

In speaking and thinking of the responsibilities of the gospel ministry, he was accustomed frequently to refer to the commission given by God to the prophet; "So thou, O son of man, I have set thee a watchman unto the house of Israel; therefore thou shalt hear the word at my mouth, and warn them from me. When I say unto the wicked man, O wicked man, thou shalt surely die; if thou dost not speak to warn the wicked from his way, that wicked man shall die in his iniquity; but his blood will I require at thy hand. Nevertheless, if thou warn the wicked of his way to turn from it; if he do not turn from his way, he shall die in his iniquity; but thou hast delivered thy soul." Ez. xxiii, 7-9.

With such a sense of ministerial responsibility, it is not to be wondered at, that fidelity in the discharge of duty, particularly characterized all his varied labors for the welfare of his people and the conversion of men. The idea which he entertained of his own responsibility, will further appear from the following passages from his memorandum:

1826, August 1. "Last week I felt the importance of sounding an alarm against sin and sinners. The duty of a watchman was deeply impressed upon my mind. I must warn; I must do it from house to house, as well as in the pulpit, whether they will hear, or whether they will forbear."

1830, March 15. "Awoke in the night, and was much impressed with my duty to warn every one I have opportunity to warn. Cried unto God on my bed for some individuals. Arose about five, and cried unto God again. I feel it now to be my indispensable duty to warn and persuade all I have opportunity, by the terror of the Lord. This day, O Lord, I will begin, thy grace assisting me, and I will endeavor to be faithful, as one that must give account."

Dr. Yale was specially faithful as a pastor, in carrying the gospel from house to house, and in endeavoring to win souls to Christ, by personal interviews. An interesting account of the manner in which he performed this part of his pastoral duties, may be found in the following extract of a letter addressed to the Rev. Mr. Brace:

KINGSBOROUGH, *April* 3, 1834.

"BROTHER BRACE—I am just now in the midst of a quarterly family visiting, which I have commenced again this year, after having been irregular about it, for two years past. My plan is to do the work in March, which I have found to be the best month in the year for this work, because people are at home and at leisure; to go out at one o'clock, and continue till about nine, and visit eight or ten families, more or less, according to circumstances. I take a brother along with me, in the afternoon, and another in the evening. We ride to the neighborhood when it is over a mile, put out our horses, and walk from house to house. This season I have been providentially hindered so that I am not more than half done. Our main business now is to stir up Christians to prayer, by talking and praying. We that visit, have a kind of protracted prayer-meeting, with little intervals, while we go from house to house—sometimes one prayer, sometimes two, sometimes three in a family, attended with reading the scriptures, remarks and conversation. I take with me a temperance pledge, and ask soon after the salutations, 'How many in the family? How many are temperance members?' Then if any are not, I ask whether they wish to be. If so, I put down their names. If not, I put up my paper, and with a kind remark or two, close this part of the business. If I find any thing in a paper that is striking, on a religious subject, especially prayer, I read it, or give the substance of it, read a little from the Bible, inquire after the religious profession of each one, and into the state of mind as to hope, pray, leave a tract, and bid good bye. It is delightful work, though pretty laborious. It tends to promote friendly feelings, soften prejudice, excite interest in religion and the good cause generally, bring people to meeting, and spread the savor of godliness over the community. I find now on this visiting, that I have lost much by remitting labors of this kind. Our population is, partially, of that transient kind which rolls from one place to another, annually, or biennially, or triennially, so that they can not be benefited unless it be done seasonably. If I visit them quarterly, I am sure to find them, and usually secure some of their good feelings. Though this is but a small matter in itself, yet it is worth a great deal more than its costs. For by a visit of half, or three-quarters of an hour, three or four times a year, their good will is secured permanently, especially if they be poor. And such visits may be the commencement of a series of thoughts in some minds, to lead the soul to the Saviour. Besides, the brother who goes with me, is benefited, is improved in his graces, feels interested in those we visit, and thus a savor of godliness is diffused in the church. In addition to this, I learn to preach more than I should in my study, and often find a text for a sermon, and a train of thought to run through the sermon itself. I confess, indeed, that the work does not seem so desirable before I begin it, and I had much rather stay at home, and attend to the closest study; but when I am in it, I feel delighted. What a wonderful being man is! In every department of duty he may be happy. Even when laboring the hardest, under the greatest pressure, amid the severest self-denial, he may be happy any where. Surely it is a good thing to be a Christian, to be altogether a Christian."

While there were none of his flock who were not cared for by their pastor, and while none were designedly passed by in his pastoral visitations, he paid particular attention to such as were in adversity, or laid aside by sickness. His feelings in respect to such found utterance in the following language:

1820, Oct 14. "Visited the oldest man in the place, who fell from a horse a few days ago, and has been speechless since, and unable to use his right side. Feel as though I had not done as well as I might, because I did not visit him sooner. Let me visit the sick hereafter as soon as I hear of their sickness, and the providence of God will permit."

1829, Sept. 22. "Went to the summit of the mountain to see a sick woman. I was glad that I went, though I walked a mile up hill and through the woods. The poor woman appeared to be glad to see me, and to be a real Christian."

The following extracts have respect to certain events which took place while engaged in ministerial labors in the county of Saratoga.

1816, Oct. 23. "In the morning spent a few hours in endeavoring to show the man with whom I lodged, some of the difficulties of confounding natural and moral ability. He seemed to be pressed some, though I do not know that he was convinced. He has been in affliction, and thinks he has religion. I should think so too, if he seemed to know the plague of his heart, and to be reconciled to God."

Oct. 25. "Dined this day without asking a blessing or returning thanks. It was not, however, through forgetfulness. The man made great complaint of his poor beef. I observed: 'Perhaps you do not think it good enough, to give thanks for it.' He replied in a low voice: 'I am not used to give thanks.' Though we had all done before him, he turned away from the table, excused his haste, rose up and left the room before the rest rose. He is a head man in supporting Universalism. I thought it did not make him a better man."

In rebuking sin, Dr. Yale was frequently very pointed and direct. Indeed, he sometimes thought, himself, that he was more pointed than was meet. Of this he speaks as follows:

1824, April 9. "An incident gave me a profitable train of thought. I reproved in the morning too sharply. A common fault with me. Thought of the divine pattern, particularly Rev. ii, 3, to commend every thing commendable, and then point out deficiencies tenderly, with encouragement to reform and make them up. Resolved to follow this pattern in all my reproofs in time to come."

At a very early period of his religious life, did Dr. Yale both dedicate himself and devote all his possessions to the service of God. This he ever kept in view; and while he cherished the feeling that God had the proprietorship of himself and all that he had, he desired also the same sentiment should be cherished by others. Few things affected him more than to see God's own people clinging to the world, as if it were the supreme object of their affection. The spirit of selfishness which sometimes appeared among Christian professors, he both deplored and rebuked. Take the following:

1830, Sept. 25. "Rode to G ——, to exchange with brother R. Called on a rich man, by the way, and dined. He and his wife are members of the church, and he is an elder. But, oh! how dead! They seemed to *suppose that gain was godliness.* Gain is their duty to make, gain is their duty to keep! And their religion consists in doing their duty. This seems to be all their duty! They made me think of the pilgrims traveling through the enchanted ground, when they saw some asleep in the arbors by the way-side. They went to them and endeavored to awake them. But one answered: 'I will pay you when I take my money.' I told them of this. I repeated again and again the direction of Paul to Timothy: '*Charge them that are rich in this world*,' &c. But the reply was, that we must use riches as God's stewards, to pay our honest debts. I was deeply grieved at their wretched condition. They must hate ministers most cordially, or they can not prophesy any good about them.

Dr. Yale was a hearty temperance man—a pioneer in the work of reform, lifting up his voice in opposition to the prevailing customs of society, when most others were mute; and his fidelity in that work, doubtless, contributed much towards the removal of that curse of man, intoxicating drinks, from the entire field of his pastoral labors.

As an illustration of his fidelity in this cause, I have extracted the following from his memorandum.

1830, Oct. 1. "This afternoon, a poor drunken man called, and wished to see me. I went down. He attempted to rise, and reached forth his hand, but failed the first time to reach mine. 'Oh, I am so lame.' He sat down and covered his face for shame. 'I am a poor, unfortunate fellow'—then covered his face again. 'I havn't been drinking any thing stronger than water and beer. My disorder makes me shake. My poor wife is very sick. Have you such a thing as rice? The doctor said she must have rice.' I did not know. I asked Angeline, and she said there was. 'I've tried at all the stores, and they have none—expect some to-day, but it is not come—if you could spare a little mite.' I told Angeline to put up a tea-cup full. 'My wife would be glad to have you come and see her.' I promised to call to-morrow. 'I've one request to make to you. I wish you would pray for me that God would have mercy on my poor soul. I should be glad to talk with you.' 'I will talk with you to-morrow.' I gave him the rice. He held it in his hand. I told him he had better put it in his pocket and go home. He did so, and started, but held by the post. In the door-way he stopped, still holding, and said: 'Good afternoon.' As I turned and went into the study, I thought I should say to the venders of strong drink: *The curse of God will rest upon you for selling strong drink to such men.* I may add: *The curse of God will rest upon you for selling strong drink at all.* Hab. ii, 15, 16.

Copied this immediately, except the name Angeline, to hand to our venders. Went out and heard a young man tell some children, that A — lay on the hill drunk —thought it would be a good time to go and present my communication. I went—found one of the young men alone, and presented it, saying it was from a friend, and desiring him to read it and present it to his partner. He looked on the superscription, viz: '*The venders of strong drink*,' and blushed, and said nothing. I turned and came away, while he was opening the letter I lifted up my heart to God on the way, and besought God especially and earnestly in my closet, to send an arrow to their hearts, and make this event and this communication a means of their salvation."

Oct. 2. "As soon as I could leave home in the morning, I went to see the sick woman—found her comfortable. The poor man hobbled in, and pretended that he had fallen and put his hip out of joint. At any rate he was carried home in a wagon. I said: 'He that being often reproved, hardeneth his neck, shall suddenly be destroyed, and that without remedy.' "

While Dr. Yale thus labored with rumsellers, to convince them of the extreme wickedness of their business, in administering to the depraved appetites of the intemperate, and in contributing to the forming of such appetites in others; he labored no less faithfully with such as indulged themselves in the use of intoxicating drinks.

1830, Jan. 19. "Rose at half-past four, and endeavored to cast my burdens on the Lord.

1. My own sins.
2. The stupid youth in my family.
3. The inquiry and prayer-meeting.
4. The disorderly members.
5. Some cruel sinners in the congregation.

Before noon I felt it my duty to go and see one disorderly member. He has kept a jug of spirits in various places, the snow-bank, the hay or straw-mow, and under the fence or a log. It has many times been found, and the report is every where, and a reproach to us all. He pretends that he hid it to keep it away from his wife, and that he thought some necessary for his health, and that it had been necessary for some others who had been sick or unwell. I tried to show him the evil, startled him some, but seemed to prevail but very little. I fear he is ruined; and yet he treated me kindly."

There were some sins which Dr. Yale believed should be treated with marked reprobation. Among these was the sin of self-murder; and such were his feelings in respect to the commission of this unnatural and heathenish crime, and such his belief as to the treatment which the self-murderer should receive, that no respect for surviving friends, and no feelings of sympathy with them even in the extremity of their sufferings, would induce him to attend his funeral. His belief was that such a man ought to be treated with particular disrespect; not because of any effect which would be produced upon the state of the dead, but for the purpose of exerting an influence upon the living. He would have men feel that there was something in this sin which was peculiarly dishonorable; believing that some might thus be restrained from its commission, who would not be restrained from other considerations. The above statement will serve to explain those passages from his memorandum, which follow:

1830, July 6. "At 4 P. M., lectured in the school house near Mr. B's. Visited a family and attended Bible class. When I came out of the Bible class, heard that L. A. had shot himself, and was dead since sunset. I saw him about four o'clock, at the blacksmith shop near where I lectured. Poor, drunken, worthless man! A sorrowful case of depravity. Oh may the Lord direct me what to do, and give me grace and wisdom to do it. Last fall he was for a time thoughtful, and attended several meetings of inquiry. But it is long since I have seen him at any meeting. '*Who maketh thee to differ from another?*' '*By the grace of God I am what I am.*' O, impress deeply on my mind the need and power of divine grace."

July 7. "In the morning Capt. S. called and requested me to attend the funeral of the poor man. I thought it my duty to decline, but promised to visit the poor family. About ten I visited them. Did not see the corpse though it lay in the room. Several neighbors were in. The mother of the poor man was there. I expressed my sense of depravity, and our liability to commit sin, our dependence upon God, and the need of divine restraints. I told Mrs. A. in the presence of all, my reasons for not attending the funeral. It seemed to me, the profanation of my sacred office, though I would treat most tenderly the feelings of survivors. I stated what God had said about Jehoiakim, a wicked king of Judah, who cut and burnt the roll, indicted by Jeremiah: 'He shall be buried with the burial of an ass, and his dead body shall be cast out, in the day to the heat, and in the night to the frost.' The feeling is a feeling of horror and such a feeling should be retained. She wept but said little. I learnt that he was brought from Johnstown yesterday intoxicated. He called at B's, and asked for spirits, but was refused. He tried at the blacksmith shop where I saw him, to get his brother to go and fill his bottle, but he would not. So he went home and shot himself."

In his personal intercourse with his people as their pastor, Dr. Yale was sometimes very pointed and searching in the communications which he made, and his wish was, to say something which should produce upon their minds a lasting and a salutary impression.

Take the following examples:

1820, Oct. 13. "Conversed with J. S. who complains of a hard heart, and seems to desire to be a Christian, but dares not submit. Among other things, I said to her: 'I am afraid you will not be saved. Your own heart, and the world, and Satan are combined for your destruction.'"

1830, March 23. "One man came to the door as I was talking with his family, but when he saw me, he went away. When I came out I saw him walking towards his shop. I followed him in and saluted him. He made little answer, and made as though he would kindle up his fire and go to work. I asked him: 'Is there not a better world than this?'

Mr. S. 'What?'

I. 'Heaven.'

Mr. S. 'It may be if any wish for it.'

I. 'Do not you wish for it?'

He went to a window, I followed, talking still. He turned away again, and I came off, bidding him good-bye."

There was a sense of great personal responsibility, frequently resting upon the mind of Dr. Yale, and which served to excite him to fidelity in his pastoral labors.

1849, April 3. "Awoke before three o'clock, and soon rose with an awful impression on my mind, that I must address persons individually on their duty to God, boarders and others, as they come in my way. Meditated on Abraham, who feared God, offering up Isaac; on Moses, who went to speak to Israel and Pharaoh; on Jeremiah who did so many painful duties, and suffered so much; on Ezekiel, who lay on one side, then on the other; on Jonah, who was at first disobedient, but afterwards went to Nineveh. In my meditations and prayers, I thought I must do my duty, faithfully and wisely; under this impression, the fear of God sustained me. I said as before, in answer to the question: 'Will you avoid what may displease God? and will you do what is agreeable to his will?' I said, I will. This involves an awful responsibility. I fear God, and would do always as he says:

> 'I follow where my Father leads,
> And he supports my steps.'

'Fear him, ye saints, and you will then have nothing else to fear.' God is leading me into eternity, and just now before I go, he calls me to duties and trials, under which he alone can sustain me."

Impressions like these were not confined to the last years of Dr. Yale's life. They were impressions which he was accustomed to cherish, and under the influence of which he went about the discharge of duty.

Take the following as an illustration:

1830, Nov. 7. "In the night I awoke and felt distressed for Mr. ——. Could not bear to think of him on a dying bed, and before the judgment seat. I was distressed for him, and felt that I must go and speak to him personally. This morning when I arose he was still in my mind, and it seemed that I could never pray again, till I had made up my mind to see and converse with him this day. I felt a struggle, but the Spirit of God evidently urged me. I agreed. Then I poured out my soul for him with tears. It seemed to be the last time for him. I entreated God to grant him his Spirit. 'For thy name's sake, O Lord, pardon my sin in neglecting my duty and aid me to do it. For thy name's sake, pardon his iniquity, for it is great. Set his sins in order before him. Cause him to feel that he is unconverted. Oh, turn him to thee. Nothing is too hard for the Lord. This is the most difficult case I know of among my people. Glorify thy name by making him a trophy of thy victorious grace. Let him be the first if it be thy will, to whom thou wilt make my preaching and my labors a blessing, in the new series of labors in which I am now engaged. Thou hast heard my prayer in regard to two important matters in relation to the revival of true religion and the removal of that light material which seems to me to be ruining souls. Oh, grant now, a revival of pure and undefiled religion in connection with my labors, preaching publicly, and from house to house, testifying to all repentance towards God, and faith towards our Lord Jesus Christ. Oh, let this man, now more than three score years old, be the one, whom thou wilt choose to display thy great power and rich grace. Give me wisdom and grace, to speak to him, and bless the endeavor. Is not his attention a little awake? Wilt thou not bless my speaking to him, to advance the work? Oh mighty God, as nothing is too hard for thee, be pleased to cause him to break off all his sins and become a humble, a broken-hearted, useful believer, and thy name shall have all the glory, while I am ashamed for my manifold neglects, these many years. Oh Lord, hear and save after so long a time, and let this one case encourage me and thy people for others. For he is of no more worth than others. Oh, let thy Spirit and grace descend upon them too. Bless me also in all the labors of this day, and make it one of the most important in my life past. As I prayed yesterday that I might do more for thy cause and for souls, than I ever did any day before, so let it be to-day. And though I be nothing, and vile, yet glorify thyself in me, through Jesus Christ, Amen.'

After this prayer, my thoughts ran on the duty of speaking to the unconverted, till it seemed to be one of the greatest favors I could do them. Then my mind was relieved. Now let me feel always when I am about to speak to an unconverted soul, that I am trying to do him the greatest favor in my power. This will make it easy. It is not for self, but for him. Surely, I would not be backward, if I were trying to show him how to gain the greatest earthly good. Why should I, when attempting to guide him to the pearl of great price?

I called at the house a little after 9 o'clock in the morning but he was not at home. Circumstances prevented me from calling again this day. But I was not easy."

Nov. 8. "All the morning felt pressed with this duty, and could not pray at all without a fixed determination to call again this day. It seemed very heavy, but it must be borne. I was fully sensible that this is one of the most difficult cases among my people, and that I must go. About three o'clock in the afternoon, I called again. He was not at home. I sat down in his family and conversed with them on religion, till he came. As soon as he came, and salutations were exchanged, I desired to speak with him alone. I expressed my sense of his kindness to me always, and then opened my mind freely with tears. He was melted, and talked freely. I came home and could pray. In the evening God gave me a second sermon to the unconverted. Then it seemed that he had begun to answer my prayer, to give me the spirit of preaching. I was afraid lest I should be lifted up. But attention to my duty, preaching publicly and from house to house to all sinners, with unceasing prayer to God, is my security. Help, Lord, for without thee I can do nothing. I wondered this afternoon, while I was going to see this man, why I could not feel so about any other. Now I know. This moment, another, a member of the church, has come to my thoughts. I must say to him, what I have felt about him some time: 'I stand in doubt of you; not for what you do, but for what you do not.' Active signs of life are not to be seen in him. Lord, give me humility. Give me the boldness which arises from humility, and a full reliance on thee."

As a pastor, Dr. Yale was specially watchful over the spiritual interests of his flock. During the period of his pastorate, they were blessed with several precious revivals of religion; and as he longed for the commencement of the work of grace previous to any particular indications of the Spirit's presence, so also did he desire the continuance of those divine operations by which alone the salvation of men can be effected. He vigilantly watched every thing which seemed to indicate that the Spirit was about to depart, and earnestly inquired after the cause. Such inquiries appear in his journal near the close of the year 1829, and at the commencement of the year 1830.

1829, Sept. 21. "About one o'clock I awoke, and being unable to sleep I came into the study, and tried to pray and search my heart, to find out what hinders God's blessing. I found it to be a fact that the work does not advance in this neighborhood among the careless. I know of no new cases of awakening, while some have gone back from their awakenings. In the south, no advances. In the west and north-west, some. In the north, appearances are increasingly favorable. But is God indeed going to leave us as we are? O how dreadful the thought! What have we done thus to provoke him? On searching, I thought I saw faintly, and prayed to see more, the following evils; pride, self-complacency, self-confidence, and remissness."

Dec. 31. "At both inquiry meetings, I felt much distressed; not so much because they were thinly attended, as because the church and all seem to give sad evidence of declension. I could say but little. Seemed desirous to pray all the time, and yet feared that my prayer, and that of my brethren was not right. Returned home with a very heavy heart, and very weary. Seemed desirous to cry to God all the time, and yet as though bound down, so as to be unable to cry at all. It was an inward crying, connected with conscious sin."

1830, Jan. 9. "Evening attended inquiry meeting. Not so many as at some times. Felt ready to sink in discouragement, because now for several weeks, I can not find or hear of one who has been converted."

Jan. 10. "Lay awake in the night, thinking of our condition. My wife told me of one young woman, reported as having passed from death unto life. This seemed to revive my hopes, and caused me to thank God and take courage. O Lord, thou art our Saviour. Save me from my sins, from all the evils of my heart. O save thy people, and save poor sinners. Move, draw, purify such as have been for weeks or months, attending meetings of inquiry."

While Dr. Yale was sincerely and devotedly attached to the doctrines and order of the Presbyterian church, yet did he most cordially extend the hand of fellowship to the various denominations of evangelical Christians, who build upon the same foundation, and rely for salvation upon the merits of the same Saviour. Yet was he sometimes exceedingly tried in his own feelings, at what seemed to him to be the spirit of proselytism in others. He did sometimes feel as if unwarrantable efforts were made to draw away disciples from among his people, and his vigilance as a pastor did not allow him to let them pass unnoticed. Yet he never was fond of controversy, nor did he ever engage in it, but when he really believed that it was demanded by fidelity to his ordination vows and a regard to the spiritual interests of his people. He was as well pleased to receive members into the church as other pastors are (if they were such members as would be likely to do honor to a Christian profession), yet it is not known, nor is it believed that he ever used an undue influence to draw away persons from other churches into his own. And that spirit of Christian courtesy, which he aways felt disposed to show to others, in this respect, he desired that others should extend to him.

After having been laid aside from the active discharge of the duties of the pastoral office, for more than a year, in consequence of an attack of paralysis, on the 23d day of June, 1852, he formally resigned his charge. To this event he had been looking forward with some degree of solicitude for several months. Even while yet possessed of his accustomed vigor, and performing his accustomed labors, his mind had been directed towards this thing by the building of a new church edifice at Gloversville, and the expectation that a portion of the people would draw off for the purpose of organizing a separate church in that village. The project did not originate from any dissatisfaction with him as their pastor, or with the church as it was then constituted; but solely from the conviction that such a measure would subserve the interests of the church, while it would contribute to their personal convenience. Dr. Yale did not at first look upon the enterprise with favor; as he apprehended that both churches, after the separation, might find themselves so crippled as to be unable to support the gospel at home, and to contribute as they had done towards sustaining the institutions of benevolence abroad. Yet he did at length become perfectly composed in respect to the operation, and when the whole had been consummated, he felt particularly comforted in view of the flattering prospects of both.

Upon his resignation having been presented to the congregation at a public meeting, a committee was appointed to prepare and present an answer, which was done in due time, and which has been here transcribed for the purpose of showing the estimate in which he was held by his own people. It is as follows, viz:

Rev. Dr. Yale:—As a committee appointed for the purpose, we enter upon the duty assigned us, to respond to your letter of resignation of your office as pastor of this church and people.

Though an expected event, it did not occur without producing, in many a bosom, mingled emotions of sensibility and regret, that a relation so long subsisting, and so fondly cherished, should in the providence of God, at length be dissolved. Your reasons for demitting the pastoral office are acquiesced in, as just and satisfactory; and we are happy to convey to you the undiminished confidence and respect entertained toward you, by the people of your late charge, and of their fervent wishes for your continued prosperity and happiness.

Your official career, whether its length be considered, extending as it does through the long period of half a century; or whether we regard its successful progress and beneficial results, has been a marked and peculiar one; and standing as we do, at the close of the first epoch in the history of this church, it would be a pleasing duty, did the time and the occasion justify, to linger awhile, amid the reminiscences of the past, and opening our minds to grateful recollections of all the ways in which our fathers and their children have been led, to gather fresh instruction and encouragement for enabling us to sustain the conflicts and trials of the future. We would go back, accompanied by the sole survivor of that little band, whose warm hearts and willing hands first established here, the institutions of the gospel. We would go back through a period, comprehending nearly two cycles of human life, during which the surges of time have whelmed, in its oblivious waves, one entire generation and the half of another. We would call up, in fond review, those devoted, faithful men and women, who staid up the hands and encouraged the heart of their youthful minister, in his early labors and trials. We would follow them in their humble but beneficent course, while, one by one, they faded, and dropped away from the circle of duty and friendship till all are gone: yet leaving as a heritage to their successors, the savor of their virtues, and their own firm and unwavering attachment to their chosen pastor.

It would be an interesting topic to treat of the importance of faithfulness in the day of small things, to show that the pioneers of the first generation had much to do, in laying the foundations of the prosperity of this church. They sowed in weakness, if not in discouragement, and their names will fade from human remembrance; but their record is on high, and multitudes in this and other lands will rejoice in the beneficent results of their faithful lives and unpretending deeds.

It would be both pleasing and profitable to trace the onward history of this church down to the present time, to inquire into the causes of its continued prosperity, with no change in its pastoral relations, and without any modification of its principles and standards of faith—while in the history of multitudes of churches in our country, mutation and change have been the rule rather than the exception—when innovating heresies have created divisions and strife, have led to the dissolution of the pastoral office, and in many instances, have uprooted and prostrated the institutions of the gospel.

It would be useful also and instructive, to learn by what forming and adapting process, through a series of years, this church and community, have been advanced to a leading position in the great work of Christian philanthropy—a church which, while it has fulfilled its mission at home, in doctrine, in practice, and in influence, has, in a manner by its beneficent benefactions, reproduced itself abroad, in the building up of religious institutions on the far continents of the east, and in the islands of the sea.

And it would be most grateful, too, to speak of the mighty influence that one human spirit, guided by noble aim, directed to worthy objects, can produce upon the interests of community and the world—but these topics must he left to an abler expositor and a more fitting occasion.

Reverend and respected sir, this communication is the last incident in your official relation to this people. Most of us behold in you, our own and our *father's friend*, endeared to us by the double tie of inherited and acquired attachment. Many now gone to their reward, and many still living, regard you as standing in the sacred relation of their spiritual father; and it will doubtless be their joy and rejoicing forever, that by the influence of your life, your character, and your instructions, they were led to the Saviour. Precious will be the reward of those who turn many to righteousness. Such reward be yours.

And now, though we look forward to years of friendly and Christian intercourse, and expect your cooperation and counsel in all that appertains to the interests of our Zion; and though we forecast with filial devotedness, our duty to watch over and soothe your declining years, yet as our pastor and guide in the way, the endeared companionship of many years has now, in the allotments of providence, come to a conclusion. Here our paths diverge, and here, with the sorrowing emotions of true hearts, we bid you farewell.

Charles Mills,
J. W. Johnson,
Elisha L. Burton,
Horace Sprague.

Rev. E. Yale, D. D.

CHAPTER X.

MEANS EMPLOYED TO PROMOTE A REVIVAL.

Seasons of revival are harvest seasons to the church. It is a truth which has been recognized by the friends of evangelical religion for a long period of years; and the Christian church has been giving her response to the prayer of the prophet: "Oh, Lord, revive thy work." It was a prayer which Dr. Yale offered as sincerely and as frequently as any other. To say that he was not a friend of revivals, would be not only to belie his profession, but contradict the evidence of a long life of devotion and piety, and of the most untiring efforts for the building up of Christ's kingdom and the conversion of men. There was no truth which he more firmly believed than that of the entire alienation of the heart from God, and the absolute necessity of its renewal by the operation of the Holy Spirit, as a preparative for future bliss. "Ye must be born again." He mourned, also; he *deeply* mourned over the state of spiritual languor which sometimes pervades the Christian church, and the absence of that divine influence which results in the conversion of men.

But in promoting religious revivals, he had no confidence in the use of such means as were calculated merely to move the passions, without either awakening the conscience, convincing the understanding, or affecting the heart. His firm conviction was, that the agency which God employs in the conversion of men, is truth, Bible truth; and that a reliance upon machinery instead of the truths of God's word, addressed to the understanding and pressed upon the conscience, was a departure from God's method of saving men. His conviction on this point he has thus expressed: "I have never, except in 1822, and about that time, nor then to any great extent, adopted human devices and expedients. Methodists, Baptists, and some Presbyterians and Congregationalists, have gone into the use of these devices. They have had great excitements, and have called them revivals. Probably God used his word as preached in truth, and in answer to the prayers of his people converted some souls. But I never could approve of these measures; and I fear that the churches have been filled up, and made to overflow with unconverted converts. Hence the low state of religion, and the worldliness of professors. Now I have been reproached by friends and every body, because I have not gone into these operations.

An entire revolution is needed among us in regard to revivals. Religious revivals among Methodists and Baptists are what they always were. But among Presbyterians and Congregationalists, they are what they were not. Half a century ago they were a very different thing, and we must return to plain truth, plain prayer, plain talk and plain duty. Oh, Lord, help me and thy people."

The above was written near the close of the year 1849.

Under date of Dec. 21, 1831, in writing to a friend in Connecticut, he uses the following language:

"I wish to know how your mind is, in the midst of the changes around you. I perceive in many of my friends a most surprising change, in regard to what have been called the 'new measures,' and I am many times ready to look round for the land-marks. I seem to think that they are about to be swept away, and yet I fear to think anything against what appears to be the work of God. As to the philosophy of our religion, except so far as evidently based on the word of God, I do not care a fig for it. But I do think I see, even in the midst of revivals, many sorrowful traces of the wisdom of men—of philosophy, falsely so called—a propensity to render the great truths of revelation more acceptable to unsanctified minds. The atonement remains; conversion remains. But where is regeneration? Where is election? Where are the decrees of God? Are we to be beaten out of these doctrines? I hope not. I am informed that some of our ministers in this state, and those, too, who have been among the most successful, are very decided in these doctrines. But of others, I am sorry to say, that moral suasion is all the influence they believe in, all they preach, and it is to be believed it is all that most of their converts know. The few doctrines of the gospel are therefore useless, not preached—they are neglected, reproached, scorned. Experience, as well as the Bible, convinces me that the *whole truth* must be held up and enjoined fully, if we would promote the cause of God. I feel the need of preaching more doctrine, even that doctrine which depraved nature hates. Men hate God, his doctrine, and everything good; and if they are truly converted they are new creatures."

In another letter, at an earlier date, in speaking of the revivals which took place in central New York in the year 1826, he says: "Yet a few things I lament—females praying in promiscuous assemblies—naming individuals publicly in prayer and preaching—resolving to retire and remain till death, or till conversion. For these things I feel grieved, and fear that sad results will follow."

His belief was that on account of these irregularities, and resort to unjustifiable means in promoting them, the glory of revivals had been greatly marred—an idea which he expressed to a correspondent during the last year of his life:

"Since 1833, revivals in this region are very much deteriorated. Many are greatly excited at times, and think, or others proclaim that they are converted. But after a few years, or even months, they need to be converted again. They know nothing. They do nothing. They are stumbling blocks. Men of sense despise them, and they despise religion."

In connection with the "measures" spoken of above, there has sometimes been gendered such a spirit of censoriousness and denunciation, as has shocked the sensibilities of sober-minded, humble Christians, and from which men who were possessed of the spirit of genuine Christianity, have involuntarily revolted. This spirit was regarded by Dr. Yale as peculiarly offensive; and he has given, in some of his letters, such an exhibition of the true spirit of revivals, as will be read both with interest and profit.

Oct. 22, 1827. "During all this year we have seen tokens for good in our congregation. Great unanimity and harmony in the church, and readiness to cooperate in the work proposed. I do trust in God that he will ere long grant us a refreshing from his presence. Indeed, though I dare not speak it aloud, yet I do think a sacred influence has been spreading over us for a number of months. But oh! our depraved hearts! A perpetual warfare of depraved nature against all that is holy, resisting even the Spirit of God. Should we be disappointed of the rich blessing, we must impute it entirely to our wicked opposition. And should God visit us with a refreshing, it will be 'not for works of righteousness which we have done.' I am more and more convinced that the real spirit of revival, is a spirit of deep reverence, awe, humility, dependence on God, divested of self-righteousness and self-seeking; and of tender, delicate, kind, faithful love to our fellow-Christians, and perishing sinners. It is such a spirit as moved Abraham to intercede for the cities of the plain; Moses to throw himself into the breach between the wrath of God and Israel; and Aaron to run between the living and the dead. It excludes boasting, self-confidence, pride, harshness, rashness, self-will, and censoriousness. In short, it is the same mind that was in Christ Jesus; the same humble and benevolent mind, ever ready to do good, deny self and make sacrifices. But you know it well."

His views of protracted meetings, he has elsewhere expressed. After all his observation and experience, his belief was that other means might be employed with better results than they. Yet, there were times, when, under proper management, he supposed that they might be productive of good.

An idea once occurred to him that there might be some utility in a protracted *prayer-meeting*. He thus expressed it in a letter to a friend:

"The thought has occurred to me lately, that it would be very desirable to labor to have such a prayer-meeting in every church as preceded the day of Pentecost; when all members were present (all that could be, and as much as they could be), with one accord, pleading the promise and expecting the result. Ten days, more or less, might be the time, until they obtained the blessing. Why should we not have such a prayer-meeting? It should be for Christians, though not excluding others. It should be for the outpouring of the Spirit. With it should be connected such instructions as clearly show all that is needful to be known about the Spirit's work, and such exhortations as might be suited to excite to fervor, activity, and perseverance. Especially should the promises of God be presented, and the infallible certainty of them urged. Perhaps in the morning at 9 o'clock, a prayer meeting might be held in each neighborhood, and, at 2 P. M., one in the meeting-house. This might be continued three or four hours, at pleasure. Then might all return to family worship, and close the day in the closet, as every one should begin it. Let the labor of all, every day, tend to one point—to be all 'of one accord, of one mind,' thinking, feeling, acting alike, so far as truth and holiness are concerned. Continue till the Spirit is poured out, then act as occasion might require.

I suppose these would be *new* measures in some respects; not in fact, but in form. Are not the essential outlines to be found in the 1st of Acts? I would by no means have any more machinery about it than is necessary to keep it in motion. But it does seem to me, that we need very much that spirit and action, which are truly after the apostolic pattern. If we do not approve of what some are doing, still we need to do something."

As might have been expected, the means which he employed for the promotion of revivals among his own people, were in accordance with those firmly established principles which are contained in the above extracts from his correspondence. First of all, he cherished the feeling of entire dependence upon the grace of God and the influence of the Holy Spirit; and frequently, did he give utterance to the sentiment which was so reverently expressed by the devout Psalmist, "My soul, wait thou only upon God; for my expectation is from him."

This idea will be illustrated by a few extracts from his diary.

1828, April 13. Sabbath. "Since meeting I have tried some to pray. Have thought of our proposed day of fasting and prayer next Saturday, *to ask help.* It seemed that the first thing would be to turn all our prayers out of doors, and look at them, and see their abominations; then to ask help in the following things, viz:

1. Preparation of heart in Christians.
2. Detection and conversion of hypocrites.
3. Conversion of heads of families belonging to us.
4. Conversion of unconverted sabbath school teachers and scholars.
5. Gathering and conversion of heads of families not belonging to any.
6. Gathering and conversion of sabbath school scholars not belonging to any.

Great work indeed!

Needful:

1. For personal benefit.
2. For the benefit of connections and associates.
3. For the benefit of the next generation.
4. For promoting the kingdom of Christ in the world.
5. For the glory of God, Father, Son and Spirit.

We ask help of the Lord.

1. He alone can afford help.
2. His word encourages us to ask of him.
3. The whole originates with him. GRACE."

1824, March 1. "Four things are needful to be prepared for a revival.

1. Ardent desire of it.
2. Gospel labor for it.
3. A sense of absolute dependence.
4. Prayer to God the only help."

July 14. "Chose my subject for a sermon, at 5 o'clock. While looking it over, four precious thoughts occurred to me:

1. It is my business to preach the gospel.

2. It is the business of my hearers to embrace it.
3. It is the business of Christians to pray for a blessing upon it.
4. It is the gracious work of God to save souls, through the preaching of the gospel."

1829, Aug. 6. "During the night I felt some anxiety on account of two things mentioned yesterday, and also on account of the fact that every holy movement among us may stop in a moment. One soul can not live without the life-giving influence of the Spirit of life. But every soul can live to which he gives life. So I may rest on this foundation. God's hand is in God's work. O my soul, what more canst thou desire? '*Father, glorify thy name.*' This has been my support. I approximate a little towards it in my feelings now. Bring my heart, O Lord, to rest on thee."

"Heard of a young man who seems to be less concerned than he was. Several are in a very critical state. Surely the Lord is very kind in showing us that we can do nothing without him. O that we might hang our helpless souls on him, and put all our trust in him. It seems to me, and I hope it does to some others, that no advances can be made unless God is pleased to work by his Holy Spirit. O Lord, enable us to feel always thus, only more and more."

Aug. 10. "It seemed as though every thing were passing away from me and others; that the Spirit was already gone, or would soon go; and that all our expectations would be disappointed. Clearly did I see, and fully realize, that nothing could be done without God."

Sept. 1. "Awoke before four in the morning. Being anxious, I arose and went into the study, where I poured out my heart to God for all I needed, especially that he would direct and order all the movements at present in the North-West. It is very comforting indeed to have a God to go to. The words of the Savior after his resurrection, which had occurred to me sabbath morning as I was going to church, and feeling my weakness, afforded me great and unspeakable comfort, viz: 'ALL POWER IS GIVEN UNTO ME IN HEAVEN AND IN EARTH.' My soul rejoiced. I gave thanks for these words. I rested on them in connection with the second psalm, as the food and comfort of my soul. I spent about an hour in committing the good cause to the Savior, and in calling upon him for help, especially for heads of families, the husbands of our pious sisters."

Aug. 2. "Was disappointed in not being favored with the labors of Mr. Wisner to-day. As I was going to the church these words occurred, '*Cursed is the man that trusteth in man, and whose heart departeth from the Lord.*' I had sinned. I saw the need of withdrawing my trust in man, and turning to the Lord. Preached in the morning on I Cor. ii, 5, '*That your faith should not stand in the wisdom of men, but in the power of God.*'"

But, while his sole dependence rested on the mighty energies of the Spirit of God; and while he ever felt that, "it is not of him that willeth, nor of him that runneth, but of God that showeth mercy," he was not of those who fly to this as an apology for the neglect of appropriate means. His principle was (as above expressed), "It is my business to preach the gospel. It is the glorious work of God to save souls."

In the use of means, his desire was to employ just such as would be calculated to produce upon the mind the conviction of one's utter helplessness and dependence; and to direct the mind to the contemplation of the grace of God as exhibited in the death and sacrifice of Christ.

He had no wish merely to excite the sympathetic emotions of the soul; to make a strong impression upon the passions; or to create unreasonable claim.

His views in these respects appear from the following:

1829, July 22. "Visited in a number of families and conversed with several under serious impressions. Some seemed not to be very deeply impressed. There appears to be a speculating spirit which will cause all seriousness to evaporate, as I fear. The Bible class this evening was very peculiar. Sixty or seventy were present, I should think, and they were uncommonly solemn. Several seemed to be much affected. I took pains to avoid exciting sympathy, as I was really apprehensive that some might weep aloud. But it was awfully solemn."

July 26. "Heard of a meeting last evening at which the supposed converts were present with some professors, and at which every thing was not conducted discreetly. Now I fear another evil, even undue animal affection. I fear this may provoke the Lord to give us up and withdraw from us. In this also I go to the Lord.

'I'll cast my burdens on his arm,
And rest upon his word.'"

It was this which created in his mind, particularly, a decided disapprobation of the efforts connected with what are ordinarily denominated camp meetings; and it was such a feeling which prompted him to make in his diary the following entry:

July 28. "Awoke before three this morning. Was agitated in view of the present state of my people, especially, in prospect of the Methodist camp meeting, three weeks hence. The thought of so many warmly excited, going to a camp meeting, seemed dreadful. I arose soon after three, and retired to my study, and committed the whole, most fully and most cordially, to God."

Not only was Dr. Yale not very much in favor of what are technically called protracted meetings, but he did not approve of the plan of very much multiplying religious meetings in any shape, during a time of revival. His reasons for this he gives at the same date with the extracts given above, as follows:

"On returning home I learned with regret that there had been a meeting in one of the houses in the neighborhood. I fear too many meetings on several accounts:

1. They do not allow time for private reading, meditation and prayer.

2. They exhaust the spirits, and prepare the way for a speedy declension.

3. They produce religious gossiping and dissipation. O Lord, save us from these evils."

His reliance, under the operations of the Spirit of God, was upon the plain, unvarnished, faithful exhibition of gospel truth; presented in public assemblies, in meetings for prayer and religious conference, and in personal, familiar conversation with individuals. A summary of the means on which he relied may be found in the following paragraphs:

1829, Aug. 3. "Church meeting at 3 P. M. A committee of fourteen were appointed to counsel and aid me. Made observations designed to show that we should mind our own business—pray in secret and in little circles—read the Bible much, much, much—say but little, and as much as possible of that little in the words of the Holy Spirit."

In presenting the truth, he seemed to rely upon the truth itself, or rather, the truth set home upon the conscience by the Spirit of God; and not upon any particular coloring which that truth might receive.

The following example is in point:

1803, Sept. 4. Sabbath. "Conference in the meeting-house at half-past four. Subject: death, the general resurrection, the final judgment and eternity. These subjects were considered in the plainest manner, and, according to the simple truth, as far as it could be conceived. I labored to avoid every circumstance which should give false alarm, and endeavored to state facts in the clear light of divine revelation. As the minds of the people were very tender, nothing further was necessary than to state the truth. As the system of doctrines was concluded at this conference, it was thought advisable to recapitulate, that all the doctrines might be seen, as it were, at one view. This meeting was very solemn."

In the above extract, mention is made of a meeting for religious conference. Such meetings were common; and this was one of the means in which he had great confidence. At some of these meetings, personal religious conversation was had with each individual present, as to the state of his own mind. More frequently some subjects were discussed which had been proposed at a previous meeting; or some case of conscience or duty considered. I will here mention a few of those subjects, merely as a sample.

"The character of God—the character of man—the way of escape from sin and misery—and the experience of Christians, especially submission to the Divine will."

"The intercessory character of Christ."

"The sum of the moral law."

"Why do mankind neglect the concerns of their souls?"

"What is godly sorrow?"

"Is there any propriety in our concluding that we can do nothing, because we are dependent on God?"

"Have we any reason to complain of God as a hard master?"

"Two cases of conscience:

1. Whether there can be grace where there is a great prevalence of sin.

2. Whether persons ought to doubt because they do not come up to the exercises of some others."

"Whether the unregenerate have anything to do." (Answered in the affirmative.)

"Three questions: What is the nature of sin? Is it an infinite evil? Is it necessarily connected with misery?"

"What is moral agency? Is man a moral agent? Is man an accountable being?"

"Are all mankind born under the covenant of works?"

"What is the covenant of redemption?"

"Three questions:

1. What remedy is provided for fallen man?

2. Who is the mediator?

3. What is his character?"

The above subjects are among those which were discussed in their religious conferences, during two or three of the first years of his ministry, during a portion of which time they enjoyed many tokens of the presence of the Holy Spirit.

Their conference meetings were among the most solemn and interesting, and useful meetings which were held. This will appear from the following account of one of them.

"Conference at 3 o'clock. Various subjects. Remarks on Luke xviii. Our Lord's question to Peter, 'Lovest thou me?' 'Behold the Lamb of God which taketh away the sin of the world.' Question, What are we to understand by the school of Christ? Remarks on this passage, 'Quench not the Spirit.' This meeting exhibited many serious countenances, and was indeed very solemn. Many shed tears, and all manifested the greatest attention. There was the most profound silence through the whole time. The eyes were generally cast down, fixed upon the speaker, or covered with the handkerchief. The power of the Spirit seemed present to bless. The tongue of the speakers could not be dumb, and several Christian friends manifested great readiness to assist. At the conclusion of the meeting the people seemed to tarry around, as though they could scarcely leave the place; and, indeed, some did stay half an hour or more, as though desirous to get more instruction."

From the subjects of discussion in these conference meetings, it may be seen, that what was specially aimed at, was to bring gospel truth in contact with the understanding, the conscience, and the heart, with the fullest conviction that God makes use of his word as the great instrument of salvation.

Sometimes, young people were requested to write on the subject which had been proposed at a previous meeting. Sometimes, in these meetings, he called upon young men to pray in turn. Meetings for prayer, by which was recognized the fact of their dependence upon God, were constantly maintained. There were some general prayer-meetings for the church. There were also prayer-meetings held in different neighborhoods, and in different parts of the congregation. There were prayer-meetings especially for youth, and prayer-meetings for females.

Dr. Yale's belief ever was, that there was an impropriety in females taking an active part in leading the devotions of promiscuous assemblies. Yet he desired always that they should be active in the sphere in which they had been placed by the providence of God. Meetings for prayer and spiritual improvement held by themselves and for their own special benefit, always met with his cordial approbation. Such meetings were held in his congregation and by the members of his church at an early period of his ministry.

Though he cherished a most vivid impression of his own personal responsibility, and though he never entertained a desire to transfer that responsibility to others, yet he did desire the cooperation of the members of the church, in his labors to promote the interests of Christ's kingdom; and he proposed various plans by which their cooperation might be secured. Not only did he call upon different individuals to attend him in his pastoral visits, but committees of the church were frequently appointed to attend to that kind of labor by themselves.

Recognizing as he did his entire dependence upon the grace of God, and feeling the need of much and fervent prayer, there were times when he particularly desired the members of the church to unite with him in seasons of private fasting and prayer, with the view to seek the special operations of the Holy Spirit.

One such instance is thus noticed:

1830, Sept. 7. "In prayer had an awful sense of the condition of this apostate world, as lying in sin, and only a few in the way of life, and these few very imperfect. Men seemed to me to be moving on in the broad way, by their hosts, under their standards; all the Pagans, the Mahomedans, the Jews, the Catholics, the Infidels, the Heretics, the irreligious of every other description. What shall I do? Lead individuals to prayer and fasting privately; then in company by sections; then the whole church. Do it speedily. Begin to bring it about to-day. I must act—speedily. Oh, Lord, direct, guide, purify me.

In the afternoon I went out and called on all the members in one district, seventeen in number, in eight families, and speak to them about a day of private fasting and prayer, to be observed this week or next, chiefly, and in all cases where it can be, next week. Nearly all promised they would do it. Some thought it very important. Some seemed taken by surprise. Read or referred to the third of Jonah, and recommended it to all. Conversed with two young women who have been thoughtful for some time. More tender than I expected to find them."

Sept. 8. "Visited six families, and engaged all the members to keep the private fast."

Sept. 9. "Visited four families. Found the members in a frame to encourage my proposal for private fasting and prayer. One member said she had felt the need of it, and thought of proposing it to the sisters, but was deterred by the fear of taking too much upon her. One woman put a paper into my hand, requesting 'prayers for her perishing soul.' This affected and encouraged me."

I will close this chapter with extracts of a letter to a friend, in which he gives a narrative of the means employed for the promotion of revival among his people, at one important period of their history:

Oct. 3, 1814. "Will you bear with me, if I tell you some of God's wonderful works in answer to prayer in this place? During four years before Oct. 1, 1813, we had a prayer-meeting a week, in the center of our settlement, with little variation as to numbers and prospects. Just one year from last evening we had a conference attended by a crowd of people, and we have had a similar one statedly on sabbath evening ever since, with few exceptions. A week or two after that time, I was walking to visit a pious family, and inquiring with myself, as I had done for some weeks before, what more I could do for the salvation of perishing sinners among the dear people of my charge. I had ascended a hill, where I had the prospect of many houses, and I said: 'In that, and that, and that house I have every reason to suppose there are souls destitute of a saving interest in Christ.' The thought was affecting, and pressed home the inquiry more powerfulyl: What can I do for their salvation? With these impressions I entered the house to which I was going, and entered into conversation on religious subjects. In the course of the conversation I made inquiries respecting religious meetings, and whether they would be willing to attend if they should be appointed. This promise struck my mind with peculiar force, Mat. xviii: 'Where two or three are gathered together in my name, there am I in the midst of them.' This seemed to be an encourgement to the smallest number that could meet.

Not long after this came to my mind, John xvi: 'Whatsoever ye shall ask the father in my name, he will give to you.' These two promises appeared to be a broad and solid foundation for prayer-meetings. At the same time it appeared very desirable that Christians should be more extensively called into action. I proposed to my brethren to divide our prayer-meeting into six. The proposal met their approbation, and immediately we established them in different parts of the place, at the same time, on Thursday of each week. I was to attend each in rotation; and in my absence, a deacon, or the oldest brother present, was to preside. Several soon came forward, who had not before prayed in public, and almost all the brethren took an active part. People attended well. A few weeks after, I heard of one who appeared to be awakened. Some weeks after that, I heard of one or two more. I visited them and found evident marks of the work of the Holy Spirit.

Through the great goodness of God, our meetings still continue, and as many as forty persons within my knowledge, entertain hope of a saving change. Many more are seriously impressed, and a remarkable solemnity rests upon the minds of the congregation in general. We think that we have seen special answers to prayer. I would gladly mention many more particulars, but I have not room, and I do not suppose that they will interest you so much as they do myself. I think, however, that I must mention these things as *an encouragement to God's people to pray.* Never have I seen so laborious—never so happy a year. Sometimes I have spent almost the whole week in conversing with people under religious exercises. The work has been very gradual, yet 'the Lord has done great things for us, whereof we are glad.' But only a small number are yet saved. Many individuals, and some whole families, seem to be entirely unmoved, 'dead in trespasses and sins.'

I feel, and hope God's people feel, that we have just as much need, and just as much encouragement to pray now, as we had a year ago; that we are dependent on God from moment to moment, that without Christ we can do nothing, and that we can do all things in his strength. 'Pray for us,' that we may 'always pray and not faint.'"

CHAPTER XI.

HIS TREATMENT OF INQUIRING SINNERS.

Though it was not the privilege of Dr. Yale to live in the midst of one constant revival of religion, and to have sinners coming to him daily or weekly, to inquire after the way of salvation; yet, during his ministry, there were different times, when a considerable number of persons looked to him for counsel and instruction, respecting their duty as inquiring sinners. The church of his charge did pass through some long seasons of religious declension; and some there were, even among his own people, who seemed at times much disposed to cast the blame upon him, notwithstanding all his pastoral fidelity, and to indulge the opinion that the reason why they were not favored with such special tokens of the divine presence as had formerly been enjoyed, was because he did not think proper to adopt those measures for the promotion of revivals, which were approved and adopted by some others. Yet it ought to be remembered that, in regard to the measures, opinions of Dr. Yale were always the same. Several most precious revivals among his people, had been enjoyed in the use of the very measures which he always approved, and which he always felt ready to employ. Why should not the same system of agencies which produced such desirable results in 1803, in 1814, in 1821, in 1829, in 1831, and in 1838, produce the same reults equally as desirable in 1849? It is to be apprehended that the reason is to be looked for somewhere else than in him, or the means which he used. How much those bickerings, and that spirit of fault-finding which was indulged in by a few of his own people, had to do with it, it might be well to inquire, and yet it is a question which I find myself unable to answer.

Yet, revivals were enjoyed; and in the course of his ministry, he was called upon to guide to Christ a large number of awakened sinners. Our present inquiry relates to the manner in which this part of his work was performed. It has been made sufficiently to appear in the preceding pages, that, his firmest conviction was that the salvation of men is secured by no other agency than that of the Spirit of God and that it is in the highest degree presumptuous in men, to think of taking the work out of his hand. He went to work under this impression, ever feeling that it was not his province to 'get up a revival;' but only to cooperate with God in the use of his appointed means.

Some idea of his method of dealing with persons under conviction, and the end which he wished to attain, may be gained by the following:

1821, June 11. "Read something in Stoddard's Guide to Christ. Directions how to treat awakened sinners.

1. Endeavor to increase their convictions.

2. Encourage them to use means in order to conversion. (I doubt some whether the view given, be perfectly correct.)

3. Direct him what course to take at present: 1, Secret prayer, 2; Avoid sin; 3, Lie open to conviction.

The tendency of all this is to lead the sinner to think he is doing all he can to be converted; that if he is not converted, it is not his own fault, and also to think he is converted when he is not.

I looked through the book and found many cases stated which I thought arose from wrong directions; but towards the end he came to the point, though I could not agree with him in thinking that the first exercise of a gracious principle is always faith in Jesus Christ. On the subject of submission, I think he is excellent. The soul is brought to submit of necessity."

He was always gratified, when, in conversing with persons under awakening, he found them sensible of the depravity and hardness of their hearts, and one thing which he always aimed at, was to deepen this impression, while he desired, at the same time, to guide their thoughts to Christ, and to encourage them to believe that, depraved and sinful as they were, they had no occasion to despair or despond. This may be seen from what follows:

1821, Dec. 24. "On Friday I was called to see a young woman who is consumptive. I found her, very unexpectedly, to be sensible of her hard heart. It was truly encouraging to see her, though she did not see that she was unwilling to accept of Christ. She seemed to be afraid that Christ would not accept of her. I pressed her to make the trial, and endeavored to make her feel that her will alone stood between her and Christ."

1820, Oct. 20. "Conversed with a woman, and found her mind very tender and thoughtful. Some conversation as follows: Do you believe that Christ is God? 'I do not suppose I believe it as I ought.' Do you believe it so as to lead you to worship him? 'I fear not.' Do you not believe him to be such a Savior as you need? 'I am such a sinner that I fear he will not have mercy on me.' The tears often rolled down her face, and she could not conceal them. After I arose up to come away, she said: 'I sometimes think when my children act bad, and will not do as I bid them, I disobey God much more than they disobey me; that he has much more reason to be angry with me than I with them.'"

1822, Feb. 1. "Yesterday I was called by a very urgent request to visit a lady over the Mohawk river—a woman who resided awhile among us, and was seriously impressed two years ago. Found her sick, and anxiously concerned for her salvation. That appeared to be her only concern. She had been concerned, more or less, ever since I conversed with her two years ago. She appeared to be sensible of her sin in some measure. I directed her to go to Christ. She was afraid he would not accept of her. She seemed somewhat surprised to hear that he was able and willing to save the greatest sinners. She said she was willing to come to him. I felt some doubtful whether she was enough acquainted with her own heart; but urged her to bring all her sins to Christ, and confess them, and put all her trust in him."

1830, Jan. 5. "At half-past four, I was up and entered into my closet, praying and mourning over my heart, and the state of my people. In the forenoon I called to see a young woman in much distress of mind. Found her fearing that there could be no mercy for her—pointed her to Isaiah lv and Mathew viii, and urged her to come and see if there were mercy; and told her there would be time enough to mourn over her desperate condition, when she had made the trial and been rejected."

1829, Aug. 7. "At evening, S. A. called, in much distress. She was evidently inclining to look very much at her own heart, and thinking that she felt nothing, while she was very much distressed. I inquired of her concerning certain facts, which she acknowledged. Such as these: 'Do you not feel much afraid of God's wrath?' 'I do some.' 'Do you not feel that you deserve it?' 'I do.' 'Have you not broken all his commandments?' 'I have.' 'Do you not feel that your heart is at enmity against God?' 'I do not know that I have felt that.' 'Have you not sometimes felt envious, when you have heard that others have obtained hope?' 'Yes.' 'Have you not felt hard towards God for taking them and leaving you?' 'I have.' 'Have you not sometimes thought it vain for you to strive any more, and that you would give it up?' 'I have thought so, but I have thought this the last time.'"

Then I endeavored to show her the evil of such a

state of mind, and of such exercises, and to turn her mind entirely to the Lord Jesus Christ. I endeavored to set his excellencies before her, and to commend him to her acceptance."

The last extract is an illustration of the manner in which he sought to call out the feelings of inquirers, so that he might have a correct understanding of the state of their minds, and that they also might be assisted in obtaining a correct view of themselves.

Another extract will illustrate the same point.

1831, Sept. 20. "I conversed with a little girl, nine years old. 'Do you love Christ?' 'I hope so.' 'Did you always love Christ?' 'No sir.' 'How do you know you are a sinner by nature?' 'My parents told me so.' 'Did you ever read any such thing in the Bible?' 'Yes, sir.' 'Do you remember any passage which teaches you this?' 'By Adam all are sinners.' '*By one man sin entered into the world, and death by sin, and so death passed upon all men, for that all have sinned.*' 'Is this the passage you refer to?' 'Yes, sir.' 'Did you ever reject Christ?' 'Yes, sir." 'How?' 'He commands me to come to him, but I would not. I put off till another time.' 'You are a sinner—how can a sinner be saved?' 'By Christ.' 'Can you repeat a passage of scripture which teaches that?' 'He is able to save all that come to him.' 'What is it to come to him?' 'To believe on him.' 'Well, to come to him and to believe on him are the same thing—can you tell me what that means?' After a little pause, 'I suppose it is to desire him as the Savior.' 'How can you know that Christ will save such as come to him?' 'He says he will, in the Bible.' 'Can you tell what his words are?' '*Come unto me, all ye that labor and are heavy laden, and I will give you rest.*'

"I was surprised at her understanding and answers; '*Out of the mouth of babes and sucklings, thou hast perfected praise.*'"

He was always accustomed to urge upon inquiring sinners, a prompt and an immediate compliance with the requisitions of the gospel; not believing himself, and not wishing to have them believe, that their dependence upon God's grace was any valid excuse for their impenitence.

1822, Nov. 1. "Conversed with four young women, one of whom wept much, and the others were solemn. I proposed to call again in six days, and that they should repent and believe the gospel within that time. I felt that all would be vain without the Spirit of God, and prayed for it."

The following presents several cases which, in their nature were very different, and which required very different treatment.

1822, Sept. 16. "Conversed with two girls alone. They told their feelings freely. Very much alike. Very natural. Thought they loved God, and desired to be religious, and could become better. I told them to read Romans iii, 10–18, and viii, 1–8.

"Evening. Had conversation with two others with whom I had often conversed before. Both were lingering. One seemed to have lost almost all her convictions through enmity and envy. Told her I thought I should soon be compelled to give her up as forsaken of the Spirit of God. The other had appeared to be broken down lately, by the conversion of a companion. I must make special efforts with these as very difficult cases.

"Conversed also with a member of the church, who is desponding and tempted. She was engaged at the commencement of the revival, but soon turned her attention to herself, was determined to know her state before any other work—soon gave up her hope—now wishes for no treatment but as an impenitent sinner. I had learned before that she had thus prescribed to God, and warned her of it. Two or three times I had seen her without saying any thing. Sabbath day she desired me to call. This evening she opened her mind freely. I told her what I thought—I believed her exercises were truly Christian. She was very much disappointed."

Oct. 17. "Conversed with the church member mentioned above. Tried the effect of pressing to repent of sin, on her own ground. Saw that she was often overwhelmed with grief, and ready to sink."

Oct. 18. "Conversed again with the above named member, being very doubtful whether the conversation the preceding day was judicious. I found her very sorrowful. I conversed much, and endeavored to show her wherein she had erred in the beginning, by prescribing to God. She listened with unusual attention."

In the following brief passages, are mentioned several cases which show a great diversity of feeling.

1822, Sept. 17. "Conversed with E. G., a woman of color—professor. I found her in great distress because she did not believe God's work, here going on. She could not rejoice as formerly in hearing of the conversion of sinners. She was afraid they were deceived. She doubted whether she had any religion. Directed her to prayer and holy activity. She wept.

J. D., thoughtful, but confused. Resting on inability. Endeavored to show him that he must repent and believe the gospel. Did not succeed in moving him.

R. C., hoping. Many words. Little depth. Must converse privately with him.

Mrs. H., last week I found her thinking that she was doing well. I told her to read Romans iii, and other places. She had read that passage, and seemed convinced."

Though he says in one of the above extracts that he told the person spoken of, that he "believed her exercises were truly Christian," it was not his ordinary practice to address such language to those with whom he conversed. He deeply realized the deceitfulness of the human heart, and the danger of deception in regard to one's religious experience. He believed it better to have no hope than a false one; and he preferred to have persons discover from the exercises of their own minds, compared with the exhibition of Christian character contained in God's word, that they had experienced a change, than to tell them his own convictions in the case, even though he might gain an evidence that they had become the subjects of God's renewing grace. Of this there is evidence in abundance.

1830, June 8. "Conversed with a young lady, and found out her case. She has heard that some entertain hope for her, while she has no evidence to satisfy herself, and fears she shall thereby be fatally deceived. She wept. I directed her to admit the possibility of what had been suggested, merely for the purpose of examining her case. That seemed to be precisely the point, and she seemed to be glad of the interview."

1829, Sept. 12. Found one who is praying for the Spirit, to become as she ought to be in truth and holiness, endeavoring to do good to the souls of friends and relatives. Yet she indulges no hope of an interest in Christ. It is certainly much better to have religion without knowing it, or thinking of it, than to have a hope but no religion."

In view of the fact that it is by the operations of the Spirit of God, that the sinner is converted, it was always a matter of great solicitude with him, that the Spirit be not provoked to withdraw his influences, and thereby leave the man who was once awakened, to return to his former state of worldiness and stupidity. Any indication of the Spirit's withdrawal, filled him with fearful apprehensions.

1829, Aug. 5. "Heard of one young woman, whom I conversed with a few days ago, who is now said to be losing her impressions, and becoming stupid. This is another trial. But I have been talking on a most encouraging theme; '*Is anything too hard for the Lord?*' When should I be tried if not when I have a test which shaves the bone? Well, be my heart staid on the Lord."

1849, April 3. "Three young ladies called to converse about their souls. Their impressions do not seem to be deep. I warned them against three dangers going back, false hope, and despair."

The question often arises whether it is proper to direct inquiring sinners to pray. Inquirers themselves often apologize for their neglect of this duty from the professed belief that their impenitent prayers will only tend to deepen their condemnation. The reader may wish to know the views which were entertained on this point by Dr. Yale. They appear from the following two or three sentences.

1828, June 5. "Mrs. C. engaged to pray for herself every day this month, on condition that I would pray for her. This I am to do. Now I begin."

1822, Oct. 19. "Conversed with a young lady, who told me she did not pray every day, because she thought her prayers did no good. I warned her against talking with the wicked, that it is vain to serve God and unprofitable to pray to him."

While he never refused to pray for others, and while in fact, he prayed for them much when they knew nothing of it, he desired that they would depend neither upon his prayers nor their own; nor indeed upon any thing but the grace of God through Christ; and whenever such a tendency was discoverable, it was pointedly rebuked; as may be seen in the following incident: "A young man came to me with tears, and desired me to pray for him. I said; 'Cursed is the man that trusteth in man, and maketh flesh his arm.' Yet I promised to pray for him, while I warned him not to rely upon any thing but Christ."

Though Dr. Yale had great quickness of apprehension in respect to the grounds on which individuals rested their hopes, and though he had an uncommon acuteness in detecting the fallacy of a delusive experience, yet he was never accustomed to speak with much confidence of the supposed religious experience of professed converts. And whenever he saw a man resting upon an evidence which was manifestely delusive, it filled him with inexpressible pain. We have one or two cases in point.

1826, Aug. 4. "Called at the house of Mr. M., a very sick man. Was told by his daughter that he was attending to all his worldly concerns as carefully, and as regularly, and with as much composure, as if he were going a journey. I observed that the great business of eternity was most important to be done. She said she had conversed with him about his future state, and he appeared to be very easy and ready to die. He said he had found something when he was sick twelve years ago, that gave him comfort now. How was I struck at hearing this! I knew the fact twelve years ago. I knew also that soon after his recovery at that time, he had relapsed, and had lived these twelve years utterly regardless of religion. Many times had I endeavored to converse with him, but he was stupid and obstinate, and for some time had appeared to be settled down stupidly on something else besides religion. I observed to his daughter that we ought to be very cautious on what we build our hopes for eternity, and went on to express my opinion about such vain hopes. His wife and daughter seemed to agree with me. I did not see the man at all. What a dreadful condition is he in!

1829, Oct. 27. "Met ten or twelve who have hope, and questioned them very concisely about the state of their minds. One young man related his experience in the following manner. Some years ago he had been converted, as he supposed, and joined the church, though of another denomination. After awhile he lost his religion and withdrew from the church, that he might not be under restraint. Several years he lived in this way. Within a few weeks he has been awakened and alarmed, resolved to try to get religion, read, prayed, &c. Two weeks ago, or a little more, in prayer obtained relief. The next night dreamed that he was in his father's house in a chamber, very dirty with brick, and mortar, &c., which he was to cleanse. It was a difficult work, but he cleansed it. When he awoke his dream seemed to indicate that his heart had been cleansed by being renewed. Reflecting upon it, he was affected with the goodness of God in having mercy on such a sinner, and was led to rejoice and praise him for his goodness.

I was very much surprised at the evident marks of delusion in the experience which he related. I said nothing, and felt as though I wished to tell him privately, that he must have better experience, or have no evidence of grace. I was struck very much at the striking contrast between his experience and that of all the rest who had expressed their views. O how deplorable is such a religion! and the influence it has upon the mind! It seems to destroy the mind, so that truth can never get hold of it again, without almost a miracle." O Lord, deliver us from delusion."

At a church meeting held two days after this occurrence, for the examination of candidates, he says that he advised this young man not to offer himself; who "consented, though not without much reluctance."

Moreover, he did not often speak with very great confidence of a change, even when he thought that he had good reason to hope. Nor did he like to hear it from others.

1831, July 8. A protracted meeting at West Galway. "Some special attention has been manifested for some weeks; and during the meeting it has been more publicly and strikingly manifest. I was pleased with most of the exercises, except speaking with confidence of the new converts, and of *many* that were anxious. The former I think always unjustifiable, because we know nothing only that they profess to have experienced a change. And the latter savors more of ostentation than of real benefit."

But though he would not speak confidently of their experience, he was always ready to give them wholesome advice, and to assist them in coming to an intelligent decision concerning their religious state.

1829, Aug. 31. "A young man called to see me. His anxiety was very great. He had obtained hope sometime ago, I believe at the camp meeting, but was full of confusion, not knowing what to do. I could not attempt to solve his doubt, but directed him to Exodus xxxiv, the name of God proclaimed; to Romans iii, depravity; the latter part of Romans iii, salvation; and to Romans viii, the privileges of believers."

Aug. 15. "A young man called on me in great distress. He seemed to be only just alive. May the Lord indeed subdue his heart to himself.

"At 7 o'clock, I met the young converts. Spent some time in conversing on Ephesians ii, 1–10, in giving them counsel, and in inquiring what they consider as evidence of grace in themselves. Every one gave some mark. They generally appeared well. But it was to me a very solemn and anxious meeting. I took occasion to remark to them about the pilgrim's progress—how some who set out on pilgrimage, turn out of the way, or turn back, some at one place, and some at another. What would become of them it would be impossible to tell. Time would show. I cautioned them particularly to be careful of their conduct, as many eyes are upon them. But of two things in particular:

1. To cherish desires for the salvation of others, against all temptations.

2. To be very careful in conversing with them, to conduct with tenderness, humility and delicacy."

When a person is supposed to have met with a change of heart, or when he supposes himself that he has met with such a change, his mind is usually occupied with the question of making a public profession of his faith by connecting himself with the visible church of Christ. This duty was always recognized by Dr. Yale; and he sometimes had occasion to bewail the delinquency, in this respect, of some who supposed themselves, and were supposed by others, to have passed from death unto life. His feelings on this subject, we find thus expressed in his diary, under date of Dec. 14, 1829:

"The meeting, at Mr. Ward's, was very solemn. I expressed a wish that all who have hope, would give up their hope or profess religion at the next sacrament; that all sleeping Christians and lingering sinners would move out of the way, in the same time, and no more be stumbling blocks. I urged earnestly present duty by the high authority of God."

Yet, it was never his practice to recommend a hasty profession of religion, without having some time and opportunity to test the reality of the supposed conversion. But, if there were to be discovered marks of a genuine change, if there were evidences of Christian meekness, and an humble reliance upon the merits of Christ for salvation, connected with a manifest desire to acknowledge Christ before the world, he encouraged the applicant to go forward in the discharge of duty.

1829, Sept. 5. "About 10 o'clock, a young lady called and conversed, and expressed a desire to unite with the church. Among other questions, I asked her, 'Do you deserve to be punished forever?' She said, 'Yes, sir,' 'But what have you done to deserve a punishment so dreadful?' 'I have rebelled against my Maker?' That is reason enough, you need not give any more. She conversed with great simplicity; and I told her to do her duty, as I could not advise her to do anything else. If she felt it a duty, and wished to unite with the church, she might do as she wished."

While he desired the enlargement of the church, and fully believed it to be both the duty and privilege of genuine converts, to connect themselves with the people of God, by a public profession of their faith; yet was he not so anxious for the increase of their numbers as to encourage such to come forward as did not seem to be prepared.

1829, Oct. 29. "I entreated the Lord to send us such, and such only, to offer themselves to the church, as he approves, and will own and bless. Our strength is not in numbers, but in the grace of God. Much will depend upon the disposals of his providence at such a time as this."

I will close this chapter, by a connected and somewhat lengthy account of the manner in which he treated one particular case—a case of more than common interest.

1829, July 16. "The young man who boards with us returned home about 8 o'clock, and told us that L. C. had passed a sleepless night. Soon after, Mr. C., his father, sent his youngest son to request me to visit him. I tried to pray. I went, pensive and solemn, yet inwardly rejoicing in hope of God's mercy. Found him on the bed, in an agony of distress, holding his heart and turning every way. I asked him, 'What troubles you?' He replied, 'O, trouble enough.' His father pointed me to Phil. iv, 19, as a passage L. had just read. I inquired whether such a rich passage, though not written in reference to such wants as his, would not afford him all he needed? 'Yes, if I could believe.' I took Hartford Hymns, and read the 43d with some comments, right to his case; but unbelief was the evil. I named John iii, and some other passages; and turned down several leaves of the Bible. Prayed. Got him up out of bed. Conversed a little with his father, and a few others, and came away. Marvelous work, O God! Clearly and fully he shows his own hand. Has he heard my prayer, so far as to begin to revive his work in his own time and way, and for his own glory? Will the Lord indeed visit us? Will he use me as his instrument? Lord, here am I—all I am; all I can do; all I have. To thee, all holy is thy name. O Lord, glorify thy name. In prayer at Mr. C's, this was all my plea. O that God would secure all the glory. Yet, I know not what he will do. O Lord, revive thy work. O Lord, glorify thy name!"

July 22d. "I found L. C. in a very peculiar state of mind. I went to him at his work, and said, 'I wish to speak with you a few minutes.' 'Well,' said he, 'I am glad to see somebody to talk with.' We went into the orchard, and he sat down on the ground, while I leaned over the trunk of a bending apple tree. There he conversed very freely, stated his views of his own mind, as altogether sinful, and of Christ as altogether able and willing to save, and of himself as willing to come to Christ, only he feared he had not that sense of things which he ought to have. He appeared very calm and reconciled, with a countenance lighted up with a little smile, of which he was unconscious. I could not help thinking he was '*in his right mind*,' in the most important sense. Yet I said not a word to him, intimating my thoughts, nor did any such thought seem to have entered his mind."

Sept. 11. "Heard that L. C. is indulging a hope, and is cheerful and comfortable. This is a blessing, indeed. I have been well satisfied of his reconciliation to God, ever since my conversation with him under the apple tree."

Sept. 18. "At evening, L. C. called. He readily entered into the views and feelings of the sacred writers; but could not allow that he felt as they did, because he was not a good man.

'Suppose,' said I to him, 'I should be a deceived soul, thinking myself a Christian without being one. Suppose I should undertake to examine myself, and say, I feel as David, and Peter, and other good men, because all good men feel alike, and I am a good man; would that be fair reasoning?' 'No.'

'Suppose, I should say, I am not a good man, and, therefore, I do not feel as David, and Peter, and others; would that be fair reasoning?' 'No.'

'We must then compare our exercises with the exercises of good men, and see whether they are the same.' To this he assented. Then the conversation became peculiarly interesting. He needed cordials, as he had been sinking in despondency."

Oct. 23. "A young man, L. C., called in the evening, who appears to be established, though trembling."

Oct. 26. "Heard that L. C. had been greatly cheered and animated on the sabbath, as though he had entered into a new world. Said it was the first sermon he had ever heard. On returning home, found several young men, and among them L. C. He appeared with remarkable humility, and asked advice as to his duty. It seemed as though God intended to glorify himself by such instruments as he pleases. Let his name be glorified."

The reader may be interested to know, that this same L. C. afterwards entered upon a life of decided piety; that after having pursued a course of literary and theological studies, he entered the ministry with great promise and flattering prospects of usefulness; that he preached with acceptance and profit for a season; but in the providence of God, was soon called upon to lay aside his armor, and while yet possessed of the ardor of youth, suspended his chosen employment of preaching the gospel of Christ to his fellow-men, and entered upon the rewards of the just.

CHAPTER XII.

HIS SHINING EXAMPLE.

"Let your conversation be as it becometh the gospel of Christ." Such was the injunction of the spirit of inspiration—and it was an injunction which met with a remarkable fulfillment in the every-day deportment of Dr. Yale. It may be truly said that his godly walk was a constant comment upon his public preaching. The world judges of religion by the demeanor of those who profess it. Nor would religion suffer as it now does, if all its professors were as uniformly consistent in their deportment as was Dr. Yale. "*He was a burning and a shining light.*"

In looking at him as a pattern for imitation, there is a great variety of aspects in which his character may be regarded, and in respect to which he might safely be looked upon as a model. We are expected to imitate only what is *visible* in man; because that is all which comes before us. But when we are permitted to look at the secret spings which set the whole outward machinery in motion, when we look at the inward workings of that strong, ever-present, all-controlling piety which was in constant operation in the mind of Dr. Yale, we feel as if there was something for us to seek after, which is more worthy of the aspirations of the immortal mind, than any outward manifestations either of the feelings or the principles of piety. There was a hidden fire which, in his bosom, was always kept burning, and which was daily rekindled at the altar of prayer, by which his entire outward deportment was modified and controlled. The first thing to be sought is the kindling up of that hidden fire; and then may be expected the outward manifestation.

Dr. Yale's example was worthy of imitation, as it respects the whole tenor of his conversation. His entire life was a life of holy walk with God, and all his communications were such as savored of the piety of his heart. "His speech was always with grace, seasoned with salt." It has been said of him that he never said a foolish thing. He was often cheerful; but never light and trifling. Nor did he ever indulge in foolish jesting, or in such sallies of wit as did not accord with the seriousness of his profession. In his conversation he always sought to introduce such topics as would be a source of improvement either to the minds or the hearts of those who were present; and in his intercourse with the young, his aim seemed to have been to say something which they would be likely to remember to their profit.

There are probably few men who have set a closer watch over their own heart than he. It was his constant practice to keep up the most intimate communion with himself; and to take particular notice of the operations of his own mind. And at whatever time, and in whatever circumstances he was conscious of any departure from the perfect standard of the Bible, even though it were only in his thoughts or feelings, he was sure to check himself and repent. As a man of great self-vigilance and earnest prayer, his example was particularly worthy of regard. And though these traits of his character have been somewhat illustrated in former chapters, yet it may not be improper, as a further illustration, to introduce in this connection, a few more brief extracts from his memorandum.

1826. Aug. 6. "Soon after four when I awoke this morning, this text was in my mind: '*Give no place to the devil.*' It was in my mind when it began to rove towards worldly objects. He is desirous of a place. If he can get one, he will improve it greatly to our detriment or to our ruin. So he did with our first parents; and so he has done with millions.

'Give no place to the devil.'

1. Allow no sin. 2. Omit no duty. 3. Indulge no remissness. 4. Admit no discouragement.

Alas; it is not so with me. I am very guilty, and this sense of guilt increases my discouragement. Yet, my duty and my privilege are to repair to Jesus Christ who saves sinners. May his grace be sufficient for me. But does the devil fear us at all? What is there in or about us, that he fears? Our wisdom? Our goodnes? Our power? None. He regards them all as rotten wood. Our Lord and Savior is the only one that he fears."

1829, Aug. 11. "Though I saw so much occasion to be anxious, yet I was not anxious, last evening or this morning. It seemed as though God had deserted me, and left me to myself. On searching a little, I found the terrible proud feelings and thoughts of last week had probably been the cause. How desperately deceitful and wicked is my heart! I begged and entreated God to purify and cleanse me. In reading the book of Numbers in family worship, I observed, what I have often observed before, that the offerer of any sacrifice, or one that sprinkled the water of purification, was unclean until the even. How strikingly this signifies, that after all that we do, we remain unholy until the even of life, as long as we live. Thanks be to God that holiness comes in the morning of life eternal. O for perfect holiness! Lord God, cleanse me and make me perfectly holy."

While Dr. Yale has set us such a shining example, as to the fervor of his devotions, and his desires for a state of perfect assimilation to Christ; there was also a great degree of self-jealousy in respect to the motives of his conduct, which deserves to be imitated by all the people of God.

1826, June 26. "Found myself unable to get my mind composed to my subject all day. In the evening I felt what I said. But through the day my heart was not spiritual or heavenly, but backward in every thing good. This morning I feel guilty, fear desertion, must fly to Christ, even if I do fear it is all selfish, for fear of judgment if I do not do right. Yet, if it is all selfish, I need Christ the more. No righteousness but his. What should I do without this? How hopeless my condition!"

Jan. 30. Brother Davis, in his prayer with me, prayed that we might have such a revival here, as we never saw. I said, Amen. Since I fear spiritual ambition and pride, O Lord deliver me from these dreadful evils."

There was, indeed, no part of his shining example which is more worthy of imitation, than the strict scrutiny which he maintained over his own religious character, and the singleness of his motives in the discharge of the duties of religion.

1841, June 1. "Felt this morning the need of conversion. As Christ said to Peter (Luke xxii, 32), 'When thou art converted strengthen thy brethren.' The inquiry arose strongly in my mind: Do I not need conversion, and all my people with me?

1. *In Conversation.* From worldly, to religious. From superficial to profound. From external to internal; and from formal to spiritual. From little to much; and from circumstantial to direct.

2. *In self-examination.* Is it not true that this exercise has gone almost into disuse with me? Alas! I see at once, when I begin to look at my practice, that self-examination is infrequent, not often as it should be; undecided, i. e., not brought always or often to a point, in which I say that I am a Christian, or that I am not, or that I do not know. Every day should I try myself, and beg God to try me, and then record the decision. Now I am conscious that the great matter is uncertain. It ought not to be so. What! uncertain whether I shall forever shine in heaven, or burn in hell! Great God, awaken my soul, and convert me from this negligent course of conduct.

3. *In reading the word of God.* I read it, to be sure; and generally three times a day. But do I always feed upon it? Sometimes it is sweet to my taste: yea, sweeter than honey to my mouth. I am often directed, encouraged, strengthened, as well as warned, reproved, and rebuked by the word; but I would never look into it without some deep and lasting impression, according to my state and wants at the time. It is not always so. Alas! I sometimes read the word, but receive no impression. The word is like the flight of a bird, or the path of a ship through the waters, leaving no trace behind.

4. *In motives.* Let it be my aim to please God—to be and do as he will. Then the approval of conscience in the sight of God is to be sought. In my retirement, in my thoughts and feelings, I am to be such as an enlightened and correct and tender conscience will approve. The good opinion of my fellow creatures is desirable, if it favor me, for the same reasons that God and conscience do; otherwise, their hatred is better than their love. How small a matter it is to be judged of man's judgment! How little does man know of the thoughts, feelings, motives! How often should I be ashamed and confounded, if men knew my heart! Oh, let me aim to be much more pure within than I am without, that I may be blessed with the pure in heart and see God. Mat. xxiii, 26: 'Thou blind Pharisee! cleanse first that which is within the cup and platter, that the outside of them may be clean also.'

It is written, 'whether ye eat or drink, or whatsoever ye do, do all to the glory of God.' God is the infinite one; infinite in all possible perfections, and he is therefore, in himself, worthy of all the devotion of my heart, and soul, and mind, and strength. To him must I have regard in all things, first of all, and supremely, even as though there were no other being in the universe. 'Of him and through him, and to him are all things; to whom be glory forever.'

5. *In the design of living.* Surely the design of living should not be merely to live—to exist. Nor to enjoy life. Nor to become rich. Nor to be renowned. Nor to obtain, possess, and enjoy power. Oh, how mean are such objects! how far below the design which becomes me! I am destined to exist forever. I can know, love, enjoy, serve and praise God. Should I not then live for this end? Not prepare to do it hereafter; but to do it now. I am also to glorify God my Redeemer. As I expect everything from him, I may devote every thing to him. I am bought with a price, am not my own, and therefore to him I will devote all. To do good to men, to their bodies, to their souls, for time, for eternity. In short, live with the same design as good men *always* live.'

'I have glorified thee on the earth, have finished the work which thou gavest me to do.' 'My sheep hear my voice.' 'No man liveth to himself.' 'Set your affections on things above, not on things on the earth.' 'For ye are dead, and your life is hid with Christ in God.'"

With such motives in view, and with such a course of conduct marked out for himself, it need not be wondered at that he submitted himself to the strictest regimen. Whatever might be the government to which others were brought to submit, with him, *self*-government was regarded as most important. He ever acted on the principle of denying himself the use of every thing which he believed to interfere with his duty to God, to dampen the ardor of his devotions, or to detract from his usefulness. As he labored hard, he was usually blessed with a good appetite for his food, and at times, when he felt dull and found a flagging in his religious feelings, he was disposed to attribute it to his having partaken of too hearty a meal, and then would he resolve to be more abstemious in future.

For some years he had accustomed himself to the use of tobacco, as very many do still. But, becoming apprehensive that even this indulgence might interfere with his devotions, he resolutely abandoned it.

Of this he speaks as follows:

1822, April 7. "I have been thinking how my prayers are not heard. It grieves me. Yet I say the Lord is right. How can I expect such prayers to be heard? While I had my pipe in my mouth it came to me, Will you give up smoking for a spirit of prayer? Yes, I answered at once, if that will be of any avail. On further consideration it seemed to me inconsistent and shameful for me to be smoking. I have laid away my pipe, and I think I shall not soon use it again. This is not to buy the Spirit. It may be a little self-denial. Oh, may the Spirit teach me to pray, and to live to the glory of God. Amen."

His purpose was formed, and from that time, the use of the pipe, and indeed the use of tobacco in all its forms, was entirely abandoned. Nor was it in the use of this thing only that he practiced self-denial. His aim was to carry out the principle of self-crucifixion in all things inconsistent with a life of entire devotion to the service of God.

1827, April 14. "It is evident that there must be many crucifixions of the flesh with the affections and lusts.

1. *Indulgence.* Various luxurious affections must be crucified. So my heart has decreed. To-day, too, that they may not crucify my Lord to-morrow.

2 *Negligence in regard to souls.* It is true that I am very guilty.

3. *Remissness in regard to charitable institutions.*

4. *Remissness in regard to spiritual graces.*

These are a kind of negative sins, except the first. But they arise from positive sins—undue affection for earthly things—conveniencies—the comforts of life—the praise of men. These must be crucified; and from this time forward, I must, by divine grace, be bold, intrepid, carrying forward the work openly, and with confidence in God."

In a portion of the above extracts, we have had our attention directed to that hidden fire of which mention was made at the opening of this chapter. We see the power by which he was impelled in the discharge of duty. It was this inward light which broke out, and blazed, and shone in a remarkably uniform and consistent Christian deportment.

Dr. Yale was remarkable for his improvement of time. He looked upon time as a talent given by God, and which is to be improved for his glory. His purpose was to employ even its fragments to some good purpose; and his aim to make long days and short nights. Indeed, some of his most intimate friends were of the opinion that he did not allow himself that amount of repose which the demands of nature really required.

His habits of *punctuality* were such as to command our admiration. It was his settled purpose to meet all his engagements, if it was within the range of possibilities; and to fulfill all his appointments at the hour. In one instance, at least, when the road was so blocked up with snow between his dwelling and the church as to render it impassable, he went to the house of God on snow-shoes, and preached to the few who were able to assemble. His pains-taking to meet his engagements were so great, that he seldom failed; yet there were some occasions when he speaks of such a failure with regret; e. g:

1808, Nov. 22. "The weather being extremely bad, I did not go to conference, although I started. But I was afterwards sorry that I had not gone, because three or four persons attended."

And while he was so punctual and faithful in the fulfillment of his own appointments, and in his attendance upon meetings for public religious worship, he was sometimes deeply grieved at the remissness and delinquency of others. Of this, frequent mention is made in his journal, such as the following:

"Was displeased at several things; but especially at the late hour of my people's coming to prayer-meeting; must be guarded lest I be vexed."

Again: "At 8 o'clock started and went to Broadalbin, to attend a meeting of a committee of the Bible Society. Only two members out of eight were present; but other gentlemen by invitation, met and acted. Some were so late that it retarded the whole business. Oh, when will men be punctual in the work of the Lord! His business should be done with all our heart, and with all our soul."

CHAPTER XIII.

HIS ENTIRE DEVOTEDNESS TO THE SERVICE OF GOD.

There is an end for which every man is supposed to live. The end for which Dr. Yale lived, and which he was accustomed ever to keep before his mind, was not that which seems to be uppermost in the minds of many others. It was not to make money. It was not to gain the friendship of the world. It was not to enjoy the pleasures of sense. It is not asserted that he was free from the desire to possess and enjoy a competence of this world's goods—nor that he was altogether indifferent to the applause of his fellows,—nor that he did not find in himself such like passions as mar the peace and detract from the enjoyment of other experienced Christians. These, and things like these, were the cause of his deepest sorrow; and these did he regard as his most inveterate foes.

There were times, too, when he was particularly perplexed with his pecuniary affairs; and when it was with the utmost difficulty that he was enabled to meet his pecuniary engagements, and to make the necessary provision for his family. For many years he had the occupancy of a small farm, the most of which belonged to the people of his charge, and the use of which constituted a part of his stipend; and though the labor on this farm was performed mostly by others, yet it necessarily occupied a portion of his time and thoughts. Still, his mind was ever upon his appropriate work as a minister of Christ; and it was his earnest desire to be free from all worldly care, so as that he might devote his undivided energies to the upbuilding of Christ's kingdom and the salvation of men. There are numerous entries in his diary in which his feelings on this subject are expressed, a few of which are here transcribed:

1822, Jan. 25. "Have just finished the life of Henry Martyn. 'He was truly a burning and a shining light.'

How unceasing his blaze till on the 16th of Oct., 1812, his brightness was no more seen below, but began to shine with the spirits before the throne. What shall I now imitate in him?

1. His entire devotion to Christ.
2. His attention to the word of God.
3. His spirit of prayer.
4. His unquenchable zeal, tempered with the purest love and the most unmoved patience.
5. His activity and perseverance.
6. His faithfulness to God and to men.
7. His meetness to live or to die.

All these I can imitate, while his genius, his learning, and many other accomplishments are entirely beyond my reach. Were all ministers such devoted men, how rapidly would the word of God advance!"

1823, Sept. 20. "I have been overwhelmed this morning with a sense of my distance from God, with negligence of my soul, my family, my church, my people, and others. I have every thing to do, and yet I do nothing. I have been looking for a better time to be more spiritual and devoted, but am convinced that I ought not to defer it another day. Now is the time, and now I begin. I have no new covenant to make. It is made already, and has been repeatedly renewed. I am bound and I trust God will give me all the grace I need. I am to aim at perfect truth, and perfect holiness, and perfect obedience, and as much usefulness as possible, and to do all to the glory of God. Let the promise of the Spirit in the 14th of John be my precious encouragement."

Oct. 16. "By request, preached for Dr. Hosack a fast sermon in prospect of the sacrament. Fear the want of the true spirit of fasting and prayer on such occasions. In returning home had very pleasant meditations, on these words: 'Father, glorify thy name.'

It seemed delightful to think that God does glorify his name. I longed to be wholly employed in his service; that I might glorify him in body, spirit, time, talents, all things; and that all mine and the whole world might glorify his name. Yet I was conscious of great defects, and afraid of self-deception in what I thought my real desires and wishes."

1824, Jan. 25. "In the afternoon visited a sick young man. Very low, and sinking fast; has spoken but once to-day. On returning home in the evening at 9 o'clock, found that I had been sent for again to see the dying youth. Went and found him dead. All my work with him is ended. But I have not done all my duty. I fear he is lost. It is time for me to awake, and take care of souls. Much concerned when abed, thinking how I should dispose of my business, so as to devote myself wholly to souls, and live as I ought."

Jan. 27. "While reading, I felt much the importance of disposing of all my business as fast as possible, and giving myself wholly to my work. I hope it will not be a momentary pang, but an abiding impression. I thought I should communicate to my leading men the important design of relinquishing entirely my tuition of scholars as soon as my present engagement can be fulfilled, or dispensed with, with a view to excite them to build an academy. That I should dispose of all my farming business in some way or other. That I should find some body to take the business of various societies, as much as possible, and as soon as possible. Then nothing to do but to promote the welfare of souls, and of Christ's kingdom, directly and with all my might. Oh that the Lord would direct and aid me, and that I might give myself up wholly to seek the salvation of all my people. This is a great work, which has never been effected in any place. The time must come. Will not God use me as an instrument? Oh! I dread the evils of my heart. Lord God purify my soul, and help me to devote all to thee."

1827, May 1. "The season has been so extremely unpleasant, and my avocations so numerous, that I find myself at the commencement of this month in a very different position from what I expected. I had hoped the business of the Bible Society and of domestic missions would have been nearly completed. But it is scarcely begun. My temporal buisness is also in a bad state, owing to the same cause. To-morrow I am to start for a ministers' meeting and preach; and the next day to attend Presbytery in Schenectady; and the next week to start on a journey to Lenox, to be absent two weeks. I feel altogether unfit for duties so numerous, so various and so arduous. At the same time my people and others around me are going to destruction. It is, however, some support that I may come to God, and look to him. Yet I am conscious of so much neglect of him, and his word, and his grace, that I have not all the confidence in him, which would enable me to take fast hold of his strength and grace. I find it to be a fact that when I read the Bible with care, and meditate and pray, and truly seek God and maintain intercourse with him, I can proceed in my course with some vigor and resolution. But when grace declines in my soul I can do nothing for God.

How different is my situation from what it was twelve years ago! Then the business of my parish was almost my only business, and I sighed for more. Now I am overwhelmed with business abroad, and am compelled to neglect my business at home. Yet time urges on his chariot wheels at a most tremendous rate. Soon shall I be at the end of my race. Let me give up entirely and forever all thoughts of worldly attainment, and make it my whole business to live to the glory of God, and the benefit of my generation. Eternity is before me. Oh, may the whole weight of eternal concerns rest upon my soul. The Lord work all my work in me."

May 7. "This morning I could not come to God. Did not feel right. A cloud between God and my soul. Oh, may I be washed in the fountain. Poor souls around me are greatly neglected. Oh that God would grant me grace to serve him with all my powers."

July 1. Sabbath. "Did not awake this morning in season to attend the prayer-meeting. Felt very sorry. Was up too late last evening reading a newspaper. Thus have I lost a privilege which I have constantly enjoyed while at home for nearly three months. By divine grace, I hope to recover this disadvantage. In secret prayer I most solemnly besought God to revive his work in his own time and way, and so as to glorify his name, and to prepare me to be used in any way which might subserve the purpose; either by laying me in the grave, or laying me on a bed of sickness, or in any other way most agreeable to his will, yet I besought him to use me in the work, if he could do it, and yet answer his most holy purpose. My mind was very solemn in view of these things, and I felt the need of grace to fit me for the answer to my prayer."

Dr. Yale sometimes excited himself to fidelity in the service of God, by a reference to the fidelity of the men of the world. Take an example:

1821, Nov. 1. "Read in the life of Nelson, after the battle of the Nile, 'Whilst a ray of reason remains, my heart and my hand shall ever be exerted for the benefit of my king and country.' How much better is King Jesus, and the country of heaven! and yet how far do I fall short in my zeal and devotion, of the zeal and devotion of that man, who served only an earthly king and country! I am ashamed of myself, and yet what do I do for the honor of my King and country? Did his king honor him with a peerage? and his country with a pension of £2000 for himself and his two next heirs? What has my king to bestow upon his faithful servants? A crown of glory. What a contrast between Nelson's services and mine! What a contrast between the reward of Christ's servants, and of king George's!"

There were certain periods, the return of which Dr. Yale was accustomed frequently to observe with great interest. I allude particularly to the anniversary of his birth, and the commencement of the year. At each of these periods, it was not uncommon for him to enter upon his memorandum some very interesting reflections. Some of these entries are very much in point in this place, as expressive of his entire devotion to the cause of Christ. I propose to give a single example from each.

June 15, 1841. "I am this day three score and one

years old. Set it apart as a day of fasting and prayer, with a view to look over my affairs, ask help of God, and look out for time to come. I find on looking back on my past life, very little comfort, except that I see much of the Lord's goodness. My own life appears to me very odious. The grace of God is so much the greater. How little do I for God or souls! My neglect is my great sin. My present feelings lead me to despair of ever doing any good. May I not utterly despair? How can I do any good? How can such a mass of stupidness, folly, and sin, ever do any good? But I have a little hope that God will do some good by me. Let me ask him. He has said, 'Ask, and it shall be given you.' What a promise! I will ask that he will do good by me. I have been before God and entreated that he would make me as a little child; sensible of weakness, attentive to instruction, docile, unaspiring, ready to yield to my Father's directions, and receive his counsels, and do as he pleases. O Lord, do make me as a little child. Use me to do a little good. If it be only to hew wood, or draw water, or dig the earth, or carry a tract, or speak to a child, or any thing thou pleasest, yet condescend to use me to do some good. Use me to do good to my wife, to the inmates of my family, to the little lad, to West and his, to schools, to sabbath schools, to families, to the church, to the congregation, to my friends, to the nation, to the heathen. God has placed me so that I can be used thus, if he please to use me. Wilt thou allow me to preach thy word again? May I aid in collecting means to send the gospel to others? Will God use me in these services, or any other? I think I feel willing. After all my neglect, how merciful to be employed again. He has used me for good, and I have been proud of it. After all my pride of heart, on account of what he has done for me and by me, will he allow me to be used by him any more? What an infinite mercy! I will try, O help me! Work in me and by me. Make me low, and keep me low. I hold myself in readiness to obey the first intimations of thy will. Lord, move me right.

Have prayed for others. God, the Savior, said to Peter, 'I have prayed for thee.' He now intercedes. He says, 'Pray for the peace of Jerusalem.' 'Pray one for another.' May I be used to do good in prayer. O bless my dear wife and make her useful. She has already been very useful to me. She has helped me much. Make her useful still. Make all my relations useful. Make the church useful. Have mercy on such as are out of the way. Help such as are trying to reclaim them. Bless the sabbath school, the church, all thy servants, my friends; make them all useful. Humble me and all, and let thy name be praised and glorified. Amen.

"God has helped me this day. May he help me always. O my covenant God, fill me with thy Spirit; and then shall I be useful."

1822, Jan. 1. Half-past five. "I am raised from my bed to see the opening of a new year. What a prospect is before me! How uncertain to me are the events of it! Before the end of this year, many now on earth will be in heaven—many in hell. Where shall I be? It is not for me to know. My business is, to be ready for heaven—ready to do or suffer the will of God on earth. Shall I see a revival? How can I know? It is none of my business. It is mine to seek, and labor, and pray for it—every day. To go about the work of God in confidence of its importance, and in reliance upon his grace. I am to observe this as a day of fasting and prayer, with the express design of humbling myself and seeking the blessing of God, and especially with reference to a revival. May I be truly humbled and prayerful. I am afraid that I shall not pray aright. Grace only can give me what I need. I intend by the grace of God to seek him like Jacob. O how weak am I! Yet how ready am I to excuse myself! Lord, help me. Prayed for the Holy Spirit; O how unworthy of it. But if unworthiness hinders, I can obtain no favor. God has expressed a willingness to bestow this. But as it is the greatest favor, it must be sought according to its worth. No sacrifice, no effort is too great to be continued. My soul said, 'I will sacrifice any thing, and I will do any thing in my power to obtain the Holy Spirit. It did not lie, so far as I know it; but I know my heart is so depraved that I shall do nothing, unless God work in me both to will and to do.

"I prayed for the Spirit upon my people. And still must I continue to pray. It is attainable. May my heart be right with God—like Daniel.

Progress of the day.—"I have taken a partial review of all my life. I see what it is. Sin; folly. The ground on which I stand is this. I am condemned. I see it, I feel it. I own my sin, and take up arms against it. I stand with God and his holy law; I oppose my sin as he does, though not in degree. I carry the dead body with me. But I rely on Christ alone as my Savior. I need no other. I desire no other. 'My beloved is mine'—mine in his doctrine—merit—friendship—kingdom. 'And I am his.' His in my person—affections—service—and to be made happy by him. His blood atones for me. His Spirit purifies me. His Father pardons and justifies me. I am not my own. I wish to be the Lord's forever. This is the ground on which I stand. I am imperfect and feel abased. I am sinful, and loathe myself. I am helpless, and Christ is all my hope. May he own me. I trust he does. May he use me in his service. I trust he does. May he fit me for for heaven and take me home. I trust he will.

Two things I desire. 1. To live *with* God this year. 2. To live *to* God this year. To live *with* him in daily prayer, meditation, reading the Bible, and holy nearness. To live *to* him in motives and obedience. All for God. Refuse what would keep me from him and hinder my obedience. Do what may promote his glory.

5 in the evening. Have renewed my covenant, I hope with all my heart. Have made some preparation for the business of the year, by making out each day of the month and week, as I have done three years before. I have also endeavored to come near to God, to wrestle with him. He has graciously condescended to show me how. By considering the promises and pleading them.

If I have a promise to the case, plead it—as for instance, for the conversion of the world, or Christ's promise to be with his ministers, or his promise to meet with his people in his house, or where two or three meet to pray, or individual prayer for the Holy Ghost, or prayer for the sick. But if no particular promise comes to the case, then take the more general, which includes the particular. Thus he has promised that all shall know him, from the least to the greatest. This must be plead in particular cases. This is a precious privilege. O may I improve it like Jacob.

Why does not the believer wrestle with God in every prayer? 1. Because he does not see and feel the blessing needed as Jacob did. 2. Because we do not really believe that God will grant it. 3. Because we do not expect him to grant it soon."

Within a few months after his conversion he not only made a public profession of his faith in Christ by uniting himself with the visible church; but he solemnly entered into a secret covenant with God by adopting for himself one of those forms which are contained in Doddridge's Rise and Progress of Religion in the Soul. This covenant was transcribed with a few verbal alterations, and was first subscribed on the 20th of November, 1799. Nor was it the less his own because it was originally drafted by another. The entire purport of this covenant was the most unreserved dedication of himself to God and to his service, with all that he was and all that he had. The covenant itself was copied at length and incorporated in the discourse which was preached at his funeral, and which may be found at the close of this volume.

That Dr. Yale was accustomed constantly keep the obligations of that covenant before his mind, appears from the fact that he ordinarily reviewed it twice a year, in the most solemn and impressive manner. That the reader may have a still further exhibition of the undying spirit of devotion to the service of God, which ever dwelt in his breast, I will here transcribe some passages in which a renewal of this covenant is contained.

1842, Jan. 1. "Another new year dawns. I have received great mercy during the past. Every sabbath was I not only able to preach, but I did preach at least one sermon and generally three. Now as I enter on another year I know not what awaits me. But I feel it to be a duty and a privilege to be in covenant with God: to have him for my father, my redeemer, and sanctifier: to devote all I am, all I have, and all I can, to his service and glory. I am very imperfect and very sinful, and often fail in fulfilling my engagements. But this is a covenant of grace. Christ is my only righteousness. The Spirit is my only helper and comforter. The Father of mercies is gracious and merciful, and for his Son's sake blots out iniquity, and transgression, and sin. O Lord, I desire no more than is contained in thy covenant. Make me as I should be, and accept me, living or dying, and use me for thine own glory, now and ever. Amen. Elisha Yale."

1842, June 15. "This day I am three score and two years old. How much mercy have I received; God has fed me all my life long. God has blessed me much. His grace has restrained me from many sins, and enabled me to do a little in his service, yet what I have been doing is only putting in my little oar to row the boat which for ages has been passing down the stream of time, freighted with immortal beings bound to glory. Soon I cease. God raises up others. Every one has his day. We are but agents and stewards. God by us carries on his work. May I do his holy will while I stay here, and find mercy in Christ when I go home and be no more. By grace I am saved, and hope ever and forever to serve and enjoy him, 'who hath saved me and called me with a holy calling,' &c. Now I need all the blessings of the new covenant. Now I am desirous to live more holy and devoted. But there is nothing in my flesh but sin. All my hope is in the covenanted mercies of God through Jesus Christ, to whom with the Father and the Holy Spirit be all honor and glory, might and dominion for ever, Amen. Elisha Yale."

June 15, 1846. "I am kept alive until this time, and am this day three score and six years old. I have been looking back on all the way in which the Lord has brought me, and can not help wondering at all his mercy and truth. God has been faithful. He is faithful. He will be faithful. Forgive all my unfaithfulness, O my covenant God. Now I most cordially renew this covenant. Now when I am old and gray headed cast me not off. Renew my strength day by day with all might by thy spirit in the inner man, that I may be strong in the Lord and in the power of his might. While I can not do some things which I once did, may I have grace to do what I am better able to do. Thus I consecrate all anew to thee, and O do thou quicken me and help me, for thy great name's sake, to do thy will and trust thy grace and hope in thy mercy. I have failed of seeing God's glorious work as I had hoped, and have no way but to do my duty steadily, and trust God to work his own work according to his own will. Now I am thine, and to thy name be all the glory for ever and ever, Amen. Elisha Yale."

June 15, 1848. "Between 4 and 6 A. M. I rose at four and have been praising God for his wonderful goodness to me during three score and eight years. Looking on my own history I see it to be a series of strange action. During nineteen years I lived without God. During forty-nine, nearly, I have been wandering and returning, backsliding and recovering, halting and springing forward. Thus have I proved, a thousand times twice told, my helplessness and sinfulness. But God has been my merciful Father, my loving Brother, my unfailing Comforter. Again I give all to thee according to this covenant. May I be entirely thine. During this year thus far I have had great trials, and great supports. God has dealt bountifully with me in regard to temporal things, and has given me more and more experience of his faithfulness in all things. A few drops of salvation have fallen. O may the shower come, and the great rain of his strength to save souls. Now, O thou infinite fountain of love, fill me with all thy fullness, and help me to live entirely for thee. Amen. E. Yale."

The above are only a few out of more than a hundred similar records in which he made a semi-annual dedication of all his powers and all his possessions to God. The practice was continued to the very last; and the last act of the kind took place on the 1st day of January, 1853, which was but nine days before his death. This last entry has nothing in it of greater interest than many others, and possesses peculiar interest only from the time at which it was made. I will give only one other very brief extract from his diary as illustrative of his entire devotion to the service of God.

1830. Aug. 22. "This day I have felt more deeply than ever before the Saviour's words, Rev. ii, 10: "BE THOU FAITHFUL UNTO DEATH, AND I WILL GIVE THEE A CROWN OF LIFE."

To-day I begin by the grace of God, and proceed every day faithful to God, to the church, to my people, to my friends, to all men, to my own soul, O Lord, help me in all that I need. Amen."

CHAPTER XIV.

THE DUTIES AND RESPONSIBILITIES OF THE GOSPEL MINISTRY.

"I had rather be a minister of the gospel than to be president of the United States." This is a remark which Dr. Yale was often heard to utter. He regarded it as a higher honor. Regarding, as he did, the commission of the gospel minister as having been issued, and sealed and ratified by God himself, he considered it as more honorable to hold that commission, than to be promoted to the very highest position within the gift of prince or people. It was not the honor of wearing high-sounding titles; or of securing worldly applause;

or of receiving a large stipend, after which he aspired. It was rather the honor of being a coworker with God in the salvation of men.

To this he alludes in a letter to a friend under date of October 8, 1830:

"It is your highest honor to have your children employed in the family and cause of Christ. What an unspeakable privilege, if they may but be allowed to wash the feet of his servants—to carry their shoes—to give them water! They would think themselves honored to be even known by the president of the United States; more to be in some important offices; but much more, to be ambassadors of a foreign court. *Now, then, we are ambassadors for Christ.* Let us try to estimate this honor and privilege. Lord Nelson viewed it as his highest honor to serve his king and country. The new French king has sworn what you and I would not dare to do—'to act in all things with a sole view to the interests, happiness and glory of the French people.' What a dreadful temptation to be a king! Thank God that we are sworn, *to act in all things with a sole view to the interests, happiness and glory of the Redeemer's kingdom.* This oath does not hurt my conscience. But the forgetfulness, stupidness, and remissness of my life in regard to it, many times makes me afraid."

There was nothing, the thought of which seemed to fill him with greater horror, than the doom of an unfaithful minister. There is one passage in his diary in which his feelings on this point are clearly expressed. It is as follows:

1835, April 2. "Rev. Mr. ——, called in the afternoon and spent an hour or two. He is in serious trouble in regard to his people. Very little religion among them, and, with the form of godliness, prejudiced against its power. How sad the effects of an unfaithful ministry, such as has evidently been that of his predecessor! I have often feared, and sometimes shuddered with horror at the thought of such a ministry as his. And yet I know that I am by no means out of danger from my own unfaithfulness. What a contrast between the man I have referred to above, and Dr. Hyde! The judgment day will show it in all its striking colors. Not for ten thousand worlds would I be in the place of that unfaithful man. And yet I know that I am very unfaithful myself."

And as he had such a view of the fearful responsibilities of a gospel minister, he fully realized the truth that no man ought to engage in that work, or aspire after that honor unless he was clearly called to it in the providence and by the grace of God. He believed that there was such a thing as a call to the gospel ministry, and that this call was of God. Yet he did not suppose that the knowledge of it was communicated to man by special revelation, or by dreams, or apparitions. All these he looked upon as miserable delusions, as will appear from what follows:

1829, Dec. 7. "Mr. M. came home and staid with us. He gave an account of an attention in a sabbath school which he conducts in the wilderness eight or ten miles off. Six scholars followed him home last sabbath, and wished to know what they should do to be saved. He thinks it his duty to preach, but is not qualified and sees no way to be qualified. Soon after his conversion he had an offer of aid to get an education, but says he was too proud to accept it. The Lord has been against him ever since; he has lost all his property, and thinks he never shall do his duty and be happy till he does preach. He has long entreated the Lord to show him his duty in a dream, or some other way, so as to satisfy him. Recently he had a dream, very remarkable, as he thinks, and considers that he must preach. He has written on two subjects and spoken to the people. He has thought of connecting himself with some other church where qualifications are less than among Presbyterians; but he thinks he can not give up his principles. His case seems to be very critical. I felt disturbed about it, but endeavored to commit it unto the Lord."

Dec. 8. "Conversed much with Mr. M. Read to him the 23d of Jeremiah, and made remarks on dreams, and also told him of a poor, deluded man, who thought some years ago that he must preach, and brought the 74th Psalm to show me that he ought to break down the carved work of self-righteousness with axes and hammers. This seemed to stagger Mr. M. some. I lent him Mr. Scott's life, and sent him away. Truly this is very trying. The Lord direct."

There are some hints on the subject of a call to the ministry, contained in a letter to a friend, which may not be out of place here. The letter is dated May 16, 1837. He writes as follows:

"You know it was my great desire that you should have been prepared to preach the glorious gospel of our Lord Jesus Christ. This is the greatest work in which man can engage; and therefore while it demands our most serious consideration in regard to its importance, it also demands our most serious attention to the requisite qualifications. The more you simplify the subject, the easier will be the answer. Is it then the will of the Lord that you should preach the gospel? This is all you need inquire about. If it be his will you can know it by humble prayer, and attentive consideration. 'In all thy ways acknowledge him, and he shall direct thy paths.' 'If any man lack wisdom, let him ask of God, who giveth to all men liberally and upbraideth not, and it shall be given him.' It is desirable to know exactly what is the will of God, and then we can be at peace when we do it. A few years ago, as you may remember, it was a serious inquiry with me, whether I should leave my pastoral charge, and devote my life to the great work of endeavoring to get more laborers in the harvest. I laid the case before God, and was confident that he would direct me. So after about six weeks my way was made so plain that I could see no prospect of accomplishing what seemed to me essential to my success if I engaged in the work. Yet the trial did me good, though I am now in the same place I have been in thirty-four years. We expect no miracles, no voice, or vision from heaven to direct us, and yet God does give his humble followers an answer of peace. Pray much. Have no will about it. Be ready to do any thing God requires. Lean not to your own understanding.

It has long been a settled point with me, that the Lord Jesus has an immensely great work to do in this world. In this he uses the cooperation of his people; some in one part of the work, and some in another. And it is the business of his servants, not to choose what part of the work they will do but to engage in doing the very work to which he calls them. Some are to serve him in one way, and some in another; but every one according to his several ability. One is to supply the place of seeing, another of hearing, &c., &c. Nor can any one member say to the other, "I have no need of you."

Many good men misjudge very much in regard to themselves. I knew a man with a family about ten years ago. He had a fluent speech and a good amount of zeal; but he was ignorant. He wished to know my mind. I gave it with the utmost frankness. It did not suit him. He went into another part of the state, where he studied some, and was licensed and began to preach. For a year or two he preached about there in some of the new settlements; but became miserably poor, and the last I heard he was sick, and he and his family in such a state of want, that they were likely to be sent to the poor house.

I do not know that it would be wise in me to say all I know and think on the subject of the ministry just now. But this I say, that in my opinion, the church is suffering more at present from incompetent ministers, than from all other causes put together. Many, I trust, are good men who have run before they are sent. Here I trust you will not misapprehend me. I do not suppose that any amount of learning can qualify a man to preach the gospel. It is the grace of God which is the root. Yet men must be able to preach, or they are not called to the work. In the present state of our country and of the world, amid the pressing calls for ministers, the greatest curse upon the church and the world must be novices, puffed up with their own importance, falling into the snare of the devil, and leading others after them."

Upon the views which he entertained in respect to the duties and responsibilities of the gospel ministry, his whole life was a faithful commentary. Those who knew the man, and who were familiar with his fidelity in the discharge of his official duties, could not fail to receive the impression, that he felt a responsibility resting upon himself of no ordinary character. This feeling also was clearly expressed in a letter addressed to Rev. Cyrus Yale, from which I will here extract a few passages:

July 1, 1828. "Every minister, every Christian, is admonished to work while the day lasts, not only because the night cometh in which no man can work, but also, because the people pass away, and nothing more can be done for them. Many times I seem to stand in amazement. All are going. I am going. Few are prepared. Every one is impressing his sinful likeness on those around him. The impression remains; it is carried into eternity, or it is restamped upon others *in perpetuum!* To act, to speak, even to think, in such circumstances, is too great for finite man. Yet, to act, to speak, to think, and that for others too, is the business of a minister. I seem to see myself produced and reproduced ten thousand times, in moral resemblance; and perpetuated to the end of time. O what a prospect will open to us in eternity! A word, dropped and forgotten by us, fell upon the ear of a child, or a stranger, and caused his ruin. A word on our tongue, and kept back through sinful fear, let pass a soul it might have reclaimed. What, if Jesus had been intimidated when he knew the murderous thoughts of the scribes and Pharisees, while the man with a withered hand was before him! How had the poor man been disappointed! What a tribute of glory had God lost! What a forfeiture of our confidence in Jesus! But he was not intimidated. The man was not disappointed. God did not fail of his glory. Jesus did not forfeit our confidence. He remains our bright example, to show that good must be done when it ought to be done, and that events must be left with God. Could I warm up my own cold heart to my duty by writing these solemn truths, one sinner more might be saved. But what are we? How great is our work! How much remains to be done! I look over my ministry sometimes with deep sorrow, when I find only about ten on an average hopefully converted by my ministry, in a year. May the Lord impart to you and to me more spiritual life, and ministerial fidelity and activity. Our cause is before us, our time short. If we do any thing it must be done quickly. We need your prayers. May you be blessed in all things.

Yours, ELISHA YALE."

At the ordination or installation of his younger brethren, Dr. Yale was frequently called upon, as the organ of the Presbytery, to deliver to them that charge which is required on such occasions by the constitution of the Presbyterian church. This charge is expected to contain some delineation of the responsibilities of the ministerial office, and the particular duties of those by whom this office is held. By transcribing here one of those charges, in extenso, a more full and comprehensive view of this subject may be obtained, than could be secured in any other way. It was first delivered at Malta, on the 7th day of February, 1821, at the ordination of the Rev. Joseph Bracket; and the substance of it was delivered on two other occasions afterwards. It is as follows:

[CHARGE.]

"*My dear Brother:* It was but a few days ago that I was by the grave of a beloved Christian minister, who had just finished his work, and laid down his commission at the feet of Jesus. In view of that grave I would now address you, in the name of Christ, at your entrance upon the duties of this sacred office. Of all the undertakings of men, none are more important than the work to which you are this day set apart and consecrated. Its appointment is not of men, but God. The investiture of the office is by human hands; but the office itself is of Divine authority. The doctrines you are to teach are not the investigations of reason, but the dictates of inspiration. The duties you are to enjoin are not the commandments of men, but the laws of Jehovah. The threatenings you are to denounce are not the expressions of human displeasure, but the thunders of divine wrath. The promises you are to present for the encouragement of the convinçed and desponding, are not the fancies of theoretic philanthropy, but the overflowings of God's unbounded goodness and mercy. Your embassy is from God to men; from the wise and good Ruler of the universe to a portion of his rebellious subjects; and the proposals you are to make from his word are to be the unalterable terms of life and death. The results of your ministry are not to be the happiness or the misery of empires and ages, but the happiness or the misery of immortal beings forever.

"Having consecrated you to this great work, 'we have given to you the right hand of fellowship, to take part with us in this ministry;' and in giving you that right hand, we have pledged ourselves to our utmost efforts for your aid in the duties and conflicts of your ministry. But, sir, we have to leave with you our solemn charge, to fulfill the duties of your office.

"We have not ordained you to be a magistrate, a counsellor at law, a physician, a husbandman, or an artisan; but we have ordained you to be a minister of Jesus Christ, and installed you as the pastor of this church. In the words of Paul to the elders of Ephesus, we address you, 'Take heed, therefore, unto thyself, and to all the flock over which the Holy Ghost hath made thee an overseer to feed the church of God, which he hath purchased with his own blood.'

"We charge you, therefore, *first of all, to be faithful in maintaining personal religion.*

"Feel yourself a poor, undone sinner, more worthy of hell than heaven, and of the curse than the blessing of God. As such, rely only on the blood of Christ for pardon, and the grace of the Holy Ghost for sanctification. You will thus rest on the only sure support of the soul. Live near to God in habitual meditation, and prayer, and faith, and love, and hope. You will thus live in the enjoyment of God. Crown your religion with a blameless and useful deportment in the occupations of every day. For 'a bishop must be blameless, vigilant, sober, of good behavior, given to hospitality, apt to teach; not given to wine, no striker, not greedy of filthy lucre; but patient, not a brawler, not covetous. Moreover, he must have a good report of them that are without; lest he fall into reproach and the snare of the devil.'

"Personal and experimental religion will enable you to show your people in what it consists, and to direct, and warn, and comfort them, as they may need. As a minister also, you will have this peculiar advantage when you speak from your own experience, that you will speak with the assurance which arises from feeling as well as demonstration; for what a man feels powerfully he will express with assurance. And a minister of Christ is to be, not merely an organ by which God communicates his will to men, but an active agent, engaged in doing that will and deeply concerned to see it done by others. He is not only to serve up food well prepared for others, but to feed upon the same for his own satisfaction and nourishment. Be sure, therefore, that you believe, and love, and practice, and enjoy that holy religion which you wish your people to believe, and love, and practice, and enjoy.

"We charge you in the next place, *to preach the gospel.* This is to be the main business of your life. You will need to look to the Lord Jesus Christ for his teaching and guidance, that he may lead you into the mysteries of his religion, and enable you to preach the unsearchable riches of his grace. Pray before you study, that you may study to please God and be useful to men. Study before you preach, that you may preach according to the mind of Christ. Whatever attention you may see fit to give to your style and diction, let it be only with the holy view of making your sermons more effectual to the good of souls. Feed not the flock of God with sound, and shadows and flowers, instead of the nutritious milk, and the substantial meat of the word. Meet with firmness that popular presumption that a minister can preach without preparation; and yet, be always prepared to preach, when the providence of God makes it your duty. And in your preparation you will always remember, that the best sermon is that which is best adapted to glorify Christ and save the souls of men. Give every part of the Word of God a due share of your attention, that you may be a preacher of the whole. Incline not to theoretical speculation; and while you endeavor to explain all that needs and is capable of explanation, do not endeavor to make your people understand all mysteries. Treat theological subjects with all the understanding and all the force you possess, but treat them at the same time as resting upon the broad basis of revelation. Dare to believe, and dare to preach, all that you find supported by the authority of God's Word; for that authority will bear you out before men, and before the tribunal of Jehovah. Dwell chiefly on the peculiarities of the Gospel; for in them lies chiefly its peculiar excellence. What it maintains in common with philosophy, is not its glory; but what it maintains as peculiar to itself. I mean the justification of a believing sinner only by the righteousness of the Lord Jesus Christ, and the sanctification of a sinner by the power of the Holy Ghost. Have no communion with that pretended reason or philosophy which would lead to a doubt of these fundamental principles of the gospel; neither commune with those as Christians who deny them.

Be a plain preacher also, and let it be always your aim to exhibit your subject and not yourself. Endeavor, moreover, without ceasing to have and to feel the genuine spirit of your work, the spirit of preaching, under the influences of the Holy Ghost. For (to adopt the language of the pious and excellent Brainard), 'When ministers feel those special gracious influences on their hearts, it wonderfully assists them to come at the consciences of men, and, as it were, to handle them with hands; whereas, without them, whatever reason and oratory we make use of, we do but make use of stumps instead of hands.'

"To sum up all that we would say on the subject of preaching, we add, in the words of Paul to Timothy, 'We charge thee, therefore, before God, and the Lord Jesus Christ, who shall judge the quick and the dead at his appearing and his kingdom, preach the word, be instant in season, out of season; reprove, rebuke, exhort, with all long-suffering and doctrine.'

"We charge you, further, dear brother, *with regard to the care of the church.* 'Feed my sheep,' says the Good Shepherd, and 'feed my lambs.' This requires attention not only to the wholesome doctrine you are to preach, but to the holy discipline you are to exercise. As to those already in the church, you are to see that they do not go astray; and if they go astray, to bring them back and see that they continue steadfast unto the end. As to those hereafter to be admitted, be careful that they be sound in the faith, experimental in their views and feelings, and blameless in their deportment. Guard well the door of the sheepfold, and use every precaution to admit all the sheep and the lambs, and exclude every intruder. The strength of the church does not consist in its numbers, or its wealth, but in its purity and spirituality, and obedience to Christ. Be especially careful to use all your influence in the support of 'elders that rule well,' knowing that rulers will not maintain a greater degree of purity in the church than they maintain in themselves.

"We charge you, moreover, to fulfill the duties of your office *in regard to the higher judicatories of the church.* It is "by the laying on of the hands of the Presbytery" that ministers are set apart and consecrated to their work, and Paul's charge to Timothy, as a member of the Presbytery, and through him to every other member, is in these solemn words: "Lay hands suddenly on no man, neither be partaker of other men's sins; keep thyself pure." This judicatory is the guardian of the church's purity. If the Presbytery ordain men without sufficient proof of piety, soundness in the faith, holiness of practice, and ability to teach, they neglect this apostolic charge, and participate in the errors and scandals which such men introduce. To prevent this evil so far as your own efforts are concerned, be always present at the sessions of this judicatory and of the Synod, when not prevented by the providence of God. When present, endeavor to "maintain the unity of the Spirit in the bond of peace." Submit to their constitutional decisions; for genuine Christian liberty and independence and fidelity are always consistent with due subordination to the constituted authorities of the church, and we are never authorized to depart from them, till we are satisfied on good grounds that they are incorrigibly corrupt, and that God calls us to "come out from among them." At the same time, act as an honest, faithful, and valiant man. Agree with your brethren in all things so far as they agree with the word of God; and be not afraid to disagree with them, if you believe in your heart that they depart from that word. For the word of God is the citadel of the church, and when we surrender that we surrender all.

Finally, dear sir, we *charge you to be faithful to all the souls committed to your trust.* We know very well that you will find it difficult to do every thing you desire to do for the salvation of such of your beloved people as have yet no interest in the Lord Jesus Christ. We can fancy ourselves placed by your side in your study, observing your concern for those immortal beings, that are perishing in sin. We hear your sighs, and see your tears. In the tender anxiety of your heart you say: "What more can I do to save them from sin and death? What new means shall I try to awaken them? On what subject shall I preach and how shall I preach to do them good?' We see you on your knees, and observe you pouring out your sorrows into the bosom of your Savior. Brother, we know your soul will be ready to sink under the weight of your charge, and we would not needlessly increase that weight; but we must be faithful to you, that we may not be guilty should your people perish through your neglect. Behold your people that are yet in sin. They are dying. Be assured that the soul of every one that dies without Christ, sinks directly down into hell. It sinks directly down into hell. It sinks directly down into hell. Listen for a moment and hear the words of Jehovah to you in respect to this part of your people. ‘Son of man, I have made thee a watchman’—unto this congregation —‘therefore hear the word at my mouth, and give them warning from me. When I say unto the wicked, thou shalt surely die, and thou givest him not warning, nor speakest to warn the wicked from his wicked way to save his life; the same wicked man shall die in his iniquity; but his blood will I require at thine hand. Yet if thou warn the wicked and he turn not from his wickedness nor from his wicked way, he shall die in his iniquity; but thou hast delivered thy soul.’

Do you say in your heart, and are you ready to exclaim: ‘Who is sufficient for these things?’ Call to mind for your encouragement, the grace of God, by which you may be enabled to do all things, though in yourself you are nothing and can do nothing. Jesus, our Lord and our God, whom we love, and serve, and adore, and in whom we trust, has not left us without support and comfort in this ministry. And now, brother, as you are about to take part with us in this ministry, so take part with us in this consolation: ‘Lo I am with you always,’ saith the Savior, ‘even unto the end of the world.’ ‘Amen,’ said the evangelist. Thus do we also say. Even so, Lord Jesus, even so be with us, and with this thy servant and our brother. Amen.”

The want of permanency in the pastoral relation, or the frequent dismissal and removal of ministers, in certain sections of our country, has become proverbial, and very many have been mourning over the evils incident to such a state of things. Dr. Yale was among the number who consider the practice as fraught with disaster; and his views are expressed in the following brief extracts from his correspondence. The first letter from which these extracts are taken, was written to a friend in the western part of New York, and the other to a correspondent in Connecticut.

"I did not forget your worthy minister Mr. F., but had not room on the other page to mention him. Hope he is recovered before now. Take good care of him, and keep him long. I am well satisfied that the frequent change of ministers is a great evil both to ministers and people. To the former it prevents generally the building up of a character. Exceptions there may be; but generally a character is to be like the growth of an oak, or a cedar; slow and gradual, but sure and lasting. Ministers who are often changing, attain not the most desirable character. Then people become restive and feverish, find fault, and deprive themselves and their children, and their grandchildren, of the wisdom, counsels and example of age and experience. Congregations become unstable, and are often broken and divided. Certain Christian graces have not time to grow, even if they exist. Such as patience, forbearance, long-suffering, forgiveness, and the like. People also fail to be united as they should be."

This letter was written near the close of his life; and the other in the year 1826.

"You mention the unpleasant circumstance of the dismission of brother B. He has been in the region beyond us, and seems afraid that education societies are overacting. But the dismission of ministers is a very frequent and very painful occurrence in this region. I can tell you a story which will make your ears tingle. Nine ministers dismissed and one removed by death within three years. I do not know but I shall be dismissed myself. It is dreadful. We do not know the lesson—'Bear and forbear.' Our congregations suffer amazingly from these changes. Even if they obtain as good ministers as they lose, they do not regain the confidence they lost, as to the integrity of the ministerial character. I do hope the time will never come when Connecticut will be like York State in regard to the changing of ministers. Our condition is most miserable."

CHAPTER XV.

PASTORAL COMMUNICATIONS.

Though Dr. Yale ordinarily enjoyed such vigorous health that he was enabled to perform a vast amount of labor, there were times in which, through bodily infirmity, he was so far laid aside as to be obliged to suspend the active performance of the ministerial work. This was the case in the year 1835; during which year, for several months, he found himself altogether unable to engage in the labors of the pulpit; and frequently found it injurious even to associate very much with his friends. During this period, however, while his pulpit was supplied by others, he did occasionally send to the congregation some "pastoral communications," which were read by the person who occupied the pulpit for the day. And as these communications contain facts of the deepest interest, I have thought it best to give them a place in this volume. In this chapter will be found communications of this character, not only of the date above mentioned, but some also that were written at a much later period of his ministry. They will be inserted in the order in which they were written.

PASTORAL COMMUNICATIONS.

No. I.

Read April 12, 1835, P. M.

Statements and Requests.

"The pastor of this church, being unable to speak much, invites attention to the following communication:

"On the last week in January, I had symptoms of scarlet fever, especially in an affection of the throat. This, in connection with a chronic catarrh, produced hoarseness and a weakness at the lungs, which rendered public speaking difficult. During the last week in March, I experienced two slight paralytic affections. After consultation it was thought best to use means to prevent the recurrence of such affections. It is hoped that the means may be blessed to produce the desired result. But, at present, it is thought prudent to avoid much public speaking. The congregation will please to receive this as a concise statement of the nature of my affliction, and as an apology for ceasing to perform public services for a season.

"Allow me to call your attention to two facts which seem worthy of a little notice. The first time I preached in this congregation, being then an entire stranger, was on the first sabbath, the third day of April, 1803. The last time I preached was the last sabbath of March, being the 29th day, 1835. Thus *thirty-two* years were completed, even to a sabbath, from the time I preached the first, till I preached the last sermon in this house. Whether the Lord will allow an unfaithful servant, as I have been in many things, to preach to you again, is one of the secret things which belong to him. My first sermon to the congregation then worshiping here, was founded on the text, John iii, 16, 'For God so loved the world that he gave his only begotten Son, that whosoever believeth in him should not perish, but have everlasting life.' My last was on the text, Jeremiah xxxii, 33, 'They have turned to me the back, and not the face.'

"The sermon last sabbath, the first in April, when I was present, but unable to preach (I mean the sermon in the afternoon), seemed to me particularly appropriate, and was on the text, I Thess. v, 25, 'Brethren, pray for us.' If an apostle needed and desired the prayers of his brethren; how much more do ministers of inferior grace and qualifications. Allow me, then, to ask of the church, of every member in particular, the same precious favor. Were I only a member among the members, in a feeble condition, I would consider this as a precious favor. But, much more, in the relation of a minister to the members, do I need; and, therefore, would I earnestly ask an interest in your prayers.

ELISHA YALE."

PASTORAL COMMUNICATIONS.

No. II.

Read April 19, 1835, P. M.

Revivals.

Ps. cxi, 4, "He hath made his wonderful works to be remembered."

"While unable to speak much, I would be doing what I can for the cause of Christ and the welfare of the congregation. The revivals of religion among us, during the thirty-two years of my ministry, merit our attention. If these are genuine, they are the work of God. They are not the least of his works; but they must be ranked among his wonderful works. These are to be remembered by us. He will cause them to be remembered in the ages of eternity; for this is one design in the conversion of sinners: Eph. ii, 7, 'That in the ages to come he might show the exceeding riches of his grace, in his kindness toward us through Christ Jesus.'

"Before I preached in this place, God was evidently preparing the way for a revival. In the year 1802, the word of God was preached several months. And I have been told by the pious, that they felt an unusual spirit of prayer during that year. The final judgment alone will reveal what God was then doing to prepare the way for his glorious appearing to revive his work in the year following.

"I stated the last sabbath that I commenced my labors here the first sabbath in April, 1803. During that week, God evidently commenced a revival. I wondered at it then, and have wondered at it always. But he had prepared the way before, and all that was needful was that some one should speak to the dry bones, and thus be instrumental of their beginning to shake. God did evidently appear then in Zion to do his wonderful work. In following years about seventy united with the church, as the fruits of that revival; numbers of whom have proved by the trials of thirty years, that they do love our Lord Jesus Christ, in sincerity.

"During eight or nine succeeding years, we passed through the furnace of affliction. We were afflicted in the church, and in the congregation. In both respects we were sometimes almost ready to despair even of life. We found trouble and sorrow. But again God had pity for his great Name's sake, and again he performed his wonderful works.

"Near the close of the year 1813, he appeared to build up Zion. During the year 1814, he wrought marvellously; nor did he cease till near the close of 1815. About eighty became members of the church in those and following years, who may be justly reckoned as the fruits of that revival.

"In the year 1819 and 1820, he sent down upon us a refreshing shower, though it did not water all our field. About twenty joined the church as the result. Perhaps, we may say, that the wonderful works of God then commenced, did not cease entirely till we were favored with a general revival in the year 1822. About fifty became members in consequence of that precious refreshing from the presence of the Lord.

"Seven years rolled away with no general attention after this till the year 1829, when God was pleased to visit us again. About eighty united with the church in a few years following, chiefly from the members of the sabbath school.

"Once more, in 1832, a partial shower was enjoyed, issuing in the addition of about thirty-five to our number. The whole number who have joined our church as the fruit of these six revivals, so far as I can fairly estimate them from the church records, is about three hundred and thirty-five. Besides these, sixty-five have joined it by letter, or as the fruits of particular acts of

God's power, at seasons when there was no general revival. There were thirty-nine members when the church was organized in the year 1804. And including those, the whole number of members of this church during thirty-two years, has been four hundred and thirty-nine. Thus God in his wonderful mercy has, in this period of time, added unto us, *four hundred.*

"I record these things that we may call his wonderful works to remembrance. 'O that men would praise the Lord for his goodness, and for his wonderful works to the children of men.' 'Are his mercies clean gone forever! And will he be favorable no more? Hath the Lord forgotten to be gracious? Hath he in anger shut up his tender mercies?'

"But I forbid this hopeless thought,
This dark, despairing frame;
Remembering what thy hand hath wrought,
Thy hand is still the same."

PASTORAL COMMUNICATIONS.

No. III.

Read April 26, 1835.

Declensions.

Psalm cvii, 39: "Again they are minished and brought low, through oppression, affliction and sorrow."

"The last sabbath I gave you a concise statement of the revivals of religion among us during thirty-two years past. Those were verdant and delightful spots in the field of my labors. But this is a changeable world. As man is by nature wholly opposed to God, and as even Christians retain much that is sinful, there is an incessant influence of sin, always counteracting the work of God, so that declension has followed revival in every period of our history. And we have reason to lament that it is so everywhere, and in all ages of the world. Revivals have never yet been continual and perpetual, in any portion or period of the church. I design to-day to give some notices of the declensions among us.

"In the year 1804, there were added to the church forty-five members. From that time there was a gradual decline in the number of additions, till the year 1808, during which there were none added. That year is marked in the records as a barren year. That was the lowest ebb to which the church has been reduced. Though in the year before one had been excluded, yet no bad effect was produced upon the church. But the year 1808 was eminently a year of trials and distress, divisions and animosities. We were, indeed, 'minished and brought low, through oppression, affliction and sorrow.' From that year there was a gradual increase, though in 1814 we were constrained to cut off another member. But this took place not long before there were many additions, although there had been but two in that year before this calamitous event. In 1814, there were added twenty-six; and in 1815, thirty-one. In 1816, we were tried again by the exclusion of one, and the unchristian conduct of another. In 1818, another member was excluded, and but three were added; and that year was the lowest point to which the church was reduced from the year 1815 till the year 1822.

In 1819 there were added seven. In 1820, ten. In 1821, twelve. In 1822, thirty-one. In 1823, twelve. The declension continued down to 1826. For from the beginning of June till the 27th of Dec., 1825, more than six months, the church were troubled with four cases of discipline, which resulted in suspension. The lowest point, therefore, may be considered as being at the close of the year 1825, and the beginning of the year 1826. This is about the central point between 1822 and 1829, two years of precious revival. From the beginning of 1826 there was a gradual rising again, till the revival in 1829, in which year there were added thirty-five. In 1830, twenty-seven. In 1831, twenty-three. In 1832, twenty-three. In 1833, sixteen. And although we were obliged to suspend one in the year 1831, it did not operate to produce much excitement, and though it was painful, so far as the individual was concerned, yet it was not disastrous to the church.

"As the result of our affliction and sorrow thus far, we have been constrained to exclude four members, and suspend six; total, ten, who remain, if living, in a state of separation from us. Others have fallen, and caused affliction and sorrow to themselves and others; but have generally been reclaimed and restored. I will mention some of the offences which have caused us trouble and sorrow. Transgressions of the 3d commandment, of the 4th commandment, of the 7th commandment, of the 8th commandment, of the 9th commandment and of the 10th commandment. Also the sin of intemperance. More cases of discipline have occurred for this, than for any other offense. And yet, covetuousness has caused us more trouble than all others. I mean cases in which property has been concerned as the subject of contention among the members.

"Under a sense of our sins and imperfections we are called upon to humble ourselves, while we give thanks at the remembrance of the Lord's mercies. I would close this communication with a single remark. As it is one to which I attach much importance, I hope it will be remembered by all the members, and especially by all who are in the days of their youth. The rema k is this, that *every member of the church should dread more to be a troubler of Israel, than to be dead.* Better expressed thus: *Every member should dread more than death to be a troubler of Israel.* As said our Savior: 'It is better for a man that a mill-stone be hanged about his neck, and he be cast into the sea, than to offend one of these little ones.'"

PASTORAL COMMUNICATIONS.

NO. IV.

Read May 3, 1835.

Various attitudes and aspects of the church.

During thirty years, there must be varieties in the state of the church, both internal and external; the former appear to the omniscient eye only, while the latter are the subject of human observation. Varieties in the external state of the church are, of course, those only which I am now to notice. These may be comprised under four heads, viz: the church at the lowest point of depression; in a state of gradual revival; at the highest point of elevation; and in a state of gradual declension.

1. *The church at the lowest point of depression.*

At that point this church has been three times during these years; in 1808 when none were added; in 1818, when three only were added, and one excluded; and in 1826, after four had been suspended, and three only were added. We were distressed within ourselves. Some of our own household were ensnared by the adversary of God and man, and we were constrained to exercise the rod of discipline. As this is always painful to the tender and faithful parent, so is it to the church. We always took up the rod with reluctance, only when we were compelled to it, and could no longer enjoy peace and unity, and purity in the church without it. Not that these were the only times of the exercise of discipline in the church; but these gave us the most trouble.

We felt grieved, and pained, and ashamed at the scandals which were among us; and knew of no way but to endeavor to reclaim, or to put away the offenders. With great reluctance we engaged in the work, and went through it. At times, it seemed as though the church would be rent in pieces and scattered. But I believe we never lost a member in consequence of doing our duty. On the contrary, while we seemed to be bleeding under our wounds, and almost ashamed to look up; while it would seem that the enemies of the church would triumph, an unseen hand preserved us, and we were not utterly cast down and destroyed, neither was our heritage given to reproach.

2. *The church in a state of gradual revival.*

In our low condition we looked round on ourselves, and said: 'By whom shall Jacob arise, for he is small?' We sighed and looked upward. We looked upon the condition and character of God's enemies, and heard a voice from the word of God, saying: 'Can these bones live?' We replied: 'Oh, Lord God, thou knowest.' We began to call on the name of the Lord: Oh, Lord revive thy work.' 'Wilt thou not revive us again?' And we said: 'Oh that the salvation of Israel were come out of Zion. Endeavors were made to instruct and guide the young, and to engage the attention of others to religion, and their own spiritual welfare.

Our progress was slow, for it was all up hill. It was a very difficult thing to get our own hearts engaged in the work. Often did our praying seem like no prayer, and our endeavors of little or no use; for the impenitent thronged the broad road, and the church came reluctantly and slowly 'to the help of the Lord against the mighty.'

Yet our progress was onward and upward. We put away occasions of scandal, and engaged in the work of reformation, and in various endeavors to arouse the attention of the careless, and instruct and impress the young. A careful attention to the truth—to experimental and practical religion, always marked the progress of the church in her ascent upwards, and more than ordinary prayer was deemed indispensable. Two things seemed to be deeply impressed upon the church: 1, That every thing must be done that God requires; 2, That by his Spirit alone could we be revived. At the same time a tenderness of feeling was very manifest; such tenderness as was often attended by the starting tear, when the worth of the soul, and the work of the Lord, were subjects of thought or conversation. And while known sin was put away, and known duty carefully performed, the inquiry was often made: What shall be done to enjoy a revival?

3. *The church at the highest point of elevation.*

At length it was manifest that God had commenced his great and glorious work of converting sinners. Deep solemnity rested on the countenances of many. The tear of tender concern fell down upon the cheek. The inquiry was made: 'What shall I do?' Some rejoiced in hope. Some were filled with greater anxiety, and others with enmity and anger, because they heard of the joy and peace of such as believed. The church in general became greatly encouraged and animated, and were ready to say as Israel of old: 'When the Lord turned again the captivity of Zion, we were like them that dream. Then was our mouth filled with laughter, and our tongue with singing.' And as there 'was great joy' in the city of Samaria when Jesus was preached and believed on, so was there great joy among us at the revival of the Lord's work. Then had the church 'light, and gladness, and joy, and honor.'

4. *The church in a state of gradual declension.*

In view of the mighty power of God, exercised evidently in answer to prayer, and in blessing the means of grace, we felt and said that if the church would only continue to pray and labor, God would continue to revive his work. True as this saying may be, I have observed that the church has uniformly begun to decline, as soon as we have begun to talk about it. Perhaps, for a time, more zeal, and more activity have been manifest, than at any preceding period; but the declension has been uniformly manifest at this point. Instead of laboring and praying as we ought, we have talked about laboring and praying, and calculated on much that we should be able to do. We labored and prayed in a very different manner from what we did when rising from the dust, under a sense of our great sinfulness and extreme unworthiness. Conversions became less frequent. By degrees all declined, and we sunk down into a good opinion of ourselves. Lower than this, we needed not to descend. But we descended lower and lower, till we arrived at the lowest point already described. Are we not nearly at the same point now? And may we not inquire again: 'By whom shall Jacob arise, for he is small?' "

PASTORAL COMMUNICATIONS.

NO. V.

Read May 24, 1835.

Cause of Revivals.

" I have stated facts respecting revivals and declensions, and also respecting the attitudes and aspects of the church, during thirty-two years past. And there is no doubt that we look with the deepest interest on those seasons, 'few indeed, and far beetween,' in which we have been thus highly favored. If we see not that the very existence, yet certainly we see that the increase and prosperity and usefulness of church, are owing chiefly to those revivals. And now, if we desire one spiritual favor more than another, it is that we may enjoy a revival of pure and undefiled religion. Surely I may appeal to every pious feeling in the church that our hearts' desire and prayer to God, is, that he would revive us again, and cause us to rejoice in him.

"Were the inquiry, 'Who made the world?' No sober man would think of but one answer. The heavens and the earth, and all things that live and move and breathe in this wide world, 'are the work of his hand.' 'He spake, and it was done.' They existed when they were bidden, but not of themselves. They existed when God spake, but it was not the word that caused them to exist. The word was the token, but God himself was the cause. Were the inquiry, 'Who causes all to continue in being?' No rational, sober man, who believes the Bible, would think of ascribing continuance in being to any other cause. We may talk about the laws which govern matter, yet, they are nothing more than the established modes of God's operation. So we speak of the cultivation and the growth of every sort of vegetable, but we mean by it no more than that God causes every vegetable to grow by that mode of cultivation. It is true of every thing, that 'neither is he that planteth, nor he that watereth any thing, but God that giveth the increase.' In no sense whatever, is any creature or any thing more than an agent, or instrument, by which God works. He does not cause the grass to grow for the cattle, or the grain for man, except according to established laws; but, at the same time, it is he only that causes them to grow.

"In the animal world, every thing propagates its kind, in the way appointed, and in no other; but God is just as entirely the cause of every living thing as he was of the first living thing that ever existed.

"In regard to the Holy Scriptures, men thought, and felt and wrote, but they thought, and felt and wrote as 'they were moved by the Holy Ghost.' So that 'all scripture is given by inspiration of God.'

"When Moses lifted up his rod over the Red sea, the waters were divided; but God divided them. 'Jordan was driven back.' 'But what ailed thee, O Jordan, that thou wast driven back?' 'The waters saw thee, O God, the waters saw thee, they were afraid, the depths also were troubled.' God did it. The same is true of every miracle. It was not the clay on the eyes of the blind man, nor his washing in the pool of Siloam, but the power of the Lord Jesus Christ that opened his eyes.

"But what has this to do in showing the cause of a revival of religion? One thing, and one only—*it teaches us how to understand the language of God's word.* This is all the use I would make of it. The argument from analogy is by no means conclusive, in any case where we can have any better. In this case we have all we need, or could reasonably desire. But we may find a similarity in the use of language in regard to all the works of God, and this may help us to understand its meaning in regard to his work in a revival of religion.

"We are to keep in mind, on this subject, that a genuine revival of religion is connected with the increase of grace in Christians, and the conversion of the ungodly. That the Holy Ghost is the sole cause of these effects and results, appears from express declaration, from the work actually done, from the acknowledgment of the pious, and from their prayers.

1. "*The express declaration of Scripture.*

"Men are said to be '*created* in Christ Jesus unto good works;' to be 'born, not of blood, nor of the will of the flesh, nor of the will of man, but of God.' It is said, 'that which is born of the flesh is flesh, and that which is born of the Spirit is spirit.' 'Not by works of righteousness which we have done, but according to his mercy he saved us, by the washing of regeneration and renewing of the Holy Ghost.' 'You hath he quickened who were dead in trespasses and sins.' 'It is the Spirit that quickeneth, the flesh profiteth nothing.' 'Work out your own salvation with fear and trembling, for it is God that worketh in you both to will and to do of his good pleasure.' 'Not by might, nor by power, but by my Spirit, saith the Lord of hosts.'

"In these divine declarations, four great works are comprised, which none but God can do. One is creation; another is the beginning of existence at the birth; another is giving life to the dead; and the other is producing a willing mind, and an obedient life. I am not aware that stronger expressions than these are used in the Word of God, to show the power of God in any of his works. As God works in Christians to will and to do all that they will and do, that is good; and as he creates and regenerates, and revives those that are in a state of nature, he is the cause and the sole cause of a revival of religion. All that men do in the cause, though done as God would have it done, is nothing more than his way of doing his own work. 'It is the same Spirit that worketh all in all.' Men will and do what God requires, but he worketh all their work in them. 'It is not of him that willeth, nor of him that runneth, but of God that showeth mercy.' The same is evident:

2. "*From the work actually done.*

"Is it compared to creation? God only can create. Is it resurrection from the dead? God only can raise the dead. Is it the beginning of spiritual life? God only is the author and giver of life. Is it to turn an obstinate will, and cause the disobedient to do their duty? God only inclines the will to what it is by nature disinclined. Nor does any one become obedient till he is made willing to obey. And, hence, that saying is verified, 'Thy people shall be willing in the day of thy power.'

3. "*The acknowledgment of the pious proves that the Spirit causes revivals.*

"On this point we are not to appeal to any man on earth. We are all to compare ourselves with those examples which God has given us in his Word. Not that there are no pious people on earth. But as there are vast differences of opinions and views among people who are reputed to be pious, we may not be entirely safe in appealing to the living. On the contrary, we are perfectly safe in appealing to those examples which are presented to us in the Word of God. What do they say? 'Not by works of righteousness which we have done, but according to his mercy he saved us by the washing of regeneration and renewing of the Holy Ghost.' Again, 'who hath saved us, and called us, with an holy calling, not according to our works, but according to his own purpose and grace, which was given us in Christ Jesus before the world began.' Hence, they say: 'Not unto us, not unto us, but unto thy name give glory, for thy mercy and for thy truth's sake.'

4. "*The same is proved by the prayers of the pious.*

"They do not pray that men may revive religion, but that God would do it. Said David, 'Create in me a clean heart, O God, and renew a right spirit within me.' Others prayed, 'Turn us, O God of our salvation, and we shall be turned.' 'O Lord, revive thy work.' 'Wilt thou not revive us again, that thy people may rejoice in thee?' Said Paul, 'My heart's desire and prayer to God for Israel is, that they may be saved.' 'These all continued with one accord in prayer and supplication.' For what did they pray? For the promise of the Father, the Holy Spirit.

"But surely, I need say no more. Nor would I have said so much, but to impress upon our minds one of the most important truths of the Bible, and one which is the hope of the church. It is the Spirit of the living God, the third person of the adorable Trinity, who causes every genuine revival of religion. To him let us look; to him let us give all the glory."

As every thing is regarded with particular interest which appertains to the work of God's grace in the revival of religion, I will here give a few extracts from a letter to a friend, giving some account of the revival which has been spoken of as enjoyed in the year 1822. It was written in October of that year.

"During last winter there was more than ordinary solemnity on many minds, especially in our conference of young people. In March and April I visited almost all my people. No special seriousness, yet a disposition to listen. I felt very much the need of divine grace. When at Philadelphia, in May, my mind often turned with strong desire and not without tears, to the state of my people. When I came home in June, I was very low indeed, as to spiritual activity and enjoyment. I found my brother at my house from Charlotte—from the midst of a revival among his people—warm and vigorous. He spent two sabbaths with me, and preached nine or ten sermons. His labors were blessed. A few were awakened before he went away. As the church began to awake and arise, so sinners were awakened. Soon one or two were hopefully converted. In a few weeks many were awakened. The first week in August was memorable. Thirteen were the hopeful trophies of victorious grace. Since that time we have had hopeful conversions every week till the last. Many are yet serious—some lingering—some, I fear, turning back—and some making progress. Between fifty and sixty are rejoicing in hope. In one family there are six hopeful converts; in another, three; another, four; another, four; another, nine, &c. Hitherto the attention has been chiefly in three sections, and in a small number of families, compared with the whole. The work is less powerful in some parts, but is extending to others. We have been harrassed by the devil. He has roared like a lion, hissed like a serpent, spread terror and dismay like an infernal fiend, and transformed himself into an angel of light. Pray for us; you know the anxieties and trials of a revival.

Believe me to be yours most affectionately,

ELISHA YALE."

After Dr. Yale was disabled by paralysis, in the spring of 1851, he sent to his people a number of short communications, which were rendered interesting from the cirumstances under which they were written, and the spirit which they breathed. Two or three of those communications will here be given:

March 30th, Lord's Day, 1851.

"THE PASTOR TO THE PEOPLE.—Unite with me in thanking our Heavenly Father, in so far answering your prayers, that I enjoy peace, great peace, and sometimes perfect peace. Still continue to pray that God would make me willing to be just what he would have me to be; and, especially, that he would fill me with his Spirit, and cause all the graces of the Spirit to abound; namely, 'love, joy, peace, long-suffering, gentleness, goodness, faith, meekness, temperance,' and that he would grant me the passive graces also, namely, submission and cordial resignation, so that I may, as the apostle James, says, 'Count it all joy when I fall into divers temptations;' and with the apostle Paul, 'We glory in tribulation also, knowing that tribulation worketh patience; and patience, experience; and experience, hope; and hope maketh not ashamed, because the love of God is shed abroad in our hearts by the Holy Ghost, which is given unto us.'

"In regard to the wants of the people, I have only to repeat what I requested you to pray for, and that you confidently expect that our Heavenly Father will grant our request: because his all-sufficiency is infinite, his love unbounded, and his truth immutable. His word can not fail any more than he can cease to be God. And he says, 'Open thy mouth wide, and I will fill it.'

"In answer to your kind inquiry about the shattered earthern pitcher, it may be enough to say, 'Ye see how large a letter I have written with my own hand.'

"ELISHA YALE."

"*April* 27, 1851.

"THE PASTOR TO THE PEOPLE.—Thanks to you for an interest in your prayers. Thanks, above all, to him who gives a spirit of prayer and the answer. Continue to pray without ceasing, for the same blessings referred to in the first communication, namely, for a pastor after God's own heart—for the peace, purity, and prosperity of the church—for decision of all true converts to God—for the destruction of all vain hopes—for the universal practice of family religion—for the conversion of impenitent sinners, of all sorts and ages—and for me, that God would make me willing to be just what he would have me to be.

ELISHA YALE, Pastor."

At the communion season observed by the church on the first sabbath in May, there seem to have been some additions to the number of the communicants; and on that occasion a communication was directed particularly to the newly received members. It is as follows:

May 4, 1851.

"A few words from the pastor to those who have now been received into the church.

"BELOVED.—We bid you welcome to our Father's household. Welcome to the provisions of his table. Welcome to all the privileges of his house. You have now witnessed a good confession of faith. *Abide in the truth.* You have entered into an everlasting covenant with God and his people. Be faithful to the *vows* of your covenant. Expect your fellow-members to be faithful to theirs. Be sure that *God* is faithful, and will fulfill all his promises. You have entered into a city that is set on a hill, which can not be hid. All eyes are upon you. 'Let your light so shine before men, that they may see your good works, and glorify your Father which is in heaven.' Abound in 'the fruits of the Spirit, which are *love, joy, peace, long-suffering, gentleness, goodness, faith, meekness, temperance.*' Be not content to bring forth thirty-fold, or sixty-fold, but aim at a *hundred.* Remember the saying of our Lord Jesus, 'Herein is my Father glorified, that ye bear *much fruit*, so shall ye be my disciples.' Be *vigilant*, be *sober;* for your warfare is not with flesh and blood, but with principalities and powers. 'Take unto you the whole armor of God, that ye may be able to stand in the evil day. Praying always with all prayer and supplication in the Spirit, and watching thereunto with all perseverance and supplication for all saints.'

"For your direction and encouragement in prayer, lay up in your hearts what Christ taught his disciples in the eleventh chapter of Luke, the thirteenth verse. We commend you to God and to the word of his grace, which is able to save your souls. Finally, to you and the whole church, we say, '*be of good comfort, be of one mind, live in peace, and the God of peace and comfort shall be with you. Amen.*'"

CHAPTER XVI.

INTERESTING INCIDENTS.

The ear of Dr. Yale was always open to hear whatever might serve to magnify the grace of God, or to illustrate the spirit and power of the Christian religion, or to show the depravity and wickedness of the human heart. Some such things found a place in his memorandum, a portion of which occurred under his own observation and in connection with his pastoral labors; and a portion he received from friends, and recorded for his own benefit and the benefit of others. A record of some of these incidents may be useful as illustrating the operations of divine grace in the salvation of men, while they also illustrate the character of him by whom the memorial was originally preserved.

For this purpose the following extracts have been made from his memorandum:

1803, July 7. "A brief account of persons under serious impressions, who have wished for particular conversation.

Mrs. B. was the first. She was deeply affected with a sense of her guilt and danger; felt a very great burden; but after about a week felt it in some measure removed. Here she obtained a little glimpse of hope. But being in a very doubtful state, complained bitterly of the stubbornness of her heart. She thought she had been convinced, but was about to be left to stupidity and hardness of heart. This continued some time, till through much bodily weakness and temptation of Satan, she was driven to total despair; in which state she remains at this day. She thinks that misery eternal is her portion.

Capt. I. was made thoughtful a short time afterwards. He was afraid that it was with him too late, as he had passed his fiftieth year. In this state he continued some time, seriously inquiring. He now hopes with great fear and trembling.

Mrs. H., who had been a professor many years, was brought to serious inquiry into the grounds of her hope. She feared that she had been always wrong.

Mr. G. had at various times been serious for many years; but now saw that his work was not done. But he feared, and does still, that he never felt any true conviction. An unfeeling heart.

Miss A. G. has been brought to serious consideration, wonders at her stupidity and folly, but does not think herself impressed as she ought to be. A hard heart.

Mrs. H. thought that she had been wrong all her days; that she had much work to do, and had done nothing. A hard heart.

Mr. B. appears very much affected with a sense of his danger. He says that he knows himself to be a sinner, but that he is under no true conviction, and fears that as he has but a short time to live in the world, he shall never feel as he ought."

Aug. 2. "Conference at 3 o'clock. The meeting exhibited many serious countenances, and was indeed very solemn. Many shed tears. Mr. S., who happened to come to the house about the conclusion of the meeting, seemed to be in the greatest horror of conscience.

He acknowledges himself the greatest of sinners—and appears to be under temptation—has not been to the sanctuary for several sabbaths, through temptation. I told him there was mercy even for him, as there was for Paul; but he turned about, shed tears, stood a minute, shook his head, and went away apparently in very great anguish. He acknowledges the truths of the gospel, but says they pierce him through with the keenest horror."

1824, April 3. "At three, I visited a family, and conversed with some solemnity, and prayed with them. The pious mother told me, with tears in her eyes, that she had felt desires for a revival. An old man, the father of all in this family, seems very much changed from what he was two years ago.

He has left off the dreadful habit of drinking and is sober and diligent in business. He is reformed. Called at another neighbor's, the one mentioned as having had that dreadful sense of sin. Designed only to converse with R., but the woman after a few minutes, said: 'F.'s wife wishes to see you in the other room.' I went in. She immediately began to express her doubts and fears that she had no religion. Said that she had thought of requesting to be cast out of the church as a hypocrite. It was a solemn time, though I could not but rejoice at this concern."

THE PIOUS INDIAN WOMAN.

The following account of a pious Indian woman presents a remarkable exhibition of the power of God's grace; and for this purpose the memorial of it appears to have been preserved. He us tells that he received the narrative originally from the late Judge McMartin, of Broadalbin, than whom no informant could have been more reliable.

The record is as follows:

1820, Dec. 15. "In conversation with Judge McMartin on Wednesday evening, he related the following facts which he had himself witnessed:

'When I was residing in the town of Palatine,' said he, 'a number of years ago, I became acquainted with an Indian woman of the Stockbridge tribe, who came with several others of her tribe, and resided awhile in that town, for the purpose of making brooms and baskets. She could read, and had a copy of the New Testament which she valued above all price. When she was not reading it, she would not lay it down out of her reach, but kept it always in some part of her clothing. She was often reading it to herself when surrounded with company, and I observed that she retired frequently, but cautiously, for religious purposes; but whenever she was seen at her devotions and knew it, she ceased immediately. She was very careful to keep the sabbath holy, and would go out of the room when improper conversation was indulged; even though she was obliged to go away into a cold room, or into the fields. She could sing a number of psalms and hymns, which she did frequently with a very melodious voice, though extremely low, so as to be unnoticed, and attract as little attention as possible. I endeavored to converse with her as often as I could, but her modesty made her unwilling to say much, and what little she did say was usually so low as to be scarcely intelligible. But the following anecdote was the most remarkable thing that I ever observed in her, and gave me an exalted idea of the noble character of her mind, and the sincerity of her religion.

'She had a son who has since been employed as a missionary. This son had business in company with several chiefs of his tribe, with the legislature at Albany. On his way he passed through the town where his mother resided, and spent a day or two with a bad woman whom he had brought from home with him, and behaved in a manner very unbecoming. After his return from Albany, he visited his mother, who was then at the house where I resided. I knew that she had heard of his bad conduct, and was extremely grieved on account of it. I expected she would talk with him, and intimated to the mistress of the family that it would be desirable to leave them alone for a season, that she might discharge her duty without any embarrassment. This was done; and as I had a great desire to witness the interview, I placed myself unobserved, where I could hear the most that passed. The mother and the son being thus alone, not a word was spoken for the space of half or three-quarters of an hour. Tears, and sighs, and sobs seemed to deprive the mother of the power of utterance; and the son was kept silent by conscious guilt and filial veneration. At length the flood of her sorrows passed away, and being able to speak she said to her son: 'Hendrick, you have grieved the heart of your mother.' A pause of eight or ten minutes ensued, which would have been an awful silence, if it had not been interrupted by sobs, and sighs, and tears. Then she said: 'Hendrick, you knew better than to keep company with that bad woman.' A pause ensued as before, attended with bitter weeping. Having recovered herself again, she said: 'Hendrick, you will bring down the gray hairs of your mother with sorrow to the grave.' At hearing these words, Hendrick burst into tears, and mingled his sighs with those of his mother. After a little time he recovered from the burst of passion, and said: 'Mother, can you forgive me?' She replied: 'Hendrick, it is easy for me to forgive you, but you must be forgiven of one greater than I.' After a short pause she added: 'Hendrick, will you promise not to go back with that bad woman?' He paused for a time, but at length said: 'Mother, I will not go back with her.' 'Hendrick, I forgive you,' she added, 'you have healed the heart of your mother.' "

INCIDENTS IN CONNECTICUT.

In the year 1821, there was a very interesting revival of religion in several towns in the state of Connecticut. In the spring of that year, Dr. Yale paid a visit to some of his friends there, at their earnest solicitation, and spent several days engaged in active ministerial labors, and efforts to advance the cause. His diary contains a record of several interesting cases which occurred in connection with that revival, by the perusal of which it is believed that the reader may be both interested and profited.

1821, May 23. "Some remarkable cases have been mentioned to me which show the power and grace of God. A young man belonging to a pious family, whose father and mother and sister belonged to the household of faith, had been thoughtful at times for years, but more especially during last autumn and winter. Though the marked seriousness of his countenance had attracted the notice of others, he did not intend to reveal the feelings of his heart. At an evening meeting early in March, his whole attention was arrested, and he returned home with a burden too heavy to bear. His father, and mother, and sister were present, but he did not at once reveal his feelings, though his distress was such that he supposed that they must know it.

He walked the room several times with both hands clasped round his breast, and bending forward as if ready to fall to the earth. He cried out: 'Oh, my dear parents, my sister, do you not care if I perish? I am going directly into hell. I shall be there before morning. Do pray for me. I want every one of you to pray for me alone.' He shook each of them by the hand, and bid them farewell as for the last time, and retired with a candle to his own room, expecting soon to perish beyond the reach of mercy. It was a sleepless house, and a night long to be remembered. Every one was crying for help to him who only doeth wonders. He that heareth prayer gave ear to his people's supplications. The young man read, and reflected, and cried to God who was angry with him, to have mercy upon him. About midnight he obtained relief, and went out to call his friends to rejoice with him, and praise God for this great deliverance. In the morning he told his minister what great things the Lord had done for him, and went from house to house, through that day, and day after day, warning his companions, and beseeching them to flee from the wrath to come.

A man of middle age who had been very careless

and inattentive to public worship, was offended greatly at the doctrine of election. He conversed one day with a particular friend of his on that doctrine. Both agreed in condemning it. Not long after his convictions returned with greater force and frequency; and he was convinced of the truth of that doctrine. He determined the same day to see his friend and endeavor to convince him of the error he was in, by telling him his own convictions. His friend, in the meantime, had been brought down, and had submitted at the feet of Jesus, without his knowledge. He went to a religious meeting at the north part of the town, where his friend resided, and there became distressed beyond measure. At the close, he went across the way to his friend's house, which he reached in extreme agony, and threw himself into his friend's arms exclaiming: 'Oh, do pray for me. I fear my case is hopeless, and I am lost for ever.' His friend told him he was glad to see him in that condition, and urged him to submit to God and give up himself to his disposal. This he was shortly enabled to do, and began to rejoice in the hope of the glory of God.

An infidel who had treated all religion with contempt, was addressed by his minister with just a word as he passed him to visit some pious friends in the house. The minister thought no more of it, but it went to the heart of the infidel. The next morning he applied to one of the deacons, with the solemn and interesting inquiry of the jailor: 'What must I do?' He was told as the jailor had been long before. He is now very different from what he was, and gives good evidence of having passed from death unto life."

THE INTEMPERATE PROFESSOR.

I will further mention a few interesting incidents which occurred in his own field of labor, and among the people of his pastoral charge. One was the case of an intemperate professor of religion, who, in prospect of an exchange of worlds, was filled with the deepest anguish.

1827, Dec. 8. "I called to see a neighbor, a professor

for many years, though not of this church, an intemperate man but of strong mind, and naturally of good sense, who was sick of dropsy in the chest, not long to live; but without hope, and on the borders of eternal despair. He desired me to read the 14th chapter of Ezekiel, as applicable to him. 'He that setteth up his idols in his heart, and putteth the stumbling block of his iniquity before his face, and cometh to inquire of a prophet, I will answer that man by myself. I will cut him off, and he shall be a sign,' &c. He wished to know whether there could be any mercy for such an one? I told him that our business is to repent, and believe the gospel, and be sure of mercy to such, and to no others. He dwelt also on Proverbs i, 24: 'Because I have called,' &c. 'I call unto him now, but he does not hear me, even as he called upon me and I did not hear. I have often gone to that meeting house with my idol set up in my heart. Now I am afraid the Lord will cut me off, and make me a sign. After I am dead they will say: That man is a sign, because he set up his idol in his heart,' &c.

Surely this is a fearful case. He seems to me like one of the foolish virgins: 'Give us of your oil for our lamps have gone out.'

THE TEMPTED PROFESSOR.

A certain member of the church was exceedingly depressed in her feelings on account of not having had those manifestations of the divine favor at the communion table, which she desired.

1822, Nov. 1. "Conversed with Mrs. L., who lately united with the church. In trouble. On the day of her reception she set up this mark, that if she should have the manifestations of divine grace, she was a Christian; if not she was a hypocrite. She had nothing. I asked her if that was laid down in the Bible as a mark of divine grace.

Nov. 19. Visited Mrs. L., who is in a state of temptation. I gave her notice before, and desired her to give me an account of her state. Before she offered herself to be examined, she had doubts of her state, and hesitated whether she ought not to wait until she had become more established. Some of her relatives advised her to go forward, if she could, lest she should hinder others. Her daughter offered herself, and finally she and her husband ventured. Still she was doubtful whether she should actually unite with the church. She feared, on the one hand, that she should be fatally deluded if she did unite; and on the other, that she might be the means of harm, or neglect her duty, if she did not. She had heard people tell of great light and comfort in that ordinance, and she concluded that if she was a Christian, she should have special manifestations of divine light and love at the Lord's table. She went forward. But while she was standing in the broad aisle, and attending to the confession, &c., it seemed to come to her mind, 'You are Judas.' This harrassed her grievously all day. She had no comfort at the table. Down, therefore, she fell, for she had not the sign of a true Christian.

She looked back to past times. She remembered the morning after she obtained hope, and how the thought then came to her: 'Now, if you are a Christian, you will have to pray as long as you live;' and how heavy and burdensome it appeared then. Then it was suggested: 'Now these things together prove that you were deceived like Judas.' Being very offensive in the sight of God, she thought she would not pray. The Bible was all against her. She could not bear to read it. At intervals she had some little light and comfort for a moment, but it would not stay. Often did she lament because she could not be put back where she was before she united with the church, and before she obtained a hope. But even then she knew not what else to do than she had done. This thought sometimes distressed her: 'Why did not God keep me from committing these sins?' Then she would think how much more happy others were, while she was full of trouble."

Young people are fond of mirth and amusement, and even Christian professors often take liberties in such matters which ill-become the disciples of Christ. Nor is it uncommon for them to justify themselves in so doing. It is therefore pleasant to see such conscientious scruples in young profesosrs, and such an operation of Christian principle, as appears in the following:

1831, March 5. "N. C., a young member received at our last communion, called in distress, on account of having gone to a sleigh-ride, in company of many other young people, both professors and others. Her views were very correct. She said she could not get near to God, that she felt she had sinned in not doing all in her power, that she feared others would think religion of little worth, that she could not speak to them with confidence, that she could not address her sabbath scholars as she should. She wished to know what she should do. I told her to confess to her Savior, and to individuals, as she had opportunity, and to state her views and feelings to her companions."

CHAPTER XVII.

HIS REGARD FOR THE SABBATH.

Dr. Yale was one of those who believe that "the sabbath was made for man." He regarded it as a most imperative duty resting upon all men, to sanctify the sabbath by a holy resting all that day, even from such worldly employments and recreations as are lawful on other days; and spending the whole time in the public and private exercise of God's worship, except so much as is to be taken up in the works of necessity and mercy."

There was no truth of which he had a deeper conviction, than that man most directly and certainly advances his own well-being by a proper observance of God's holy day. He was taught to respect the sabbath from his earliest youth; and though he afterwards deeply lamented that he did not properly sanctify it in the days of his youthful folly, and that he did sometimes indulge in things of which he was afterwards sincerely ashamed; yet he seems even from the days of his childhood to have imbibed the sentiment which he ever after cherished as one of the main pillars of Christian faith, that the observance of the sabbath is both intimately connected with our success in the ordinary business of life, and most essential for the promotion of the interests of the church and the salvation of men.

A conscious defect as to its observance in his own case, even though it were only in thought, or in the lack of that spiritual frame of mind which he desired, was ever to himself a cause of extreme regret, and the want of success in the business of the week, he sometimes attributed to his not having properly sanctified the sabbath. Let me here again give some extracts from his journal.

1828, May 3. "It has been this week much as I expected it would be, from my manner of spending the last sabbath. Truly it is the greatest folly as well as sin to spend the sabbath in vanity and spiritual inactivity. It injures the whole week. I have been so much occupied as hardly to find time to pray. Very much dissipated in thought. What need have I to watch and pray!"

It was this principle which he endeavored to carry out in his own practice, and which he also earnestly inculcated on his people. He was always deeply distressed at the desecration of the sabbath by others, and there was a time when this gave him, perhaps, more trouble in the church than any thing else. The business in which a portion of the members were engaged, called them frequently away from home; and some of them, in those days, thought themselves justified in prosecuting their journeys on the Lord's day. At least the temptation was so strong that it was not always resisted. Against this sin did Dr. Yale set his face as a flint; and members who had been guilty of such a course of conduct, upon the fact becoming known, were sure to be called to account; until at length this form of sin, as far as repsects the members of that church, ceased to exist. His views and feelings in this matter may be learned from what follows:

1822, Jan. 19, *Saturday morning*. "Awaked in distress on account of our situation. Know not what to do. Am resolved on one thing—to do all I can to save the sabbath. We are not prepared for the Lord's supper. I do not like to put it off. I fear I shall not be able to know what to do, and shall have occasion to meet the people like Ezra, when many had married strange wives.

Evening.—I have preached a sacramental lecture on these words: 'Confess your faults one to another, and pray one for another, that ye may be healed. After service I desired the church to stay. I stated my trials about the sacrament on account of the violations of the sabbath. I did not specify particular cases, but mentioned that there were many, that they were various—that I had been enumerating several different pleas—that I could not say that it would be expedient to receive any public confession—that I wished that subject at present to be kept out of sight and that we should attend to our duty. After I had done, one young woman came to me, and desired to know if I referred to her in any thing that I had said. She was much agitated and excused herself; but I did not know that she was guilty. I told her, however, that if I thought she was guilty, I should speak to her about it. I have been troubled some since I came home lest my measures should not be found prudent. But I am satisfied that the cause is good, and that religion must stand or fall with it. I expect to see the effect of it to-morrow. I expect several will keep away from the table, perhaps even from the house of God. But I have said that I would die for the sabbath, or live with it. Here, oh Lord, I am at thy disposal. Oh, strengthen me. I stand with thee, and thy law, and thy word. Oh, direct me, that I may conduct just as I ought to conduct. I feel that I have Ezra's work in some measure. May I have his spirit, and his helpers. Remember me, oh, my God, for good.' This is a conflict, and 'in the Lord only have I righteousness and strength.'

Review and Reflections.—This has been a painful week. Had it brought me near to God, it had been salutary. It appears that God has taken me at my word, and is emptying me in earnest. Amen. Only let me be filled with his grace. This is all I need after being emptied, and that is the design of being emptied."

Sabbath morning, July 20. "The subject of the sabbath occupies my mind, and I have thought of this resolution, as suitable for every Christian and the whole church; viz:

Resolved to abstain from traveling and other exercises, both of speech and action, which are of a nature to prevent the spiritual use of the sabbath; and to adopt this rule, viz: In time of temptation not to inquire whether we *may be indulged* in doing this or that, but whether God *requires* us to do it, and to regulate ourselves according to the deliberate and prayerful decision of the question in the light of God's word and the prospects of eternity."

March 16. "Went to church meeting at 2 o'clock, with a heavy heart, not knowing what would be the result. Had seen no other of the brethren. Had not prayed as I ought. Many came. The meeting was solemn and interesting. God was there and melted every heart. All were agreed. God has preserved and honored the sabbath. To him be all the glory. Amen."

March 17. "Very much fatigued, and went to bed early last night, and rested well. Thankful every time I awaked for the goodness of God yesterday. My heart is comforted amidst my labors."

1828, Feb. 18, Monday. "In the forenoon a man called, who came from Milton, sabbath morning. Came to Fonda's Bush and attended church, and then came here after meeting. I set before him the evil of such conduct, and gave him a tract on sabbath occupations, the same that I gave to the teamster yesterday."

The extracts which follow may serve to give us some idea of his own conscientiousness in respect to sabbath consecration:

1824, Nov. 7. "This afternoon I have preached on sanctifying the Lord's day, especially in thought. I endeavored to show what thoughts were wrong, and the best means to prevent them. Conscience is the point at which I aimed. I reached my own in some measure. I feel very guilty of worldly thoughts on the sabbath. I feel as though I had long provoked God, and injured my own soul, and the souls of others. My sabbaths for a long time have not been as they were once. Now I set myself to seek the grace of God in this respect, and to use every exertion to sanctify the Lord's day, in that *little world* which is within me. May the Lord afford me help. I do now solemnly brand worldly thoughts on the sabbath as *sinful.* Lord, help me to banish them. Amen."

Nov. 29. "Yesterday after meeting I could not pray. In the night could not sleep well. Examined and found I had not kept the sabbath as I ought. Having received two letters I read them both, though knowing the import of one, I needed not to read it, and the thoughts of the other should have been put away. Thus I sinned, and God hid his face from me. I endeavored to humble myself this morning, and seek pradon."

Among his papers has been found one which, in his own peculiar style, presents his estimate of the advantages of a proper observance of the sabbath; and I feel sure that the reader will be pleased to have his thoughts on this subject, clothed with his language. This paper is as follows:

THE BEST MARKET DAY.

This is the day in which we can gain the best things in the greatest abundance. No doubt of this. Suppose that on one day of the week, and one only, gold, precious jewels, the best provisions, the most desirable raiment, and other most important articles could be found in the market, and in the greatest abundance; would not that be the best market day? Up early then and away to the market. Take with you all the means which you can command, and vessels in abundance to bring home your gain. Be earnest to find the best stalls, and to obtain the best articles. Be diligent to improve every moment and secure the best opportunities, and continue as long as the day lasts, or while the market is open. And when you return home be careful and watchful that nothing be lost or stolen.

This day is the sabbath. On this day God keeps open a market. At his house treasures abound, altogether the richest and the best. During the whole twenty-four hours, may we come to seek supplies; but about four hours in the middle of the time is most favorable. Then he keeps open house, where all may come and buy freely, without money and without price. His servants are there and all things are ready and in order. He invites, 'Ho, every one that thirsteth, come ye to the waters; and he that hath no money, come ye, buy and eat; yea, come, buy wine and milk, without money and without price" Isa. lv, 1.

But without a figure. The sabbath is the day to be improved above all others for the special purposes for which it was designed. It is set apart from other days. God drew around it a guard, saying, this within is holy ground. Rest here from ordinary pursuits. Tread not upon this spot with unholy feet. It is sanctified. A peculiar blessing rests upon it. On this day commune with God, and with one another, on the greatest and best things. When Israel came out of Egypt, God added new reasons, even his wonders in delivering them from bondage. When the Lord Jesus rose from the dead God changed the day from the seventh to the first, for the purpose of celebrating that great event, and adding new themes of thought, gratitude and praise. And now, in the ends of the world, he tells us there is a rest, a sabbatism, which remains for the people of God. So that, while creation calls us to contemplate God's wonders as the first, and providence as the second, and redemption as the third, the future glory of heaven completes and closes the whole. Thus does the sabbath afford us time and opportunity for the highest mental improvement and enjoyment. The common affairs of life, labors for the things that perish, are laid aside. The usual opportunities and means of improving the mind in useful knowledge, in literature and science aer laid aside also. And the attention and time are wholly devoted to know God and Jesus Christ whom he hath sent. In these sacred studies God opens the book of creation, and we may read in the heavens and the earth. He opens the book of providence, every day's work of which presents additional views of his wisdom, power and love. He opens the book of revelation, in which he throws light on parts of his other books which are obscure, and opens new views of himself, of which in his book of creation there is not the slightest trace, not a line or a letter.

The book of experience, also, lies open to our inspection, in which we may read of the dealings of God with us, and of the influences of our fellows upon us, either for good or for evil. Besides these books, which are open on this day especially, as we have special time and opportunity, God sends his servants, specially qualified and commissioned to assist us in our endeavors to become wise unto salvation. In the midst of his redeemed from among men, his chosen, his friends, we may appear, to attend upon the instructions of his servants, and unite with them in celebrating his praise, calling upon his name for all we need, studying his holy oracles, and laying up in heaven durable riches and righteousness.

Is not this, then, the best market day? On what other can we find so much of equal value, or so many means, opportunities and helps to attain it? Do we not also observe that they who do not improve the sabbath remain destitute of these purest, best, richest treasures? Other things they may have. But of these they remain destitute. And when they come to leave the world, they are wretched and miserable, and poor and blind, and naked. Many times they know it; but if not, it is a reality. Let nothing, therefore, hinder the improvement of God's holy day for the attainment of its legitimate objects—the treasures of heaven and preparation for their enjoyment. Proposals may be made to you from the thoughtless, the idle, the vicious; your friends, your neighbors, your enemies; pretended religionists, or the despiser of all sacred things, but regard them not. Tell them as Nehemiah, 'I am doing a great work so that I can not come down. Why should the work cease, while I leave it, and come down to you?'

SABBATH OCCUPATIONS.

"It is impossible to keep the sabbath well without suitable means of improving it. Among these we may notice the following:

1. Public worship, including its accompaniments.
2. Secret worship, including its accompaniments.
3. Family worship, including its accompaniments.
4. Reading—the most holy books—first of all the Bible.
5. Meditations—including the putting them upon paper.
6. Conversation—most holy, heavenly.
7. Teaching and learning. It is the duty of some to engage in teaching divine things on the sabbath—of others to engage in learning.
8. Exercise—such as duty requires in the care of domestic animals, children, &c. Such as may be necessary to take us to the house of God, or any place where we can give or obtain instruction.
9. Making collections for the poor, I Cor. xvi, 1, 2.

'Welcome sweet day of rest,
That saw the Lord arise;
Welcome to this reviving breast,
And these rejoicing eyes.'

'Is there not a cause?' said David to his elder brother. David had just come to the army. He had seen and heard the giant. He had felt a noble indignation that no Israelite had gone to meet him. He was inquiring what should be done for the man that killed him. He had said, 'Let no man's heart faint because of him. I will go against him.' His brother Eliab, stung with the reproach cast upon him, though not intentionally, but necessarily, by the words of the stripling, said, 'With whom hast thou left those few sheep?' &c. David modestly and meekly replied, 'Is there not a cause?' As though he had said, Did not my father send me? &c. Is there not a cause why I am here?

So may the lover of the sabbath ask, Is there not a cause for saying, 'Welcome sweet day of rest?' Do you not go forth and take pains to meet a distinguished man who appears in your region, your town, or city? We say, 'The king himself comes near'—even Jesus, the King of kings, and the Lord of lords. Is there not a cause for saying, 'Welcome?' Do you not think much of a day of feasting, of the good food, the pleasant associations, the pleasant and profitable discourse? Our King himself comes near. Nor does he come empty. But he comes, 'To feast his saints.'

'Then may we sit and see him here,
And love, and praise and pray.'

Is there not a cause? You delight in your company, feasting, converse. We in ours. 'Welcome sweet day of rest' Again we say, 'Welcome.'"

CHAPTER XVIII.

HIS GREAT INDUSTRY.

As Dr. Yale had a specific end for which he lived, he was very laborious in his efforts to attain that end. He did not enter the ministry because he regarded it as a life of ease, nor did he ever feel a disposition to wrap himself up in his mantle and spend his days in idleness. His purpose was to fill up every day and every hour—first in the closet, then in the study and the prayer meeting, and the Bible class, and the conference room, and the family, and the public assembly; always doing something with the design of advancing the great end for which he lived. He was truly in labors abundant. To illustrate this position is the design of the present chapter—and it will be done altogether by extracts from his memorandum and his correspondence. I will first transcribe the record of the labors of a single day, and then of a week, and of a month successively."

1830, June 3. "At 8 o'clock I set out to visit the north-west district. I visited twelve families, rode about twelve miles, lectured at four after catechising a number of children at a school, attended a Bible class in the evening at another school-house, and returned home about half-past nine."

1816, Dec. 21. "Rode sixteen miles and preached at the funeral of a child. Returned home at evening. If the value of my services were to be reckoned according to the *quantity*, my time this week would not be considered useless. I have traveled a hundred miles, preached six times besides the sabbath, in as many different places, made ten family visits, written several letters, and revised a sermon for the press. But I feel as though I had robbed my own people to supply the destitute in this region of desolation. Greatly are ministers needed in this region."

1824, Feb. 2. "Returned home and attended the monthly concert in the evening. Very cold and unpleasant, so that only a few attended. Thus have I finished the work of seven days, in which I have rode a hundred and ten miles, preached six sermons, attended one funeral, two prayer meetings, distributed six Bibles, and a number of tracts, and had intercourse with about twenty families. I have to lament my want of a spirit of prayer and nearness to God. I sometimes fear that all is vain for want of that holy intercourse with God, which is the life of all religion and action."

1822, April 27. "During the week I have done a considerable part of that work which has been long on hand, viz. reviewing and arranging church records. I have visited twenty-seven families, and written two sermons, and attended a church conference, besides the conference of young people. How rapidly my time rolls away! How soon will all be over, and the business of eternity commenced!"

1828, March 1. "This week I have preached six sermons; on the sabbath, three; on Tuesday evening, one; on Thursday, one; to-day, one. Have attended ministers' meeting, Bible Society, a fast, a church meeting, two Bible classes, and rode twenty-four miles. O that God would bless my labors and crown them with success."

Review of a month:

1829, March 31. "Have administered the Lord's Supper once, admitted two young men to communion, baptised five children, preached seventeen sermons, visited sixty families, wrote four sermons in full, obtained ninety-two dollars in subscription for domestic missions, attended three prayer meetings, including concert, eight Bible classes, two funerals, two weddings, visited four schools, heard one sermon, rode about a hundred miles, attended a ministers' meeting and two meetings to promote the interests of the Bible Society, and received many visits. This makes a show, but O what reason have I to be humbled and to lament my want of grace, humility, love, piety, faith. I have spent much time with my people, and some of it profitably; some, I fear, unprofitably. I see no revival. Lord, help or we perish."

Dr. Yale performed a vast amount of labor among his people by way of pastoral visitations; sometimes by himself alone, and sometimes in company with some one of the members of the church. Of this, such like notices as the following are found in his journal:

1828, March 3. "The visiting committee met, and agreed to go with me; one on Wednesday, and the other on Thursday."

March 5. "Early in the morning, with brother M., I started to visit one section. We visited ten families. In the evening attended Bible class at Capt. Jones's. A good number, more than ever before, present. Very weary, but much encouraged to think my plan can be carried into effect."

March 6. Early, brother M. and I rode to the North West Corner, six miles, and during the day visited fourteen families. In the evening attended Bible Class at Mr. L's. Very much encouraged to-day, though weary, to think my plan can be effected. If twenty-four families can be visited in two days, a hundred and twenty may be in ten, especially as we have visited some of the most distant. But, O, what a deplorable condition are many poor parents and children in! The Lord be pleased to show us what to do for them, and especially for their poor children."

March 11. Went out early and visited twenty-three families in one district. Only five members of our church in those families. Only two families where prayer is regularly offered. Only four families that attend any church with any tolerable regularity. Four habitual drunkards, and several other hard drinkers. Found one little bit of Tom Paine's toe-nail—vile trash, in a poor wretch. The number of children is not very large, as most of the families are young. O Lord, my eyes are unto thee, for I know not what to do."

March 13. "Spent the day in visiting about eighteen families. Found much more encouragement than in any other neighborhood. Think some will be got out to church without much difficulty, and that several sabbath school scholars will be added to our classes. Felt fully convinced of the necessity, propriety and utility of my work, though very laborious. I am now about half done, having visited about seventy-five families. I think I shall finish next week, by divine help. May the Lord prosper this work."

March 15. "During this week I have in three days visited forty-eight families. Thus, by the divine blessing my work can be done. O may I be directed as to what I shall do next."

There were times when Dr. Yale felt exceedingly pressed with the multiplicity of his engagements, and the amount of business which demanded his attention. A single example:

1823, Oct. 9. "In my feeble state of health my duties and cares press upon me; but I try sometimes to cast my burdens on the Lord. I have great and difficult business on hand. Care of my soul—care of my family—care of students—care of my church and people—defence of the gospel against error—irregularities of a member—Bible Society—Tract Society—Domestic Missions. I have to solicit subscriptions for the last, at home and in Charlton; also at home for the Bible Society—I have to converse with many, and defend the gospel—I have to preach soon on a sacramental occasion—I am appointed to preach an ordination sermon in Albany. O Lord, give me strength, wisdom, grace, humility. How different is it with me now from what it was ten years ago! Then I desired more business. Now I am burdened with it. O may I rest on God, and do all I can."

If any should be disposed to inquire how he was able to accomplish so much, it is doubtless to be found in the fact, that while he reduced every thing to a system, he took care to improve all his tim e to the best advantage Yet it is true that in the midst of all his industry, and when laboring to the utmost of his abilities, he frequently regarded himself as doing but little, and deeply bewailed his own remissness. We may see this in two or three sentences in a letter to a friend:

"I plod along, doing a little and a little, and hoping to do more. But I shall be in my grave long before I have done my duty. It is often a great grief to me that I do so little, and see so little done by my means. Sometimes I murmur at God, and sometimes I loathe and abhor myself. But one thing comforts me in some of my lucid moments—that this good cause will live, and flourish and triumph, when I am dead. Glorious truth,

I am confident that you rejoice in this, in regard to yourself; and may not you, and I, and our brethren truly rejoice, that we shall rest from our labors, and see our avior raise up wiser, better, holier men, to gain 'the crown of all the earth.'"

The sense which he cherished of his own remissness, is expressed in the following paragraph from his diary:

1830, Nov. 7. "Felt this morning an increase of guilt for neglecting time and opportunity. Oh, how much good might I have done, had I improved every time and every opportunity, even the least! I confessed my sin, and entreated forgiveness. *Now by the help of God, I will improve time and opportunity, even the least.* This is my duty. Let grace enable me to keep it always in mind."

This last resolution is, in fact, only expressive of the principle on which he had been accustomed to act heretofore; and from the following extracts we may see the perfect system to which he had every thing reduced:

1821, Aug. 8, Wednesday morning. "'Gird up the loins of your mind,' I Peter, i, 13. These words came to me as soon as I awaked. I felt that I had let the reins loose for a long time, as to rising, as to devotion, as to the management of my time and my business, and my intercourse with my fellow men. I felt the need of immediate reformation. I arose, and reflected, and resolved and prayed. For I know these must be joined together. Rise at 5 o'clock, or before, uniformly. Half an hour in reading, meditation and prayer. Half an hour for breakfast and family worship. Four hours in study, composing sermons or attending to some other study of importance. All the time lost from this to be carefully regained the first opportunity. One hour for attention to domestic concerns. One half hour to reading the word of God, meditation and prayer. One hour in hearing recitations. One half hour in dining.

At one the afternoon begins. Monday, Tuesday, Wednesday, three hours among my people, or otherwise engaged in company. Half-past four, recitation, one hour. Sup at half-past five, half an hour. At six, the evening begins. Three hours among my people instead of three in the afternoon. This to make up the time. Otherwise read. At 9 o'clock family worship, close with half an hour's private devotion, including a review of the day.

Thursday afternoon devoted to visiting and religious conference or prayer, or lecture. The evening may be substituted. Hear no recitations on Thursday unless I go out in the evening, or have failed on some other day.

Friday afternoon, receive such visits as my people may see fit to make me. Evening, to singing, and hearing my students' composition or speaking, when not engaged in company.

Saturday afternoon to conversing with serious persons, or serious Christians, or making up deficiencies in the business of the week. Evening to meditation and prayer —preparation for the Sabbath—general review."

In all his arrangements, Dr. Yale was particularly systematic, though the order of his arrangements was not always the same. An arrangement somewhat different from the above appears in the following:

June 15, 1826. This being my birth day, I thought it needful to set it apart for special prayer, with a view to seek wisdom and grace for myself and my people; more especially to digest a plan of operations which may tend more systematically and effectually to secure the great ends of the ministry. Renewed my covenant with God.

Resolved, To spend one hour in the morning and one in the evening, every day in reading the more devotional parts of the word of God, in prayer, meditation and contemplation, and the reading of such books as are of a devotional character, and suited to promote personal piety. The hour in the morning to commence ordinarily at 5 o'clock, and the hour in the evening at sun-set. When this can not be done, some other hour in each division of the day to be secured.

Resolved, To spend one hour each day in suitable attention to domestic concerns that every thing may have a due and seasonable share of attention; the hour to be ordinarily the next after family worship in the morning. When that is not practicable, some other hour, and when need requires on some special occasions, there may be more time at once, but as rarely as possible in the morning.

Resolved, To spend one hour each day in preparation for the pulpit; that hour to commence ordinarily at 9 o'clock in the morning. To be made up in case of failure, in the use of the first unappropriated hour.

Resolved, To spend one honr each day in the study of theology systematically, reading, writing, &c., that hour ordinarily to commence at ten in the morning.

Resolved, To spend an hour each day in the cultivation of general literature and the improvement of the mind generally; that hour ordinarily to commence at eleven in the morning.

Resolved, To spend one hour each day in visiting my people, on religious subjects exclusively; that hour to commence at 2 o'clock P. M. But when more convenient, two or three hours consecutively may be thus employed. This one hour to be exclusive of all other intercourse, and as spiritual as possible.

Seven hours each day are stated, and the business assigned to each is to be considered as the order of the day, viz:

Two hours for devotion—one hour for domestic concerns—one for preparation for the pulpit—one for the study of sytematic theology — one for the cultivation of general literature—one for religious visits.

Nor were these empty resolutions, made to be lost sight of as soon as they were made. His aim was to carry them out to the very letter, though in some instances he found this to be attended with great difficulty. Yet whenever he failed he was accustomed to notice the failure with great particularity. Such failures are noticed in the following:

1826, June 25. "On Monday I finished the report of the Bible Society and attended to the order of the day in all things except evening prayer. Tuesday attended to business, but not to the order of the day except evening prayer. I did not neglect all devotional exercises on Monday evening and Tuesday morning, but could find no opportunity for the usual exercise in full. Wednesday and Thursday very diligent and recovered all."

Sabbath morning, July 2. "The week past was very much like the last sabbath. I did not prosper in any thing. That sabbath's influence ran through all the week. Monday, Tuesday and Wednesday occupied with company, and I found it extremely difficult to attend to the appropriate business of every hour. My deficiencies are not made up, though I tried hard on Friday and Saturday. My work is up and two weeks yet in advance. But my devotions except in the morning, are behind for three seasons, and my visits for five, and my study of theology and general literature for two each. It is hard struggling indeed. Oh, how much do I need the grace of our Lord Jesus Christ!"

While Dr. Yale was always glad to see his friends, and while he was ever ready to attend to the calls of such as had business of importance to transact, with his peculiarly industrious habits, it is not to be wondered at that he was sometimes greatly tried at those interruptions which he was compelled, occasionally at least, to meet.

This is well expressed in the extracts which follow:

1830, Dec. 17. "Near 12 o'clock, M. J., a minister who is going about from place to place, with little to do, called on me. He seems to be a good man, and is said to preach well; but he is somewhat wild. I felt tried at the interruption, but thought of Mr. Newton's saying, 'No man knocks at my door but I think God sent him. Another, 'The man who wants to see me, is the man whom I want to see.'"

1831, Jan. 6. "It seems as though I should never do any more business in the way of study. But I must remember that, 'The man who wants to see me is the man whom I want to see.' And 'when a man knocks at my door, let me think that God sent him.' Oh, let me live and breathe pure the air of heaven."

CHAPTER XIX.

HIS DOMESTIC HABITS.

If we would understand a man's real character we must look at him at home. When one goes abroad, he may be expected to change his apparel. We are to look at him in his every day clothes, if we would know what he is. At home a man acts under less restraint, and it is there that his heart is turned inside out. Men have often seen Dr. Yale in the pulpit, in the prayer meeting, in the Bible class, in the meetings of ecclesiastical bodies; have watched his movements while engaged in efforts to promote the institutions of benevolence; and have regarded his example as preeminently worthy of imitation. But let us stop awhile at his dwelling—look at him in the social circle, in his intercourse with his family, in his management of his secular affairs, and in the discharge of the varied duties of domestic life. The quaint saying sometimes used, "A saint abroad and a devil at home," could never have been appropriately applied to him. His saintly character shone with as much lustre in the bosom of his own family, and in his every day deportment among his domestics, as it did in the performance of the more public duties of his ministerial office.

In the management of his pecuniary affairs, he always acted on the principle of the most rigid economy. In his expenditures, indeed, he was never parsimonious or stingy; he never refused to procure things which were really necessary and useful, for the sake of saving expense. There was in him nothing which in the remotest degree, partook of a miserly disposition. Yet did he religiously abstain from the purchase of those articles which were not in themselves useful, and of which he did not himself stand in need. From the earliest period he kept the most accurate account of all his receipts and expenditures; and was ever careful that the former should not be exceeded by the latter. He noted down every bushel of grain which he bought, and every barrel of flour and every article of apparel. When on a journey, every item of expense, even the most minute, was carefully registered; and at the end of the year, his receipts and his expenditures were all carefully looked over and the difference between them ascertained. Though he lived, at least a considerable portion of his life, upon a small salary, and though there were times when he was greatly straitened and embarrassed in regard to his pecuniary affairs; yet he always contrived to live within his means; he never contracted a debt without a reasonable expectation of being able to pay it; and by good husbandry and the help of an excellent companion, he was enabled always to have the necessaries and many of the luxuries of life for the comfort of his family and the entertainment of his friends.

Dr. Yale may be said to have been "given to hospitality." His friends were always welcome at his table; and the stranger who was in circumstances of want, and deserving of sympathy, was never turned away from his door, without having occasion to be thankful for kindnesses received.

While he was specially devoted to his appropriate work as a minister of Christ, he was accustomed to superintend his own domestic affairs. He was sometimes assisted in the care of his domestic animals, and in other ways, by young men who were admitted into his family, for the purpose of deriving assistance from him in procuring an education; and while he occupied the parsonage, the most of the labor in the cultivation of the land was performed by others; yet did he with his own hand perform many of those services about the barn, and in the garden, which are sometimes committed to others.

Shoveling paths about his premises in the winter, and tending his garden in the summer, was labor which he seldom called upon others to perform. He never thought it a disgrace for any man to work; and though manual labor was by no means that to which he devoted his time or in which he expended his energies; yet did he never consider it a disparagement to engage in such labor when circumstances required it. At the earliest dawn of the morning was he employed in something useful. Rising with the lark, even while most others were holding communion with the goddess of sleep, it was not uncommon for the sound of the saw at the wood-pile, to proclaim his habits of industry.

He was always exceedingly grieved in view of the frequent dismissal of ministers from their people, for the want of a competent support; regarding it as indicating a lack in the people of a proper estimate of the gospel, or in the ministry, of those habits of frugality and economy which are so much to be desired.

On this point has he expressed himself in his correspondence with a friend; and I feel disposed to give place here to a few extracts, inasmuch as they serve to exemplify so clearly the principles on which he managed his own secular affairs. He writes as follows under date of October 2, 1816:

"The new doctrine supported by Mr. B. and others, of which you speak, I believe is not so new as the age in which we live. 'God hath ordained that they who preach the gospel, should live of the gospel.' But has he ordained that they shall ride in elegant carriages, be drawn by the finest horses, clothed in the most costly array, dwell in the most spacious mansions, fill their houses with the best furniture, and load their tables with the most sumptuous provisions? I think that in order to maintain consistency, and to keep the dust off their feet, when they have once shaken it off, they must reduce their expenses to the gospel scale. I am satisfied, sir, that our good Christian brethren will not be far behind us in their exertions to build up Christ's kingdom.

But with what face can a minister complain for want of support, when his *useless* or *superfluous* possessions would support him one, two, three or four years? Not that a minister is to be reduced to bare necessities, but let him be frugal."

In another letter, written a little later, we find the following:

"Were we always suitably sensible of the all-sufficiency of God should we ever distrust his providence? But O, how much do I think of my wants! how little of my mercies! how much less of him that has given all that was good for me, and has promised to 'withhold no good thing from them that walk uprightly.' I do not know but such anxious thoughts sometimes knock at brother B's door—for he has written once or twice about small salaries, dismission of ministers for want of adequate support, &c. But I believe my friend is some like one who formerly said, 'I have learned in whatsoever state therewith I am, to be content.' So he says to these knockers, 'There is no place for you in my house.' Keep 'em out, good brother, keep 'em out; the good hand of God which has fed you all your life long, will always have something to give you and yours, while it continues to feed the ravens. As to being dismissed for want of support, I suppose I might have been so dismissed ten times before now, if I could have found so many new places to settle in; but I think when I begin to feel a little uneasy, of an old proverb, 'As a bird that wandereth from her nest, so is a man that wandereth from his place.' Though I have need enough of Christian resignation, yet it has been fixed in my mind ever since I entered upon the work of the ministry, that I should have no abiding city on this side heaven; that I should go whither and stay where my Master directs, and remove when he calls me away. I trust he sent me to this place; I came freely: I am willing to stay as long as he finds me employment and support here; and as willing to go whenever he calls me away. As to salaries, I believe it would be far better for ministers to preach them down than to preach them up —not so much by diminishing their demands, as by removing the causes of them. And what are those causes? Extravagance in consuming, and improvidence in securing the necessaries of life. And what are the causes of those causes? The extravagance and pride of the people. The former raises them above their ministers, the latter is ashamed to see them poor. Let ministers preach down these vices in their people, and they will live as well and be as useful, with a small salary as a large one. I call them vices, for I consider them so in their own nature, and the fruitful sources of the complaints both of ministers and people."

In his family, while Dr. Yale never put on the aspect of moroseness, he was always serious and sedate. He never said any thing silly or unbecoming his profession; but his conversation was always instructive and useful. He was always particularly guarded against making censorious remarks about others, even such as were doing their utmost to destroy his peace and mar his usefulness. During the few last years of his life, especially, his conversation in the domestic circle was almost exclusively on the subject of religion. During most of the time for many years, did he have under his care and at his table, a number of young men or boys who were mostly occupied in literary pursuits or in studies preparatory for college. In associating with these youth, it always seemed to be his object so to direct the conversation as that they might receive some useful information, or that some salutary religious impression might be made upon their minds. The proper education of children he always regarded as of primary importance; and whenever he associated with the young whether in his own family or elsewhere, he aimed to say something which they would afterwards remember to their profit. The youth in his family he was careful to instruct in the things of religion. He faithfully and diligently taught them the truths contained in the Shorter Catechism; for many years they committed a verse of scripture each day, which was recited at the table during the morning meal, and he afforded such assistance as the case required, to the members of the family, in familiarizing themselves with those parts of the sacred text which constituted the lessons of the sabbath school.

As an illustration of the fidelity with which he sometimes dealt with those under his care, I have transcribed the following from his memorandum:

1845, June 22, Sabbath. "Since meeting I have been attending to the sabbath school lesson for the next sabbath. Ps., xcii, 9: 'For lo, thine enemies, oh, Lord, for lo, thine enemies shall perish.' I was hearing the lad Elisha say the lesson, and repeating it, when an impression came and I asked him: Do you believe it? He said he did. Are you God's enemy? 'I suppose I am.' Do you believe it? He thought he did. No, you do not believe it. If you believed you had a serpent in your stomach, would you not be concerned about it? 'I should.' Would you not be inquiring: 'What shall I do?' Would you not go to Dr. Peake and ask if he could not do something for you? Now, the devil, the old serpent, is in your heart, and you do not believe it. He manifested some alarm. I pressed him; but every word I said pressed my own conscience. You do not believe. No, I do not. If I did believe that every impenitent sinner had the devil in his heart, and was God's enemy, and would certainly perish, I should not, I could not live as I do. My faith is dead. It produces no works. Is not God now hearing prayer for the Spirit, by convincing me of unbelief? This is the very thing. The Spirit is come. The Spirit now makes me feel my deadness in regard to faith. Do I now desire to have God pour out his Spirit upon me? Then shall I hear his reproof. Then shall I do as my convictions tend. Is not this the beginning? Is not this a little speck of a cloud? Oh, that God would add to it; for I am so dead that I can hardly say: 'Lord, I believe, help thou mine unbelief.'"

In their morning devotions in the family, each reader had his Bible, and each took his turn in reading, thereby securing a more close attention to the word of God than would have been likely to be secured in any other way. It was expected that the whole household should be present at family worship; and it was his wish, also, that these services should be participated in by laborers in his employ. It was hardly to have been expected that persons in his employment and in his presence, would often be guilty of grossly vulgar or profane language—but a story is told of one, to this effect, that at one time a man in his employ became very much irritated at some thing, and uttered an oath in the presence both of himself and some youth who were then residing in his family.

Dr. Yale says to him somewhat as follows: "Mr. C., when we swear, we won't swear before the boys." The man felt the rebuke, received it kindly, and remembered it ever afterwards.

At his own table, Dr. Yale was always in the habit of having two religious services, the one at the commencement, and the other at the conclusion of the meal. This practice he maintained to the last, although the second religious service at the table had gone so extensively into disuse. He deprecated the practice of rising from the table at the close of a meal, without giving a formal expression of thanks to the Giver of all good for the blessings received.

His sentiments on this point he uttered in a letter to a friend under date of Aug. 15, 1852, as follows:

"In the families of Christians and ministers, one exercise of devotion at the table operates rather worse in general where I have been, than it did in your family. Rarely are the members together at the table, or the family altar. It grieved me greatly to see this irregularity. What a little thing is the neglect of giving thanks at the table, instead of asking a blessing and giving thanks! What a little thing! How great an evil! With many families, even religious, where they have prayer and reading the word morning and evening, some of the members, sons or daughters, or some of both, are never present at the same time; and as to family instruction, it is out of the question. My soul has cried in the night over these evils. If there is not a change, religion will die out. In more than thirty families where I have been at table within three months, only two have been regular. Those two have two exercises at the table. All are present when the blessing is asked. All are present when thanks are returned. And when family worship is attended they are all present. There is no need of a bell or a call to get them together. For they are together, and ready to read and give attention to prayer. What a terrible influence this irregularity has upon the Christian family and community! No wonder the bands of parental authority are feeble. Children despise the religion which is eaten up by the world. Can I expect to effect a change—to dip out the waters of the St. Lawrence with a thimble? I will try to do what I can, and God is able to do the work. Will you not help me?"

CHAPTER XX.

HIS PULPIT PREPARATIONS AND THE CHARACTER OF HIS PREACHING.

As to the amount of labor bestowed upon his preparations for the pulpit, there was no uniformity. There were times when he was so much occupied with a great variety of other duties, and his studies were so much interrupted that he found it impossible to bestow as much labor upon the preparation of his sermons as he desired. Sometimes he preached extemporaneously. Sometimes he wrote but the introduction and heads of his discourses. On some of these occasions he preached with much comfort to himself, as well as profit to others; while at other times he speaks of his own want of enjoyment in his ministrations, and expresses his apprehensions that but little good had been accomplished. He was accustomed however, very generally, both in the early and later years of his ministry, to write out a large portion of his public discourses. He felt the need of careful preparation for the pulpit, to such an extent that, in systematizing his labors, he designated particular portions of time to be employed in this specific business.

Thus: 1828, April 1. "A month for study. By the help of God I am going to spend two hours every day, except the sabbath, in the entire and exclusive business of preparing sermons. If I am hindered at the appointed time, then the next two I can command. Lord, help me in this work."

The following rules for the composition of a sermon, may also be found in his diary, viz: "In every sermon consider well the meaning of the text. What is opposed to it—whom it may favor—whom it may oppose—what good it may offer or secure to some—what evil it may portend to others—how the glory of God is affected by it."

As it respects the character of his pulpit performances, they were generally estimated much more highly by others than they were by himself. To a great extent he had a poor opinion of his own preaching—which he expressed in the following terms:

1827, Dec. 9. Sabbath. "This has been a peculiar day —so slippery that few could get to the house of God, and rainy too. I have preached as well as I could, but it seemed to be good for nothing. I found no comfort in my own soul, and seemed to give neither comfort nor concern to others. Indeed, I do not know what is the matter with my preaching. It must be that it is wrong. Were it good for any thing, surely it would do some body good. But now it does seem to do nobody any good. I am searching to find out its essential defects. It seems to me one is that my sermons are generally too long, and not sufficiently pointed. But I am thinking that the main is, that I am not preaching experimentally, but mechanically. I am not near to God, but very far off. Now, what shall I do? I am thinking that I must live for heaven—live in heaven—have my heart there. As Mr. Baxter says: 'Live a heavenly life on earth.'"

1836, May 15. "The attendance at church was good, and I tried to preach, both morning and afternoon. Since meeting I have been reading Payson, and feel altogether ashamed. Indeed, I felt very much ashamed when I returned from the house of God. It grieved me some to occupy the time and attention of so many people, with such poor services. Is it not time to be in earnest to change my course? I have lamented it long, but I see not the least change, except that my family visiting breaks in upon my course of worldliness. The Lord show and direct me what to do, and how to do it. I can not live so. It is not living at all."

In the following, while he expresses the low opinion which he entertained of himself as a preacher, he also expresses his sense of dependence upon the assisting grace of God.

It is found under date of Oct. 30, 1839.

NEED OF PRAYER.

"'Without me,' says the Savior, 'ye can do nothing.' Should I then attempt any thing without him? How presumptuous? Can I choose a text, adapted to the wants of my people, without his counsel? Let me then, always say: 'Give me wisdom from above.' Can I understand the text? Can I unfold it, can I apply it, without the influence of his Spirit, to give me understanding, skill and energy? Can I speak so as to gain attention, awaken the mind, arouse the conscience, move the heart, or do any good at all, without the Spirit and power of Christ?

Oh, then, let me before I prepare, while I am preparing, after I am prepared, and when I am preaching, lift up my heart continually to God. And when I have ended my sermon, let me as soon as possible throw myself before the mercy-seat, and pour out my heart to God, sa ng: 'Forgive what is amiss, accept what can be accepted, bless what is useful.'

How many sermons have I preached which seem to have been powerless! I have never heard from them as having done any good. This is truly a grief to my heart. This makes me lament over my insufficiency, and cry unto God for pardon. How can I bear to continue in this way? I long to have my preaching blessed. I cry unto God but he seems not to regard me. Formerly, at times, my preaching seemed to do good. But of late it has been less efficacious. My soul is often cast down within me, and I fear my preaching will no more be owned of God and blessed. This fear makes me go to the pulpit with feelings of distress and dismay. Oh, that God would remember me in mercy. Oh that God would forgive all my sins, remove what hinders, teach me how to speak, give me the spirit of preaching, and crown my preaching with success. Oh, how happy should I be, if I could be so aided and blessed that every sermon might do some good. I am willing to study deeply, to meditate day and night. But how can I bear to be laboriously engaged in doing nothing? Lord, wilt thou not show me wherein I have offended—wherein I am deficient? Wilt thou not help me, and from this time crown my preaching with thy blessing? I know I am a poor preacher. I feel that I am far inferior to my neighboring brethren, generally, and yet, I fear I think too highly of myself. Oh, cause me to lie as low as I ought, and condescend to forgive all my sins, and bless my poor preaching for some good. Oh, let me not be a cumberer of the ground. Let me not stand in the way of some one whom thou couldst employ in this place to better purpose. But oh! while I am allowed to live in the world, and to speak in thy name, enable me so to speak as to please thee, and enjoy thy blessing. 'For thy name's sake, O Lord, pardon mine iniquity, for it is great,' and from this time forward bless me indeed in preaching the gospel. And thy name shall have all the glory. Amen."

Dr. Yale, however, was both a very acceptable and very useful preacher. He made no attempt at oratorical flourish in his pulpit performances. His preaching was always plain, simple, evangelical, practical. He sought not so much to move the passions, as to enlighten the understanding. Rather, it was his purpose, by means of truth addressed to the understanding, to affect the heart and to call into exercise religious affections. He was always bold and fearless in his defense of that system of truth which he believed to be taught in the word of God, though he never indulged himself in vague philosophical speculations. It was no part of his desire to give offense to any portion of his hearer; yet did he never suppress the truth for the sake of gaining applause. He planted himself upon the rock of eternal truth, and while he kept in view the old landmarks, and adhered most firmly to those truths which have heretofore been regarded as lying at the foundation of the gospel method of salvation through Christ, he was shocked at those fine-spun theories which were sometimes advocated by others, and those speculations which seemed to threaten the purity and peace of the Christian church. His language to a correspondent on this subject was as follows: 'Who does not know that philosophical dogmas are the source of most theological errors? How sadly is the human mind carried away! Wave rolls over wave, and one system is carried away after another. So it has been. So it is. So it will be. I trust you are in no danger. Pray for the peace of Jerusalem." Again, he says: "When a man, however great, or learned, or wise, or good he may be, lays down philosophical dogmas at the foundation of things, he will be sure to lead others to destruction as the stream of time flows, and his dogmas can be seized by the devil, and one of his agents employed to sustain and extend it. Alas! how much evil has already been done by philosophy falsely so called! God be praised that you and I are little men—that we have never known enough to be wiser than that which is written—never been exalted enough to be flattered. We have been plodding along with our Bibles in our hands, content to labor hard to live, and do a little. We have not found it needful to make great discoveries in theology, being satisfied that the good things of the gospel were as well understood in Paul's day as they are now. We are happy in our comparative ignorance."

Such being the sentiments of Dr. Yale, as to the dangers connected with philosophical speculations in religion, the reader hardly need be told, that in all his instructions he adhered closely to the obvious teachings of the word of God. He regarded God as exercising the supreme government of the world; guiding the affairs of nations, and directing the destiny of individuals according to his own pleasure, and accomplishing his own purposes in the administration of his government. This truth he was accustomed to exhibit, as taught in the sacred volume, for the purpose of honoring God and setting the crown upon his head, as King Supreme over all. He dwelt much upon those great leading doctrines of the gospel which serve to illustrate the plan of salvation through Christ. Man, a sinner—depravity inherited from Adam as the federal head of his posterity, and as their representative in the covenant of works—the sinner exposed to the curse of God and the pains of an eternal hell, in consequence of his apostacy—the indispensable necessity of a thorough and radical change, through the operations of the Holy Spirit—the sovereignty of God's grace in the bestowment of spiritual as well as temporal blessings—the vicarious sacrifice and all-sufficient righteousness of the Lord Jesus Christ as the only Savior of guilty men—and the duty and obligations of men to repent of sin and believe on the Lord Jesus for salvation. To this might be added, the necessity of personal holiness as a prerequisite for heaven, and the Christian's responsibility as to a life of obedience to God's law, and devotion to his service. While he believed and preached that man is altogether dependent upon a divine influence for every holy feeling, and every holy purpose, and ability to perform every holy act, he neither believed nor preached that this dependence was an excuse for his continued impenitence and rejection of Christ. It was, therefore, his constant practice to warn the stupid, careless, worldly, impenitent sinner, and to call upon him to repent and turn to God. Indeed, he was frequently very pointed and direct in his appeals to the impenitent, if possible, to awaken them from their slumbers, and to excite them to seek salvation through Christ. When God said to the wicked, "O wicked man, thou shalt surely die," he never refrained from giving the echo to this voice of God.

The duties and responsibilities of Christians, and their obligations to live to the glory of God and the spiritual well-being of their fellow-men, also constituted a frequent theme of discourse. He felt, and it was his aim to make others feel, that, "Man's chief end is to glorify God." "None of us liveth to himself, and no man dieth to himself."

Regarding the understanding as the inlet to the heart, he endeavored so to present the truth as that it should be the means of spiritual illumination; but regarding the conscience as man's divinely-appointed monitor, to check him in his course of folly, and excite him to the practice of virtue; he sought also to awaken it from its slumbers and to stir it up to fidelity in the discharge of its duty.

This may be shown by a single brief extract:

1821, Oct. 14. "Rose before 5 o'clock. The importance of aiming at the conscience, pressed on my mind. Conscience is a tender part which people wish to hide. Conscience is the tender part which delicate feelings dread to wound. Conscience is the vulnerable part of man. If I reach it, the person will either love me better, or hate me worse, and will certainly fear me. It is to be assailed with fidelity, but not with rudeness. It is to be as much alone as circumstances will admit. It is to be in such a manner as to leave no chance for blaming my motives or conduct. Let it be my study in all my preaching and conversation, to reach the conscience. I think too, that Christ is to be my example."

I will close this chapter by giving the outlines of two sermons, for the double purpose of exhibiting the way in which he frequently made his preparation for the pulpit, and of showing the interesting manner in which he was accustomed to present truth, in his ordinary ministrations among his own people. The outlines here given are all that were written of these discourses.

The first was a sermon addressed to the youth of his congregation, and was preached May 8, 1842. It is as follows:

TO YOUNG PEOPLE.

On the Influence of True Religion upon their Happiness.

Proverbs iv, 1: "Hear, ye children, the instruction of a father, and attend to know understanding."

If every youth, if every child, would commit to memory this interesting chapter, I doubt not that they would derive from it substantial and lasting benefit. Its recommendations are so appropriate, so beautifully expressed, and pressed home with such energy, that they must be salutary. In addressing my young friends at this time, I intend to refer you to the history of forty years past, among ourselves, to show you that true religion has a happy influence upon the young. The whole number of members in that period has been five hundred and eighty-four. Before I came, forty. Since added, five hundred and forty-four. Of these, two hundred and seventy-three were youth, unmarried at the time of their joining the church. Two hundred and seventy-one, others. So that more than half of all that have joined this church in my time, have been young persons. Of these two hundred and seventy-three, thirty-four have departed this life, six have been excluded and not restored, eight have joined other denominations, and seventy-seven have been regularly dismissed to other churches in communion with us; so that now a hundred and forty-eight remain. Of the whole number, ten have been ministers of the gospel in the Congregational or Presbyterian church; one has been a Baptist preacher, one a Lutheran, and one an Episcopalian. One of the ten was a missionary to the Cherokees, and one of the brethren was a missionary printer at the Sandwich Islands. Most of the ministers are now employed in good congregations, or in other services of much usefulness, while one is not. The Rev. J. Leonard Case died one month after his ordination at Kingston. Seven are in a course of preparation for public usefulness. Of the one hundred and forty-eight who remain among us, much of our spiritual strength consists. If they were removed, more than half of our church would be removed. In addition to this, it is very proper to observe, that many other young persons have been connected with us, though they had commenced their family relationship before they joined the church. There has, indeed, been a variety of character and condition among those who thus began to serve God in the days of their youth. But in general, the influence of their religion has been salutary upon them. It has afforded them more happiness than any thing else that they have enjoyed.

I have been with many of them in their decline, their sickness, and their death. What was it which supported and comforted them in that trying season? Was it the world? Was it infidelity? O! it was the glorious gospel of the blessed God.

Others have passed through, or are now passing through, the afflicting scenes of their pilgrimage. What is their support now? For the present, what is their comfort? For the future, what is their hope?

Numbers are engaged with others in trying to build up the Redeemer's kingdom. Would they give up their privilege for all the world? Numbers of young members feel it to be a part of their happiness to aid in diffusing the savor of divine grace through the world. And many rejoice in the Lord always, and sometimes 'with joy unspeakable.' A kind spirit is manifest—they do love the Lord, and his people, and souls.

Now, from what source does this happiness, this peace, and this hope arise? I think I can tell you. Having from my youth been intimately acquainted with religion, I think I can tell you something about it. May I say, as Solomon, though not with his wisdom, 'Hear, ye children, the instruction of a father, and attend to know understanding.' Let me then tell you plainly what God recommends to your attention, as well worthy of your chief concern.

1. *First of all that you give your heart to the Lord.*

You know that this is the very thing which you believe to be needful. You have no opinion of any religion which is heartless. Neither has God any regard to any other. To give your heart is to withdraw your affection from other objects, and set it on God and the things of God. Hence, 'ye must be born again.'

2. *Embrace the Savior as he is offered in the gospel.*

3. *Study the holy oracles that you may understand them.*

Do not merely give the Bible a cursory reading. Let it be your deep and intimate study. Let every opportunity be embraced to become acquainted with the Word of God. 'Hear;' 'attend to know.' Let it be one part of the business of life.

4. *When you have once embraced religion, be consistent.* I will venture to say that in this remark I agree with you entirely. You believe in a religion which lasts—which is constant. Find your happiness in religion. For true religion makes the professor happy. It is but a poor substitute for true religion which makes it needful 'to go abroad for joy.' As I heard an aged saint say once, when he was detained from the house of God: 'I need not go abroad for joy,' &c. Allow me to say, young friends, that fond as I once was of the enjoyments common to youth, I never once, so far as I remember, had the least inclination to return to the forsaken pleasures of folly. The employments and comforts of religion have always been enough for me, since I knew what they were. Let me earnestly recommend, therefore, to all young Christians, to find your happiness as well as hope in religion. Let me ask you as did the amiable Nevins: 'Does your religion make you happy?' If not, either your religion is not of the right kind, or you have not enough of it.

Bear in mind continually that you need to become acquainted with a holy and infinite God.

That you have much to do to regulate your own selves.

That you must overcome temptations.

That your happiness in heaven must be in God.

Dare, then, my young friends to take your part with

God. I know the dazzling influence of the world; but it is only tinsel. Dare to love God supremely. Come out boldly always on the side of the Savior. Become intimately acquainted with the Bible. Be wholly, at all times, and for ever a Christian. Think of the noble and amiable Joseph. Set Daniel before you as worthy of special estimation. Calculate on a short life. Expect soon to be in heaven. While you live, live for one purpose—'to glorify God.'"

The following are the outlines of a discourse preached on the 5th day of June, 1842, at the funeral of Stephen Gillett, Esq., a venerable and much esteeemed member of the church; and is principally valuable on account of the exhibition which it contains of Christian character:

PEACE AND REST FOR THE UPRIGHT.

Isaiah, lii, 2: "He shall enter into peace: They shall rest in their beds, each one walking in his uprightness."

"'The souls of believers at their death are made perfect in holiness,' &c. They may fall in battle, as fell Josiah in the midst of his days—not forty; or by the sword of persecution, as James the brother of John; stoned, as Stephen; or just entering the field of labor, as was one of our young men; or while preparing to be useful; or in old age, after years of pain. They may die deeply lamented, or unlamented.

In the case of our venerable friend whom we this day, &c.

Long was he ready and waiting, kept here not so much on his own account as on the account of friends. Perhaps we sometimes inquire: What good can there be in the continuance of an aged and infirm man, almost deaf and blind? And it may be profitable to answer such an inquiry. Good to himself, in the exercise of patience, submission and humble waiting for God's counsel. I happen to know something in this case. Two or three years ago, under many infirmities and pains, he was uneasy, and said some things which seemed to be not entirely consistent with the best Christian feeling. A book was sent him: the life of the Rev. William Tennent. I was the bearer of that book, and pointed him particularly to a conversation between Mr. Tennent, the good Mr. Whitefield, and others. He read that discourse often, and with great interest and benefit. Many times did he afterwards repeat it in my hearing, and express much gratitude that he had read it. He felt reproved, and often and humbly confessed that he had been wrong. Thus the graces were exercised.

But more especially is good designed to others. My intimate acquaintance with the friends, more especially the children, enables me to speak on this subject with the more freedom. I know that they have honored their father and their mother. God has seen fit to try them. It has been a long and severe trial. Imperfection, doubtless, they are conscious of—if they were not, they would not answer my good opinion of them. The infirmities of their father have been specially for the trial of their filial affection—of their disposition to honor God and their parents—in circumstances of inconvenience, toil, care—of their patience, submission, confidence.

But trials have an end. When all the designs of God are answered—all his work done—the result.

1. '*He shall enter into peace.*' 'Mark the perfect man'—'peace.' The bar which breaks up our cell may be heavy, and its strokes terrible. The enemy may have power to distress the weary soul, so weak. God has not promised that our passage through the dark valley shall be easy. Even our elder brother suffered extremely.

But peace—It does not mean peace in this life, though a universal grace—'love, joy, peace'—'great peace.' But '*shall enter into peace.*' In this world peace is within us. In the other we enter into peace—the state beyond the boundaries of time. 'In my Father's house.' 'We know that.' 'I go to prepare a place'—it is not the quietus of the soul. It is not a purgatory of the soul—winds—waters—fires. But the rest which remaineth—beyond the reach of the enemy—want—care —fear. To the thief on the cross. 'To-day,' Moses and Elijah—Abraham, Isaac and Jacob. The beggar—the spirits of just men—'do immediately pass into glory."

2. '*They shall rest in their beds.*'

After the toils of the day, our beds. Their bed—very painful labor—distressing trials. David fled. A hard struggle—a long delay—a dreadful conflict—distressing pain, poverty, want, cruelty. Lazarus.

But the night comes. The bed is prepared—a good bed. Sleep in Jesus. All have a bed equally comfortable. They talk of kings and great men lying in state. The king of Madagascar with ten thousand silver dollars; but be the bed of the righteous what it may it will be equally easy to all. The angels keep them. The body of Moses—rest to the weary body, while the soul rests. Both are provided for, and taken care of till another glorious period.

3. *The character.* 'Each one walking in his uprightness.' The expression comes back to the singular—character personal—every one—'uprightness.' Moral uprightness is included—but not the thing. Though in this respect as much might be said of our father, now deceased, as almost any man. Remarkable for uprightness—inoffensive—of sound judgment—of great impartiality—candor. Few enemies—very few.

Full of self-righteousness till about thirty-nine years ago. He was alive without the law—might as well live as any one.

But his character was then formed anew. Describe the upright in him. I will tell you how he viewed the matter.

Supreme regard to God's word. Of sound judgment, correct argument. Yet he used his judgment and reason to understand God's word. He referred every thing to this test. He would not believe any doctrine not taught there. He aimed to believe every doctrine there taught. All scripture—he loved it. It dwelt in him. More precious than gold. Once asked: 'How does a Christian feel towards God's word?' He answered:

'Why, he feels just as I do.' He read it as long as he could see. He heard it as long as he could hear. He repeated it when he could neither see nor hear. He meditated upon it when he could do neither. How he wished he had attended to it during the first fifty years of his life!

From the word he learned,

The worthlessness of his own righteousness.

The preciousness of the righteousness of Christ.

The inward righteousness wrought by the Holy Spirit.

The outward righteousnesss of a holy life.

Thus he walked in his uprightness.

He was very jealous over himself.

He was careful in self-examination.

He was a cordial friend to the church.

He was a lover of good men and of good things.

In one word, he was an humble follower of the Lamb of God.

I can not help thinking this day of others of our fathers. Can not name them all now. But the associatoin is so strong in regard to some, that they seem to pass before my mind's eye in close connection. I seem to see and hear them again in the prayer-meeting, the sanctuary, the church-meeting, and at the Lord's table. Though men, sinful men, yet were they washed. I seem to see and hear Judson, and Hall, and Steele, and Giles, and Thrall, and Gillett, and numbers of others. I wish I could see them again. They once were in our assemblies. But they have entered into peace. They rest in their bed. Let us follow them as they followed Christ. Nor shall I forget that mother in Israel. She prayed for us.

Now let me say in conclusion to these friends, especially to the children. The memory of these friends is consecrated for your benefit. You need not go any farther than to the word of God and their example to know what true religion is—being taught by the Spirit, and the piety of these departed saints always before your eyes."

CHAPTER XXI.

INTERESTING VIEWS OF SCRIPTURE TRUTH.

Few men are closer and more diligent students of the word of God, than was Dr. Yale. He made the Bible the study of every day, and its contents he received as food for the soul. It might have been expected that a man with such a mind, and such a heart would have had many thoughts on the great variety of subjects embraced in the volume of inspiration, of the deepest interest and the greatest practical utility. He is not known to have written any thing like a connected commentary of any part of the sacred volume, yet in addition to the great number of written sermons which were the product of his pen, there were many brief comments, connected with practical reflections, on isolated passages of scripture, scattered through his memorandum, a selection from which I have felt disposed to present for the satisfaction and profit of the reader.

BRIEF COMMENTS ON SELECT PASSAGES OF SCRIPTURE.

I Timothy, iii, 6: "'*Not a novice.*' Cherish the thought after any performance that you have *done well;* and you are a *proud* novice. Cherish the thought that men will think you have done well, and that they will praise you for it and you are a *vain* novice. Aim at doing so well, when, an opportunity offers, that you may cherish the thought of doing well, and you are an *ambitious* novice. Feel inwardly sorry when another is commended for doing well, and wish to detract from his merit, and you are an *envious* novice. People may aim in making their minister a novice, by commending him. A minister may encourage them to make him a novice, by allowing them to commend him. Let some judicious and faithful man point out my real faults and my real abilities —but privately—not as a judge or a critic, but as a Christian. . Let some one report to me faithfully the opinion of men of sense, but of no religion. Let some other one tell me the opinion of my bitterest enemies.

Prov. xv, 8: 'The sacrifice of the wicked is abomination to the Lord.' Much more prayer. What prayer?

1, Of ostentation; 2, Self-righteousness; 3, Weariness; 4, Self-complacency; 5, Conditions—that is, expecting that God will give us so much good for so much prayer.

'But the prayer of the upright is his delight.'

Who are the upright? What prayer is the delight of God?

1, Of a broken heart; 2, Of a cordial friendship. Of such as view it a great privilege. Not *must;* but *may.*

Mat. iv, 8, 9: 'Again the devil taketh him up into an exceeding high mountain, and showeth him all the kingdoms of the world and the glory of them; and saith unto him, All these things will I give thee, if thou wilt fall down and worship me.'

For what a small matter apparently did the devil offer the world! Only do me this little favor, and I will give you the whole world! A WORLD for an act of worship! Impudence unparalleled! to offer Christ the world, made and upheld and possessed by himself, to induce him to worship the devil—to commit high treason against God in favor of the vilest usurper in existence, doomed to hopeless ruin! But this is worthy of the devil. What will he not attempt? Oh, God! deliver the world from his temptations.

John, xx, 20: 'And when he had so said, he showed unto them his hands and his side. Then were the disciples glad when they had seen the Lord.'

Thy hands, blessed Jesus, were nailed to the cross. Thy side was pierced with the spear. Dost thou show me thy hands and thy side? Those are the same that were crucified. These wounds prove thy love, and my sin: thy love in dying for me; my sin which procured thy death. Dost thou thus give me assurances of these amazing facts? Lord, I am redeemed. I am thine. What wilt thou have me to do? To thee I devote myself, and my all, to be for ever used for thy service and glory.

John, xx, 21: 'Then said Jesus to them again. Peace be unto you; as my Father hath sent me, even so send I you.'

Peace. Not false, but the peace of God, which the world can not give, or take away. How sweet the accent to the troubled heart! As the same voice calmed the blusterings of the whirlwind and composed the rollings of the billows, so it calms the storms of the soul. '*Peace.*' How seasonable to the disciples! They had, in the hour of trial, been ready to give up all for lost. But now, not only is hope restored, but assurance that all is perfectly safe, causes the mind to settle down in peace, not as the stagnant pool, but as the deep and placid and pure river.

'*So send I you.*' Into the world on a message of love, proceeding from love, to produce a return of love, and thus to destroy the work of the devil. Here, oh, thou dying, living Savior, do we behold the true origin and spirit of missions. Thy Father was the author; thou wast the first missionary; thy mission was from heaven to earth; thy message was mercy. Now thou dost act the part of thy Father's love, in sending thy missionaries; they act thy love in becoming missionaries; thy message is their message, and it is the theme of angelic anthems. 'Glory to God in the highest, and on earth peace, good will to men.'

John, xx, 23: 'Whosesoever sins ye remit, they are remitted unto them; and whosesoever sins ye retain, they are retained.'

Did Christ give his disciples power to forgive, or to retain sins? So say the Catholics, and on this saying build the most terrible system of spiritual tyranny. But it was well asked: 'Who can forgive sins but God only?' Though they who asked it denied that Christ had the authority, and thus went contrary to known facts, by which he proved his authority; yet they reasoned correctly that God only has authority to forgive sin. He gave his disciples authority, acting in his name, and under the inspiration of the Holy Ghost, to settle the only terms on which sins can be forgiven. He also gave them and all his ministers authority to declare the same, and to administer censure, or absolution in the church accordingly. Further than that he gave them no authority, and any claim to it is spiritual usurpation.

Psalms, xxxvii, 8: 'Trust in the Lord and do good; so shalt thou dwell in the land, and verily thou shalt be fed.'

A very encouraging subject. Let me go on with my work, just in the way of duty, never fearing that I shall have a place to live or work to do, or support in doing it. All I need is to please the Lord, and trust him.

'Fear him, ye saints, and you will then
'Have nothing else to fear:
'Come, make his service your delight,
'He'll make your wants his care.'

Psalms, lxxxiv, 11: 'For the Lord is a sun and shield the Lord will give grace and glory; no good thing will he withhold from them that walk uprightly.'

As a sun, he is my light. As a shield, he is my defense. As he gives grace, he will sanctify my soul, and help me through all my labors and pilgrimage. As he gives glory, he will crown all his grace with eternal life above. As he will withhold no good thing from them that walk uprightly, I may ask all I need; for I do receive righteousness from the Lord Jesus to justify me, and he works in me to will and to do of his good pleasure. Surely it is very delightful to find a word so precious, and so entirely adapted to my case.

Psalms lxxxvi, 5: 'For thou, Lord, *art* good, and ready to forgive; and plenteous in mercy unto all them that call upon thee.'

What sweet and precious words! *The Lord is good.* In himself he is infinitely good. In his word he is good. In all his dealings with his people he is good. And in all his dealings with his enemies he is good, no less than in all his dealings with his friends. The same goodness counteracts, restrains and punishes the one, which guides, encourages, and rewards the other. *He is ready to forgive* as his name imports, forgiving iniquity, transgression and sin. So he readily pardons every one that forsakes his evil way. I do not wish to be forgiven while I continue in my evil way; for of what possible use would this be to me, or any one? My sins would instantly incur more wrath. But in the Lord's merciful way I trust I am forgiven through Jesus Christ our Lord.

And plenteous in mercy unto all that call upon him.

Mercy I need. Oh how precious is it that I can have Plenty of mercy, when I call upon the Lord! Plenty of mercy! As much as I need or can desire. Surely I will open my mouth wide, and pant for his mercy, and receive an abundant supply.

Acts, i, 4: 'And being assembled together with them, commanded them that they should not depart from Jerusalem, but wait for the promise of the Father, which, saith he, ye have heard of me.'

But why remain at Jerusalem, that wicked city, that bloody city so often stained with the blood of the prophets, and still smoking and red with his own blood? Why not send them away to some distant place, at least till the storm had abated which had then begun to rage? There may be reasons which have not occurred to me, but the following seem very evident.

1. The witnesses of the crucifixion and of the resurrection were on that spot.

2. The conflict was begun, and the power of Christ could best be shown in the face of his enemies.

3. The wickedness of the people gave opportunity for the exercise of the richer grace.

Acts, i, 8: 'But ye shall receive power after that the Holy Ghost is come upon you; and ye shall be witnesses unto me, both in Jerusalem, and in all Judea, and in Samaria, and unto the uttermost parts of the earth.'

Christianity is founded on testimony, not on the positions and deductions of reason. God has spoken. He has delivered his communications to us by chosen witnesses. All we have to inquire into is the credibility of the witnesses, and the import of their testimony. In this method God meets the adversary in the place where he met and ruined our race—in the forum of truth. God had there made his will known; but the devil said, It is not true. Man believed him and died. Now God comes with testimony to prove his holy designs and plans of salvation. The witnesses testify what he has taught them. They give us all the data we need. And now, 'He that believed shall be saved, and he that believeth not shall be damned.'

Acts, i, 9: 'And when he had spoken these things, while they beheld, he was taken up; and a cloud received him out of their sight.'

Highly favored auditors! listening to the words of him who spake as never man spake! Of him, too, raised from the sepulcher, and proved to be their Lord by infallible signs! But now what do we behold? Not a chariot and horses of fire, sent down to take him up, as Elijah; but himself, without any aid, or attendant, and without any effort, ascending upward, till received by a cloud which intercepted their view.

Acts, i, 10. "And while they looked steadfastly towards heaven as he went up, behold two men stood by them in white apparel."

Well might they look intently up into heaven, while their Lord was ascending. Such a miracle had they never seen before. In a moment all their hopes of an earthly kingdom vanished away, and heaven seemed to be their home, where their all was received.

Acts, i, 11. "Which also said, ye men of Galilee, why stand ye gazing up into heaven, this same Jesus which is taken up from you into heaven, shall so come in like manner as ye have seen him go into heaven."

How did they know they were men of Galilee? Doubtless they had been with them before, though invisible. "Are they not all ministering spirits?" Kind friends, they then made themselves visible, and addressed the disciples to give them important information, such as they needed, but such as they could attain only by special revelation. "*He shall come again.*" They specify no time, for the angels in heaven did not then know it. But they specify the fact. *He shall come again, according to what manner,* ye have seen him go into heaven—*manifestly*, for every eye shall see him—*bodily*, as he took the same body to heaven which he had on earth—*supernaturally*, as it was not common for bodies of men to pass through the air, but the Lord was then passing up through the air, and he would come again in the air, into which his followers shall be caught up to meet him *in a cloud; "Behold he cometh in a cloud."* Yet doubtless incomparably more glory will attend him, when he comes again. Then he will appear in the glory of the Father. Then shall come all the holy angels with him. Then shall he sit upon the throne of his glory. Then shall all nations be gathered before him. Then, O then, shall even the splendor of the sun be darkness, in the presence of his glory. Delightful prospect! Oh how reasonable that he should be thus exalted, who was so deeply abased? Awake up, my soul, be ready to meet him; lift up thine eyes, hasten forward, become holy, wash thy robes, and make them white in his precious blood."

The following paper has been transcribed for two reasons—on account of its intrinsic value, and on account of the novel and peculiarly interesting manner in which important truth is presented.

THE CHRISTIAN LADDER.

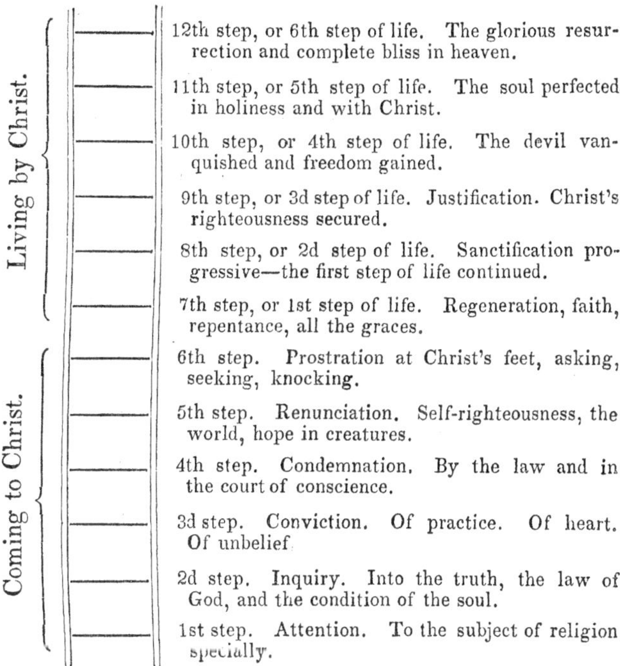

John xiv, 6. "I am the way, and the truth, and the life; no man cometh under the Father but my me."

Mat. xi, 28. "Come unto me all ye that labor and are heavy laden, and I will give you rest."

John vi, 57. "As the living Father hath sent me, and I live by the Father, so he that eateth me, even he shall live by me."

John x, 28. "And I give into them eternal life."

DESCRIPTION OF THE LADDER.

1st. step. *Attention.* This is needful to any movement of the mind towards Christ; and the attention is arrested in ways innumerable, and by means and agencies very surprising. Ten persons, giving an account of what first called their attention permanently to the subject of religion, stated the matter thus:

One said—" A friend invited me to attend a religious meeting."

Another—" I heard my grandfather pray for the conversion of youth."

A third—" I thought I had been called often, but had grieved the spirit, and might be left to perish."

A fourth—" I refused to give my consent that a minister should pray me."

A fifth—" My mother told me of a youth who had been hopefully converted."

A sixth—" A Christian friend often talked with me, and entreated me with tears to come to Christ.

A seventh—" I heard remarks on these words: ' The Spirit and the bride say come,' &c."

An eighth—" A Christian friend in the church, after service, conversed with me often for a year."

A ninth—" My father, when I was quite young, told me of a number of my age, who were serious."

A tenth—" At a social visit, a young man, not then a Christian, told me of a religious revival."

At one time the Lord Jesus said to a man sitting at the receipt of custom: " Follow me." At another, he said to one who had climbed a tree to see him: " Make haste and come down." Nicodemus was excited by the miracles he witnessed; the woman of Samaria by the discourse at the well; the thousands on the day of Pentecost by the Spirit's miraculous operations; Saul of Tarsus, by the great light from heaven; the people of Samaria by the preaching of Christ by Philip. Indeed, the incidents are innumerable, which the Lord uses to awaken the attention of sinners. Then they take the first step towards Christ. But from this, multitudes recede, and return again to their state of insensibility. Some, however, proceed and take the

2d step. *Inquiry*. At first they may feel no great anxiety, but they wish to know something more on the subject. They read, or hear, with new interest. The truth, the law, the gospel, Christ, their own character and condition, the scenes of futurity, lead their thoughts; and while they think, they become concerned and anxious. At length they ask: "What shall I do?" Though from this state many turn again, yet some fear to go back. Destruction is behind them, while they see no way of escape.

The 3d step is *conviction*. This takes place more or less as soon as one begins to inquire. The law of God requires perfect obedience in thought, word and deed. The painful assurance of the inquirer is, that he has not obeyed the law. The commandment comes with power. It makes him feel the evil of many wicked acts, and especially of the neglect of his duty. He breaks off his outward sins, and begins to do many duties. But as he proceeds, he finds that the streams of sin proceed from the fountain within, out of the heart. Evil thoughts are *actions* in the sight of the Holy and Omniscient One; and so are the emotions, affections, and passions. A fountain that sends forth bitter water, is bitter. "The carnal mind is enmity against God; for it is not subject to the law of God, neither indeed can be." Hence all within is found to be wrong. "Every imagination of the thoughts of the heart is only evil continually." At the bottom of all is unbelief; deep seated and deep rooted. Especially unbelief in regard to the Lord Jesus Christ — disregard, or contempt, or opposition. So deeply was the seed planted by our first parents when they believed the devil rather than God. That wicked one said: "Ye shall not surely die." From that moment the seed of unbelief germinated in the soul, and successive harvests have been reaped by all succeeding generations. Hence said the Savior (John xvi), "When he is come, he will reprove the world of sin—of sin because they believe not on me." Hence the convicted soul finds itself in a state of deep and desperate sin—*unwilling to come to Christ.*

As the Lord said to the Jews: "Ye will not come to me that ye might have life." John v, 40. The sinner, in this state, hears about faith, but does not understand it. He is invited to come to Christ, but he does not move toward him. He often thinks that he would go any where and do any thing, if he could come to Christ; but he knows not how to come, and no one can tell him so that he can understand. His distress is often great, and yet it many times seems to him that he feels nothing. His heart is very hard. No hreatenings, no promises can move him. And he cries out: "What shall I do?" This inquiry is greatly in advance of his inquiry at the 2d step. Then he was not *very anxious* while asking what he should do. But now he is like the thousands to whom Peter preached on the day of Pentecost; like Saul of Tarsus, and the jailor, and others. For now he feels his sin, and knows not what to do.

4th step. *Condemnation.* The law of God is now come. It is the word of the Great King. It is a messenger of death. For the sinner is already convicted. "The law is holy, and the commandment holy and just and good; but I am carnal, sold under sin." God pronounces the sentence of condemnation—"Cursed is every one that continueth not in all things, which are written in the book of the law, to do them." This sentence is echoed in the court of conscience—"Thou art the man." "Cursed art thou, for thou hast not continued in all things, which are written in the book of the law to do them." "All is right too, on the part of God, but thou art wrong. Thou deservest eternal death." This conscience is a "son of thunder," and the poor soul quakes. Nor is there any way to escape.

5th step. *Renunciation.* Self is undone. Works are dead. Self-righteousness is but filthy rags. The brave world is only a deceiver. Neither self nor any creature can afford the least relief. All are given up, and the soul despairs of help from any created being or thing, in the universe.

6th step. *Prostration at the feet of Jesus.* All the heavens are veiled in blackness. All creatures, were they present, would stand by in silence. The Lord Jesus, the bright and glorious Emanuel has life. The prostrate soul cries: "Lord I am vile;" "Never did a good deed; no, not one." "All is selfish in my endeavors after salvation. I have had no regard to thee, only for my own sake. Even my prayer has been sin. My heart is not right." "Create in me a clean heart, oh God; and renew a right spirit within me." "For thy name's sake pardon mine iniquity, for it is great." "Shouldst thou cast me away I could not justly complain. But I cast myself on thy mercy." "God be merciful to me a sinner."

LIFE IN CHRIST.

1st step. *Regeneration.* "A new heart also will I give you, and a new spirit will I put within you; and I will take away the stony heart out of your flesh, and I will give you a heart of flesh. And I will put my Spirit within you, and cause you to walk in my statutes, and ye shall keep my judgments and do them. Ye shall be my people, and I will be your God. Ye shall remember your own evil ways, and your doings that were not good, and shall loathe yourselves in your own sight for your iniquities, and for your abominations. Not for your sakes do I this, saith the Lord God, be it known unto you; be ashamed and confounded for your own ways." Ez. xxxvi. Thus Emanuel says to the prostrate sinner: "*Live.*" "The Spirit quickeneth." "You hath be quickened who were dead in tresspasses and sins." From the moment faith in Christ exists, the soul is united to him as the branch is united to the vine, and lives by faith. Godly sorrow worketh repentance unto salvation not to be repented of; and love, with all the Christian graces, begins to move, adorn and beautify the soul. Surely this is a new creature; "old things are passed away; behold, all things are become new."

2d step. *Sanctification progressive. The first step continued.* When the soul is renewed and lives, and all the graces of the Spirit exist, a new series of exercises and actions is commenced. The new creature acts anew. The Savior prays: " Sanctify them through thy truth." And though this is a progressive work, continued as long as they live in the world, yet as it succeeds regeneration, we may consider it as the second step of life, though in a very important sense it is not complete till the close of life. We must by all means maintain that *progress* is made in the divine life.

The first step must be followed by another. "For this is the will of God, even your sanctification." And this consists in " the increase of holiness." Nor is any other perseverance of any use. If a person seems to be a new creature, and after a little season loses all life in the cause of Christ, " what doth it profit?" If he have faith at all, it is only a dead faith. There must be a second step as certainly as the first, in all cases when the soul is truly regenerated. For the path of the just is onward.

3d step. *Justification.* In some sense justification is co-ordinate with regeneration. In another sense it follows it. For, as we have seen, the soul is first regenerated and becomes a new creature. Then it is united to Christ by a living faith, and by faith we become entitled to an interest in the righteousness of Christ. His righteousness thus received and reckoned to our account, becomes ours in such a sense that God freely pardons all our sins and accepts us as righteous in his sight, only for the sake of Christ's righteousness. Thus the believer is justified: " Therefore, being justified by faith, we have peace with God through our Lord Jesus Christ." This is an important and an essential step in the way of life. For this, and this only, delivers us from that death which is the penalty of the law. This only secures that life, to us, which is endless happiness in heaven. " There is, therefore, now no condemnation to them that are in Christ Jesus, who walk not after the flesh but after the

Spirit." Rom. viii, 1. "Whoso eateth my flesh and drinketh my blood, hath eternal life; and I will raise him up at the last day." John vi, 54. More than justification is contained in eternal life, but justification is one essential item.

4th step. *The devil vanquished.* "The god of this world blinds the eyes of them that believe not;" but Christ opens the eyes of believers. The strong man armed keepeth his palace; but Christ "binds the strong man and spoils his house." The devil leads men "captive at his will," but Christ delivers the captive and lets him go free. The devil draws by the cords of sin, every one of his followers to death, but Christ draws the believer with bands of love, and gives him life. Many and sore are satan's temptations; but Christ is able and he will succor the tempted believer and make a way for his escape. Thus Christ delivers from all the power of the devil, and secures to the believer, the beginning, the continuance, and the perfection of life. For by his own death, "he destroys him that has the power of death, that is the devil."

5th step. *The soul perfected and with Christ.* "Be ye holy, for I am holy." This is the will of God, even your sanctification." "Being confident of this very thing, that he which hath begun a good work in you, will perform it until the day of Jesus Christ." Hence we read of "the general assembly and church of the first born which are written in heaven, and the spirits of just men made perfect." The first born, written in heaven, are believers on earth; the spirits of just men made perfect are believers in glory. Such are Abraham, Isaac, and Jacob. Such are all true believers when they leave the body. As said Christ to the penitent thief: "This day shall thou be with me in Paradise." Hence said the apostle Paul; "I have a desire to depart and to be with Christ, which is far better."

6th step. *A glorious resurrection and complete happiness in heaven.* That the soul will meet the body again, raised from the dead, and formed like unto Christ's glorious body, and be complete both in holiness and glory, is as sure as the word of God. Therefore, it can by no means be doubted. Then will life be complete. Believers will be forever with the Lord. This is the summit of the climax—the last step of the ladder. Ascending this, the dark places are all left behind and below. Enemies no more assail us. Dangers never again make us afraid. We step forth upon the heavenly plains; we see the new canopy; we walk the golden streets; we drink the crystal fountains; we pluck the fruit of the living tree; we behold the glory of God and the Lamb; we join the song of the innumerable multitude, saying, "Worthy is the Lamb that was slain, to receive power, and riches, and wisdom, and strength, and honor, and glory, and blessing."

CHAPTER XXII.

PLANS OF USEFULNESS.

"The liberal deviseth liberal things," and the man whose heart is so absorbed with the idea of doing good as was that of Dr. Yale, will be pondering upon the best method of accomplishing the object had in view. He was distinguished for his plans, and purposes, and efforts to advance the interests of his fellow-men, and to promote the glory of God. Nor were the plans which he devised merely plans to be talked over and then laid aside; but such as he endeavored to put into execution. Moreover, they were not plans for others only to execute, while he himself shrunk from the labor which their execution required. True, indeed, he sought to enlist the co-operation of his brethren; and one thing in which he particularly excelled was in exciting others to active efforts for the building up of the church of Christ and the advancement of the well-being of men. His desire was that all the men in the church should be *working* men; and perhaps he was enabled to attain this end to a greater extent than most of his brethren in the ministry. Yet, while he wished to call forth the energies of others, he was always willing and forward to expend his own.

Among the objects which enlisted his affections, there was none in which he felt a deeper interest, than the proper training of the young. In the child he saw the man in miniature, and felt the importance of imparting such a bent and of communicating such information to the mind, as that he might be qualified to occupy a position of honor and usefulness in after life. His heart ached at the sight of children growing up in ignorance and vice; and hence the schemes which he devised for their mental and moral improvement. It was as early as the year 1807 that he proposed for the consideration of the church, "the wretched situation of many poor children growing up in ignorance;" and a *Female Charitable Society* was formed and went into operation, for the purpose of aiding in their education. For many years after his settlement as a pastor, he was in the habit frequently of visiting the district schools within the bounds of his congregation for the purpose of catechetical instruction. It was common for more or less of the parents to be present on such occasions, and the children were expected to recite such portions of the Assembly's Shorter Catechism as they had previously committed to memory. If there were children in the district whose parents were unwilling that they should receive instruction in that catechism, they were passed over in the recitation. This practice was continued until a change in the school law of the state rendered its expediency a matter of doubt, and the object had in view was to some extent attained by the establishment of the Sabbath School. There is no question but that this practice was of great practical utility; and to it may be attributed much of that personal influence which he gained over the minds of the youth of his congregation, and the firmness which most of them have ever after manifested in their adherance to that system of truth which they were then taught to believe.

The number in attendance, of course, might be expected to vary according to circumstances; but at times the attendance was numerous and the interest manifested great.

By one or two extracts from his journal, perhaps we may be able to have a better understanding of this matter than we could otherwise obtain.

1817, June 13. "Finished adjusting my accounts with circulating libraries, and catechised a school; present, twenty-eight children. I have now catechised seven schools in which there are two hundred and twenty children that attended catechising. Four of these schools are under the care of pious females who pray with them daily, except one, and if she does not, she is greatly tried and distressed at her neglect. God is truly very merciful and kind to grant the little children such excellent instructors."

Sept. 14. Sabbath. "Preached a sermon to parents, catechised upwards of a hundred children in the intermission, and preached a short sermon to children."

It hardly need be said that upon the establishment of sabbath schools, they received his warmest sympathies, and his most cordial support. He took special pains to secure the attendance of as large a number of the youth and children of the congregation as possible; and indeed, this was one thing which he aimed at in his pastoral visitations.

In devising plans for the welfare of others and the edification of the church, it was his wish to call forth the energies and secure the co-operation of the membership. The way in which this was sought will appear from the following:

1823, Dec. 13. In the evening visited a poor intemperate man. Conversed with him and his wife. Thought of a plan to do him good. Main principle, prayer for the Holy Spirit. Main means, Christian association and influence. Endeavor to get three or four Christian brethren associated to labor with him and for him—to visit him often—to draw him to meetings and to better company—good books. May the Lord direct and bless."

Dec. 14. "Have thought over a plan to draw men to the gospel. Associate three or four Christians, and induce them to labor for the salvation of one, on the plan mentioned above. I do trust the Spirit has directed me to this. I have long been inquiring what I should do. May the Lord direct and, bless. O for faith!"

Dec. 17. "Last evening I met with a few members of the church in the North Eastern district. Endeavored to press three things—doctrine, assurance, labor for souls; by each seeking to be instrumental of saving one, by contributing as the Lord prospers us."

Similar efforts to call into action the members of the church, are spoken of also at a period somewhat earlier.

1821, Sept. 23. "In the evening a church prayer-meeting was attended at the meeting house. Many members were present and some others; though it was designed for none but members. Two proposals were made, to be carried into effect between this and Thursday evening when we are to have another meeting. 1. To consider one half hour. 2. To converse individually with at least one member of the church not present this evening. Pressed the importance of opening the door of the church to admit Him to revive his work—can be done only by a majority—to do nothing is to vote against it."

Oct. 22. "Proposed at the close of the meeting yesterday, that every one should pray for a revival last evening at 8 o'clock, who felt the need of it—and that every one who did not, should mourn over a stupid heart. At that hour I did little else but mourn. It seemed as though God had shut out my prayer."

In laboring to promote the spiritual interests of his people, while he relied upon gospel truth as the instrument, and God's Spirit as the agent, he was accustomed to narrate in public, greatly to the edification and comfort of the pious, any facts which had recently come to his knowledge, respecting the progress of the work of grace in other sections of the church. In the early part of the year 1821, he spent a few days in the state of Connecticut, in the midst of a glorious revival of religion—and upon his return, he made such communications to his people in regard to the displays of God's grace in the salvation of men there, as were calculated to excite their warmest Christian emotions. Of this, mention is made in the following sentences from his memorandum.

1821, May 27. Sabbath. "The Lord has helped me, I hope, this day. Though poorly prepared in every sense, I think I did look to God for his aid, and he gave ear unto me. The people were many and attentive. When I stated facts, in particular cases, they shed tears in profusion."

In the cause of Temperance, Dr. Yale may be considered as having been a pioneer. In this, he was in advance of most of the men of his generation. It is not affirmed that he was the *originator* of that movement, which has done so much for the present generation in saving men from the untold miseries which result from a free and unrestrained use of intoxicating drinks. But if he did not *originate* the movement, he was certainly far in advance of most other men in endeavoring to promote it.

As to his own individual habits, he rigidly abstained from the use, as a beverage, of all intoxicating drinks, when most others indulged it. He advocated the cause of total abstinence, when most others were either silent or opposed. And he boldly carried the subject into the pulpit, and fearlessly preached against the prevailing customs of the day, even when he knew he would not only subject himself to the ridicule of the lovers of strong drink, but also cross the path of many of his dearest friends. He tells us that the battle on this subject, was fought among the people of his charge, as early as the year 1814. In a letter written on the 14th of May of this year, he speaks of this subject in the following terms.

"Happy indeed I am to hear of revivals of religion, and that you have hopes in your region that the millennial glory is rapidly approaching, and that you hear the distant rumbling of Messiah's wheels. I think every minister, and every Christian should ask himself, what more can I do for the hastening of this glorious day? You can not think what a doleful region I live in, some parts of which are almost as destitute of the gospel as the dominions of Juggernaut. Intemperance shakes his deadly sceptre over the county of Montgomery. I have attempted to establish a moral and benevolent society in my own parish; but you can not think how much opposition it meets. But its friends are not discouraged. I heard it said a few days ago as coming from a man employed in a store, that not *one-half* the quantity of spirits had been sold in that store since the establishment of our society, that there was before. If this be true in six months, amid great opposition, may we not be encouraged?"

What is called above "a moral and benevolent society," had for its object, among other things, the promotion of the public weal in the disuse of alcoholic drinks. It is true that the pledge exacted of its members was not the same as that which has been adopted since, nor was the position taken the same as that which has since been taken by temperance societies: but it was a beginning in the work, and all which, at that time of moral blindness on this subject, could be effected. Nor was he discouraged, so as to cease his advocacy of the cause, on account of the opposition which it was destined to encounter. The subject was frequently spoken of in his public discourses; and on the 4th of July 1820 (which was several years before the general temperance effort commenced in the country) he preached before the society above named, a sermon, a copy of which was requested for publication, in which the very ground was taken which was afterwards taken so successfully by others, and the very arguments employed which were afterwards employed with so much effect, in opposition to the then prevalent habit of using intoxicating liquors as a beverage.

And when the general movement on this subject commenced in the country, he (as might have been anticipated) was one of its foremost and most effective advocates. He plead the cause in sermons and public addresses, both at home and abroad; and attentively marked its progress. When men began to discontinue its use in their public gatherings, and on other occasions on which it had been common, he hailed it with thanksgiving and gladness. He spoke of it thus:—

1829, June 3. "Heard the very good news that one of our principal men, a few days ago, raised a building without spirits. The Lord is giving force to conscience."

June 4. "Heard that the same man has employed two carpenters all the season, without spirits, giving them sixpence per day instead of it. I can not be thankful enough for this. Heard also, to-day, of another man who has taken down an old barn, and set up a large new one, without spirits. His chief carpenter said it should not be raised without, and some drunken neighbors joined with him, and said they would not help. But when the day came, not a man failed and the building went up without any difficulty. Thus a victory over sin has again been gained."

Sept. 7. At the training, the company, with but one dissenting voice, voted out ardent spirits. Oh! what shall I say!"

These extracts are worth preserving, principally for the purpose of marking the change which a few years have made in the opinions and practice of the public in respect to the use of alcoholic beverages. Unless such facts were chronicled somewhere, coming generations could hardly be made to believe that during the first quarter of the nineteenth century, and before, men were so much enslaved to rum, that without it no enterprise of importance could be undertaken or carried on.

Among what Dr. Yale called his unfinished works, there is an article on this subject, which I have felt disposed to copy—both on account of the ingenuity which it evinces, and for the purpose of showing the views of the writer. It is as follows:—

BALAAM AND BALAK, OR THE VENDER AND THE BUYER.

Balak, the rum-lover, sent to Balaam the money-lover, and said: There is a people come from the land of many waters, so numerous that they cover the face of the earth, and they are very much opposed to me, so that if they continue to increase, I shall not be able without shame, if able at all, to drink any more rum or even whiskey. For they are a very stiff, precise, tyrannical people, and intend to unite church and state, so that none of our pleasant, jovial, and honorable company shall ever more enjoy ourselves as we have in times past. Come now, Balaam, try by your wisdom and goodness to contrive some way to rid me of these people, for they are the most troublesome of all people. And I doubt not that you will be able to say or do something to remove them. For the words which you speak are good, and you are every where known as a good man and a wise counselor.

Then Balaam, the money-lover, sent to Balak, the rum-seller, and said: The people who come against you are numerous indeed, and increasing; and I should be glad to help you against them, if it could be done safely. But I am fully satisfied that they are a blessed people, and that I must not say or do a single thing against them.

This answer did not satisfy Balak, the rum-lover at all. He supposed that Balaam the money-lover only desired to get more money from him. Therefore he sent the second time and said: Let nothing hinder you, good Balaam, from coming to me; for I will promote you to great honor and will do whatsoever you say to me. Only come, and help me against these people from the land of many waters.

When Balaam, the money-lover, heard this second message, and saw that such rich rewards were offered him, he set himself to prove that *light is sometimes darkness*, and *evil good;* especially when much money and honor are to be gained. Therefore he made up his mind to go with the messengers of Balak, the rum-drinker, and endeavor to do all he could to get money and honor.

So Balaam, the money-lover, came to Balak, the rum-lover, and was received very gladly, though not without a gentle rebuke for not coming the first time he was sent for.

These two being met together, they consulted in what manner they might prevail against the people who came from the land of many waters.

After due consultation, Balak the rum-lover, brought Balaam, the money-lover, to the high places of Bacchus, that he might prepare a sacrifice to their God, and watch the movements of the water-people.

And Balaam said to Balak: "Build me here seven distilleries, and prepare seven hundred thousand barrels of rum, and seven hundred thousand barrels of whiskey." And Balak prepared them.

Then said Balaam, the money-lover, to Balak, the rum-lover: "Deal out now abundantly to all the people that love rum and whiskey. For the people from the land of many waters will increase, if you do not pour out the rum and whiskey abundantly, and keep the merry ones well filled with drink. I will go and see if the Lord will not favor us against the cold water people."

So Balaam, the money-lover, went to seek counsel against the people from the land of many waters. And when he returned he found Balak the rum-lover standing by his distilleries, his rum and his whiskey; and all the chief men who love rum and whiskey stood with him.

Then said Balaam the money-lover, 'Balak the rum-lover has brought me from the mountains afar off, to curse and defy the people that come from the land of many waters. But how shall I curse whom the Lord hath not cursed? Or how shall I defy whom the Lord hath not defied? I see them in the highest stations, and among the wisest and best of men. The people shall be a peculiar people, not subject to the evils which most grievously afflict the rum-lovers. They shall greatly increase and become mighty; and all the rum-lovers and the money-lovers shall desire to be as prosperous and happy as the people from the land of many waters.'

And Balak, the rum-lover, said to Balaam, the money-lover: 'What hast thou done unto me? I sent for thee to curse my enemies, and lo, thou hast blessed them altogether.'

And Balaam, the money-lover, said to Balak, the rum-lover, 'I said before, that I must be careful what I speak.'

Then said Balak, 'Come to another place and curse the people from thence.'

Then they came to another place, and Balak built seven distilleries, and prepared seven hundred thousand barrels of rum and seven hundred thousand barrels of whiskey.

When Balaam consulted to find something to say in favor of Balak, and against the cold water people, he was greatly disappointed, and returned to publish his own confusion. For he said, 'God is not a man, that he should lie, nor the son of man that he should repent. Hath he said, and shall he not do it? Or hath he spoken and shall he not make it good?' 'Light is not darkness, nor is good evil.' The truth must be told, and it is this, and must prevail. The cause of the people from the land of many waters is a good cause; and that of the rum-lovers is an evil cause. There is no perverse design in the cause of the water people; it is all in the cause of the rum-lovers. The water-people make men free; but the rum-people make themselves slaves.'

But Balak, the rum-lover, said: 'Neither bless them at all, nor curse them at all. Come, and I will bring thee to another place.'

'Build me here,' said Balaam, 'seven distilleries, and and prepare seven hundred thousand barrels of rum, and seven hundred thousand barrels of whiskey.'

Now Balaam lifted up his eyes, and saw the cold water people abiding in their comfortable dwellings, abounding in peace and plenty, and he said: 'How goodly are your dwellings, oh people that abstain from strong drink! As the valleys are spread forth, and as gardens by the river-side, so are the abodes of the temperate people in their beauty. Cursed be he that curseth the people from the land of many waters, and blessed be he that blesseth them.'

Then Balak's anger was kindled against Balaam, and he smote his hands together, and said: 'I called thee to curse my enemies, and lo, thou hast blessed them these three times. Therefore, now, flee to thy place: I thought to promote thee to great honor, but the Lord hath kept thee back from honor.' And Balaam said: 'If Balak would give me his house full of silver and gold, I *can not* go beyond the commandment of the Lord.'

'But, come now, I will advertise thee what will become of the rum-lovers in the latter days.'

His views of legislative action, and the propriety of a law prohibiting the sale of intoxicating drinks, are expressed in the following brief extracts of a letter to a friend under date of Oct. 15, 1851:

"From what Agricola writes, I think he will go strong for the Maine law. That is the thing. Too long have we been dealing with men. England has been doing the same a hundred and fifty years, with about the same results. Now God in his wisdom and mercy has put it into the heart of Maine to adopt the very thing. Total abstinence has saved all that have practiced it. Total destruction will annihilate the whole thing. As the former never did any harm, so neither will the latter. As men find their pleasure in something besides intoxicating liquors, so will they find use for their money in something besides traffic in the drunkard's drink. It is now thirty-eight years since I began to speak and act on this subject. I have seen great things. There is no place now in this town north of the village of Johnstown where it is publicly sold."

It has been already said that Dr. Yale was a very close and diligent student of the word of God, and he seems to have adopted something in the form of the "verse system" in his family, many years before it is known to have been adopted to any considerable extent by others. He was strongly impressed with the utility of the practice of committing to memory one verse daily of the sacred scriptures. The introduction of this system into his own family is mentioned in the following extract from his memorandum.

1821, March 23. "Began last Saturday morning to attend to the scriptures more in my family. Each one to recite a passage at prayer-time, from the portion read at the previous season; and each one in rotation to recite a passage at the table. May the word of God dwell in us richly in all wisdom. Oh Lord, awaken our souls."

The peculiar advantages of this system he thus sets forth in his journal under date of January 16, 1832:

"I think the verse-a-day system has peculiar advantages.

1. It is so easy, that it encourages effort.
2. It is so simple, that all can attain it.
3. It is so pure, that no objection can be made to it. Nothing but the word of God.
4. It is so impartial, that the word of God is regarded in its connection.
5. It is so universal, that it may be adopted by all persons, in all places, of all employments.
6. It is so concise, that it takes up but little time, and that which may thus be saved.
7. It is so frequent in occurrence that much will be attained, almost imperceptibly.
8. It is so opportune, that it furnishes materials of thought when alone, and of conversation in company.

How admirable are the ways of God! He first caused his word to be sent throughout the families of the earth, and then taught them this peculiar way of securing the blessings it contains."

The estimate which he placed upon this practice, may also be gathered from the following scrap of original poetry, which he wrote in the album of two of his young friends, only a few months before his death.

EIGHTEEN THOUSAND VERSES IN FIFTY YEARS.

One verse a day, from God's own word,
Implanted deep in memory's soil,
Will make thee joyous in the Lord,
And richly pay thee for thy toil.

In fifty years the sum will swell
To twice nine thousand truly told;
Nor aught on earth will pay so well,
No, not the richest mines of gold.

If storms and darkness o'er thee roll,
And terrors shake thine heart with fear,
Some precious truth will calm thy soul,
And give thee proof that Christ is near.

When on the verge of life you stand,
Just by the sea that has no shore,
Then may you take your Saviour's hand,
To be with him and die no more.

As on your pillow for repose,
You gently lay your weary head,
Fear not, if night your time should close,
And morn should find your spirit fled.

As the mind of Dr. Yale was so much occupied with thoughts respecting the extension and prosperity of the kingdom of Christ, the inquiry frequently arose, why has not this kingdom already become universal, and, by what means is this end to be attained? Of this he speaks in the following terms:

1830, April 14. "Awoke at four, and arose soon. Was led to reflect upon the slow progress of religion in the world. Why is it? God promised to Moses, 'As truly as I live, all the earth shall be filled with the glory of the Lord.' Not yet done—why not? 'After that, in the wisdom of God, the world by wisdom knew not God, it pleased God by the foolishness of preaching to save them that believe.' When God works alone, as in creation, it is soon done. But, when moral agents, angels, men, devils, work, they must have time. God extends his plans so as to give them full scope to develop their characters—time necessary—many and various actions and events necessary; God knows at first how they will act, and how long, and what way they will take to show themselves. He fixes all things accordingly, they show to themselves and others what he knew before. So contingency and immutability are both secured. Our wisdom is, to do as he directs; then all is well with us, and with such other beings as accord with God. The disobedient are comprised in the divine plan; but all in them tends to confusion. The sentiments of men often cross the Lord. He corrects them. He did so when on earth. His disciples often met and overthrew error. Paul disputed in the schools; certain philosophers of the Epicureans, and of the Stoics encountered him. At this day, philosophy is in the way of the gospel. It corrupts the religion of many to the very core. Let me read the New Testament through, expressly to find out the points in which Christ and the apostles crossed error and sin—the points in which the people or their teachers varied from sound doctrine, and the holy law, and the blessed gospel."

How shall the kingdom of Christ be extended throughout the world, was a question which presented itself to the mind of Dr. Yale with absorbing interest. It was a question on which he thought much, and of which he often spoke. He once made mention of certain principles to be observed in this matter, which are of very great importance. As follows:

" 1. *To commune with prayer and holy conversation with Christians, individually, till they, with me, enter fully into the mind of Christ, and make it our business to promote his kingdom.*

2. *To feel, and to endeavor to make others feel, that we are under no obligations to solve the devil's problems.*

Such as: How came Adam's posterity to be sinners in him? or, how can sinners be to blame, if they can not change their own hearts? or, how can decrees and free agency agree? or, how can sinners repent and believe when dependent on God?

Deut. xxix, 29. 'Secret things belong to the Lord our God.'

3. *Never to allow the least despondency, when engaged in the work of the Lord.*

4. *To found everything on the word of God, whether I address saints or sinners; that they may not stand in the wisdom of men, but in the power of God.*

The word of man is of but little weight; but who can resist the word of God?

5. *To visit every family four times in a year; viz: once a quarter, in March, June, September, and December.*"

The Christian reader may remember, that in the month of May, 1843, a missionary convention was held in the city of New York, the design of which was, to endeavor to unite and call forth the energies of various denominations of evangelical Christians, in the work of evangelizing the work. The hope was that by uniting the energies of different bodies of Christians, to a certain extent, as they are in some of the great catholic institutions of the land, more might be done in this important enterprise. And though the results hoped for from that convention were not realised, the object aimed at was a noble one. In this thing, Dr. Yale was one of the prime movers, and he had more to do, perhaps, than any other individual in calling it. In the ardor of his Christian feeling, the chariot wheels of the gospel seemed to move too slow, and he felt that the Christian church was far from doing all her duty in this work. What he thought should be aimed at, was, the evangelizing of the present generation of the heathen, by the present generation of Christians. Some interesting thoughts on this subject are contained in a letter, written to the Rev. Cyrus Yale, of New Hartford, Connecticut, under date of January 11, 1843, as follows:

"Never before did I see so much discouragement as to sustaining the cause of God, as at the present moment. The American Board is running down deeper in debt than ever before, and all our societies seem to be approaching to bankruptcy. Now is the time to look up; now we cease from man. Our resources fail as in the days of Haggai. Then they carried out much, and brought in little. They 'earned wages to put it into a bag with holes.' Wherefore? Because they suffered the house of the Lord to lie in waste. So now the church in America suffers the house of the Lord to lie waste. The heathen cry for help, but we send it not. They perish, because we send not the gospel; and we perish, because we shut up the gospel at home. We do not well. If we tarry thus, some evil will befall us, more than has befallen us already. Let us then lift up our cry to heaven, that the Lord would have mercy upon us, that we perish not, while we leave others to perish. Our convention is not yet; but we are making arrangements to hold one during the anniversaries in May, in New York. The Tract Society, at their late convention, have made an advance, such as we wish; and have given us a partial specimen of what we hope to attain. We hope to enlist as many as nine denominations in the work, and to co-operate on principles as general as those of the Tract Society. Will you not co-operate with us, and aid us in the great work of enlisting the whole world of evangelized Christians to send the gospel to the *present generation of perishing men*? This seems to be our duty. Is it not our duty? Should not you, and I, and every minister of Christ, and every believer, make it our business to evangelize all nations during this generation? Were all Christians and ministers fully engaged in this, might it not be done? Were we as devoted, as laborious, as self-denying, and as willing to suffer as Christ was, could it not be done? I am morally certain of it; are you not also morally sure of it? If it be so, then what follows? Shall not you and I do what we can? Shall we not enlist as many as we can? Will not you, my beloved one, feel that this is your work as a minister of the gospel? Will you not do what you can, by yourself, alone? Will you not enlist other ministers? Is it not needful to speak often one to another?

Are you not answerable for that talent of writing, which the Lord has enabled you to acquire? Is not some paper in Connecticut open to you? Will you not do what you can to wake up Connecticut to this great enterprise? When the wicked are pouring out a deluge of pollution to destroy the hope of our land, will not you do what you can to meet the torrent? I am persuaded, that in our beloved country the struggle is between life and death. Shall we and our people continue to possess the fair heritage of the Lord, or shall it be wrested from us by his enemies? The gospel in its purity, in its power, public and private, is the only thing that can save us. But we increase not the power of the gospel by concentrating its force; on the contrary, by diffusing it, as far as possible, its power prevails. Hence, persecution sends Christians abroad every where, preaching the word; and it may be, that you and I may yet live to eye the fire kindled, which shall scatter American Christians all over the world. Then will the gospel be spread; better for us, and the world, that it be done in this was, than that it be not done at all."

CHAPTER XXIII.

HIS INTEREST IN THE CAUSE OF BENEVOLENCE.

There was no truth of which Dr. Yale had a deeper conviction, than that gifts without grace are of no avail. And among the graces of the Christian, he seemed disposed to set that first, which was set first by the Apostle. I am understood here to refer to *charity*—charity in its true evangelical sense, as meaning both love to God and benevolence to man. His heart bled over human woes and human ignorance; and he most sincerely wished to relieve the one and instruct the other. On the subject of Christian benevolence he had no hobby; but regarded with favor every thing which seemed calculated to meliorate the condition of man or promote the glory of God. His sympathies were also frequently excited by things which he found among his own people, or at least, among those who lived in the territory embraced in his congregation. He was not of those who extend their vision so far as that they can not see objects near at home. He wept over the miseries of men in other lands, and in other climes—and he wept also over the miseries of such as lived within the field of his own pastoral labors.

The reader may be interested in the description which he gave himself of this field, many years ago; that it may be contrasted with what it has become at the close of his ministerial life. Such a description is found in letters written to his correspondents in the state of Connecticut. The first from which I extract was written to Rev. Cyrus Yale, of New Hartford, as follows:

KINGSBOROUGH, *Jan.* 18, 1815.

"MY DEAR COUSIN,

I suppose you are by this time set down among your people, and comfortably surrounded by your little family. I rejoice in the favorable prospects before you, and hope your life may be long, and through the whole of it useful and happy. There is a striking contrast between your situation and mine. Your people are numerous, mine are comparatively few; yours are established in steady and regular habits, mine are forming their habits; yours have been favored with eminent ministers, mine have had but one before myself, and him but a few years; yours are a people of wealth, mine are comparatively poor: you are in a neighborhood of able divines of the same denomination, habits and sentiments; I am surrounded with hedges and wolves, and have but few counsellors within many miles; you have somebody on every side to hold you up, but I have many who would not lament at my fall; you are in the heart of good old Connecticut, but I am in the regions of that state whose very name is almost a reproach. Doubtless it is all well—the Master knows where to employ his workmen to the best advantage; and some may be useful in cutting up bushes and rolling stones, who would do nothing at all in polishing and varnishing. "In a great house there are many vessels," but they are all good in their place; and the kettle to put over the fire is no less needful than the china upon the table. Indeed I believe I may think it a great privilege that God can find any work at all that I am fit to do, and that he can fit me to do any. He is marvelous in working, and even an ass's colt may be of some service 'when the Lord hath need of him.' I am sometimes distressed and perplexed, but never in despair."

In another letter written to the same, July 1, 1828, he speaks as follows:

"I have been long trying to get people to meeting, and with some success. Our sabbath school, including teachers, contains more than three hundred; but we need many, many more. Sixty or seventy families attend meeting very little any where. They are not like your families, stable and firm as the rocks and hills on which they build their dwellings, but they are comparable to the flocks of black birds, which pitch down into the fields, and roll and roll from place to place, till they take wing and soar into other fields. How little good can be done to such a flying population! We have about a hundred families that are pretty stable, but of the whole population in this place, more than one third has changed within eleven years."

The labors of the gospel minister are much more arduous in many places, in consequence of the division of the church into so many different sects, and the prejudices which exist among them. This was one difficulty with which Dr. Yale had to contend, and of which he speaks under date of Oct. 1, 1817, as follows:

"I see a great field around me, which needs immense labor; and while the work is only beginning it remains undone. Ministerial labor in this region is attended with many difficulties, compared with Connecticut. Here our exertions are almost isolated. We have the Dutch religion, and the Scotch religion, and the English religion, and each of these subdivided. Some of us are endeavoring to throw down the walls, but too many think the Lord will dwell only in a square house, and that too, erected by such sacred hands as theirs. Not long since, a candidate from Dr. Mason's school was asked by a good Dutchman, in one of our neighboring towns, if he did not think the Dutch church was one of the two witnesses of whom we read in the Revelations. He answered that he did not know but it was. "And what church do you think the most likely to be the other witness?" "Why, sir, I think it is the Associate Reformed." I hope you will pardon my story telling. I mention this fact to give you some idea of the prejudices which prevail in some parts of our country, and in this region renders the work of the ministry very laborious.

Lest, however, some may think it was only the exterior of the building which was so forbidding, while all was fair and inviting within, let us take a look at the interior, that we may have a more correct and intelligent idea of the whole. There were "regions lying beyond," which were emphatically regions of darkness. So also there were many dark spots within. We may enter the building by the following introduction of Dr. Yale.

1829, Nov. 17. "Visited five families. In these five families, I could not discern the least degree of spiritual life. One of them contained thirteen souls, and did not contain a single reader. They have been here only since last spring. They seem dirty, and filthy, and lazy as heathen. Another family just come, very stupid, no Bible—but they say they left it where they came from, not expecting to stay long. I conversed on the third of John, especially about the brazen serpent. They gave attention. Their daughter thanked me for calling. As to the family that can not read, I know not what to do. They will not go abroad to get instruction, and it is extremely difficult to give any where they are. Saw one benefit of distributing tracts. It interests Christians in the welfare of such families.

In another family where neither the man nor the woman can read, the man a drunkard, and the woman a swearer, where two years ago I was treated rudely, I was now treated very kindly, heard no complaints of neighbors or Christians, and was listened to with profound attention, after they had smoked their pipes. They even appeared to be solemnized. And were it not that little is to be hoped for from such, I should almost hope some good might be done. But God alone can do it. May he glorify his name."

From the above extracts, the reader will see that the field which Dr. Yale was called to cultivate, was not always like a watered garden, at least in all its extent. There were objects even here which excited his deepest sympathy, and in his care for them he was perfectly willing to adopt the maxim which is so grossly abused, while it contains so much truth, that "charity bigins at home." He did not pass by the heathen at his own door-sill, while he strained his vision to look at the condition of those in Burmah or China. Nor did he feel justified in withholding his sympathies from the heathen abroad because there were also heathen at home.

The interest which he felt in the cause of temperance has already been spoken of. He also felt very great interest in the cause of African colonization, regarding it as eminently calculated to better the condition of the degraded and oppressed sons of Ham. I know, indeed, that he has sometimes been charged with indifference to the wrongs endured by the African race, because he did not sympathize with the principles and measures of some of those men and societies of men who have seemed to regard themselves the exclusive friends of the slave. But though he saw nothing in the movements of the so-called "abolitionists" to call forth his sympathies, he was no friend to the institution of American slavery; and the emancipation of the slave, in such circumstances as to make liberty a blessing, and in connection with such a training as to qualify the liberated for the duties of freemen, he regarded as a thing very much to be desired. Yet while he was free to say that he saw no promise of good from the measures of the abolitionists, he believed that the objects of the colonization society were preeminently philanthropic, and that there was the promise of the happiest results from the measures which they had adopted. His feelings on this subject are very briefly stated in a letter to a friend, dated April 23, 1847. Thus:

"I have had some thought of taking opportunity to visit the refugees in Canada. But I have recently learned enough, from the American Missionary, to satisfy me of their condition. This notice being given by friends is to be relied on. If the condition of the emigrants to Liberia were as wretched, and as likely to continue so, I would never again lift a finger to aid them. But the contrast is most marvelous. Depending as I do on the notice of their friends in Canada, and on the notices of all who write about Liberia, I am satisfied that, while the condition of the former has enough in it of ignorance and wretchedness, that of the latter is encouraging beyond any thing which has ever been realized before, or in any part of the world, by the colored people. I think, therefore, I shall not go to Canada."

Dr. Yale's interest in those great national evangelical enterprises which have secured the cooperation of American Christians for the last few years, is widely known. The circulation of religious tracts he regarded as well calculated to promote the interests of man—the operations of the sabbath school met with his cordial approbation—and the cause of education, in all its varied branches, he considered as intimately connected with the prosperity of the community and the welfare of individuals.

In the organization of the Bible society in the county where he lived, and in its support and progress, he took a very prominent part. It is believed to have been chiefly through his instrumentality that this society was first formed. He corresponded with influential men in various sections of the county—he sought personal interviews with them on the subject—he prepared an address to the people of the county in relation to this matter, and caused it to be published and circulated—he secured the calling of a meeting for this purpose, which was held in the court house in the village of Johnstown on the 21st day of Dec. 1816; at which time a society was formed by the adoption of a constitution which appears to have been previously prepared by himself. And after it was formed he took much pains, and performed much labor to promote its interests. He was its chief executive officer for the period of twenty-nine years, and performed its duties with the utmost fidelity. Besides attending to its correspondence, preparing its reports and looking after their publication and distribution, he put forth a vast amount of effort to advance the cause by visiting the various towns of the county, holding public meetings, making public addresses, and sometimes by calling personally upon individuals, and exciting them to activity in the cause. Moreover he was himself a Bible distributor; and on the 27th day of September, 1811, which was more than five years before the Montgomery county Bible society was organized, he received for distribution fifty copies of the Bible from Oneida county.

In promoting the interests of the Bible soeiety in the county, not only during the first years of its existence, but for many years afterwards, while he put forth very great efforts, he met with many and great discouragements. As a single illustration of this fact, I will here transcribe a few passages from his memorandum.

1830, Feb. 9. "Started at nine o'clock to visit N., to promote the interests of the Bible society. Found the case very difficult, the people greatly tormented by divisions, animosities, parties, masonry, &c. At evening Mr. Wood and I attended a meeting at which he preached. When we went into the school house, there was no light except what the stove imparted; at the door several boys and young men were standing, and talking, and laughing. I sat down in the dark and felt distressed. Very few members of the church were present. The whole scene seemed strikingly emblematical of the condition of the people—covered with darkness, cold, indifferent, stupid, asleep, dead. In the family where we lodged, the father, and mother, and a young man, are members of the church—but scarcely a word on the subject of religion, or our business. In the morning the young man went about his work, and gave us very little reason to hope that he would do any thing. We left papers, requesting them to read them, and appointed to preach again next week on Wednesday evening. In the morning, called on several young people and left reports of the Bible society, and told them our object. We called on Elder S. and made arrangements for future operations. He seemed to be cordial in his feelings, and ready to do any thing in his power."

Feb. 17. "Rode to N. and preached. Few present. The meeting was even more chilling than the one last week. Deplorable state! By invitation a few gentlemen came in in the morning. We conversed much with them. A little impression seemed to be made. But their state is dreadful. Oh how dreadful! Darkness visible and tangible. Came home heavy in regard to that people."

The above extracts are given for the simple purpose of giving the reader some idea of the difficulties and discouragements which he had to encounter at that period, in his efforts to advance the cause on which his heart was so much set. Nor was this a solitary instance, nor the place alluded to above the only place where such discouragements were met. Such things were quite too common. It is gratifying, however, to be able to inform the reader, that the above description would not apply to that place at the present time. Religion is now comparatively prosperous in that community, and there is now one of our most efficient branch Bible societies.

It was at the very time when his benevolent mind was occupied with the subject of the formation of the county Bible society, that he was also using his influence for the formation of a society for domestic missions, to embrace the counties of Montgomery and Saratoga. In his journal there is the following entry, under the date of Oct. 8, 1816.

"Prepared the constitution of the Montgomery and Saratoga Auxiliary Missionary Society, and a short address with it for printing."

In the cause of domestic missions he felt the deepest interest. For many of the first years of his ministry there were extensive wastes in the immediate vicinity of his own field of labor, and he frequently made missionary tours into destitute neighborhoods: while he also took special pains to secure both missionaries and the means of their support.

After the matter had been under consideration for several years, a board of domestic missions was formed in August 1821, by the Presbytery of Albany, of which, Dr. Yale was then a member—and he was appointed its corresponding secretary. He held this office as long as that board had an existence, and until it was dissolved with the view of a more direct cooperation of the Presbytery with the Board of Missions of the General Assembly. He found this to be an arduous business. It taxed much of his energy—as it devolved upon him both to direct the labors of missionaries, and to do much towards securing the funds necessary for their support. These missionaries were frequent guests in his own family, and received from him all needful direction and encouragement. But it was enough if he could but thereby promote the interests of Christ's church, and aid in the salvation of men. As a single illustration of his labors in this matter, and of the spirit by which he was actuated, the following brief extracts have been made from his memorandum.

1824, Jan. 30. "About 10 A. M. started for Stratford in company of Deacon Giles and Philo Mills. Arrived a little before sun-set. Attended a prayer meeting in the evening."

Saturday, January 31. "Rode about five miles to the most remote house in the settlement on the north.

Returned in the snow and called at almost every house to distribute tracts. Preached in the evening a sacramental lecture at a school house, well filled, though the weather was uncomfortable."

Sabbath, Feb. 1. "The wind had blown through the night, and I found the light snow sifted over my clothes in the morning; for the house was made of logs and the crevices were not all filled. Preached at half past ten to two rooms full of people. Preached also in the afternoon, after administering the Lord's supper Preached in the evening at a school house in another part of the settlement."

May 3. "Rode to Palatine, fifteen miles, met Mr. Knight, Mr. Johnston, and the elders and trustees of Palatine congregation. Made the proposals of the Presbytery to them, which were accepted—gave Mr. Johnston directions to go to Knox, and returned home, weary, weary, weary, and yet very thankful for the openings of kind Providence, and the prospects of a minister at Palatine Admired and praised God for what he was doing by means of our Missionary Board."

Yet, while Dr. Yale was an American in his feelings, and loved his country with the affection of a true hearted patriot, he felt that there were others also who demanded his sympathies, in addition to those who were enclosed within the geographical limits of the United States. He remembered the words of the Lord Jesus when he said: "The field is the world." "Go ye, therefore, and teach all nations, baptizing them in the name of the Father, and of the Son, and of the Holy Ghost." There was a time when, in his own mind, he agitated the inquiry as to his duty to engage personally in Missionary labors abroad. On this subject we find in his memorandum the following paragraphs:

1820, October 24. "Found news of an earnest request for a Mission among the Great Osages of the Missouri. Many queries during the night whether I ought not to offer myself. Felt unqualified and embarrassed, and as though the labor would be almost too great for my strength and resolution—but I felt a degree of willingness."

October 26. "Have laid the queries respecting the mission to rest in this way: that I do not see my way clear to go, though I should not hesitate as to inclination. I pray the Lord to send by whom he will send."

But though he was led to the conclusion that he was not called upon himself to enter the foreign field, he did feel that he was to do what he could to advance the cause, and to sustain others whom the Great Head of the church should see fit to raise up and send forth. While he contributed from his own resources for these various objects of benevolence, he devised means and put forth efforts to secure contributions from others: and the deep interest which he felt in the cause may be seen in the following sentences from his correspondence. In a letter to his friend, the Rev. Mr. Brace, under date of July 2, 1842, he holds the following language.

"I have many things to say to you, but I can not with pen and ink communicate the tenth that I wish on the subject of the Redeemer's kingdom, which certainly does lie nearer my heart than any other. It seems that I do every day feel it more, while I seem to do nothing worthy of a subject which demands and enjoys an angel's powers and good will. If you have recieved Mr. Bingham's *Ambassador*, you know a little of what a few wish to do, while the world lies in the wicked one, and we do little to save souls from eternal death. Brother Brace, let us pray and labor with the hope of being instrumental of saving millions. I *say* millions. I *mean* millions. May the Lord give us more grace, wisdom, diligence, blessing. Amen."

In another letter, written just a year later than the one from which the above extracts were made, he expresses his strong sense of ministerial responsibility, and the responsibility of ecclesiastical bodies, in respect to the evangelizing of the world. Thus:

"I wonder what the General Association of Connecticut mean, when they spend a whole session, and say not a word about evangelizing the world. I am amazed at them, and at the other ecclesiastical bodies. They seem not to understand their commission. With what are they charged? Is it only to take care of the little state of Connecticut? Does their commission extend no farther? Will the Lord say "Well done" to a laborer who does not even attempt to do the greater part of his work? Where is the spirit which animated Samuel John Mills, Jr.? Had all our ministers and ourselves the same spirit, would not the world soon be filled with the knowledge of the Lord? If Connecticut river possessed the properties of rendering every human being immortal and happy, as soon as bathed in its waters, and if the people of Connecticut were charged by their Maker to publish the joyful tidings to all the world, would they think they had done their duty, when they had told the people of the state of the properties of that river? If they should collect their holiest men together to devise ways and means to publish the joyful tidings, would you be satisfied that those men had done their duty, when they returned home after one week's session and had not said a word about their main business? So have your General Association been doing this year. So have some other bodies been doing. Are you not amazed at their rashness? How dare they thus disregard the dying command of their risen Lord and Saviour? It seems to me that Christ's ministers have forgotten their duty. They spend day after day talking about slavery about which he has given them no charge, and go home without saying a word about spreading the gospel all over the world, which is their main business! Brother Brace, "these things ought not so to be." Let the world be evangelized, and the world will be healed. But there is no other healing stream. O let the world hear of the river of water of life. Does not that heal the soul? How can we keep back the glorious truth? Why need we be a thousand ages in telling the world of the river of salvation? Was there ever such another strange thing in the universe of God, as there has been in this world for eighteen hundred years? The Son of God crucified for the world, and yet unknown to the world! His command to publish it to the world, and yet his servants silent as death! Is it not amazing? Tuesday of last week a letter was read in the meeting of our Bible Society from a man who was a convert last winter. He had given a dollar, but afterwards his conscience smote him because he had done no more to send that Bible to others, while he felt it to be the principal means of his own salvation. So he paid ten instead of one. The old school General Assembly took up the subject and *said* something. Yet I fear that little was *done*. So we pass on year after year, while twenty millions of souls go unsaved into eternity! Brother Brace, farewell. Let us do our part of this great work, even if we do it alone. I know of no other way toplease our Lord.

Respect and love, much and strong, to Mrs. B. and all yours. E. YALE.

Nor was Dr. Yale's interest in these matters comparable to wind, or of that evanescent character which vanishes into smoke. It did not expend itself in eloquent words and pathetic sentiments, while all the zeal which is felt, dies away with the sound, and nothing is done or attempted more than there would have been if no eloquent appeals had been made. Would we understand the depth of that interest which he felt in the various objects of benevolence which make their appeals to the friends of Christ, we need to look at the self-denying efforts which he put forth to advance them. In the course of his pastorate he spent days, and even weeks in going from house to house and personally soliciting donations for these various objects of Christian philanthropy. If the reader desires to hold communion with him on this subject, to be let into the inner chambers of his heart, so as to understand the feelings under which he acted, and to attend him upon some of his tours for the collection of funds, I am happy in being able to gratify him. Read the following:

1823, Oct. 20. "Having invited and requested the members of the domestic missionary society to meet this evening to consult about raising $125, about twelve met and agreed that it would be best to undertake it immediately. Twenty dollars were subscribed. Thus about one-sixth part is secured. Now I shall try to raise $20 every day this week. I feel some anxiety, but I think it is the cause of God, and that I can trust him. I do hope, love to his cause and the good of my fellow men move me. Oh God, purify me from all selfish views, and give me success."

Oct. 21. "Felt an anxiety this morning on this subject, but was enabled freely to plead the cause before my Lord and Savior. In the afternoon went out with the hope of obtaining $20 more; but was disappointed in that I did not find but just one man at home. He and his wife gave me four dollars, which was all I gained. Yet, I thank God, I am not discouraged."

Oct. 22. "In view of my labors in soliciting subscriptions I felt disagreeable for a time, but was enabled to feel that all hearts are in the Lord's hand, and that he can turn them and make them willing. Went out trusting in God. Obtained $20·50. In four instances where I might have called, or did call, I did not find them at home. In one case a man and his wife gave me six dollars very cheerfully. In another, a man from whom I did not expect much gave me six dollars very pleasantly. In another, a man from whom I had expected something, gave me nothing but objections. These I answered very easily, and yet he kept objecting. I finally concluded that his heart was too small, and his mind too ignorant to be wrought upon. Thank my gracious Savior, I was enabled to converse with composure. I left him, saying that he was under no obligation except to God, and that the matter rested between him and his Maker. He said he would think of it. I felt more sorrow for him than I did for myself. Poor man! I afterward learned that he lets out money at fourteen per cent."

Oct. 27. "Spent the day in raising subscriptions. Very kindly received, and successful. Raised more than $30 this day. The sum now amounts to $84, and I think the remainder will be raised without difficulty.

The Lord has been very kind indeed, and blessed be his name. He has blessed and strengthened me, and I now feel ready to talk with almost any man I meet."

The various benevolent societies of the day, found in him a zealous cooperator; nor were the accredited agents of these societies refused a hearing from his pulpit. Yet there were times, when the number and claims of these several societies, were a trial even to him. On this subject we find in his diary, the following interesting reflections:

1824, May 12. "SOCIETIES.—I have been tried because they are so numerous, and require so much time and care. But the thought struck me this morning: *What if there were none?* Then suppose you saw the wants of men just as you do now—that you felt an ardent desire to relieve them—that you exerted your own powers and made your own sacrifices—would you not wish others to aid you? Would you not endeavor to obtain their aid? Should you obtain it, what would be the result? *Societies.* Now they are ready to your hand—what is to be done? Shall they be neglected? Then where is your desire to do good? Take them as they are, be thankful for them, go on laboring in them, and trusting in God."

As the soldier has joy when he gains a battle, and the husbandman when he reaps a harvest, so also does one who truly loves the cause of Christian benevolence rejoice in its prosperity. In this we have another illustration of the interest which was felt in this matter by Dr. Yale. It is expressed in the following paragraph:

1829, March 10. "Yesterday and to-day I have seen and admired the goodness of God in directing and prospering my new plan to obtain donations for domestic missions, as a work of faith and labor of love. He seemed to be opening the heart. Oh that he would indeed increase and strengthen faith and love greatly. These are greatly needed. Oh Lord, move our hearts."

1830, Aug. 24. "Rev. Mr. Weed called about nine o'clock. We prayed together for wisdom, grace, and blessing. We went out and had a most delightful day.

One man was ready as soon as he understood our object, and subscribed a hundred dollars. This was not all. He expressed views of the subject and of provision for his children, of the most enlarged kind. We called on some others, and found much good feeling. Oh, how glad I was, and I hope thankful for the grace of God bestowed upon him. Oh that it might be bestowed upon all my people."

Aug. 25. "We called on several, and with my own obtained $140, so that in two days we have raised $250; and yet, there are only six subscribers. I am truly surprised at it. I bless God for it. I apprehended great trials in connection with it, and I hope and pray for great grace. I know that God is able to sustain us, and to make all grace abound."

Aug. 26. "In the morning found trials arising on account of the stand we have been taking, so much in advance of what we have been. The enemy will roar. Some that have professed to be friends may fail. Many may say it is extravagant. Motives may be questioned. But my mind runs immediately to Christ,—'Ye know the grace,' &c.,—to the apostles—primitive Christians—the word of God—living by faith—a man that should die—a Christian. I prayed that I might be a Christian—like Christ—like the apostles. Blessed be God, it helped me to pray—to cast my care on him. The Lord answereth the requests of his people in truth and terror—truth to them—terror to his enemies. Oh let me go after him through the sea. Let this church follow. Oh God, cause us to be Christians."

When, however, a soldier loses a battle, and the husbandman fails in a harvest, he is filled with grief. So also did the interest which was felt by Dr. Yale in the cause of benevolence, sometimes show itself by his grief on account of the apathy of some of its professed friends, and the want of success which attended his efforts to advance it. Take a single illustration, among the many which might be given.

1830, Aug. 27. "To-day Brother Weed and I went to B. to endeavor to finish an important work there.

Found some individuals of importance entirely indisposed—moved by nothing, even such as profess to be friends—elders. Very few at the meeting. Only one of these few seemed desirous to act. One person who had subscribed forty dollars desired to draw back, because his family, his wife and daughters were averse to it. It was indeed a grievous disappointment. We returned home in deep sorrow for the miserable condition of our brethren. After our return we called on one from whom we expected twenty-five or thirty dollars, who did not subscribe any thing, though he promised to give something.""

CHAPTER XXIV.

MEANS USED TO PROMOTE MISSIONARY OPERATIONS AMONG HIS PEOPLE.

For a number of years past the congregation of which Dr. Yale was pastor, has contributed for benevolent purposes, perhaps, more in proportion to their means, than most other congregations; and the inquiry has often been suggested, how has this desirable end been attained? This is certainly a question of considerable interest, and one also of great practical importance. There can be no doubt, that very much of that spirit of enlarged benevolence, which has been there developed for years past, is to be attributed to the enlightened zeal and judicious labors of their pastor. It has not been of spontaneous growth there, any more than in other places; but the results have been realized as the fruit of long-continued and persevering efforts. Time was when that people fell very far below $1,500 a year, as the medium, or even the maximum of their gifts for benevolent purposes; and that point was attained by degrees, and as the result of much fervent prayer, and much hard labor on the part of their spiritual guide and leader. And, much as they have given at times, Dr. Yale steadily maintained that, instead of exceeding their obligations, they did by no means come up to them.

This idea is clearly expressed in the following:

1829, January 1, Tuesday. "Rose before five this morning, renewed my covenant with God, and went to a prayer-meeting at sun-rise (very interesting indeed). Made arrangements with all my might for the evening. This evening a number of men have met to consult, and to raise contributions for foreign missions. Not so much feeling and liberality as I could wish. One subscribed fifty dollars. This is good, compared with former times; but it is not good compared with our duty. I fear the judgments of God. Two hundred and twenty-four dollars and fifty cents were subscribed on the spot. But O, how much do we need the grace of God! I feel indeed cast down in my soul, because of the hardness which is too manifest by many. My heart is not right. I am not near to God. I need very much to draw near to God. O thou who art the hope and portion of my soul, do not let me fall. Save me. Purify me. Fit me for thy service. Glorify thyself in me through Jesus Christ."

January 2. "Felt anxious in the night for fear we should fail greatly. One important man was not at the meeting, and another whom I expected very much, was not there. Feared the workings of ambition and vanity in my mind. Sought God and obtained relief; especially in reading Psalm xlvi: '*God is our refuge and strength, a very present help in trouble.*' Good words, and comfortable words. In the morning I went to one of the brethren who was absent, and he had his mind made up to give fifteen dollars. I rejoiced. I went in the afternoon to see the other, but he was not at home. Felt comforted some."

It was by no means always that contributions of $100, or of $50, or of $10, were secured from individuals; and, in fact, such contributions were formerly unknown. He was himself greatly surprised on one occasion, at the receipt of $10, for missionary purposes, from one of the wealthy men of his congregation. This circumstance is thus noticed in his journal:

1831, February 11, 4 o'clock. "A singular event has just occurred. An aged man who has much property just came into the study, and, after some inquiry, handed me $10, for foreign missions. Surely the heart of every man is in the hand of the Lord, as the rivers of water. He turneth it as he will."

Under date of September 30, of the same year, we find the following, in relation to the same man:

"Mr. —— called and gave me $10 more for foreign missions, making $30 during this year. I admire the dealings of God with this man. He shows that the silver and the gold are his. Surely all hearts are in his hands."

In this matter the first thing with Dr. Yale was to cultivate among his people the spirit of missions. The spirit of missions he regarded as the spirit of Christ. His desire was that every Christian believer should feel that there was an object for which he ought to live, more worthy of the pursuit of Christ's disciples than merely to amass wealth or to attain the good things of the present world. One great object of his ministry was to impress this sentiment upon the mind, and to urge Christian professors to live in view of it. The beneficial results of missionary efforts he was not accustomed to measure by the amount of contributions secured, so much as by their tendency to create or to foster a missionary spirit. His estimate of the spirit of missions may be seen in the following brief extracts from a letter to a friend, written as early as 1818.

"What do you think, Brother B., of the Moravian brethren? Of that spirit which could make them resolve to sell themselves for slaves, and work among negroes to save souls? Of that spirit which animated them to dash among the ice mountains of Greenland and Labrador, and abide in those inhospitable climes, and sell their small pittance of coffee to procure food for widows and orphans? Is not this the spirit which came from heaven with the *Great Missionary* who was sent by the Father? Did not this spirit move Paul, when he said to the Thessalonian saints: "Being affectionately desirous of you, we were willing to have imparted unto you, not the gospel of God only, but also our own souls, because ye were dear unto us?" Oh, for such apostles, for such ministers, for such Christians! Were all such, the unregenerate would find no refuge, but by flying to Christ, or to the dark abodes of infidelity. I fear our Lord and Master will not highly approve of many things which some of his professed followers think innocent and even very needful. Do you know the man, Brother B., who is in fact willing to act to the full extent of the principles he professes to believe? I do not know whether others are tried as I am, but really I am at times distressed because I do not go to the utmost possible extent in self-denial to build up Christ's kingdom and save souls from ruin."

The above passages indicate the spirit which animated his own bosom, and which he endeavored to instil into the bosoms of others. Nor did he ever have the least apprehension that the spirit of benevolence in the church in respect to missionary operations abroad, would interfere in the least unfavorably with the support of religious institutions at home. The man that feeds the hungry beggar, will not be likely to neglect to provide for his own children. His views on this subject will appear from a few passages from another letter to the same correspondent, under date of April 1, 1825.

"My people are advancing to a noble spirit. They have presented me with about $60·00 this year to enable me to obtain a horse. They paid $150·00 last year for domestic missions, and subscribed about $75·00 for the benefit of the Jews, to be paid next Monday. This week they have raised a monthly subscription for one year in aid of the A. B. C. F. M. exceeding $100·00, and we expect it will rise to two hundred or more. This is for the year, to be paid monthly, or quarterly. I mention this to show how I expect to live among my people, while I devote my whole time to ministerial duty, and also to say to you, my good brother B., that I think the support of foreign missions the best means in the world to make a people liberal. Nothing so much enlarges the views as to fix the limit of your action at the boundary of the world, and cast your eye often over the perishing population which lies between you and this boundary. Nothing so effectually breaks up the frost of a selfish heart; nothing warms so deep the recesses of the soul; nothing moves it so powerfully to action. Being thus affected, men do not think so much of five dollars in charity, as they did once of one dollar to support their own minister. I will presume upon your patience and your love so much as to state a few facts. I know two contiguous congregations in this state. Both support Presbyterian ministers of nearly equal salaries. The one is twice as able as the other as to property. The more able does next to nothing for foreign missions, for domestic missions, for education, or for the Jews; and is in debt to its own minister from a thousand to fifteen hundred dollars. The less able pays more annually for charitable objects than for the support of its minister, and pays the salary of their minister punctually, and helps him besides whenever he needs. How true the words of the Holy Book; "There is that scattereth and yet increaseth, and there is that withholdeth more than is meet, and it tendeth to poverty."

There is also a passage in his diary under date of March 21, 1833, which expresses his estimate of an enlarged spirit of benevolence above that of the most liberal pecuniary contributions. It is as follows:

"At 2 o'clock P. M., attended a meeting for the promotion of benevolence. The traveling was bad, and yet numbers attended from different and remote sections of the church. There appeared to be a good and delightful feeling. There were $12 on paper before, and the addition to day was $668·75, making in all $680·75. O that I might be thankful for this token of divine goodness. May the Lord purify our hearts. O may the blessed Spirit dwell with us. O Lord, in infinite mercy, fill our hearts with holy love. For if we give all our goods to feed the poor, and have not charity, we are nothing. O give us a humble, prayerful, benevolent heart, and we shall be blessed. I do beseech thee, do not deny this. O leave us not to barrenness of soul while we open our hand."

There was no truth of which Dr. Yale was more fully persuaded, or which he desired more deeply to impress upon the minds of others than this, that the object of life was not to make money, and that this was altogether unworthy of the pursuit of an immortal mind. Impressed with this idea it was that he sometimes sharply rebuked that over-eagerness which is frequently manifested by men to make money for the purpose of making and possessing it. For the same reason, he looked with a sort of holy abhorrence upon the panic which has pervaded the community for a few years past, for California gold.

Soon after the excitement first broke out in the country (a portion of his own people being affected by it) like a faithful sentinel, he sounded the note of alarm, and in a public discourse gave free utterance to the sentiments of his own mind on this subject. His views are also expressed in his correspondence with a friend, a few extracts from which on this subject will here be given.

"What a sad thing to go to California after gold! Had they gone to give away gold for the salvation of the poor, ignorant, perishing souls in California, neither father nor mother need have felt much concern about them. But now they are likely to be ruined both for this world and the world to come. If they get gold to any great amount, it will almost certainly make them indolent and worthless in time, and ruin them in eternity as a matter of course. If they get none of any amount, they will come home (if they come at all) disappointed, ashamed, depraved in their habits, unsteady, and less inclined to work than before. Like the gambler, they will be vexed at their loss, and try some way to make it up. O, it is a sad business.

I have wondered how good people could ever encourage the enterprise in any way whatever."

Again he says:

"Your statements about the Californians are truly appaling to one who regards the soul more than money. Alas! how many will lay their bones there! How many will wreck their characters there! How many who return, will be worse than soldiers from the army! How many will be corrupted and ruined by the gold they obtain! How many will lose their souls to all eternity in consequence of that desire to be speedily rich! Yet they say to me, "Is it not lawful?" To be sure it is. But is every thing expedient that is lawful? A man need not destroy himself in a business because it is not forbidden. Not one in a hundred will ever be benefited by the enterprise which has taken them to California. 'He that gathereth by labor shall increase.'"

Again he writes:

"California has made fools of multitudes, and ruined thousands both for this world and the future. More good has come from Plymouth-rock than a thousand years will produce from California. Men seem to pay no attention to history in regard to rich mining countries. They seem not to know that a rich mining country never enriched its inhabitants. They have forgotten, or never knew, that Spain and Portugal were ruined by the riches of America. They have forgotten, or never knew that stern virtue had its cradle in the barren regions of New England; and that like causes will produce like effects. The riches of a place are its charms with most people; its virtues and intelligence with few. Your brother E. is probably a specimen of the best of Californians. Half that go there die. Half of the remainder lose their health. Nine out of ten had nothing else to lose, as they had neither money nor morals. Half of one tenth lose what they had of either, and a few remain unscathed, if they return. But none, even of those who get wealth, make any addition to their moral worth. O, it is a desperate enterprise, from which every wise man should keep far away."

Such were the views which he ever cherished of efforts to get gold merely for the sake of having it, or for the sake of using it only for the pleasure or aggrandisement of its possessor, without regard to the interests of religion, or the welfare of others. These views he wished to impress upon his people; and to the success which attended his labors in this respect may be traced whatever of the spirit of missions is found to exist among them—at least whatever exists there above what may be found in other portions of the church. And while he labored to promote the spirit of missions among his people, he labored to promote only that which he possessed himself. He evidently acted upon the principle that strong feeling in himself might result in producing similar feeling in others. When he spoke of Christian responsibility, and the duty of God's people to live and labor for the extension of Christ's kingdom, he spoke only the feelings of his own heart—and when he called upon others to make sacrifices to promote the great objects of Christian beneficence, he required of them nothing beyond what he was willing himself to perform, Thus he sought to infuse his own spirit into others by frequently presenting the subject from the sacred desk, and by holding meetings during the week for prayer and consultation in respect to their individual responsibilities. It was his wish also to keep his people informed in respect to the benevolent operations of the day. For this purpose he was accustomed to narrate interesting facts in his public discourses, and the missionary prayer meetings; while he took special pains to introduce into the families belonging to his congregation such periodicals as would give them suc h informatio as he thought it important for them to receive. In doing this he sometimes assumed some personal pecuniary responsibilities, as may be seen in what follows:

1830. March 29. "In the morning, in thinking over charitable objects, felt it to be my duty to take measures to procure and circulate such publications as give light in regard to them. It will cost me more than twenty dollars, but I must lay myself out for God's service, and trust him to enable me to bear the expense. Wrote for six copies of the Missionary Herald, and for six of the Tract Magazine."

While he prayed himself and excited others to pray for the blessing of God to rest upon the missionary enterprise, he desired that all might feel the inconsistency of praying for these things while they neglected the use of appropriate means. His doctrine was that prayers and alms should always be conjoined; and that it was only mocking God, to offer a heartless prayer, while no corresponding means were employed to secure the end contemplated. Moreover he fully believed that there was nothing lost by a judicious and liberal bestowment of funds upon the real objects of charity. He was never afraid to trust Providence; nor did he fear the fulfillment of the promise: "Honor the Lord with thy substance, and with the first fruits of all thine increase: So shall thy barns be filled with plenty, and thy presses shall burst out with new wine."

Interesting thoughts on this subject, together with a statement of some interesting facts are found in a letter of his, written on the 1st of January, 1841.

"I fear I am an egotist, but you partly compel me. I am surprised to see the contributions of my people. Many have enquired the causes, but I have not attempted to tell them. Since your last I have thought on the subject some, but am unable to tell why it is that they do as they do, unless it be divine grace shed down on very simple means, if means they may be called. For many years, I have given a tenth of my income annually for benevolent purposes, though few knew it. Numbers become acquainted with the operations of the day, and feel as all Christians do when enlightened to see the state of facts. This is about all I can say. Never before have I been so much surprised as at the close of 1840. Eleven hundred dollars or more for the Bible Society. Six hundred dollars for foreign missions. One hundred and ninety for colonization, and a little for other purposes, amounting to more than $1,900.

And yet the pecuniary pressure has been tremendous. Almost all our people have been pressed, and I, never so much before. Yet we keep along. Some among us fail; but as yet not one who has ever contributed much. Is not this marvelous? When one such does fail, I will tell you, if you and I live. Never yet have I known one of my contributors to fail. God may try us in this way. If he does, it will be to correct our pride, or some other evil propensity."

Dr. Yale was accustomed oftentimes to mark the providences of God, in furnishing him with means in unexpected ways, to meet his engagements for benevolent purposes.

Take the following as an example:

1830, Dec. 21. "Attended a wedding and received $7·44, so only fifty-six cents remain to be made up of all that I gave away on Monday. Such special providences require special acknowledgments, so I devoted the whole to the Lord. As he teaches me to venture for him, so may I learn to do it. I have never ventured so much as this year, and I have never seen so much of his goodness in meeting me and supplying my wants. He deals very bountifully with me.

'I'll praise him for all that is past,
And trust him for all that's to come.'"

The scale by which he graduated his donations for the various objects of Christian benevolence, is contained in the preceding extracts—not less than one-tenth of all his income. He did not always wait until the money was actually received, but frequently pledged specific sums beforehand, with a reliance upon the kind providence of God for means to meet his engagements.

1834, Jan. 8. "Now one week is gone. I have looked over all my pecuniary accounts of the last year, and find that the Lord has given me, as actually received, $698·01, coming within $1·99 of ten fold the amount ($70) which I subscribed for benevolent purposes. This surely is near enough. And doubtless if I had put down every thing (as I have probably forgotten some), it would have exceeded $700. Oh, how wonderful is the goodness and righteousness of the Lord!

P. S. On further attention I found my income $730."

In this same year Dr. Yale received an invitation to enter upon another and a different field of labor, in which he was expected to receive an increase of salary. For a while his mind was somewhat disturbed by the proposition, and thinking that he might perhaps regard it as a duty to accept it, he records the following resolution in respect to the disposition of the salary which he might receive:

"A tenth-part of all the Lord gives me is devoted, till it amounts to $700 a year, and then all over that sum to go into my contributions for benevolent objects."

In the preceding pages it has been said that Dr. Yale was peculiarly systematic in all his arrangements, and he was not less systematic in his contributions for purposes of Christian charity, than in other things. His views of systematic benevolence he thus expresses in a letter to a friend, dated December 15, 1852, which was less than a month before his death:

"Your affairs interest us very much, and we are glad to have you notice them minutely. We are glad to see you do right and go straight forward whether people like it or not. That is the way to build up a reputation that is worth having. Every little adds to it and strengthens it. You may never be rich. We hope you never will be. The rich are commonly worthless, and many times pernicious. The way is to pray as Agur, and to do good as you go along, a little and often as you have ability and opportunity. Perhaps it may be as well, for the present, to say little of what you do; but do it whether others do the like or not. It will work like leaven, not the less for being hid, and will show itself in due season. Go on steadily, and do what you can systematically. You may talk of the Bible principles while you act upon them. You will see others begin gradually to act upon the same, and will rejoice in the goodness which you behold. I have not seen all I wish, nor all I hope to see of God's goodness in giving the people and my friends a mind to work, but I see some acting, as I think, wisely.

Some of my friends have blamed me for doing too much. They have said, 'You should lay up for your old age, and a rainy day.' So I do—but not in the way which they most approve. My motto is, 'Trust in the Lord and do good; so shalt thou dwell in the land, and verily thou shalt be fed.' My supplies are not laid up in California gold, nor in bank stock, nor in bonds and mortgages, but in the promises of God. Are not these better than the promises of men? Thieves care nothing for these, and would not rob me if they could, nor could they rob me if they would."

In this, as in other things, he commended to others only that which he was willing to practice himself. In fact, Dr. Yale always preached by example, and there were not among all his people any who gave more willingly, or more freely, or more liberally, in proportion to their means, than he. There is a principle which is well understood, that men are not apt to rise above the mark at which they aim, and in his efforts to promote the various objects of Christian benevolence, Dr. Yale always kept this principle in view. Therefore it was that he set his mark high, and devised and proposed liberal things.

1832, March 5. "Attended a meeting for conversation previous to the monthly concert. A goodly number present. It was thought best to endeavor to raise $1,000 this year for charitable objects, and to devote $150 to constitute me a life director of the American Bible Society, and $500 to support a missionary in foreig lands. Upwards of $600 were subscribed. My soul did magnify the Lord, and rejoice in God my Savior. I think I felt some like David, when he said, 'What am I and my people, that we should be able to offer after this sort?'"

In his efforts to promote the cause of benevolence among his people, various plans were proposed at different times, and various courses pursued.

In the year 1821, he mentions the following:

"Plans of benevolence now agitated in the church.

1. To educate a young man with a view to the ministry.

2. To cultivate a common missionary field of four acres.

3. To cultivate private portions for the same purpose.

4. To prepare a box of clothing."

And in the following year we find the following entry in his memorandum:

"This evening attended a meeting of such as assisted in cultivating the missionary fields. Prospects favorable. Obtained subscriptions the current year to the amount of one acre."

But though he speaks thus encouragingly of the cultivation of a missionary field, it is understood to have been an experiment which did not succeed very well, and was consequently soon abandoned.

In his efforts to collect funds for benevolent purposes, he frequently made personal application to individuals, to solicit both their contributions and cooperation. Sometimes also he entered the names of individuals in a little book which he kept for the purpose, with the intention of putting forth some special effort to induce them to give to some particular object of benevolence, somewhat in proportion to what he supposed to be their ability. Thus:

1834, June 17. "I have entered the name of D. C., in my little diary. My object is to endeavor to assist him to become a life director of the American Bible society, by his contributing $150. I spoke to him and prayed for him. By the help of God it can be done. All hearts are in his hand. The silver and the gold are his."

June 18. "I have entered the name of T—— L. in my little diary. My object is to endeavor to aid him to become a life director of the County Bible Society, by his contributing $50 to its funds; and then to enjoy his society and aid in advancing the cause among others. The Lord can graciously enable him to enjoy this privilege."

June 24. "I have entered the name of D. P. in my little diary, with a view to aid him in becoming a life director of the American Bible Society by his contributing $150 to its funds. Will not the Lord grant me success?"

Sometimes after a public presentation of the cause, cards were passed through the congregation on the sabbath for the purpose of giving each individual an opportunity to put down what he felt disposed to give, and in some cases the results were quite satisfactory.

It is not, however, to be supposed that Dr. Yale made a righteousness of these charitable contributions. Nothing could be farther from the truth. After all the liberality manifested by his people in sustaining the various objects of benevolence, he felt the deepest anxiety, lest many of them should after all fail of securing their own personal salvation. On this subject he employs the following language, in a letter to a friend. After speaking of some liberal contributions which they had made, he says:

"I fear my own heart while I record these facts about the liberality of my people. I admire the good providence of God, which enables them to do it, and his rich grace which inclines them to do it. And after all I fear that some of them will be lost. Oh what a dreadful thought! to do so much for the gospel, through the common grace of the gospel, and then perish for want of the special grace of the gospel. I am amazed when I think of it. I think that as soon as the money for the arrearage is raised I shall endeavor to set these things before them in as solemn a manner as I can. For some of the worst feelings of the human heart may be nourished by such things—spiritual pride and self-righteousness—and it may be love of the world besides. Oh, I fear lest our pride should bring us low. I am amazed to see what God has done for us; and yet the great thing remains undone. If the heart is not sanctified to God, all will perish."

For a number of successive years he was accustomed to attend the annual meetings of the A. B. C. F. M., of which he was a corporate member. Those were meetings for which he had the highest relish; not on account of the business transactions connected with them, so much as the devotional spirit with which they were conducted, and the object for which they were held.

At these meetings he felt as if he was sitting in heavenly places. Here he obtained the renewal of his spiritual strength; he received a fresh baptism to the missionary work; his heart was annointed afresh with that spiritual unction, the import of which he well understood; and when he returned to the people of his charge and the field of his labor, his custom was to endeavor to excite anew a missionary spirit among them. This he ordinarily did by giving them a more or less extended account of the doings of the meeting and of the state of the missions under their care, and by communicating such missionary intelligence as seemed to him to be desirable.

I have thought that the reader would be both gratified and profited by the perusal of one of the discourses which he preached on these occasions.

Though the one which is here given contains no particular statements of the condition of the heathen world, or the progress of the missionary cause; yet in the circumstances of the case, it was evidently well calculated to excite a missionary spirit, and to cause his hearers to feel somewhat as if they were themselves occupying the places of which he spoke. It was preached on the 26th day of September, 1847, upon his return from the meeting which had been held at Buffalo, a short time before.

The discourse, as far as written, is as follows:

HEAVENLY PLACES.

Eph. ii, 6. "And hath raised us up together, and made us sit together in heavenly places in Christ Jesus."

Heavenly country, heavenly Jerusalem, heavenly things, heavenly places, are phrases used in the word of God, to denote things and places different from the common things and places of this world. Mankind are not born in heavenly places. For both Jews and Gentiles, all men, are "by nature children of wrath." And you hath he quickened who were dead in trespasses and sins; Wherein in time passed ye walked according to the course of this world, according to the prince of the power of the air, the spirit that now worketh in the children of disobedience: Among whom also we all had our conversation in times past, in the lusts of our flesh, fulfilling the desires of the flesh and of the mind; and were by nature the children of wrath even as others." And those who are favored to sit with Christ and one another, in heavenly places, are raised up by him from the state of sin and death in which all are born.

The heavenly places are places in heaven, where Christ sitteth at the right hand of God. And they are places on earth, which resemble places in heaven, where Christians meet Christ and one another, to do his will and enjoy his favor.

A Christian family is a heavenly place.

A social circle for prayer and praise is a heavenly place.

The house of God is a heavenly place.

The table of the Lord is a heavenly place.

But the real heavenly place is heaven itself, where Christ is.

HEAVENLY PLACES AT BUFFALO.

It was not the city—though it was *in* the city. Nor were all the people of the city, or that were in the city, in the heavenly places. But heavenly places were there. And there were people in the heavenly places.

It is my intention to give you some thoughts on the communion season on Thursday the 9th day of September.

1. It was a great and exclusive assembly.

The house in which we met was large; with large galleries on three sides, and a session room opening into the front gallery. All parts were filled; the platform around the pulpit and the pulpit with its stairs; the slips on the right and left, and in the front; the galleries and the session room. Besides all these, many were standing who could not find a seat. There was no room for spectators. All were communicants. Notice had been previously given that none could be accommodated but communicants.

I felt sorry for those who were excluded, while I wondered to find myself there, admitted into that great multitude. So it was a great and exclusive assembly.

Not that the lines were daawn precisely where they will be drawn on the last day in the heavenly places above. How affecting the thought that the searcher of hearts himself will not only be there, but his eye will fall on every one destitute of a wedding garment, and he will say; "Friend, how camest thou in hither, not having a wedding garment?" What an exclusion will that be! On the other hand, how deeply did every humble soul, in the heavenly places at Buffalo, say, "Lord, why was I a guest?"

> "Why was I made to hear thy voice,
> And enter while there's room,
> While thousands make a wretched choice,
> And rather starve than come?'

2. In those heavenly places, the *assembly was from every quarter, and from afar.*

They came from the East, and from the West, and from the North, and from the South. From Maine to Missouri; from Canada to the southern states. From Europe, Asia, Africa, and the islands of the sea. At the same time we thought of Missionaries and their churches assembled in other heavenly places, at seventy-three missionary stations. Though absent in body, they were all present in spirit. Who in those heavenly places could help thinking of that great Assembly to which all believers look—in the true heavenly places, when they "shall come from the east, and west, and shall sit down with Abraham, and Isaac, and Jacob, in the kingdom of God."

3. In those heavenly places, the *assembly was made up of the excellent of the earth.*

There were men and women who had spent many a toilsome year in far distant lands, toiling amid all the privations, discouragement, and opposition, which heathenism and barbarism, and the untold evils which the wicked one could invent. There were some who had literally made themselves poor, to make others rich. With the loss of all things earthly, they had given the Bible to those who had not known it, and proclaimed the Lord Jesus as their all-sufficient Saviour. It was an honor to sit by their side. There was one who had fled for the sake of the gospel from father, and mother, and kindred, and home—an Armenian from Constantinople. There was a widow wearing the weeds of mourning for a missionary husband who had toiled among the distant Indians, to pour into their dark minds the rays of divine light. There were those who had given liberally of their hard earnings to supply the lack of service in others far more able; yet never grudging the gift, but desirous to give even more. There were hundreds of ministers of the gospel from various sections of the country, whose high duty it is to invite their fellows to the gospel salvation, and to make it known to the world. There were excellent men, high in office and station, whose official duty leads them to guide thousands of youthful minds in the paths of literature, science, morals, or divinity; or to adjudicate between conflicting claims at the seats of justice. But all were one in Christ Jesus. All were in their places. And among the most distinguished civilians were some engaged in serving the elements of bread and wine to the multitudes of their brethren. But some were not there, who on former occasions had delighted to enjoy the precious season—now gone to the heavenly places above. Some wept at the thought that we should here see their faces no more. And yet they seemed to be gone only a little before us, to enter into the joy of our Lord.

4. In those heavenly places, *all minds were directed to one object.*

We were not assembled to look at one another. The hymns, the prayers, the addresses, the bread, the wine, all pointed to one object. Christ was in our midst. He was evidently set forth, crucified among us. All eyes, all thoughts, all desires, all hopes were centered in him. But for him we had not been there. To him our souls were consecrated, as by him they had been redeemed. 'God who is rich in mercy, even when we were dead in sins, had quickened us together with Christ, and had raised us up together, and made us sit together in heavenly places in Christ Jesus.' Could we then think of any other? All that vast assembly were attracted by him alone. We beheld by faith and adored him as our God. We beheld and embraced him as our Savior. We admired and became familiar with him as our brother. All our hearts and all our tongues were engaged in giving him thanks. A little foretaste of the heavenly things themselves was then realized. How vast the interest in the heavenly places above, when all shall be gathered together in one, from every kindred, and tongue, and people! Then, indeed, will they all be one with Christ, and Christ will be all in all.

I could not help comparing the innumerable multitude of believers on earth to the vast assemblage of waters that are always rushing down the great cataract. From far distant springs, thousands of miles apart from the point at which they rush down into the fathomless abyss, the drops fall, the springs gush forth, the rills meander, the streams collect their stores, the lakes expand, and the whole accumulated body rushes on, and then, at the fall, thunder down.

So the innumerable multitude of believers, from regions far more distant than Niagara's most distant springs, take their rise, flow on, and flow together down into the ocean of eternity. Would you not fear being lost in such an assemblage? How small is a drop in that cataract of waters! Yet not so small as you or I in the whole multitude of believers, that have been, now are, and shall be!

5. In those heavenly places, *we received impressions favorable to humility.*

'A drop of a bucket.' Such are the nations. Isaiah xl, 15. How small then is one individual particle of that drop!

'Oh, God, how infinite art thou!
What worthless worms are we!'

In those heavenly places we feel as nothing. Then comparing that vast assembly with the 'General Assembly and church of the first born that are written in heaven,' we feel comparatively less as the assembly becomes greater, till we become inconceivably small and insignificant. I was ready to ask, what will become of me, even if so happy at last as to have some place among the happy ones? Where shall I be? What shall I do? I behold around me as far as the eye can reach, a dense mass of holy and shining eyes, and beyond all that I can see, I am sure the mass stretches away, like the starry firmament, and like the ocean's waters. Oh, God, forget me not.

But this is not all. How unreasonably soever I may have magnified myself, I am compelled to feel that there are many in these heavenly places, who are wiser, and greater, and more holy, and more useful to men, and acceptable to God than I am. How much more will there be such in the heavenly places themselves.

More than this. God is all in all. Created beings, angels, men, and all together, are inexpressibly small before God. And he has said: 'The loftiness of man shall be bowed down, and the haughtiness of men shall be made low, and the Lord alone shall be exalted in that day.' 'Behold, I am vile.' 'God be merciful to me a sinner.' If I am not ever hereafter a humble man, it will not be for the want of impressions favorable to humility.

6. In those heavenly places, *we were excited to attempt more in spreading the gospel and glorifying Christ.*

Our salvation is all in the gospel. So is the salvation of every child of Adam. Every one in this vast assembly, in the whole church invisible, is saved by the gospel and only by the gospel. Oh, how deep are our obligations to the gospel! Must our fellows in sin perish without it? Is this the only fountain whose waters heal the nations? Cut out channels and let them flow. Are the unevangelized perishing? Run, send, fly quickly, before they die. Shall toil, or means, or son, or daughter, or self be withheld, when the soul is in jeopardy? Anew we consecrate ourselves, our powers, our influence, our all to this great work. Is it not our business on earth? Why do we live at all, but to make known this gospel to save men, and glorify Christ? All the redeemed every where, and of every age, are like us in these heavenly places. And others need the same gospel as much as we. And Christ will be glorified in them as in us. For we are in these heavenly places, and shall be in those above, 'to show in the ages to come the exceeding riches of his grace in his kindness towards us through Christ Jesus. More than this we can not say or do.

'Salvation! let the echo fly
'The spacious earth around,
'While all the armies of the sky
'Conspire to raise the sound.'"

The reader will not infer from the above that Dr. Yale was such an enthusiast, or that he was so baptized with the spirit of fanaticism, as to imagine that all who participated in such services as those here alluded to, were necessarily Christians. Lest such an inference might be drawn by some of his own people, in the afternoon of the same day in which the above discourse was delivered, he preached from the passage found in Acts viii, 21: "Thou hast neither part nor lot in this matter, for thy heart is not right in the sight of God."

This discourse he introduces in the following manner: "Possibly some may infer from what I have said about the heavenly places at Buffalo, and the blessed privilege of being there, that I think all who were in those heavenly places were Christians. But I think no such thing, as you will quickly perceive when you attend to what I am about to say." He then proceeds,

I. To describe the fair professor.

II. To show why he has neither part nor lot in the great salvation.

The Christian public have long felt a desire to know how Dr. Yale managed to secure from his people, such liberal contributions for purposes of Christian charity, and my object in this chapter has been to endeavor to answer the inquiry.

The first and primary reason may be found in his own breast. A stream is not expected to rise higher than the fountain from which it flows, and the feelings of a people ordinarily will be neither more intense nor more self-sacrificing than those of their spiritual leader.

He felt strongly himself, and was enabled to impart some of his own feelings to others. He was willing to make personal sacrifices for the promotion of this object, and by his example and his instructions, was he enabled to induce others to make sacrifices also.

In these labors he sometimes met with obstacles which it was difficult to overcome: yet did he never desist from the effort as long as there was any hope of success. Sometimes also was he encouraged by instances of unexpected liberality. Instances have been somewhat numerous in which, without any solicitation on his part, individuals have handed him large sums as donations for some object of Christian beneficence. Among others, we find a record like this made in the winter of 1837: "When I was passing a house on Thursday morning I was asked in. An aged man put a piece of paper rolled up into my hand, and said there was a little for the good cause. On opening it I found a $100 bill for foreign missions."

This was at the time that he was engaged in securing funds for the building of a new chuurch edifice for the benefit of his own people, and the circumstance seems to have nerved him up to new energy, and to have inspired him with yet stronger confidence in God. In view of it he says: "The Lord shows me that the silver and the gold are his. One rich man told me in the morning, just after I had received the $100 and while I had it in my pocket, that the money could not be raised. I felt however that it could be raised. Thus the Lord encouraged my heart.

CHAPTER XXV.

HIS HAPPY OLD AGE.

The evening of life is sometimes overcast with dark and gloomy shades. Men who, in their prime, have been both pious, and active, and useful, when the sun of life declines, and their pulse becomes feeble and their steps languid, do sometimes become imbecile and unhappy. But to this Dr. Yale was a remarkable exception. It is believed that there are few men who have retained their cheerfulness of temper, and their uniform suavity of manners, and their perfect submission to the will of God, in their last days, to the same degree that he did. In him was fulfilled the divine promise in a remarkable manner. "They shall bring forth fruit in old age, they shall be fat and flourishing; To show that the Lord is upright; he is my rock and there is no unrighteousness in him." "Even to your old age I am he; and even to hoar hairs will I carry you: I have made, and I will bear; even I will carry, and will deliver you."

Dr. Yale performed the duties of a pastor with great fidelity until about the middle of March 1851, when he was laid aside by paralysis. Probably there was no year during his whole pastorate in which he performed a greater amount of labor, than the one which immediately preceded. Now, however, he became so prostrated as to be incapable of active exertions for months; yet was he in a most devoted, and spiritual, and heavenly frame of mind, up to the moment of his departure.

It has already been stated, that, soon after he first became a subject of grace, he formally entered into a secret covenant with God, by adopting as his own one of those forms which may be found in Doddridge's Rise and Progress.

It has also been stated that he ordinarily renewed that covenant twice a year. This he did, in the most solemn manner, four times after he was laid aside from active ministerial labor; and that the state of his mind during this period may be more fully understood, these several acts of covenanting with God will be here transcribed.

June 15, 1851. "I am alive now on my birth day, aged seventy-one—tried in a new way—paralytic—have not preached in just thirteen weeks—from March 16. But God's mercy has been very great, and his grace and goodness abundant. I have been afflicted with very little pain—taken but litle medicine—and have enjoyed great peace and comfort. This covenant has been useful to me. I rely on Jehovah Jesus only and simply. For all that's to come I rely solely on him. Apparently near death, I cast myself on him. I have feared only one thing—sin—a deceitful heart. Against this none but Jesus can do me any good. It is all I have and all I need to find in him righteousness and strength. So I renew this covenant. E. YALE."

Jan. 1, 1852. "I marvel that I am yet alive, and gaining every day more strength to do the will of God. His grace helps me. He is my covenant God. He is all-sufficient in every attribute, and every attribute is infinite love. He is my God in Christ, who is my righteousness and strength. By his grace I am what I am. By his grace I hope to be what he would have me to be. His covenant is 'all my salvation and all my desire.' He has not forsaken me. He will never leave nor forsake me. During the last night I thought I might be off in a moment. I left all with God. Now I live with him by the day. My book is full. I may need no more. I close with an entire consecration according to this covenant. 'Thy will be done.'
E. YALE.

June 15, 1852. "God has brought me to another birth-day. I am now three score and twelve years old. I have added another sheet to these records. I rose very early, before 4 o'clock, and bathed myself in cold water as I do every morning. Then I bowed before God with my covenant before me, and read every word of it as a prayer. It seemed all good, all right, all needful.

I viewed it in connection with Isaiah xliii, 25; the verse for the day; 'I, even I am he that blotteth out thy transgressions for mine own sake, and will not remember thy sins.' How precious! Not for my righteousness, for I have none. But because God is God, just what he is. His infinite goodness and mercy exercised towards me, is the reason, the only reason that he forgives all that I have done, or said, or thought, or felt amiss. He accepts me as redeemed. He adopts me as his child. He is my Father, my Brother, my Comforter. I am thine, O my God, in the bonds of an everlasting covenant, ordered in all things and sure. I must record thy great goodness since January 1st, of this year. By the kind providence of my God, and the help of my good friend, the Rev. Samuel W. Cozzens, I have completed my Select Verse System, got it all ready, engaged a publisher, obtained many and good recommendations, and sent it to Albany yesterday, to be published. One year ago I had given it all up, as not likely to be finished. Now it is finished, and by God's favor will be published in about three months. I have committed it to God, and to his favor do I daily commend it. I have the materials before me ready for a new work, which I shall probably call, A REVIEW OF A PASTORATE OF FORTY-EIGHT YEARS. I feel now, and wish to feel that I write on the verge of eternity—uncertain altogether how far I shall proceed. I leave all with my God, and say without reserve: 'Not as I will, but as thou wilt.' O my God, keep me in thy perfect way. Amen. ELISHA YALE."

January 1, 1853. "I marvel that I am here this day. I marvel more at the loving-kindness, and tender mercy of my covenant God. I am very comfortable in health. I have seen great things since June 15th. On the 21st of that month 78 members were dismissed to form a new church at Gloversville. On the 23d I resigned my charge. On the 27th preached my farewell sermon. Since that time a church has been formed at Gloversville, a new house of worship dedicated, and the Rev. Homer N. Dunning settled. At Kingsborough the Rev.

Edward Wall has been called, measures have been taken to change the order to Presbyterian, with a fair prospect of success, all in peace and harmony. We are become two bands, and both appear to be about equal, and likely to live. I am also provided for. My verse system which I expected three months ago is, as I suppose, just about to come from the press, stereotyped, I hope to be useful. I have finished my review of forty-eight years, but not revised it—upwards of three hundred pages. I have also finished Helps to Cultivate the Conscience, upward of 100 pages; what will be done with them I know not. I have other works on hand, I am on the verge of worlds, yet trying to do a little. I marvel. I am the Lord's. I say without reserve. 'Thy will be done,' and renew my covenant. Amen.

ELISHA YALE."

This is the last transaction of this nature in which he was ever engaged, and from the date of the last entry, it will be seen that it was but nine days previous to his death.

After his prostration by paralysis in the spring of 1851, he requested several of his young friends to come in at different times, and to write in a book which had been prepared for that purpose, things which he dictated as expressive of the existing state of his mind. Sometimes what he desired to have written, was only a few stanzas from some favorite hymn, and sometimes it was some original composition of his own—some of the reflections of his own mind. There is so much interest in some of these entries, and they are so strikingly expressive of his feelings at the time, that I have felt disposed to give a few of them to the public. This scrap-book he entitled:

THOUGHTS AND COMFORTS IN AFFLICTION.

"In the multitude of my thoughts within me, thy comforts delight my soul." Ps: xciv, 19.

"Comfort ye, comfort ye, my people, saith your God." Isaiah xl, 1.

The first entry is dated March 24, 1851, and contains the following:

"Some months ago a vain thought entered my mind, to inquire into the secret things of God—contrary to Deut. xxix, 29. What shall I do when I resign my pastoral charge? God has shown me that he can bring me into trouble, or lay me in the grave. The will of the Lord be done."

The second entry is under date of March 25, and is as follows:

JESUS CHRIST.

"How sweet the name of Jesus sounds
 In a believer's ear,
It soothes his sorrows, heals his wounds,
 And drives away his fear."

"Surely, shall one say, in the Lord have I righteousness and strength. Ps. xlv, 24: 'And this is the name whereby he shall be called, the Lord our righteousness.' Jer. xxiii, 6: 'But to him that worketh not, but believeth on him that justifieth the ungodly, his faith is counted for righteousness. Even as David also describeth the blessedness of the man unto whom God imputeth righteousness without works, Saying, Blessed are they whose iniquities are forgiven, and whose sin is covered. Blessed is the man to whom the Lord will not impute sin.' Rom. iv, 5–8.

This is all my hope."

PEACE IN ANSWER TO PRAYER. March 24, 1851.

"I asked the people to pray for me, and God has given me peace. During the last night my thoughts rested on his precious word, as it is written: 'Great peace have they that love thy law, and nothing shall offend them.' Again, 'Thou wilt keep him in perfect peace whose mind is staid on thee.' And again—the Savior's legacy: 'Peace I leave with you, my peace I give unto you; not as the world giveth, give I unto you.

Let not your heart be troubled, neither let it be afraid.' 'The doors being shut where the disciples were assembled together, for fear of the Jews, Jesus came and stood in the midst, and saith unto them, Peace be unto you.'"

A DESIRE TO BE WITH JESUS. April 25, 1851.

"Oh, when shall I see Jesus,
And reign with him above,
And from that flowing fountain,
Drink everlasting love?

When shall I be delivered
From this vain world of sin,
And with my blessed Jesus,
Drink endless pleasures in?"

"Shall I? Shall I indeed? I think I shall. For through eternal, electing love, and by his grace working in me repentance, and faith, I think I belong to him, and am included in his intercessory prayer; John xvii, 24: 'Father, I will that they also whom thou hast given me, be with me where I am; that they may behold my glory which thou hast given me; for thou lovedst me before the foundation of the world.'"

THE GOOD SHEPHERD'S CARE. April 29, 1851.

"The Lord is my shepherd; I shall not want. He maketh me to lie down in green pastures; he leadeth me beside the still waters. He restoreth my soul; he leadeth me in the paths of righteousness for his name's sake. Yea, though I walk through the valley of the shadow of death, I will fear no evil; for thou art with me; thy rod and thy staff they comfort me. Thou preparest a table before me in the presence of mine enemies; thou anointest my head with oil; my cup runneth over. Surely goodness and mercy shall follow me all the days of my life; and I will dwell in the house of the Lord forever." Ps. xxiii.

A SONG.

"The Lord is my shepherd, he makes me repose
Where the pastures in verdure are growing;
He leads me afar from the world and its woes,
Where in peace the still waters are flowing.
He strengthens my spirit, he shows me the path,
Where the arms of his love shall enfold me;
And when I walk through the dark valley of death,
His rod and his staff shall uphold me."

"He shall gather the lambs in his arms, and shal carry them in his bosom." Isa. xl, 11.

SECURITY FROM THE DEVIL.

"Many a time has that mighty and implacable enemy desired to destroy me. About the time the preceding was written, or a little before, in connection with it, I was one night extremely low and weak, and it seemed as though the wicked one would crush me down to death. At that moment the thought of the eagle on the wing sustained me. 'As an eagle stirreth up her nest, fluttereth over her young, taketh them, beareth them on her wings; so the Lord did lead him, and there was no strange God with him." Deut. xxxii, 11, 12.

I was on the eagle's wing soaring up to the very fountain of light, as the eagle towards the sun, while the enemy, as a conquered raven, was sinking down towards the earth, unable any more to rise. It seemed to me a wonderful deliverance, while the following sentiment filled my mind:

'The eagle's eye
The fount of light
Looks full in view
With pinions bright:
While far below,
With craven wing,
Sinks down the foe
A harmless thing."

The above was written with his own hand a few weeks after the time referred to, when he was so far recovered as to be able to use the pen himself.

FEELING FOR THE STEPS THAT LEAD TO HEAVEN.

"It is the body of the believer that dies. That is left in the care of friends. It is laid in the grave as in a bed, to sleep and rest until the resurrection. The *spirit* of the *believer* never dies. As the Savior says: 'Whosoever liveth aud believeth in me shall never die.' And as he has said again: 'Because I live, ye shall live also.'

I have been feeling after the *steps* by which the *spirit* ascends to heaven, and I think I have found them. It is by the word of God alone, especially the 1st chapter of John, at the beginning. 1. *Faith in God.* As he says: 'Ye believe in God.' I believe in God as infinite in all his attributes, and every attribute infinite love. 2d Step. *Faith in Christ the Savior.* As he says: '*Believe also in me.*' I believe firmly in him, as one with the Father in substance, in attributes, and love; being the same with the Father in his works, and and in his honor and glory, but especially as Emanuel, 'God with us,' the only Savior, by his sufferings, obedience, and power, giving to all believers eternal life. 3d Step. *Faith in the Father's house.* As he says: '*In my Father's house.*' This the same that Paul describes, II Cor. v, 1: "We know that if our earthly house of this tabernacle were dissolved, we have a building of God, a house not made with hands, eternal in the heavens.' This I firmly believe.

4th Step. *Faith in the many mansions.* As he says: 'In my Father's house are many mansions.' As many mansions as there are persons that belong to Christ, so that there shall be none unprovided for. 5th Step. *Faith in the preparation.* As he says: 'I go to prepare a place for you.' A great work is going on in the Father's house, preparing these mansions, and a great work is going on upon the earth, preparing his people for the mansions; so that heaven is as it was once described by a believer, a prepared place for a prepared people.

6th step. *Faith in his coming for them.* As he

says; "If I go and prepare a place for you, I will come again." He comes by his angels, who "are ministering spirits, sent forth to minister to them who shall be heirs of salvation." By them they are conducted into his presence. As it is said; "The beggar died and was carried by angels into Abraham's bosom." 7th step. *Faith in their kind reception by the Savior.* As he said; I will receive you unto myself." In this act, he welcomes them as his friends, and owns and acknowledges them before his Father and before his angels. They are now with him in heaven, according to his concluding words; "That where I am, there ye may be also."—*Written at the request of Dr. Yale May* 4, 1851.

HUMBLE CONFIDENCE IN CHRIST.

"The souls that believe, in paradise live,
And me in that number will Jesus receive.
My soul, don't delay, he calls thee away,
Rise, follow thy Savior, and bless the glad day.

No mortal doth know what he can bestow,
What light, strength, and comfort do after him go,
So onward I move to a country above,
None guesses how wondrous my journey will prove.

Great spoils I shall win from death, hell, and sin,
Midst outward afflictions shall feel Christ within,
And when I'm to die, receive me I'll cry,
For Jesus hath loved me, I can not tell why.

But this I do find, to him I am so joined,
He'll not live in glory and leave me behind,
So this is the race I am running through grace,
Henceforth till admitted to see my Lord's face."

Written May 7, 1851.

The following psalm from Dr. Watts is probably as familiar with most of my readers as the pages of the spelling book; and it is inserted in this place only as expressive of Dr. Yale's feelings for the last three or four years of his life. His mind dwelt upon it much, he repeated it often, and for several months he gave it out to be sung in the public assembly so frequently, that it was noticed and spoken of by many. He caused it to be transcribed in his Scrap Book. on the 23d of May, 1851.

DELIGHT IN GOD AND HIS WORSHIP.

"My God, permit my tongue
This joy, to call thee mine;
And let my early cries prevail,
To taste thy love divine.

For life without thy love,
No relish can afford;
No joy can be compared with this,
To serve and please the Lord.

To thee I'll lift my hands
And praise thee while I live;
Not the rich dainties of a feast
Such food and pleasure give.

In wakeful hours of night,
I call my God to mind;
I think how wise thy counsels are,
And all thy dealings kind.

Since thou hast been my help,
To thee my spirit flies;
And on thy watchful providence,
My cheerful hope relies.

The shadow of thy wings
My soul in safety keeps;
I follow where my Father leads,
And he supports my steps."

For some months before his death, though he was not able to perform much pulpit labor, he was able to do a considerable amount of labor with his pen; and he was as industriously employed, perhaps, as he was in the days of his greatest vigor. After completing his "Select Verse System," on which his heart was so much set, he wrote a work of great interest, which has been already alluded to, and which he entitled: "A Review of a Pastorate of Forty-Eight Years;" and which was completed but a few days before his death. He also commenced a work which he entitled:

"A SURVEY OF THE HEAVENLY COUNTRY ACCORDING TO THE SCRIPTURES.

Of this work, the title page, the preface, and an introduction to the first chapter, is all that he wrote. This the reader will be pleased to see just as he left it. It is as follows:

PREFACE.

With all due respect, the author would say to the reader, that this book originated in a desire to know as much as God has revealed about heaven. One year and eight months ago, March 16, 1851 (and it is now Nov. 14, 1852) a paralytic affection laid him aside from the work of the ministry entirely for five months, though he afterwards recovered so as to preach occasionally. During the first six weeks, at times, he felt as though he might pass at any time beyond the boundaries of time. He studied John 14th especially to find the steps to the kingdom of heaven. He found them. His meditations by day and by night, as he could not read, nor write, nor hear much reading or conversation, were of the most agreeable nature. Never was he happier in his life. One thing he prayed for and was answered, that *he might never dream of heaven.* He wanted no view or thought of heaven, but such as God has revealed. Being now so much recovered as to be able to write much, and read some, he has undertaken this survey for his own instruction and comfort, and presents it to the reader, hoping it may be of some little service in guiding him to such views of the better country, as God has been pleased to reveal."

CHAPTER I.

THE HEAVENLY COUNTRY A REAL LOCALITY.

"No more certain is it that there is an earth, than that there is a heaven. The proof of the former is from our senses. The proof of the latter is from revelation. God knows both perfectly. And he has given us such evidence in regard to both as is suited to them respectively. In our survey of the heavenly country we shall be guided by the word of God entirely. All else is uncertainty, and answers not the purposes of real beings, like ourselves; for we need reality. We consider,

I. THE HEAVENLY COUNTRY AS A REAL LOCALITY."

At this point he laid down his pen, and never took it up again; at least so far as it had respect to the completion of that work. Perhaps we may have cause to regret that he was not spared to put this purpose of his into execution. His maturity of thought, his familiar acquaintance with scripture truth, and the depth of his religious experience, would have peculiarly qualified him for such an undertaking. Yet, God had other purposes to accomplish, and it becomes us to bow submissive. This "survey of the heavenly country" is even now being made: but not with an eye of faith as was then proposed. His faith is changed into sight, and he is permitted to enjoy that perfection of bliss which he then only anticipated.

No one could have been in the company of Dr. Yale for an hour during the last years of his life, without being fully assured that he was possessed of an uncommon amount of personal enjoyment. Much of this enjoyment found its source in a spirit of entire submission to the will of God. In speaking to a friend during this period on the subject of resigning his pastoral charge, he says; "It is a pleasant thought to me that God determined from all eternity precisely how he would have it; and that by his grace, I would have it just as he pleases. It can not be better. I know that he will go on with his work both here, and everywhere, just as well without me as with me. My only endeavor shall be to do what I can in any way that God pleases, to finish what he has for me to do."

The peculiarly happy frame of mind which he enjoyed during the last months of his life, will appear from some extracts from his correspondence, which will here be given. The first from which these extracts are taken was dated Aug. 15, 1849. This was while he yet enjoyed health, and was performing his accustomed labor, and the first paragraph has respect to that bereavement in his family which was mentioned on a preceding page.

"Oh, how solitary we are in the absence of our loved one! How much we miss him! more, and more, and more, while to others he seems to be passing out of mind. His Bible, his mantle—little red mantle, his knife, his kite—they keep him often before us. But he sleeps a sound, long, uninterrupted sleep. The Lord said of Lazarus: 'I go to awake him out of sleep,' So will he awake our boy out of sleep. But first shall we sleep with him, and at the same moment awake when the trumpet shall sound. How time runs on! It is well to look steadily to the other world. There our 'friends and kindred dwell.' Above all, 'there God our Savior reigns.' It will be but a little while, and the earth will all fade from our view, and be so far off as to appear, if it appear at all, as some distant planet now appears. Amazing realities are just before us! How fearfully and wonderfully are we made! What changes await us! Oh may they all be 'from glory to glory!' Well may we leave this country for one so much better. Well may we leave the house we have built here, for one not made with hands. Our friends, our treasure, our all are concentrating in that world, which is emphatically the glory of all lands. Willing should we be to live, and labor, and suffer here, while God shall see fit to keep us here; but soon shall we be done, gather up all, and fly away. We 'will work while the day lasts. The night cometh when no man can work.' Let us labor then, not only to enter into his rest, but also to induce as many as we can to go with us. 'He that winneth souls is wise."

The above is from a letter to the parents of his adopted son, the death of whom is referred to. From another letter addressed to the same under date of April 15, 1850, I extract the following:

"The awful anniversary is passed since we received your letter. It occasioned us many painful thoughts, but we trust they were not any of them murmuring thoughts. It becomes us to be very humble, and to remember that our end is near. I seem to myself as borne on the steady, rapid wing of time, which will soon set me down at the door of eternity. I think I have but one thing to live for, to finish the work which the Lord has give me to do. As I see the day approaching I endeavor to double my diligence. Time seems more precarious than ever."

No part of his religious comforts, in these last months of his life, strong and abiding as they were, originated in a feeling of self-sufficiency or self-complacency. He rather kept his eye constantly directed to the cross of Christ as presenting the only ground of his hope, and he ever magnified the sovereignty of divine grace in the salvation of guilty men. This truth may be illustrated by a reference to the following paragraphs which were written some months after he was laid aside from active ministerial labor.

"God says, 'I, even I, am he that blotteth out your transgressions for mine own sake, and will not remember your sins.' What an expression! 'For mine own sake.' Not selfish; but not in any sense for our duties or deservings; entirely contrary to them all, because he is God, infinite in goodness and mercy. Hence the joy the believer feels in view of God's pardoning mercy. He (God) has done it himself, because he is good and rich in mercy. Oh, how sweet the thought of pardon as thus proceeding from our Father, who does it for his own sake! He can do it and yet maintain all his justice. He does it because he is rich in mercy. We can be willing to be pardoned on such grounds, and I know of no other on which an ingenuous soul could be willing to be pardoned. He could not at the expense of law and justice. He could not to the dishonor of God. He could not for any thing he has done. But now as God does it for his own sake, even to show how infinite his goodness and mercy are, how contrary he is to the devil's slanders, how totally different he is from all that hate him would represent, we can rejoice in being pardoned. So far from desiring to withhold any good from his creatures, as selfish ones would insinuate, he takes occasion from the extreme wickedness of man, to show a new treasure of his goodness in pardoning our transgressions. He blots out all that the pen of justice has recorded against us. Yea more, he puts them away in some hidden corner of the universe where no creature can find them; where even he, speaking after the manner of men, forgets where they are laid. Wondrous grace! Yet this is the grace of God. And it is part and parcel of that system of redemption which is the great theme of divine revelation."

The following short letter will be read with interest both on account of that spirit of acquiescence in the will of God, which it breathes, and because of the simplicity with which he speaks of the state of his health. From its date it will be seen to have been written some time after his confinement.

"KINGSBOROUGH, *May* 29, 1851.

"DEAR FRIEND:—Yours of the 20th was duly received, and I feel much obliged to you for your kind expressions. I had indeed an ill turn on the 20th of April, and was laid on the bed three or four days. Since that I have been gradually recovering. I had before attended church two half days, and last sabbath I attended the whole day and heard Mr. Ingal preach twice. I am altogether comfortable. I have no pain, no ache, sleep well, have appetite enough, though not craving, live on light food, and get strength every day, walk about with a staff or without one, can walk without limping, take a nap once a day about noon, feed the chickens, pig, and poney; but I am weak. I ride out every pleasant day, and sometimes take with me Mr. William Ward, another paralytic. I can get into the wagon and out of it without help; can drive the horse to Johnstown and back again. For ten weeks I have not preached except to those who have called upon me, with most of whom I have conversed very freely, and with much pleasure and profit to myself. I read little and write less; but I have thought out many sermons—whether I shall ever preach them in public is a secret thing. I dictate a few letters, and some other articles, singing much mentally, psalms and hymns and spiritual songs, by night when awake on my bed, and by day when I sit in my chair. I enjoy the singing of others remarkably well. I have invited those who fear God, to come and sing for me the praises of God. I am looking to a better country; have no fear of any thing but sin, which I hope is a conquered enemy and will be utterly destroyed. I thank you for your proposal of aid, but at present I have all that I need. You may expect to hear from me at the time appointed, when I shall be three score and eleven.

Your affectionate friend,

ELISHA YALE."

I will give another letter nearly entire, omitting only a few sentences in which the reader will feel no particular interest.

"KINGSBOROUGH, Feb. 16, 1852.

TO MR. C. H. WEST—Dear friend:—The sabbath did not allow me to write on the 15th, but I preached in the afternoon, being forty-nine years since I was licensed to preach the gospel. Text, Mark vi, 11: 'And whosoever shall not receive you nor hear you, when ye depart thence, shake off the dust under your feet, for a testimony against them. Verily I say unto you, it shall be more tolerable for Sodom and Gomorrah in the day of judgment, than for that city.'

I called up inanimate things as witnesses to my preaching the gospel. According to the figurative language of scripture, they will appear in the judgment and give testimony.

1. The dust on my feet and my horse's feet; 2, The buildings; 3, The bell; 4, The candles, and lamps, and lanterns; 5, The Bibles; 6, The primers; 7, The

tracts and good books; 8, The confession of faith; 9, The church covenant; 10, The church records; 11, The coffins—900 till Dec. 31, 1851; 12, The grave stones.

OBSERVATIONS.—1. *What a day is coming! 2. What consternation among unbelievers! 3. Will not all see why it will be more tolerable for Sodom? 4. Once more now I call upon you to repent and believe the gospel.*

I feel habitually that we are passing through awful scenes now, in some respects more awful than the other world; because we shall be there what we prepare to be here. Four funerals among us last week (three children and one adult). So the young die, and the old live. Yet the old must die, and die soon. There can be no mistake about this. I feel every day as though I were beyond the time appointed to man upon earth, try to be ready, and am doing, to the amount of my strength, what I am able in my way.

Time passes on with its usually steady, unremitted course, bearing all away to our long home. Your aunt said this morning, when I told her I was going to write to you, 'Oh how I do want to go and see West's folks!' I hope to be able by the time your rail road is done, to take tea with you on the evening of some future day. It seems to me as almost presumption to think of such a thing. I calculate certainly upon nothing, but to take my departure to the unseen world. That event is certain, and the time fixed, but it is a secret. Of course we have nothing to do with it, but to be always ready, and to do with our might what we find to do. So I am doing, but feel that I may be called to leave just where it is, any work in which I am engaged. I like to live so —on the verge of eternity, hoping to be soon with Christ and behold his glory, with all the redeemed.

How many friends have I there! Will they not be glad to see me come, and bid me welcome? Through boundless grace I trust it will be so. Christ is my righteousness. In him I hope to be found. I think I shall. I fear only one thing—*a deceitful heart.* God knows it, and he can save me. Grace has always been precious to me, since I felt myself a lost sinner, deserving to be cast away, unable to do the least thing acceptable to God, and dependent on his sovereign grace. But it seems more and more precious as I review all the steps it has taken with me, and consider that I am now just as dependent, and always shall be. Would I have it otherwise? Not for worlds. It is just as God would have it, and just as I would have it. God says: 'My counsel shall stand, and I will do all my pleasure.' Blessed be his name, it is my pleasure too. It is through grace I say this. I have not a rag of righteousness of my own, nor the strength of an infant. But I say, as it is written of one, Isaiah, xliv, 24: 'Surely shall one say, in the Lord have I righteousness and strength.' I am one of the ones that say thus. I have righteousness enough, and strength enough; for it is all the Lord's, and infinite. Oh how precious! No wonder that Paul said: 'God forbid that I should glory save in the cross of my Lord Jesus Christ, by whom the world is crucified unto me and I unto the world.' Here I find 'firm footing, solid rock.' It is this which gives me peace in view of all my sins, weaknesses, imperfections, and the changes around me and before me. I feel like a little child that knows just enough to run to his father for all that he wants; only with this difference, that I know that my Father's attributes are infinite, and every attribute infinite love; and his covenant with me as my God is 'ordered in all things and sure.'"

Affectionate regards to you all,

ELISHA YALE."

Another letter to the same friend was written under date of April 13, 1852, from which a few sentences will be extracted—as follows:

"I trust I am ready through grace to go to the better country, the heavenly, the home of all believers. But just as the Lord sees best. 'Wisdom and mercy guide my way.' Praise the Lord, as I do, daily, for the perfect composure with which I approach this crisis." (He here alludes to the anticipated resignation of his pastoral charge.) "The Lord keeps me in perfect peace, because my mind is staid on him. In regard to what will follow, the promise is just as good as in regard to what there is before. 'As thy day is, so shall thy strength be.' Thus there is no want of any thing. 'It is better to trust in the Lord than to put confidence in man. It is better to trust in the Lord than to put confidence in princes.' Trust him with your soul, and then you may trust him with all the rest. 'I know whom I have believed,' saith Paul. So it seems to me I can say: It is the Lord Jesus who laid down his life for us. Will he not give us all we need, since he has given himself? Has he given the greater, and will he not give the less? Did he die to redeem us from hell, and does he not live to raise us to heaven? Oh this marvelous salvation! Well may we be filled with wonder and delight. Too good, too great to be believed? No, for it is of God. He is used to doing great things. We expect him to do great things. Salvation is all a very great matter. Our salvation is only a small item of this great matter. Be the benefit ours. Be all the glory his. Magnified is the boundless grace just in proportion to the depth from which he raises us, and the height to which he exalts us; just in proportion to our worthlessness, and the price he paid for our ransom; just in proportion to the enormity of our sins, and the glory which he is preparing for us. Saved by grace. How sweet the sound! How low we lie in abasement! How high in exaltation, our Redeemer!

But my sheet is almost filled. May you be abundantly filled with all the fullness of God, both you and yours evermore.

With affectionate regard to you all,
I am, and we are ever yours,
ELISHA YALE."

The last letter which he wrote was addressed to his relative, the Rev. Cyrus Yale of West Hartford, Conn., and was finished and mailed only the day before his departure. It will be read with peculiar interest on account of the proximity of the date to the time of his exit. Here we see the man as he was when he was about to take wings and fly away. It will be perceived also that he was the same man that he had been for many years preceding. He had dwelt in the "land of Beulah" for a long time, and was only waiting for the call of the Master to take him hence. This letter breathes the same spirit that has appeared in the preceding, but possesses additional interest from the narration which it contains of his previous labors, and of his present illness. The letter is given entire with the exception of a few sentences at the commencement, which have respect to certain domestic affairs, the publication of which might be deemed injudicious.

It contains different dates, the first of which was:

January 1, 1853.

After speaking of certain changes which had taken place in the family of his friend he adds: "My changes are of a character widely different. During 1852 I resigned my pastoral charge; saw two houses of worship instead of one, two churches instead of one, two ministers instead of one, and incipient steps taken to change the name of one congregation and church from Congregational to Presbyterian, with correspondent changes in other respects. But *my great change* has not yet come. In my retirement from the work of preaching the gospel, I find myself relieved of a great burden. How kind is our Heavenly Father! 'He knoweth our frame; he rememebereth that we are dust.' He saw me unequal to my burden, and he said, 'Rest.' Yet how kind to divide the work betwen two young men!

Friday, Jan. 7. I was hoping to furnish and send off this letter in due time. On Saturday afternoon I heard a sacramental lecture, our minister being absent. On sabbath morning I preached at Gloversville, their minister being absent also. Sabbath afternoon I administered the Lord's supper alone. In the evening I attended the monthly concert in our church. Felt well, but did nothing. On Monday I did a little business in

Johnstown; felt well, but being a little out of time, I probably ate a little too much. On Tuesday morning I rose at five, and thought I never felt better in my life. I bathed as usual in cold water in my room, but felt a chill. Made haste to get warm. During thirty-six hours I had no appetite and ate nothing. Completely exhausted, very little pain except from exhaustion, which seemed almost insupportable, attended with some diarrhea, and the operation of a little medicine. Now I am comfortable, but very weak. Such complaints are rather epidemic among us, attended with very cold extremities. This has taught me how soon I may be off, and leave all behind. I wished to have things done up a little more thoroughly; but in the main I think all things are done.

Saturday, 8. Hope to be well as usual in a few days. It is well to be reminded solemnly of the end of life, and how suddenly it may come. I have thought much in months past of the world to which we are going. The removal of your Mary has called my attention anew to that subject. Do we think enough of the time to leave? Our Savior began early to tell his disciples of the things that he should suffer. They were amazingly disappointed, and Peter said:" "These things shall not come unto thee." But our Lord knew his business better than the disciples could teach him. How are Christians also broken up in their calculations! We learn by slow degrees what is the great business of life. Not to make this world our home—not to lay up our treasures here; but to trust in the Lord and do good. Christian parents learn that the great matter for themselves and for their children is to do all for the Lord, and to make it the great business of life to promote his cause and build up his kingdom. In that we have our all. In that we find an object, large enough for our greatest, our noblest desires, and that for which we may lay out our largest means, and use our most ample powers. It is living for something when we live for God. And though I can do but little, I delight in seeing my brethren in the ministry strong to labor. A letter from Brother Brace, received when was very weak, pained me while he detailed such laborI as were once common to him and me. It comforts ms while I think that the 'Lord lays aside his laborers, ane goes on with his work.' d

How kind that he allows them to rest from their labors! It comforts me to see my two young brethren enter into my labors, and dividing my work between them. Much remains to be done. I am gratified to be allowed to see in cases how people will conduct when I am gone—at funerals, in the house of God, at prayer-meetings. I have lived to see the oldest man buried, who was at the head of a family when I first came to Kingsborough. A few women are older, but I am the oldest man in the house of God, but one. In the prayer-meeting I look upon all as younger than I. Those who used to meet there to pray, are all gone. But I see how the younger ones conduct themselves. Every man whom I hear pray, has learned to pray since I commenced my work. And I think they will go on, after I meet with them no more. What a precious thought! O that prayer may never cease to be offered here as long as the sun and moon endure. Then will come the blessing, even life forevermore. I feel that I am finishing up my work. But O, how imperfect has every part of it been! "To him that worketh not, but believeth on him that justifieth the ungodly, his faith is counted for righteousness." This is the only foundation of my hope. All other hopes are perishing. My righteousnesses are all as filthy rags. But Christ is "the Lord our Righteousness." When the next quarter returns I hope to hear from you. And if the half year comes again to me, happy shall I be to communicate again with you. In this letter you see many marks of imperfection but the will must answer for the deed. Affectionate regards to you all.

ELISHA YALE."

This was the last letter he ever wrote, and this the last time which he ever subscribed his name. He literally wrote it on "the verge of worlds"—though it does not appear that he then immediately anticipated the event, more than he had done for many months preceding. He finished this letter and went with it to the post office, on Saturday afternoon. At evening he retired as usual to rest, as comfortable as he had been through the day. About 11 o'clock, he was discovered to have been seized with an apoplectic fit. Friends were called and remedies applied, and after about an hour his consciousness returned. From this time he continued conscious, and possessed of the most perfect serenity, and communicated most freely with his friends, until near four o'clock in the afternoon of the sabbath, when he went into another fit, and, without a struggle or a groan, passed into that state of celestial bliss which he had so long anticipated. His remains were interred on the succeeding Thursday in the village grave yard, by the side of his aged father, and in the midst of his people. His wish was long before expressed, that there should be placed at his grave only a plain stone of ordinary size, and to contain only the lines which he had seen fit to dictate. Many of his friends, however particularly desire to rear a monument to his memory, and which, notwithstanding his own personal wishes, may perhaps hereafter be done.

The lines which he desired to have engraved upon his tombstone were dictated at the time of his greatest feebleness, in the spring of 1851, and recorded by his particular request. After filling the blanks which were then necessarily left, they are as follows:

"ELISHA YALE
Was born at Lee, Massachusetts, June 15, 1780.
Was licensed to preach the gospel Feb. 15, 1803.
Was ordained at Kingsborough May 23, 1804.
Preached his last sermon Jan. 2, 1853.
Died Jan. 9, 1853.

Jehovah Jesus is my hope.
Hope thou in Jesus Jehovah."

The Ripe Christian Dying:

A SERMON,

PREACHED AT KINGSBOROUGH, JANUARY 13, 1853,

AT

THE FUNERAL

OF THE

REV. ELISHA YALE, D. D.

BY JEREMIAH WOOD.

SERMON.

"Thou shalt come to thy grave in a full age, like as a shock of corn cometh in in his season."—Job v, 26.

Human life may be appropriately compared to a *journey*. On our great thoroughfares we are sometimes surprised to see such a multitude of people, all crowding on to their anticipated place of destination. But the world itself is one great thoroughfare; and all its population are hurrying on, with the velocity of time to the end of their course. Men may sometimes appear to themselves to be stationary. They are surrounded by the same objects, and enjoy the same pleasures, and associate with the same friends for many successive years. And what though their whitening locks may indicate to others that they are hastening on, with rapid strides, to another and endless state of existence; yet they themselves scarce realise that this is the case.

MAN IS MIGRATORY.

It is not meant that he is passing from one *couutry* to another; but from one world to another. Not indeed that he is to range through immeasurable space, and fly from planet to planet, in his survey of the magnificent works of the great Creator. But this earth which constitutes his present habitation, like an old, dilapidated building, is to fall into decay; and he is to pass into other climes, and to be an inhabitant of another world.

In journeying, people sometimes endure many hardships, and encounter many dangers, and pass through many difficulties. There may be rough roads, and hard fare, and chilling winds, and drenching storm, and excessive fatigue. Yet, let the way-worn traveler only indulge the expectation of a safe arrival at home, and the enjoyment of its comforts; and all these things are to him the merest trifles.

So with our journey to the grave, and to the eternal world. There are hardships to be endured, there are difficulties to be overcome, there are dangers to be encountered. But what are these? Oh! what are these, if our eye can but rest on those Celestial Mansions which Christ has gone to prepare for his people; and if we can but look to them as our future and eternal *home?*

The text directs our thoughts to the consideration of our approaching end. "*Thou shalt come to thy grave in a full age, like as a shock of corn cometh in in his season.*" Observe,

I. That we are here reminded of a truth which is of universal applicability.

The truth to which I refer is, that we are all coming to the grave. It is true of the whole human family, whatsoever their pursuits, whatsoever their character, whatsoever their condition in life; the prince and the peasant, the philosopher and the idiot, the learned and the ignorant, ihe man of wealth with his millions, and the man of poverty with the merest pittance of earthly good.

It is true that people come to it in a great variety of ways. Some ride on in state and are clad in purple; while others hobble on their crutches and are clothed in sackcloth. Some wend their way with nimble step and a merry countenance; while others wet the very path which they tread with their tears, and the chief music which attends their weary footsteps, are their own deep-toned sighs and doleful groans.

Yet, in one way or another, all come to the grave. With what startling rapidity is the grave filling up! Filling up, too, with the great and the good. How greatly has this list been increased within the few past months! The statesman, and the senator, and the divine are laid equally low in the dormitory of the dead. The resting place of the one may indeed be marked by wealth. But, there they are, resting in the silent sepulcher, and awaiting the archangel's summons to awake. Ah! indeed, it is already true that the dead far outnumber the living. But, why should we dwell upon a truth which is so obvious to the most casual observer? And why complain, or be of a sorrowful countenance, in view even of this prevalent mortality? Why complain?

Is it because the senate chamber no longer resounds with the eloquence of these departed statesmen? Because the man of God no longer occupies his accustomed place in the sacred desk? Because an empty chair is found in the domestic circle, and the lips of him are sealed in death, who led the devotions of the family, and offered to God their morning and evening incense?

It is true that these vacancies are seen, and felt, and realized; but the stream of life is like the rolling of the mighty waters; the current is constantly advancing; and as those portions which are farthest in advance, glide on and dash over the bounding cataract, and are lost in the ocean beneath, others rush on to occupy the place of those which have gone before. Ah! indeed, there is a sense of desolation around the spot which has been heretofore filllled by the unconscious sleeper—a feeling of desolation in the heart of the bereaved companion, and the circle of sorrowing friends. His place is vacant, not only at home, where the lack is felt more than anywhere else; but even in the street we look for his accustomed tread, but it is not there. In the social gathering for prayer and praise we seem to wait for him to enter; but we wait in vain. We enter the house of God in which he was always found, but when we look towards the seat in which he had heretofore been seen, we are admonished that there is one less worshiper to engage in these solemn acts of devotion. We turn towards the sacred desk from which he had for many a successive year been administering consolation to God's mourning saints, and beseeching sinners to cease their rebellion and exercise the spirit of reconciliation. We look; but there seem to be mourning weeds even upon God's altar; not because the gospel has lost its charms, nor because it has ceased to be "good tidings of great joy;" but because the man—the man who had plead the cause of God and wooed sinners to Christ, has ceased from his labors, and laid him down in the grave to rest.

Yet, why should we be sorrowful? Especially at the removal of one who has filled up life in the discharge of all its duties? Who has labored in the cause of his Master until hoary age has crowned his temples? Who has left no part of the great work of life undone? Who has died in a full age, and has gone to his reward with his crown studded with the jewels which he has gathered for his Master?

Such was the case with our departed father. He did not lay aside his armor until he had fought the battle and won the victory. He did not cease to labor until the sun had gone far down beneath the western horizon. He did not claim the reward until the race had been fairly won. The sentiment of the text may with great propriety be applied to him: "*He has come to the grave in a full age, like as a shock of corn cometh in in his season.*"

But the language of the text not only reminds us of the *certainty* of our approach to the grave; but of the *peaceful* manner in which death is sometimes met. "Thou shalt *come*"—intimating that he moves on and advances nearer and nearer to his approaching end; not as it were by constraint and with fearful apprehensions of the future; but as if he felt that death had lost its sting, and that there was nothing either *in* the grave or *beyond* it for him to fear. Men are sometimes *dragged* to the grave as the culprit is dragged to the gallows. Indeed it is always very much against his will that a wicked man dies. He would live always in this world, would enjoy his farms, and his merchandise, and his gold, and his silver. And what though he often complains of the ills of life, and mourns on account of its adversities; yet there is something so much more dreadful in the anticipations of the future, that he is willing to endure them all rather than to risk the change. Oh! how dreadful is it for a wicked man to die! He feels it to be dreadful. Hence it is by force or violence that he is torn away from his present enjoyments, and ushered into the presence of an insulted, an offended God. "He shall be driven from light into darkness, and chased out of the world." "The ungodly are like the chaff which the wind driveth away."

But it is not thus that the Christian dies. It is true indeed that dying pangs are sometimes dreaded even by him. It is not to be supposed that the dying martyr takes pleasure in the rack; or that he feels no pain when his flesh is torn from his bones, or his body is dismembered by the instruments of torture. Even the immaculate Saviour appears to have shrunk from his sufferings; and as his sweat of blood was running down his agonized body, and his mind had the fullest apprehension of his approaching conflict, he said: "*Father, if it be possible, let this cup pass from me.*" Nor do we wonder that Paul should have said: "*Not that we would be unclothed, but clothed upon, that mortality may be swallowed up of life.*"

Yet is it true, that God enables his own people to meet even death with composure. The language of Christian confidence, yea, of *holy triumph*, which the dying saint is enabled to use, is: "*O death, where is thy sting? O grave, where is thy victory? Thanks be to God which giveth us the victory through our Lord Jesus Christ.*" *I have fought a good fight, I have finished my course, I have kept the faith; Henceforth there is laid up for me a crown of righteousness, which the Lord the righteous Judge shall give me at that day; And not to me only, but unto all them also that love his appearing.*"

There is a darkness about the tomb, even to the mind of the Christian believer; yet he finds by his own blessed experience that the presence of Christ can give light even in that darkness. There is a light that can penetrate the darkness of the grave; and the dying believer sings; *Though I walk though the valley of the shadow of death, I will fear no evil, for thou art with me, thy rod and thy staff they comfort me.*" The departing saint comes to the grave as an absent son comes home to his father's house. Then indeed does he experience the fulfillment of the Savior's promise to his disciples; "I will come again and receive you to myself; that where I am there ye may be also."

Observe,

II. That the period spoken of in the text at which death would come, deserves to be considered.

"IN A FULL AGE."

The most palpable import of the language perhaps may be, that he would live to be an old man. To live to an old age, perhaps is the universal desire of the human mind: and indeed in many respects it is desirable. There is something sad in the thought that the flower should be nipped in the bud; or that the swelling storm should sweep away the harvest while yet in its greenness. So is there sadness in the thought that lisping infancy or prattling childhood should be made to feel death's freezing chill, or that athletic manhood should be made to wither and die, even as the gigantic oak is upturned by the sweeping hurricane, and the towering cedar falls before the resistless tornado.

Our notions of old age, however, are all comparative. In the antediluvian age, a man of eighty was but a youth; and perhaps it will be so again in the days of the millennium. In reference to this period, the promise is, "There shall be no more thence an infant of days, nor an old man that has not filled his days; for the child shall die a hundred years old: But the sinner being a hundred years old shall be accursed. And they shall build houses and inhabit them; and they shall plant vineyards and eat the fruit of them. They shall not build and another inhabit; they shall not plant, and another eat; for as the days of a tree are the days of my people, and mine elect shall long enjoy the work of their hands." "*As the days of a tree are the days of my people.*" There is nothing in the whole vegetable kingdom which is so long-lived as a *tree*. Human life is ordinarily compared to things which are most transient and fleeting—the springing *grass*—the opening *flower*—the passing *vapor*. But it is here compared to a *tree*. There must be a mighty difference between the life of man as it *is to be* and as *it is now*.

Or, the language of the text may intimate that he would die when his life had been so spent as to answer life's great end. There is a sense in which even a young man may be said to be of "*a full age*." One man at thirty may have done more for God and the world than another at sixty. Henry Martyn, and Samuel J. Mills, and Robert Murray McCheyne, and a host of others eminent for their usefulness, died in comparative youth. Nor were Brainard, and Payson, and Nettleton, and Richmond old men. They all died with their armor on, and were cut down in the midst of their usefulness. Yet it was not until each had made his impress upon the world. Though not old in years, they were of "*a full age*."

Again: The language of the text implies that his death would be *seasonable*. "*Like as a shock of corn cometh in in his season*." The corn is gathered in its proper time. "*In his season*"—when it is *ripe*, and ready for the garner, then is the labor of the harvest performed. The husbandman is not accustomed to cut down the growing corn, ere its juices have become dried, or its kernel mature. It is true that there are some things in the vegetable world which are not suffered to ripen at all. There are noxious plants and destructive brambles, and worthless trees, which are fit only for the fire. The removal of such things sometimes becomes necessary, that they may not obstruct the growth of that which is really useful. The choking bramble must be plucked up by the roots, and the overshadowing branches of the worthless thorn must be removed.

So it is that wicked men are often cut off in the

midst of their days. They are already ripe for ruin; are already fit for the fires of perdition, and to cut short their pestilential influence in the community, God cuts them down. True, indeed, there are some of this class whom the infinite mercy of God spares to extreme old age; that his grace may be magnified in their final salvation, or his justice made still more manifest in their condemnation. So also there are pious, devoted, active, useful Christians who are called away in early life. There is a mystery about such providences, which it is impossible for us to understand, and in respect to which we feel that "God's way is in the sea, and his paths in the great waters, and his footsteps are not known." Yet God calls away none of his people until their graces are mature, and they have become ripe for heaven. Some may have been ripened sooner than others, and there may be reasons why God removes them from earth and calls them home to himself, which he has not been pleased to reveal to us. But in general the principle is doubtless true, that the death of all God's people takes place at the *proper time.*

If these things be so, then the death of the mature Christian is no more cause of grief, than the gathering of the ripened harvest. Who feels to regret when the well-loaded cart returns from the field, freighted with its sheaves? There may be an appearance of desolation about the naked field, and we may feel sad at the change which is there presented to the eye, when the golden grain has disappeared, and nought appears in its stead but the withered stubble and the dried-up roots. Yet, the song of "harvest home," has always, in all generations, been sung with feelings of gladness and joy. It is with tears that the seed is sometimes sown; but with joy that the harvest is reaped.

And what though sadness does steal over our spirits at the loneliness which hangs around the bed-chamber and the closet of our departed friends, and the place where they worshiped God in the public assembly and at the family altar—yet we will not *indulge* our grief, knowing that God has removed them hence even as the husbandman gathers in the ripened sheaves.

And now, brethren, it is not difficult for any one of us who have been acquainted with our departed father, to see how well these leading thoughts apply to him. He is dead; and in this respect has he fulfilled the universal law of nature. He has come to the grave in *peace*. It can not be said of him that he was violently *hurried* away from his earthly endearments and associations against his will. Indeed, he loved his friends as well as friends should be loved. He loved the church, and was willing to live and labor for its prosperity. He loved his *race*, and for the welfare of human kind it was that he was laborious in toil, and ceaseless in efforts, and unremitting in his exertions.

Yet he loved his God more than all, and at his bidding was he ready to rise and depart. Nor was he called away until he had lived to the full age at which it is common for man to live; he had measured his three score years and ten, and might with propriety be said to be an old man; yet until recently might it have been said that "his eye was not dim, nor his natural force abated."

And as he lived to a good old age, so also did he in his life answer life's great end. It could not be said of him in any sense, that he was a blank in the community. His influence was every where felt, and it was every where salutary. His desire always was that God might be glorified and the world benefited through his instrumentality. To this end he lived, and this result was realized.

Moreover it is true that maturity of the various Christian graces marked his character in a preeminent degree, for many of the later years of his life. It became evident to his friends that he was fast ripening for heaven, and when death came, nothing of the work of preparation remained to be done. He had his loins girt about, his staff in his hand, his lamp well-trimmed, and he was only waiting for the summons.

The estimate in which his Christian character was held in the surrounding community may be seen by the suggestions which different individuals were pleased to make as to the text which it would be proper to use at his funeral. An aged father who had been familiarly acquainted with his ministerial and personal character for nearly half a century, suggested the following:

"Mark the perfect man and behold the upright; for the end of that man is peace." Another person suggested the following, as a suitable and appropriate theme: "Know ye not that there is a prince and a great man fallen this day in Israel?" Others again had their thoughts involuntarily directed towards the scenes connected with the ascension into heaven of the prophet Elijah. They seemed to be so surrounded with a celestial atmosphere, that in view of his departure they felt disposed to cry out: "My father, my father, the chariot of Israel and the horsemen thereof." Either of these would have been peculiarly appropriate, and expressive either of his personal character, or his prominent position and influence in society, or the peaceful and triumphant manner in which he came to his end.

But this congregation are doubtless expecting that I will speak more definitely of the character and labors of their now sainted pastor. No eulogy can benefit the sleeping dead, and we know, indeed, that if he was now possessed of consciousness, he would turn away his ears when it was uttered. During all his long life of devoted piety and active usefulness, he was never heard to speak a word in praise of himself. Self-praise constituted no part of his character; and this is a feeling which found no place in his heart.

Yet we may hold up the example of the dead for the benefit of the living. We may speak of what he has been, during a long course of years, while engaged in active labors for the welfare of the church and the salvation of men, that survivors may thereby be stimulated to the same activity and zeal for the attainment of the same end.

We propose to speak of him in respect to his personal character; his ministerial fidelity; the results of his labors; and the peacefulness of his end.

1. His personal character.

It may be said of him as it was of Barnabas: "He was a good man and full of the Holy Ghost, and of faith; and much people were added to the Lord." One prominent thing which ever marked his religious character, was the spirit of unreserved devotedness to the service of God. This was manifest to all who enjoyed the privilege of his acquaintance; and it also appears from the record which he himself made respecting his religious feelings. He evidently felt that he was "not his own; and that having been bought with a price, he should glorify God in his body and in his spirit which are God's."

There has been found among his papers since his death, a small manusoript volume, written by his own hand, and bearing the following title in Latin: "*Deo devotus in vita, in morte, ad eternitatem*"—the English of which when translated is: *To God do I devote myself in life, in death, and to eternity.* In this volume there is the following narrative of his early life, and of some things connected with his ministerial labors:

"I was born at Lee, in the county of Berkshire, and state of Massachusetts, on the 15th day of June, 1780. I was the subject of many serious impressions in childhood and youth, in reading the primer, especially the dialogue between Christ, a youth, and the devil; in reading the Rev. Mr. Moody's sermon to children in a book called the School of Good Manners; in hearing of deaths and attending funerals; in reading Davies' sermon on the resurrection and final judgment; and on occasions of personal sickness. I many times prayed in secret, and was in the habit of praying. But I lived a stranger to God nineteen years. When I was about nineteen I was awakened to attend to truth, and the main principles were fixed in my mind.

One evening in the summer of 1799, I was in great distress in the chamber of my father's house at Lenox. After painful struggles I found myself very unexpectedly harmonizing in feeling with Watts' fifty-first psalm: 'Show pity Lord, oh Lord, forgive,' &c. In a few days I began to think I had experienced a change of heart. This was first suggested to me by my friend, Stephen

Wells, Jr., from a view I had given him of my exercises. But I was very much afraid of indulging the thought, especially as it was first suggested by another. Yet from that time I have continued to hope, most of the time, till this day June 15, 1825. On the 20th of October, 1799, I united with the Congregational church in Lenox, under the care of the Rev. Samuel Shepard.

November 20, 1799 I first subscribed the covenant contained in the following pages. Five months of the season following I taught school in Lenox. During that time the work of the ministry was urged upon me by Mrs. Mary, wife of the Hon. William Walker, and by an old disciple, Mr. Chapman. But though I desired it I thought it impossible ever to be qualified for that work, for want of means. But a way was opened in providence, in which it seemed possible, by the establishment of a school under the care of the Rev. Nathan Perkins of West Hartford, Connecticut.

On the 5th of May, 1800, I devoted myself to the work in solemn fasting and prayer. At that time I wrote what is recorded in the following pages under that date. I began to reside in West Hartford in June, and pursued study with all my might. I continued in West Hartford till some time in February, 1803, when I received from the North Association of Hartford county, a license to preach the gospel. I preached my first sermon in North Windsor. Afterwards I preached a few weeks at Newington. The last of March I arrived at Kingsboro'. The next week after my arrival some special attention to religion commenced. Mrs. Anna Belden, the first subject. I staid till some time in May, then was absent four weeks, chiefly in Oneida county, at Augusta. Returned and found the good work advancing. Spent the summer. In autumn and winter spent some time at Becket (Mass.) where I received a call for settlement. But I did not think it duty to accept it. In the winter of 1804, returned to Kingsboro'. From May 5th to 17th, as the time of my ordination approached, I set myself more carefully to search and try myself; but did not succeed to my mind.

May 23, 1804, 11 o'clock A. M. I was solemnly set apart to the work of the ministry, and installed pastor of the Congregational church in Kingsboro'.

Sept. 7, 1804. I was married to Tirzah Northrup, and soon removed to Kingsboro'.

A second revival commenced in 1813, and continued till 1815. Another commenced in 1819, and continued into 1820, but was not general. Another more general commenced in June, 1822, and continued through the year. This was the most rapid. In 1829 a fifth revival commenced in June, and continued several months. This was chiefly in the Bible class and sabbath school, and was very precious. In 1831 a sixth revival commenced in July and continued till October. This was chiefly in the Bible class and sabbath school; yet a number of heads of families, and some of the most unlikely were brought in. As the fruit of these two revivals, more than a hundred became members of the church under my pastoral care.

In September or October, 1838, the most general and extensive revival commenced that had ever been enjoyed among my people, and others in this place. In the year 1839, eighty-three persons became members of the church, besides many who joined Methodists and Baptists, and the Presbyterian church in Johnstown."

Mention is made in the above narrative of a covenant into which he had entered with God; and I know not how to give a more satisfactory exhibition of the religious character of the man, than by rehearsing it entire. (This covenant may be found in Doddridge's Rise and Progress of Religion, and was copied with a few verbal alterations, by Dr. Yale, and adopted as his own).

We find it as follows:

"*A secret covenant between God and my own soul, first subscribed Nov.* 20, 1799, *and transcribed for the sake of conv.nience, Nov.* 21, 1803."

"Eternal and ever blessed God, I desire to present myself before thee with deepest humiliation and abasement of soul, sensible how unworthy such a sinful worm is to appear before the Holy Majesty of Heaven, the King of kings, and the Lord of lords, and on such an occasion as this, even to enter into a covenant transaction with thee. But the scheme and plan are thine own. Thine infinite condescension offered it by thy Son, and thy grace hath inclined my heart to accept it. I come, therefore, acknowledging myself to have been a great offender; smiting on my breast and saying with the humble publican: 'God be merciful to me a sinner.' I come invited by the name of Jesus Christ thy Son, and wholly trusting in his perfect righteousness; entreating that, for his sake, thou wouldst be merciful to my unrighteousness, and wouldest no more remember my sins.

Receive, I beseech thee, thy revolted creature who is now convinced of thy right to him, and desires nothing so much as that he may be thine. This day (Nov. 20, 1799) do I, with the utmost solemnity, surrender myself to thee. I renounce all former lords that have had dominion over me; and I consecrate to thee all that I am and all that I have, the powers of my mind the members of my body, my worldly possessions, my time and my influence over others; to be all used entirely for thy glory, and resolutely employed in obedience to thy commands, as long as thou continuest me in life; with an ardent desire and humble resolution to be thine through all the endless ages of eternity; ever holding myself in an attentive posture to observe the first intimations of thy will, and ready to spring forward with zeal and joy to the immediate execution of it. To thy direction also I resign myself and all I have, to be disposed of by thee in such a manner, as thou shalt, in thine infinite wisdom, judge most subservient to the purposes of thy glory. To thee I leave the management of all events, and say without reserve: '*Not my will but thine be done;*' rejoicing with a loyal heart in thy unlimited government, as what ought to be the delight of the whole material creation.

Use me, oh Lord, as an instrument of thy service. Number me among thy peculiar people. Let me be washed in the blood of thy dear Son. Let me be clothed with his righteousness. Let me be sanctified by his

Spirit. Transform me more and more into his image. Impart to me through him all needful influences of thy purifying, cheering, and comforting Spirit, and let my life be spent under those influences, and in the light of thy glorious countenance as my Father and my God. And when the solemn hour of death comes, may I remember this thy covenant, 'well ordered in all things and sure,' as 'all my salvation and all my desire,' though every other hope and enjoyment are perishing. And do thou, oh Lord, remember it too. Look down with pity, oh my Heavenly Father, on thy languishing, dying child. Embrace me in thine everlasting arms. Put strength and confidence in my departing spirit, and receive it to the abodes of them that sleep in Jesus, peacefully and joyfully to wait the accomplishment of thy great promise to all thy people, even that of a glorious resurrection and eternal happiness in thy heavenly presence.

And if any surviving friend should, when I am in the dust, meet with this memorial of my solemn transactions with thee, may he make the engagement his own, and do thou graciously permit him to participate all the blessings of thy covenant, through Jesus the Great Mediator of it; to whom, with thee, O Father, and the Holy Spirit, be everlasting praises ascribed, by all the millions who are thus saved by thee, and by all those other celestial spirits in whose work and blessedness thou shalt call them to share. Amen.

ELISHA YALE."

What a solemn transaction was this for a man to be engaged in! And who can tell what influence it exerted upon him during the whole course of his long and useful life? Nor are we to regard it as an unmeaning transaction, done to be laid aside and forgotten as if it had not been done at all. He was in the habit frequently of calling it to mind, and ordinarily of making a solemn and formal renewel of it, twice in each year. His name is solemnly affixed to this covenant one hundred and two times; and connected commonly with some serious reflections upon the past, and sealed with the expressive AMEN.

In respect to his personal religious character it may be proper to say, that, though regarded by all his acquaintances as eminently holy, he always cherished a humiliating sense of his deep-rooted depravity, and always placed his only confidence for acceptance with God upon the grace of Christ. On this subject we find from his pen such expressions as these: "June, 15, 1847. Now 67! Can it be that I am three score and seven years old? So it is. Yet in the review of life in the light of God's law, I find an amazing amount of sin—more than I can reckon up. My heart is deceitful above all things, and desperately wicked. Yet God searches and knows all that I know about it, and much more. I have been looking over my sins before God. I find that in many things, while fair and good in the sight of men, I have been vile and bad in the sight of God." Such like expressions were as common for him as it was for him to speak; and from the products of his pen they might be produced to any extent. Feeling his entire dependence upon Divine grace, both for his personal salvation and success in his efforts for the salvation of others, he was eminently a man of *prayer*. Here it was indeed, that his strength lay. He loved the prayer-meeting. He loved the closet most of all. But we have said as much on this part of our subject as our limits will allow. We were to speak,

2. OF HIS MINISTERIAL FIDELITY.

He might be truly said to be in labors abundant. He was peculiarly systematic in all his engagements, and eminently industrious, filling up all his hours and all his minutes. He preached both publicly and from house to house, testifying to men of all classes and all grades, "repentance towards God, and faith towards our Lord Jesus Christ." In his religious sentiments he was a decided Calvinist, and he was an able defender of the system of doctrines to which that name is commonly applied. He had feelings of marked kindness to all, nor did he censoriously judge those who differed from him in religious opinions, did they but build upon Christ, the foundation, and receive the great essentials of Christianity; yet did he never withhold, or soften down the truth, for the purpose of adapting it to the palate, or the appetite, or the prejudices of his hearers. In rebuking men for sin, while he was never rash, he was always fearless and out-spoken.

His benevolence was as broad as the world. Hence did he take a lively interest in all those *schemes* of benevolence which had in view the evangelization of men, and the subjugation of the world to the dominion of Christ. The part which he took in both forming and sustaining these institutions, is known by all. In this respect he may be said to have had a world-wide fame. Liberal in his gifts himself, he encouraged liberality also in others.

But in the welfare of his *own* people he felt a *peculiar* interest. For them he lived—for them he labored, for them he prayed—for them he studied—for them he preached—for them he wept. June 15, 1850, be writes as follows: "The hour is come. I am now three score and ten years old. During all these years the Lord has kept me alive, Through all changes he has safely brought me. Well may I continue to devote myself to him, to his cause, his service, his glory. I renew this covenant this morning, with great peace, joy, and confidence. I trust God has in a great measure answered the prayer of many years; "humble me." I do feel humbled. Yet I know not all that is in my heart, and fear that pride, that imp of the devil, will even take advantage of my present comfort and confidence, to say, "I want to be somebody." O Lord, make me willing to be as I am, nothing, less than nothing. But enable me as thy servant, to trust thee for all, and to do thy will pleasantly, and cheerfully, and joyfully, looking for that blessed hope and the glorious appearing of the great God, our Savior. I have a little more work to do. I feel that I am finishing up.

One great petition remains unanswered. There were three: 1st, a flourishing academy; 2d fifteen hundred dollars a year for benevolent objects. These are answered. 3d, The salvation of all my people. This is not answered. Far from it. Can I expect it now after being 70 years old? Nothing is too hard for the Lord. God can do it. My God who has heard my other two requests, can grant this. It is great. But God loves to do great things. My prayer is unto him. Glorify thy name in the salvation of all my people. Amen."

He labored, too, as do other ministers of the gospel, under numerous discouragements; of these he often speaks. These were manifold; but we will mention but one. It was the discouragement arising from the want of apparent success in his ministry. There were times during the period of his pastoral labors, when he mourned, for several successive years, the lack of the converting influences of the Spirit. And at one time, instead of an increase of membership in the church, there was a diminution on an average of ten a year for six consecutive years. Oh, how was his pious heart saddened! How did he cry as he returned into his closet, after preaching Christ to listless hearers; "Lord, who hath believed our report?" Yet did he not desert his post, nor remit his exertions. At one time he writes: "I stand pounding upon the rock. It does not break. But I see not what else I can do." And the last few months in which he was enabled to engage in active labor, he was as toilsome, and zealous, and active, and faithful, as he had ever been through the whole course of his ministry. We were to say something,

3. OF THE RESULTS OF HIS MINISTRY.

Here we will be brief. These results can not now be told. He has been striking upon a chord which will vibrate through eternity. It is a solemn thought that to some, the gospel, as preached by him, may be "a savor of death unto death." Oh, how fearful the condition of that sinner who shall face such a pastor at the bar of God, with his heart steeled against the calls of the gospel, and his skirts crimsoned with his own blood! "Who is the cause of the ruin of this man's soul?" inquires the judge, with a voice which brings dismay to the very center of his heart. "Who is the cause of this man's ruin? Let him speak, whom I had commissioned to labor for his salvation." Hear the response: "Lord, did I not labor unremittingly for the salvation of this poor soul? Hast thou not seen the tears which I shed on his behalf? Wast thou not a witness to the anxiety which I felt, and the prayers which I offered? Did I not make use of all the arguments which could be drawn from thine ever-blessed gospel, if possible to affect his heart and induce him to break off his sins and to accept of Christ as his Savior? Lord, I did tell him of a Savior's love—I did speak to him of the fearful consequences of unbelief. I did direct his thoughts to the awful retributions of the eternal world. I told him of heaven. I told him of hell. And when he would not hear or heed the warning, I felt as if my heart would break. O God, what could I do more?" Miserable sinner! to have such an accuser at the judgment seat of Christ!

He did desire the salvation of all his flock. But though this desire of his heart was not realized, he was instrumental of the salvation of *some*. Among his papers there is one which appears to have been but recently written. It is as follows: "A PASTOR'S REVIEW OF A PASTORATE OF FORTY-EIGHT YEARS." "A painful thought at the close of this period of ministerial labor is, that *many are not saved.* Though six hundred have been added to the church under my care during this period, most of whom appeared to adorn their profession, yet some of them have caused sorrow, while hundreds more have lived, and many have died in their sins. This is for a lamentation, and will be for a lamentation. It is as appropriate for me as it was for the Messiah, to say: 'Lord, who has believed our report?' Some believed him, yet, in general, Israel was not gathered. 'He came unto his own, and his own received him not.' Having been thus grieved himself, he knows how to sympathize with the griefs of his servants. Kind Master, while deeply humbled in view of personal defects and official failures, thy servant seeks consolation in thy sympathizing bosom. Thanks for the grace bestowed upon a goodly number. Let forgiveness be extended to me in all my delinquencies, and let not the blood of lost souls be found in my skirts. The judgment seat appears in view. There is the judge enthroned. Before him are gathered all nations. My people and I are among them; some on the right hand, others on the left. We are to be judged, and then to receive our final doom. 'Great day of dread!'"

The results of his ministry! They will never be fully known until the destiny of these six hundred professed converts who have been added to this church during his pastorate, shall have been revealed. Not until the converts from heathenism, who have been gathered in through his instrumentality, shall have been numbered. Not until there shall have been a final summing up of all those instrumentalities for the salvation of men, which he has either put in motion or sustained. But, that his labors will tell upon the eternal destinies of many immortal souls, there is no room to doubt. It remains to speak,

4. OF HIS PEACEFUL END.

I feel almost disposed to regard his dying scenes as embracing a period of nearly two years. It was in March 1851, that he was laid aside from ministerial labor by paralysis. Then, and ever after, he may, with great propriety, be said to have been "on the verge of heaven." It is not easy to describe the peculiarly sweet and celestial atmosphere with which he was constantly surrounded. You who sat with him in the domestic circle, or who received those pastoral messages which were dictated by a love to souls and a regard for the glory of God, may have some conception of it.

For a considerable part of the above mentioned time, however, he was able to be abroad, and to enjoy the society of friends. He had been looking for his departure, and familiarizing himself with the thoughts of it for many successive months. The hour at length came, the hour of his release. And though he had not looked for it then, any more than he had for months before, yet it found him ready, with nothing to do but to "gather up his feet" and die.

There was one who was watching for his falling mantle. The aged pastor had prayed, that the Lord would not leave his flock without a sheperd; and he felt that his prayer had been heard. The youthful pastor had come in to receive the dying benediction of the ascending prophet. All was quiet. All was peaceful. All was serene. They held converse together as did Elijah and his pupil while they passed over Jordan to the place appointed by God for the aged patriarch's release from his toils, and his ascension to his rest. The prayer of both was the same: "I pray thee, let a double portion of thy spirit be upon me." And may we not believe the answer in both cases to have been the same—"if thou see me when I am taken from thee, it shall be so unto thee." Yes; and in each case, too, the condition was realized. All unexpectedly while they were thus talking, did the event take place. "As they went on and talked, behold there appeared a chariot of fire, and horses of fire, and parted them asunder; and Elijah went up by a whirlwind into heaven." Somewhat like this it was here. To be sure, there were no visible appearances like those which then presented themselves to the eyes of the youthful prophet. Nor was the material frame of this man of God removed into heaven; yet the attending circumstances were such as forcibly to remind one of the scenes here described; so that the youthful survivor felt well-nigh compelled to cry out in the very language of Elisha; "My father, my father, the chariot of Israel and the horsemen thereof:" and while he thus spake, he reached forth his hand to catch his mantle as it fell.

The dying scene. It was Saturday night, when all was still and quiet, that the silent tread of God's messenger approached. He laid upon him his heavy hand, and for awhile it seemed as if the hour had indeed come. But he again revived, so that for several hours he could hold communications with his friends. In these communications he uttered some most precious sentiments. You have often listened to his *living* words, and now his *dying* words (as they have been uttered) you feel anxious to hear and remember. Some of these words have been committed to paper by attending friends, and I am permitted to communicate them to you.

The following took place on Saturday night, as it has been remembered and recorded by an attendant and friend:

"After the return of consciousness from an attack of apoplexy, speaking to his physician he said: Why, it seems that all my friends are here to-night. What is the matter? The physician replied: You are a very sick man, and we are here to take care of you, and we fear that you will not be any better. It is to be feared that it is your last attack. He replied: Why, I am not concerned about that. Soon after, he said to the doctor, Do you think I shall go to night? It was replied that there was a strong probability of it. With a wonderful promptitude and cheerfulness of tone and manner, he said: *Well, let me go. I shall soon be at rest.* After a pause, he said that Romans, 4th chapter and 5th verse, had been a source of unspeakable comfort to him for the last four or five months. He continued: *Jesus is my righteousness. I have no righteousness of my own, nor ever had any.* He also made other remarks illustrative of the passage quoted.

On a friend intimating that it was a great comfort to hear him express himself as in so happy a frame, he replied: It is the Lord that comforteth. On seeing his friends gathered around his bed, he said: Well, my friends, if this is to be my last, I want you to remember that there is nothing in the whole world that is worth a straw but Christ. On being asked if he had a firm trust in Christ he replied: I am not afraid to trust in Christ. I would trust in Christ much sooner than I would trust in man. Speaking to a friend, he said: I would much rather put my trust in Christ, than in you; for you must die, but he is an unchanging, an unfailing friend. He then repeated the passage, 'Put not your trust in princes,' &c. He also repeated a verse in the 146th Psalm: 'I'll praise my Maker with my breath,' &c. And then he asked that the whole psalm might be read as an exact expression of his feelings.

The following remarks were also made on the same occasion to the friends by whom he was attended:

"You remember that the first request I made to the church after I was laid aside, was, for their prayers, that I might be willing to be just what the Lord would have me to be; and that prayer has been answered. Remember the prayer-meeting; it is one of the most important means of grace. The prayer-meeting has been one of my chief delights. Of all public exercises this has been to me next to the sanctuary. *But the closet has been my paradise on earth.*

I have never believed in the love of God to the extent that it exists. I have tried, but could not reach it. The law of God is the law of *love*. How I love that law! It is a transcript of his moral character. Oh, the fearful penalties of that law of love! How it withers up my soul when I think of the poor sinner!" (And then he wept.) "I would not for the world have the purposes, or the law of God, or the gospel of God, altered a particle. The Lord Jesus Christ was the manifestation of God in the flesh. It is no more to say we love the *law* of God than to say we love the *decrees* of God. I wish you to understand that I have done nothing aright. I have all along been trying to do right but there is no perfection. I have seen an end of all they call perfection on earth. God's law is wonderful, reaching not only to outward acts, but it takes cognizance of the thoughts, feelings, motives. God is infinite in all his attributes, and every attribute is infinite love.

I have served the Lord fifty years, and I have no more righteousness now than I had then; but I hope I have made some attainments. How different is my condition from that of the Hindoo father of whom I read lately; whose son, thinking that he had lived long enough, took him to the Ganges and suffocated him by filling his mouth with mud! Now I, in my extremity, though I have no children, receive the kind attentions of my neighbors." A friend said: "Yes, of your spiritual children." He instantly replied: "If they are my spiritual children, how wonderful the mercy of God that made them such!"

"If I should live a thousand years, I should be no better than I am now. Nothing but the righteousness of Christ can make me any thing but a condemned sinner."

Sometime after midnight, a friend observed: "It is the sabbath." Said he: "An everlasting sabbath, where congregations ne'er break up, and sabbath never ends. I have been expecting an everlasting sabbath."

After a paroxysm of pain, he exclaimed: "Shall I not drink of the cup that my father giveth me? This is the language of the Savior—how much more is it becoming a poor sinner!"

Patient, calm, though evidently a great sufferer, he would say: "I wish I could do without this groaning. I may as well go now as at any other time, if it be God's will."

Speaking of a brother in the church who lay at the point of death, he inquired if it was thought that brother W. would go that night; and then commended, in a touching manner, the long, tried, and faithful friendship of that brother to him and the church; and spoke of it as a delightful consideration, that perhaps they might be permitted to go in company, as it were, to the abodes of the blest. Speaking at another time of his critical position, he said: "I ought not, I must not ask for any thing; God will do all things right." This may account for the fact that he asked no one to pray, and was not heard to use the language of supplication himself.

This may be regarded as a remarkable circumstance, indicating in a striking manner his entire preparation for the change, and his consequent resignation to the divine disposal."

But though his friends were hourly watching for his departure, it did not take place until near the close of the sabbath. After the public exercises in the church, his successor in the pastorate (the Rev. Mr. Wall) came into his room just in time to receive his parting benediction, and to witness his ascent. Mr. Wall has kindly furnished the following account of the closing scene. "I called on Dr. Yale about a quarter before three P. M. I found him reclining on a sofa in the sitting-room. He was very weak, and was evidently suffering severely; yet perfectly self-possessed. After giving me his hand he spoke of his pain—was not so easy as he had been—the pain had changed its locality. Complained of a stricture across his breast. He frequently changed his posture for relief. On Mrs. Yale remarking that they had hoped to have been present in church this morning, he said: 'Now, Mrs. Yale, do not say one mournful thing. Things are just as I have prayed for them. The cup which my Father hath given me, shall I not drink it? Such was my prayer last sabbath at the communion; and you know Mr. Wall, we must not reject the answer to our own prayers.' After an interval, he remarked: 'I can bear this pain, and yet I can bear it only a little longer; but oh, the poor sinner! Who shall dwell with everlasting burnings? This is a question I can not answer.' He was here so affected that he wept—so that the last tears he shed were for sinners.

After rising from a reclining to a sitting posture, he remarked: "I would not give a straw for all the religion in the world, without faith in Christ. I want nothing but that. Understand me. I do not say that I don't want any more religion; but I want no other thing." Again he remarked: "That passage in Romans, iv, 5, has been very precious to me."

His last words were; "O that I could unloose this bond!" alluding to the stricture across his breast."

His last words! They have been spoken, and you have all heard them. They were truly *weighty* words; and so were very many other words which he has been speaking for many successive years. It now remains to be seen what effect will be produced by these words upon the minds of those to whom they have been addressed.

Having uttered these "last words," he settled down upon his pillow—and "was not; for God took him." "I heard a voice from heaven, saying unto me, write, Blessed are the dead which die in the Lord from henceforth; yea, saith the Spirit, that they may rest from their labors; and their works do follow them."

CONCLUSION.

I have found so much to say on this occasion, so much that I felt unwilling to suppress and found myself unable to condense, that this discourse has been uncommonly, and perhaps some may think, *unreasonably* long. Yet there are still a few things remaining, to which I must solicit your attention. And,

1. May I be allowed to address a few words of consolation to the afflicted widow?

You were permitted to journey and to sojourn with your sainted companion, from the 7th day of Sept. 1804 until the 9th day of Jan. 1853, a period of almost forty-nine years. These years have been years of mingled sorrow and joy. But while your path-way has been marked with alternate light and shade, the light has greatly preponderated. You have leaned upon his arm, you have reclined upon his bosom—you have been afflicted with his sorrows—you have joyed in his joys. You have prayed with him—you have wept with him—you have suffered with him—you have hoped with him. In prosperity, and adversity—in health, and sickness. In all seasons of hope and discouragement, you have had a unity of heart and a oneness of sentiment. You now feel afflicted; and hereafter your bed-chamber, and your dining room, and your parlor, and every other part of your dwelling will put on the appearance of vacancy, which until now, they have never worn. Yet, remember his dying words, among the last words which ever fell from his lips, and perhaps the very last which he ever addressed particularly to yourself: "Mrs Yale, do not say one mournful thing;" "*Do not say one mournful thing*"—"ONE MOURNFUL THING."

You surely have greater cause for *joy* than you have for *sorrow*. Ah! indeed there is nature's tie that can not be broken without a pang—and there is that feeling of loneliness which steals over your heart, and which is necessarily productive of a certain degree of depression. Yet are there very many things, in the circumstances of the case, which are directly calculated to administer consolation. May I just hint at a few? They are such as the following: God permitted him to live to become an old man; so that he has "come to his grave in a full age, like as a shock of corn cometh in in his season." Had he died in the meridian of life, and when his sun was high up above the horizon, the case would have been quite different from what it is now. Then, again, his death did not take place until he had become fully *prepared* for it. He was by no means taken by surprise; nor did the message find him with anything to do, as it respected his own work of preparation for his departure. He had familiarized himself as much with the thought of lying down in the grave, as he had with that of lying upon his bed.

Then think of the calmness with which he met the summons. No trepidation—no pleading for delay—no doubt as to the coming future. "*I am not concerned about that.*" "*Well—let me go.*" "*I shall soon be at rest.*"

You may also be consoled with the thought that he has not lived in vain. He has made his influence to be felt, even in the midst of the seas, and upon the other side of the earth. And oh! could you now look at the crown which encircles his brow, how would your eyes be dazzled with its lustre—studded all over as it is with those precious jewels which he has gathered for Christ. In him is fulfilled the promise: "They that be wise shall shine as the brightness of the firmament; and they that turn many to righteousness, as the stars forever, and ever."

You require no admonition from me, to live in constant readiness to meet your departed husband in heaven. For almost fifty-years, you have been traveling together; and he has come to the end of his pilgrimage, and passed over the river into the land of promise, but a little in advance of yourself. May we not believe that he will be watching and waiting for your arrival? I know that earth has its charms—Ah! yes—and heaven has *its* charms too. And whatever attractions it had for you before, these attractions are now increased. You are not to look for your husband in the grave; nor dwell too much upon the epitaph which may be chiseled upon his tombstone; but remember that his "record is on high," and that he has actually become an inhabitant of a better world. Let your mind dwell much upon that world; and as you think upon the life of prayer, and piety, and humility, and faith, and charity, and zeal and devotedness to God, which was led by him who so long bore you company in your pilgrimage, I am sure that you will make it your business to imitate his shining example. Live as he lived; pray as he prayed; repent as he repented; believe as he believed; love as he loved; weep as he wept; rejoice as he rejoiced—and then you will die as he died, and share with him in his eternal reward.

2. It will not be inappropriate for me to say something to my brethren in the ministry of reconciliation. We can but feel that a very important breach has been made upon our ranks. Our dear departed father has been, has *always* been foremost in the ranks of the hosts of the Lord. He always had on his armor; nor did he ever flinch in the day of conflict. He was forward in every good work, and was distinguished for laying plans and devising ways, in which to advance the interests of his Redeemer's kingdom. His younger brethren always prized his counsels, and were often quickened in duty by his words of encouragement.

But his place, brethren, we shall hereafter find vacant. in our social gatherings, in our ministerial associations, In our public assemblies, we may meet and depart, and meet and depart, but his well-known voice will no longer be heard. Yet, methinks there is a solemn lesson which we may learn from his whole history, as a faithful and successful laborer in the vineyard of Christ; and a solemn admonition which will be addressed to us from the marble slab which will hereafter mark the place of his repose. Could his tongue now be unloosed after what he has already seen of eternal realities, how would he stimulate his brethren in the ministry to fidelity, and zeal, and constancy in their work!

There is one sentence in that solemn covenant of his which has been repeated, with which my mind was particularly affected. "And if any surviving friend should, when I am in the dust, meet with this memorial of my solemn transactions with thee, may he make the engagement his own, and do thou graciously permit him to participate all the blessings of thy covenant, through Jesus Christ, the great mediator of it." When I first read it a thought sprung into my mind, that I was the first survivor by whom this article was read; and perhaps mine the first human eye, but his own, that had ever rested upon it. Am I to regard this, then, as the prayer of my long-tried and faithful friend, that I would take upon myself the responsibilities and obligations of this covenant? Is there any thing unreasonable in it? It is the solemn dedication of one's self entirely to God. He felt himself to have been thus dedicated; as he expressed it, on one occasion of its renewal: "May I be the Lord's every month, every week, every day, every hour, every minute." "EVERY MINUTE." Let us brethren make this sentiment our own. *Be the Lord's every minute.*

And as the veteran soldiers who have been in the hottest of the battle for many years, are called to lay aside their armor, their juniors who still have a place in the ranks, and especially those who have the honor of being *leaders* of the hosts of the Lord, should be admonished to be at their posts, with their swords always drawn and their armor always on.

3. It remains for me, now to seek to gain the ear of that portion of this vast assembly, who have constituted his former pastoral charge.

Dear friends, your deceased pastor has, for many years, cherished an habitual anxiety for the salvation of his people. The interests of your souls lay near his heart. He did not labor to make himself rich on the income which he received, but to make you happy by leading you to Christ and inducing you to secure your own salvation. He "sought not *yours* but *you.*"

The salvation of souls—how earnestly did he long for it! When many of you had no tears to shed for yourselves, he wept for you, and when in your impenitence, you offered no prayers for yourselves, he was constantly praying for you. I hazard nothing in saying that there has not been a day for nearly fifty years, in which he has not prayed for impenitent sinners in Kingsboro'. If it had been but one prayer a day, it would have amounted to more than eighteen thousand prayers. All this for sinners in Kingsboro', who will not pray for themselves. Remember, too, that it was for you that he shed the last tears which he ever shed in his life; or ever will shed. He had come just to the gate of heaven. The angels were beckoning him in. He was just about to cast off his tenement of clay, and his eye was already resting on the pearly gates of the celestial city; when he again thought as he had often thought before, of the condition of the poor sinner, and he says: "How it withers up my soul when I think of the poor sinner!" And then he wept.

The people of this congregation have heard from him many a rousing sermon, and at the final closing up of his ministry here as your pastor, he could truly say: "I take you to record this day, that I am pure from the blood of all men. For I have not shunned to declare unto you all the counsel of God."

He has preached many a rousing sermon; but he never preached with deeper tones than now. Indeed, his tongue is still, his voice is hushed, his lips are sealed, his eyes are closed; yet it seems to me that the very walls of this sanctuary continue to echo those touching appeals which, through many a by-gone year, he has been addressing the dear people of his charge. He has gone to give an account of his stewardship—an account of the manner in which he has preached. And you, hearers, will also be called to give an account of the manner in which you have heard. What is that account which you will give? What attention have you paid to his preaching? What obedience have you rendered to the truth?

It will be a fearful thing for a man to go to the judgment from Kingsboro', in a state of impenitence. How will you account for those eighteen thousand prayers? Yes, eighteen thousand twice told. How account for the thousands of sermons which he has preached, and the many personal admonitions which you have received? Are you ready to meet your pastor, face to face, before the bar of God? Are you *all* ready?

I know that God has here given him some seals to his ministry. He has made mention of six hundred as having been added to the church. Some of these are already in heaven, and some are still making their way thitherward. Hold on, brethren, hold on, sisters, your pastor has gone before to await your arrival. Most of these six hundred, he has said, "appeared to adorn their profession, yet some of them have caused sorrow." "*Some have caused sorrow.*"

He does not say who they were, or how it was done. But if any of this class are among this congregation, let me ask you seriously to think upon the course which you have felt inclined to pursue. Have you grieved the heart and brought tears into the eyes of your pious and praying pastor, by your backslidings, by your inconstancy, by your worldliness, by your neglect of duty, by your censoriousness, by your obstinacy, by your want of sympathy with your brethren or interest in the welfare of the church? It is time for you to bethink yourselves, and to return from your wanderings.

Brethren, your former leader has been called home. But God has been pleased in his mercy, to provide another. Your eye will now be upon him. When Moses was about to close up his labors as the leader of Israel, he was directed to take Joshua, the son of Nun, a man in whom was the Spirit, and to lay his hand upon him, and set him before all the congregation. Then was he to occupy the place in the armies of Israel, that had been occupied by the veteran Moses. See here your future leader; and may the youthful Joshua reap even more laurels, and gain more victories, than were ever gained by his honored predecessor.

"Now, the God of peace, that brought again from the dead, our Lord Jesus, that great Shepherd of the sheep, through the blood of the everlasting covenant, make you perfect in every good work, to do his will, working in you that which is well pleasing in his sight, through Jesus Christ, to whom be glory for ever and ever. Amen."

www.ingramcontent.com/pod-product-compliance
Lightning Source LLC
LaVergne TN
LVHW020119110826
845151LV00001B/208

* 9 7 8 1 4 2 5 5 4 2 6 0 3 *